INTERORGANIZATIONAL DECISION MAKING

INTERORGANIZATIONAL DECISION MAKING

MATTHEW TUITE
ROGER CHISHOLM
MICHAEL RADNOR

AldineTransaction
A Division of Transaction Publishers
New Brunswick (U.S.A.) and London (U.K.)

First paperback printing 2007
Copyright © 1972 by Matthew F. Tuite, Roger K. Chisholm, and Michael Radnor.

Library of Congress Catalog Number: 2007017007
ISBN: 978-0-202-30926-2
Printed in the United States of America

Library of Congress Cataloging-in-Publication Data

Interorganizational decision making / Matthew Tuite, Roger Chisholm, and
    Michael Radnor, editors.
        p. cm.
    Originally published: Chicago: Aldine Pub. Co., 1972.
    Papers mainly drawn from those read at a conference held at Northwestern
University in Feb. 1969. Includes bibliographical references and index.
    ISBN 978-0-202-30926-2 (pbk. : alk. paper)
    1. Decision making—Congresses. 2. Decentralization in management—
Congresses. 3. Interorganizational relations—Congresses. I. Tuite, Mat-
thew. II. Chisholm, Roger K. III. Radnor, Michael.

HD30.23.158   2007
658.4'03—dc22   2007017007

Preface

Interorganizational Decision Making— A Multidisciplinary Perspective

The Requirement for Interorganizational Decision Making

This volume on interorganizational decision making is a rare example of a multi- or interdisciplinary approach to a very significant theoretical problem and social issue. The effort is timely. Pervasive developments and changes in modern organizations and their salient environments have created sets of conditions for which the concept of interorganizational decision making becomes critical.

There is a growing interdependence among organizations and an increasing awareness in organizations of their openness to environment. This is manifested in their growing sensitivity to those environmental factors affecting inputs to the organization and affecting responses to (and acceptability of) outputs. For example, few firms can afford to act unilaterally in their relations with labor unions, and all recognize the importance of actual, probable, and possible governmental interventions on their decision making. There is a growing awareness of societal pressures on every aspect of organizational activity, from personnel policies, to quality of service, to waste disposal practices.

Organizations have grown in scale and scope of activities, generating far more complex forms of organizational structure as attempts are made to respond to the problems accompanying growth. A common response has been decentralization. Decentralization, while it creates certain benefits arising from subunit autonomy, in turn generates new needs for integration.[1] If the supposed benefits of decentralization are to be maintained, they must come from the development of multi-organizational rather than monolithic institutional perspectives.

1. This phenomenon is widely discussed in organization behavior literature, as, for example, Paul R. Lawrence and Jay W. Lorsch, *Organization and Environment* (Homewood, Ill.: Richard D. Irwin, Inc., 1969).

Further, organizations continue to push out their boundaries and domains in terms of sources, markets, technologies, and geography such as the growing multinational conglomerates. And governments undertake programs of larger and larger scope—for example, the design of total national (or even international) transportation systems, national resources exploitation programs, and the solution of urban and pollution problems. Under such conditions both private and public organizations find that it is the actions and programs of other specific and limited systems, rather than numerous generalized organizations, that create the constraints and parameters of their environments. In one sense this leads from competitive to collusive relationships, with all the associated negative connotations. In another sense it creates the potential for cooperation in which all parties, including the relevant parts of the environment (e.g., Society), might stand to benefit.

In essence this represents a shift in system focus from single organizations (acting as unified systems and operating in diffused environments) to large complex systems of organizations, each attempting to operate on the larger system to which it belongs, as one of several cooperating subsystems. A decision to act cooperatively is not, however, sufficient to achieve the benefits of joint decision optimalities. The interacting systems are not single decision makers but are themselves each complex systems. To succeed in their joint endeavors it is necessary for them to find means to coordinate their planning, information, and decision making systems, through multi-decision maker models, and so arrange the payoff structure such that each party can justify the joint goals on independent criteria.

This is the essence of this new field of interorganizational decision making which has only recently begun to attract wide attention. The position can be taken that this awakened interest is not merely the product of a growing theoretical enlightenment (though it certainly is also that), but more basically it is a reflection of the changing character of organizational decision making processes. The changes are spawning a whole host of problems which must be viewed in an interorganizational context.

The Theoretical Problem

Interorganizational decision making poses a complex systems problem involving technological, work flow, and complementarity relationships between subsystems. These systems may be independent organizations or departments in an organization, who may not be optimally interrelated in their interacting activities. Required are multiple, rather than the usual single, decision maker models which can describe this interrelationship and can expose to the participants the benefits from joint cooperative activity of which they may not be fully aware. This is true, either because the relationships and technological functions which join them are too complex, or because the system members may not even be completely, or partially, aware of the implications of the interactions in the system (or even in some cases that they have joint membership with certain others in a closed system). Such models should further show how a higher joint outcome could be achieved. Sometimes an interdependence (for example, between various polluters) is fully appreciated only when the larger system to which they belong, namely, Society, shows intentions of intervening to force cooperative activity through restrictive laws, taxes, and similar mechanisms.

The problems are both technological and motivational in character. They may be motivational, for example, when the participants are aware of the relationships but are constrained by personal or organizational factors from cooperating. Awareness of interrelationships may lead to a demand for analytical joint decision making models to permit the reaching of a higher joint optimum in cases where there is general agreement on objectives. In cases where there are significant differences in goals, then, as noted by March and Simon,[2] this might tend to lead to bargaining behavior. The problems are technological when work flow interdependencies determine the constraints and rewards of a relationship; as when one participant can succeed in his efforts only when the other, on whom he depends for his inputs or who receives his outputs, is fulfilling his role.

Joint decision making models must account for the conditions under which potential participants in an interorganizational decision system will perceive it desirable to enter into and stay within the system, as full participants. Implicit in this statement are the issues of time dependence and levels of participation. Ideally, dynamic models are required which will reflect both dependencies on environments which change over time and the possibility of adaptations within the system that will improve the rewards derived from the cooperative relationship. These come from actual changes in process and structure, and also through perceptual changes in which norms and values of cooperation are internalized. Since value systems and goals change over time, decision making models should, ideally, include the possibilities of monitoring such changes with appropriate adaptive responses. Further, the models should recognize that participation can vary on a continuum from zero through partial to complete. In many instances minimal levels of participation may be enforced by higher authorities—for example, the government—but the essence of the problem to be modeled lies in the requirements for achieving a higher-order participation.

The phenomenon of interorganizational decision making can be found at any systems level. A more accurate, but less familiar, description of the issues to be dealt with in this volume would be "intersystem decision making." It is the thesis of the editors (as well as the authors) of this volume that there are fundamental similarities in the phenomenon whether the interacting

2. James G. March and Herbert A. Simon, *Organizations* (New York: John Wiley & Sons, Inc., 1958).

systems are semiautonomous departments and divisions within an organization, or organizations, or multi-organization confederations, or various
system combinations. In this we accept the perspective of many General
Systems Theorists, and in particular that of James G. Miller.[3] This is not to
deny, however, the probability that differences in such variables as level of
system autonomy and character of the system structures and processes, as
one moves up and down the hierarchy of systems levels from that of the
individual to those of the nation and society will not necessitate significant
modifications in model requirements. In this first cut at this field it would
appear more useful, for now, to emphasize the commonality of the theoretical
model requirements. By the same token it is important to emphasize the
commonality, rather than to differentiate across another dimension of
systems variation, namely, institutional differences such as exist between
government and business.

Multidisciplinary Requirements

Both the applied and theoretical aspects of interorganizational decision
problems must, or should be, by definition, the subject of research and model
building by members of various disciplines in close cooperation with practitioners. The technological systems characteristics, the nature of the
economic interrelationships, the behavioral considerations in conflict,
cooperation, and bargaining call for contributions in the model-building
processes from economists, operations researchers, systems analysts,
behavioral scientists of various types, and institutionally oriented people.
The complexity of the problems requires models of a richness which can be
achieved only if all such groups are represented. Of course, this says no more
than that which was recognized by the early proponents of Operations
Research who saw the need for that work to be undertaken by interdisciplinary groups. However, such interdisciplinary activity is in practice (as
was the case in OR) an extremely rare occurrence. In most cases one is more
likely to see independent attacks on these problems either by the separate
disciplines or by the practitioners, without recognition of the vital contributions that can be obtained from others.

As such, the effort that is represented by the papers in this book and the
conference from which they were drawn can surely claim a description of
"uniqueness." All of the disciplines and groups mentioned above are represented, and there has been an attempt to interrelate the various contributions
in a mutually reinforcing and cross-fertilizing framework. The question may
be asked whether, in fact, this effort succeeds in being interdisciplinary in its
"cuts" through the problem area. In reviewing the materials one cannot but

3. James G. Miller, "Toward a General Theory for the Behavioral Sciences," *American
Psychologist*, X (1955), 513–31; and "Living Systems: Basic Concepts; Structure and Process;
Cross-Level Hypotheses," *Behavioral Science*, X (1965), 193–237; 337–79; 380–411.

come to the conclusion that the success has been only partial. A more faithful description of what was achieved would be a "multidisciplinary" attack on the problem of interorganizational decision making rather than an "interdisciplinary" one, in that there has been only a partial demonstration of how the contributions from these various different perspectives could be and are interrelated. What was done was to show how they do relate to each other in a mutually inspiring but not yet mutually interacting manner. In this respect there was failure to meet head-on the problem of achieving true interdisciplinary activity. Bringing together these disciplines and showing their mutual co-relevance is, however, an effort that it was vitally important to make. This effort may be looked upon as one of that set of first steps taking place today which may help achieve the needed level of interdisciplinary focus on important problems, a requirement of critical dimensions, as Martin Shubik so well noted in his closing address to the conference.

Structure of the Book

The papers included in the book are both theoretical and applied in emphasis. They include contributions, as already noted, from a spectrum of academic specializations and from practitioners representing several organizations. Rather than group papers by disciplines, the editors decided that readers would be better served if natural, multidisciplinary groupings of papers could be achieved.

This latter goal was accomplished by dividing the papers, first, into theoretical and applied groupings reflecting a variety of systems level and institutional examples; and second, into (*a*) those papers that emphasized the organization structure requirements of interorganizational decision making; (*b*) those that emphasized the behavioral requirements of interorganizational decision making; and (*c*) those that developed decision technologies for interorganizational decision making.

Following an introductory theoretical overview in Part I, the three-part division of structure, behavior, and decision technology was utilized in two sets of theoretical papers, in Parts II and III, and three sets of applied papers in Parts IV, V, and VI. The subject matter of the applications papers fell quite naturally into interorganizational decision problems of and between business units, between government agencies and governments, and at the business-government interface. This was, of course, not accidental since a concerted effort had been made in planning the conference at which the papers were initially read to see that such a cross-section of institutional applications was represented. The volume closes with a Postscript outlining suggestions for further theoretical and empirical work in this new field.

Acknowledgments

The program under which this particular work on interorganizational decision making was carried out has been supported for some time by a grant from the National Aeronautics and Space Administration (NGL 14–007–058). Much credit must be given to various management and management analysis personnel within NASA for their early recognition of the nature of the problems discussed in this volume and the need to support research in the area. As one of the very large government organizations that works in close contact with business organizations, particularly through their multitude of contractual and subcontractual relationships, they appreciated the need for development of multidecision-maker models where there were important interdependencies in a very complex system. One of the great achievements of NASA probably lies in the capability they have created to manage such complex systems of autonomous contractors and subcontractors while avoiding overcentralized control. Particular credit must go to Mr. Charles F. Bingham and Mr. Richard E. Stephens, who helped in the concept and organization of the conference from which these papers were largely drawn, and in the support given in making publication of this work possible; also to Mr. Philip N. Whittaker, who at the time this work was carried out was the head of procurement for NASA and is now Assistant Secretary of the Department of Defense in charge of procurement. Mr. Whittaker's paper appears in this collection.

Our gratitude is also extended to Haskel Benishay, Professor of Managerial Economics, Northwestern University, consultant in planning the Conference; to Harold Guetzkow, Gordon Scott Fulcher Professor of Decision Making, Northwestern University, who provided valuable advice at the inception of this project; and to John Schermerhorn and Harold Welsch for editorial assistance.

Contributors

David P. Baron
Northwestern University

Jacques Van Ypersele de Strihou
Electrorail Cy.
Brussels, Belgium

John M. Dutton
Southern Methodist University

William M. Evan
Professor of Sociology and Industry
The Wharton School of Finance and Commerce
University of Pennsylvania

Jerome E. Hass
Graduate School of Business and Public Administration
Cornell University

James L. Heskett
1907 Professor of Business Logistics
Graduate School of Business Administration
Harvard University

Leonid Hurwicz
Department of Economics
University of Minnesota

Kenneth O. Kortanek
Carnegie-Mellon University

Edna Loehman
Department of Agricultural Economics
University of Florida

William A. Niskanen
Institute for Defense Analysis

Howard V. Perlmutter
Wharton School of Finance and Commerce
University of Pennsylvania

Stanley Reiter
Northwestern University

Kenneth W. Thomas
Graduate School of Business Administration
University of California, Los Angeles

Matthew F. Tuite
Northwestern University

Gordon Tullock
Center for the Study of Public Choice
Virginia Polytechnic Institute and State University

Richard E. Walton
Graduate School of Business Administration
Harvard University

Roland L. Warren
Florence Heller Graduate School for Advanced Studies in Social Welfare
Brandeis University

Andrew Whinston
Krannert School of Industrial Administration
Purdue University

Philip N. Whittaker
Assistant Secretary for the Air Force

Contents

INTERORGANIZATIONAL DECISION MAKING

I

The Concept of Interorganizational Decision Making

Interorganizational decision making deals with multiple-decision-unit or joint decision problems. Decision problems are identified, here and elsewhere, as "joint" to emphasize the important role of coordinated action in determining the combined result achieved by the decision makers. "Combined result" carries with it a connotation of total payoff; yet more than that is at issue. The distribution of the total payoff among the decision units cannot be disregarded, particularly the clash of joint-interest in the total with self-interest in the individual share. Alternative possible distributions of the total payoff among individual units raises the specter of interunit conflicts, a specter of considerable importance in this discussion. While it is possible to act independently under conditions of overlapping outcome interest, or joint interest, the penalty for independent action under such conditions is usually a less than optimal joint return.

There is often an initial conflict of interest between the parties who discover that they have a joint decision problem. Each may prefer different points in the outcome possibilities set. Some resolution of this conflict must precede selection of a jointly optimal, or at least improved, combination of decisions. In the first paper of this section Tuite stresses the importance of "interventions" into the joint decision situation to reduce existing conflict. The dimensions of intervention are classified as (*a*) changes in the organization structure within which the joint decision problem must be resolved, (*b*) the motivation of problem-solving rather than bargaining behavior on the part of boundary personnel,[1] and (*c*) adjustment of the information and decision technology supporting the decision making effort. The idea that the initiation of interventions along these dimensions is required to bring about an optimal joint decision is implicit in all the papers which follow.

---

1. Boundary personnel are those individuals from each organization who engage each other in the decision making process.

The principal existing bodies of research on joint decision problems, game theory and the theory of teams, are likewise focused on conflict of interest as a deterrent to optimal joint action. These theories, however, take existing conditions of conflict as given. The nature of a theory of optimal interorganizational decision making can perhaps best be visualized in terms of similarities and differences which in turn parallel and complement game theory and the theory of teams.

Relationship to Game Theory and the Theory of Teams

The term "interorganizational decision making"[2] identifies an approach to joint decision problems which in some respects differs from the approach taken by either game theory or the theory of teams. The basic subject matter of all three is the situation in which the decision payoff to an individual decision maker depends upon both his own choice and the choice of another. In games of pure conflict (zero-sum games), interest is confined to individual payoffs. There is no way to influence the joint return. In games of mixed conflict-cooperation (nonzero-sum games) and in games of pure cooperation, individual payoffs as well as the joint return are of interest.

Game theory treats situations of pure conflict (zero-sum games), and mixed conflict-cooperation (nonzero-sum games). It accepts, as given, the state of conflict or cooperation existing between the parties. Each player is presumed to know the alternatives available to himself and the other decision makers as well as how the outcome depends on the choices each makes. It proceeds to work out "solutions" based upon "rational" behavior by each of the players under various conditions of collusion, arbitration, bargaining, side payments, and communication.

Games of pure cooperation are the subject matter of the theory of teams. Problems of perception and communication which present barriers to the achievement of a joint optimum outcome make this an interesting topic. In addition to perception and communication difficulties, other problems dealt with by the theory of teams are the amount of costly coordinating information to be purchased and the effect that alternative information patterns (organizational structures) have on the final outcome. If the players could concert their choices with certainty, without difficulty, and without cost, a cooperative game would cease to be a game.[3]

---

2. A somewhat elastic interpretation of conventional usage allows the decision units or "organizations" involved in interorganizational decision making to include combinations of profit and not-for-profit corporations; government branches, departments, and agencies; corporate operating divisions; and corporate functional departments (such as marketing and production).

3. Thomas Schelling, *The Strategy of Conflict* (Cambridge: Harvard University Press, 1963), p. 100.

Interorganizational decision making serves as a rubric more or less accurately labeling a variety of decision situations in which the interests of two or more decision units overlap. It does not include situations of pure conflict. It does not assume full knowledge of payoffs by the decision units as in game theory. Also, existing states of conflict-cooperation may be changed as a part of the decision process.

Objectives of a Theory of Interorganizational Decision Making

It might be fair to say that one objective of a theory of optimal inter-organizational decision making is to move from conditions of mixed conflict-cooperation to conditions of pure cooperation. Interorganizational decision making seeks means of facilitating the coordination of decisions between the decision units. The first step in facilitating coordination of decisions is simply to make decision makers aware of the potential increase in their collective payoff which is available to interdependent decision makers who coordinate their actions. The same barriers (perception and communication) which forestall coordination also prevent decision units from recognizing opportunities for cooperation. In addition, awareness is forestalled by the fact that the dominant focus of research on decision making continues to be on the individual decision maker acting independently. This focus on individual decision makers has contributed to a suboptimizing orientation among the subunits of any organizational entity.

Considerable effort needs to be devoted to determining the payoffs available to the parties who comprise a joint decision problem. Knowledge of these payoffs is assumed in game theory. One important dimension of this information problem, bearing directly on the amount of effort required to provide payoff information, is the choice of an organizational structure for interorganizational decision making. In its broadest dimensions the structural choice may be between centralization and decentralization. In its more refined state, the organizational structure will largely determine the cost of, and ease of access to, the information on which joint decisions will be based. The distribution of payoffs among the participants in a joint decision situation depends upon the nature of the reward and penalty system. If this important feature of the interorganizational decision structure supports cooperative action, subunits will generally tend to be motivated to coordinate.

A viable theory of interorganizational decision making would allow for:

a. Reduction of the conflict of interest which often exists between interdependent decision units and which reduces the likelihood of decisions being made which result in a maximum joint return. This conflict has organizational and/or behavioral origins. Its reduction lies in the accumulation of organizational design principles which foster interunit cooperation rather than conflict. These revised organizational structures must include factors which motivate boundary personnel to engage in mutual problem solving rather than bargaining behavior.[4]

b. Refinement of the information and decision models by which joint optimum solutions may be pursued in interdependent decision situations. The achievement of optimum results in an interorganizational decision problem rests on securing the willingness of all parties to cooperate and then in providing the information they need to coordinate their actions. These are, of course, overlapping issues. Cooperation often depends upon provision of sufficient information to convince organizational units that their best interest can be served by coordinated action. In a parallel fashion, obtaining the required information from subunits to determine an optimal joint action, and thereby to show the advantages of coordination, requires a fair degree of preliminary cooperative spirit. If subunits seek to "game" the proposed information and decision system by providing false information in order to improve their payoff potential, the system may never be able to justify coordinated action.

Reduction of Interorganizational Conflict

In attempting to move organizations from situations of mixed conflict-cooperation to situations of cooperation it is necessary to identify organizational contextual variables which are associated with conflict. Certain of these variables have been classified by Walton, Dutton, and Cafferty[5] as:

   a. Incentives to suboptimization which result from conflicts of interest among organizational units.

   b. Jurisdictional ambiguity which exists among organizational units when the boundaries on responsibility are fuzzy.

   c. The presence of obstacles to interdepartmental (or interorganizational) communication.

   d. The existence of frustrating task conditions within any or all organizational subunits.

   e. The existence of social friction within any or all organizational subunits.

Walton, *et al.*[6] sought to test the importance of the role played by each of these contextual variables in producing interdepartmental or interorganizational conflict. They measured the existence of conflict in terms of both conflictful behavior and affective states. Conflictful behavior took the form of one organizational unit's interference with the performance of another unit,

   4. K. W. Thomas, R. E. Walton, and J. M. Dutton, "Determinants of Interdepartmental Conflict," in Part II of this volume.

   5. R. E. Walton, J. M. Dutton, and T. P. Cafferty, "Organizational Context and Interdepartmental Conflict," *Administrative Science Quarterly* (December 1969).

   6. *Ibid.*

over-statement of its needs in communication with another unit, or the withholding of information in communication with another unit. Affective states took the form of annoyance or distrust exhibited by the boundary personnel of any or all units.

Of the contextual variables listed above, (b) jurisdictional ambiguity, (a) incentives to suboptimization, and (c) physical and related barriers to communication, in the order given, were the variables most strongly related to interdepartmental or interorganizational conflict. These results may be extremely important for designers of organizational structures for interorganizational decision making. In commenting on the article in which they appeared, Pondy[7] remarked that these results "can be used as guides to controlled experiments in organization design. Such experiments, and not more correlational studies, constitute the most appropriate next step in the study of organizational conflict."

Refinement of Information and Decision Models

Most interorganizational decision situations can realistically be identified as arrangements between individuals with differing goals rather than in terms of a team wherein individuals are assumed to share a common goal. Two major differences between the approach required to resolve team problems and that required for interorganizational problems stand out.

1. Information requirements in team problems are strictly for purposes of optimizing the team goal. Information economics can be expressed in terms of trade-offs. Only that marginal unit of information which contributes to the team goal in proportion to its costs is purchased. Marschak[8] expressed the team problem as an effort to find the best communication system and the best decision rules, given an objective function, a set of probabilities associated with states of nature, and a cost of communication.

Information requirements for interorganizational problems are much less tidy than for team problems. This stems from the need to include a motivational content in the information transmitted. The units must be motivated to act in the best interests of the organization. At the same time they cannot be expected to act contrary to their own unit goals.

In developing an information system for solving interorganizational problems, the analyst cannot overlook the importance of individual goals. Each unit must be made aware of its share of the joint return to coordinated action. This share must reflect the return each unit is able to achieve independently.

2. The optimal resolution of interorganizational decision problems may require an entirely revised reward-penalty system with attendant revisions in

---

7. Louis R. Pondy, "Varieties of Organizational Conflict," *Administrative Science Quarterly* (December 1969).

8. J. Marschak, "Elements of a Theory of Teams," *Management Science*, I (1955), 129.

the reporting of results. Result reporting will have to allow for side payments to correctly balance the share of results attributed to each unit. The operations analyst who attacks an interorganizational decision problem must be willing to involve himself in organizational design issues by considering not only reward-penalty issues but all those structural elements which affect the relations between boundary personnel of interacting subunits.

Development of the Concept of Interorganizational Decision Making

Part I of this volume is devoted to introducing the concept of interorganizational decision making. Tuite, in "Toward a Theory of Joint Decision Making," sets forth conditions prerequisite to coordination in interorganizational problems. The first requirement is that there be recognition by a group of decision makers that interdependencies exist among them. Second, certain "interventions" into the decision situation are generally necessary to facilitate the consideration of these interdependencies and the development of a joint solution. Interventions are classified as (*a*) the redesign of organizational structures, (*b*) the adjustment of behavioral conditions, and (*c*) the choice of a decision technology which allows the decision makers to reach or approach a joint optimum.

The papers in succeeding sections of this volume are arranged to conform to this three-part format of required interventions. Once the existence of significant interdependencies in a decision situation is recognized, attention must turn to evaluating the suitability of the organization structure, behavioral conditions, and decision technology for achieving coordinated decision making. Each section contains a paper devoted to some aspect of each of these topics.

Conflict is not the only deterrent to optimal joint decisions which must be offset by interventions. Warren deals with the notion of the salience of joint decision making, or, phrased another way, with whether the benefits to be derived from joint action are seen as being large enough to provide an incentive for the decision unit to join with other units in concerted action. In Part III Walton specifies conditions under which decision units will seek to avoid engaging in joint action. For instance, joint efforts tend to increase the visibility of each unit, thereby exposing its decisions to criticism. This is a particularly sensitive consideration for government agencies or functional departments of a firm. The relative strength of the incentives which exist to compel units to avoid interaction give an indication of the corresponding strength of the interventions which will be required to produce the likelihood of optimal joint action.

In this section of the book, Warren's paper, "The Concerting of Decisions as a Variable in Organizational Interaction" contains a set of twenty propositions or assertions regarding "concerted" or joint decision making. Within these propositions he includes an assertion that the extent of organizations' involvement in concerting their decisions extends along a continuum from the social choice context, where there is no concerting of decisions, through the formation of a coalition, which involves stronger interaction, then to a federation, and finally to the unitary context. Within the unitary context the organizational units are effectively a part of a hierarchical structure. The choice of context referred to here represents alternative organizational structure designs which may be chosen as an intervention to facilitate optimal joint decision making.

In each of the organizational contexts in which the concerting of decisions is attempted, Warren further states, the organizational units will enter voluntarily into the process only under those circumstances which are conducive to a preservation or expansion of their respective domains. Otherwise, either trade-off inducements must be offered to the units or coercive power must be exercised. The treatment of interorganizational power relationships is extended in Heskett's paper which appears in Part IV.

Warren also introduces a measure of commitment of the organization to the particular joint decision venture. Using the concept of boundary personnel, he indicates that the number of boundary personnel is a measure of how committed an organization is to a given joint decision problem. If the decision is really important, all members of an organization may become boundary personnel. Finally, Warren refers to cooperative and contest processes as polar forms of joint decision making. This terminology parallels the earlier game-theoretic references to conflict games (zero-sum) and cooperative games (theory of teams).

1

Toward a Theory of Joint Decision Making

MATTHEW F. TUITE

The Joint Decision Making Process

This paper represents an attempt to develop a conceptual framework for that class of decision problems characterized by the existence of interdependencies between the decision units. The framework will necessarily be broad since it must encompass work by economists, operations researchers, organization theorists, and behavioral scientists.

The existence of interdependencies, or externalities, in a decision situation requires coordination of the actions of the decision makers involved to ensure a result which is jointly optimal. Coordination in terms of goals or constraints, or both, may be necessary. The need for coordination can best be illustrated with some simple examples.

If two decision makers fail to consider how their goals overlap, they may view their separate return functions as

$$\text{maximize} f_1(x_i)\,(i = 1, ..., m);$$
$$\text{maximize} f_2(y_j)\,(j = 1, ..., n), \qquad (1.1)$$

where the first decision maker chooses values for the x's and the second chooses values for the y's without regard to each other. Decision makers may not consider how their goals overlap precisely because they have been given goals which do not call for coordinated decision making — or they may perceive a reward-penalty system which places no value on a coordinated effort.

The same two decision makers, upon recognition that interdependencies exist between them, may state their return functions as

$$\text{maximize}_{x_i} f_3(x_i, y_j), \text{ maximize}_{y_j} f_4(x_i, y_j)$$
$$(i = 1, ..., m; j = 1, ..., n). \qquad (1.2)$$

This research was conducted as part of the Research Program in Administration at Northwestern University which is supported by the National Aeronautics and Space Administration under grant NGL14-007-058.

9

(The coefficients of some y's in f_3, and of some x's in f_4, may be zero.) Each decision maker continues to control his own decision variables (the first chooses values for the x's and the second chooses values for the y's), but through communication and coordination in establishing values for the decision variables the joint (or combined) return in equation (1.2) is greater than the joint return in equation (1.1).

Another alternative is for one decision maker, or a third party, to be placed in, or to assume, authority for establishing values for all variables. This form of coordination can be expressed as

$$\underset{x_i, y_j}{\text{maximize}} \left[f_3(x_i, y_j) + f_4(x_i, y_j) \right]$$

$$(i = 1, ..., m; j = 1, ..., n). \tag{1.3}$$

Here again, the joint return from coordinated action (equation [1.3]) should be greater than the return in equation (1.1).

If two decision makers fail to consider the constraints they impose on each other, they may make their respective decisions under the following conditions:

$$\text{maximize } f_1(x_i)$$

$$\text{subject to } \sum_{i=1}^{m} \alpha_{ik} x_i \leq b_k - \sum_{j=1}^{n} \beta_{jk} y_j = c_k$$

$$(k = 1, ..., p);$$

$$\text{maximize } f_2(y_j)$$

$$\text{subject to } \sum_{j=1}^{n} a_{jk} y_j \leq d_k - \sum_{i=1}^{m} e_{ik} x_i = g_k$$

$$(k = 1, ..., q). \tag{1.4}$$

Without coordinated action, each decision maker "accepts as given" the constraining influence of the other decision maker's actions.

These same decision makers, through communication and coordination of their actions, can change their respective decision problems to:

$$\text{maximize } f_1(x_i)$$
$$\text{subject to } c_k(x_i, y_j) \leq b_k$$
$$(i = 1, ..., m; j = 1, ..., n; k = 1, ..., p);$$

$$\text{maximize } f_2(y_j)$$
$$\text{subject to } g_k(x_i, y_j) \leq d_k$$
$$(i = 1, ..., m; j = 1, ..., n; k = 1, ..., q).$$

By coordinating the choice of values for the decision variables they are able to ensure the feasibility as well as the optimality of their joint decisions.

The coordination of decision situations involving interdependencies will hereafter be referred to as "joint" decision making whether one or several individuals or decision units acquire or assume the task of coordination.

Further, we will define the joint decision making process as comprising three steps:

1. Recognition that interdependencies exist between the decision units.
2. An intervention which facilitates consideration of these interdependencies in the decision-making process.
3. Selection of a technology for making the decision.

The sections which follow will treat these steps in turn.

In this definition of the joint decision process, an intervention refers to the action necessary to facilitate the participation of all decision units in a co-ordinated effort. Implementation of the decision to engage in coordinated action is assumed to be an integral part of the facilitation step. That is, facilitation of joint action cannot be said to have occurred unless it is sub-sequently possible to make a joint decision. It is not, however, implied that the joint decision will be optimal. Optimality will depend upon the decision technology selected, the nature of the problem, and the skill of the decision maker or makers.

Technology refers to the pattern of information exchange and to the struc-ture of authority chosen for reaching the joint decision. Information can be centralized or decentralized, freely exchanged or rationed, while authority ranges between centralized and decentralized. These concepts will be elabor-ated on in the section of the paper devoted to joint decision technologies.

Recognition That Interdependencies Exist

Decision problems are commonly stated in terms of a decision maker faced with the selection of optimal values for the variables under his control. Ideally a decision model will be created which will indicate preferred values for the decision variables. Such models include constraints and parameters which represent the decision environment. Seldom is explicit recognition given to the fact that the constraints and parameters of the model have resulted, or in the future will result, from the actions of other decision makers.

If decision makers act independently in situations in which interdepen-dencies exist, the decisions of one create constraints or parameters for the other. If the same decision makers coordinate their action, an increase in joint rewards, or a "collective good," can be obtained. The forms such coordination may take and the variety of ways in which coordination can be brought about will be specified presently. For the moment it will suffice to say that before efforts to bring about coordinated action can be initiated, at least one of the decision makers or an interested third party must become aware of the potential joint rewards for coordination (or penalties for noncoordination).

Decision problems involving interdependencies exist both within an indi-vidual organization and between autonomous organizations. An increasingly complex and rapidly expanding society has created many joint decision problems at the interorganizational level. Joint taxpayer-government-business interests are evident in problems of air and water pollution; inter-government cooperation is essential for equitable sharing of common-defense needs;[1,2] interagency coordination is often neglected in providing community health and social services;[3] intricate channels for the distribution of goods involving numerous production, transportation, and marketing organizations require coordination;[4] and educational alliances hold potential for improved teaching if they can indeed be formed.[5]

At the intraorganizational level the trend toward merger and the formation of conglomerates has increased the number of interdivisional externality problems faced by the managers charged with coordinating the resulting diversified giants. Between departments and functional areas of firms the potential for joint decision making remains, perhaps, even less developed than at interorganizational and interdivisional levels. For example, a study of the role of purchasing agents[6] revealed little evidence of joint decision making between purchasing agents and engineering personnel or between purchasing agents and production schedulers. While many of the purchasing agents interviewed were aware of opportunities for substantial cost savings, realization of these savings required that they be allowed to suggest alternative materials or parts to use, or changes in specifications, or redesign of components, or changes in the timing of purchases, or changes in lot sizes. However, the reward-penalty system, in most of the companies studied, was structured in such a way that this interaction was discouraged. As a further consequence of this goal structure, the motivation of the purchasing agents for seeking greater influence in decision making was not to maximize profits, but rather to enhance their own power position in the organization.

Facilitating the Consideration of Interdependencies in Decision Making

Once there is recognition of the potential for joint decision making, an "intervention" into the decision situation is generally necessary to set the stage for coordinated action. "Intervention" connotes the type of deliberate

1. J. van Ypersele de Strihou, "Sharing the Defense Burden Among Western Allies," *Review of Economics and Statistics*, XXXXIX (November 1967).

2. M. Olson and R. Zeckhauser, "Collective Goods, Comparative Advantage and Alliance Efficiency," Roland N. McKean (ed.), *Issues in Defense Economics*, National Bureau of Education Research (New York: Columbia University Press, 1967).

3. Sol Levine, Paul E. White, and Benjamin D. Paul, "Community Interorganizational Problems in Providing Medical Care and Social Services," *American Journal of Public Health*, CIII (August 1963).

4. J. L. Heskett and Ronald H. Ballou, "Logistical Planning in Inter-Organization Systems," in M. P. Hottenstein and R. W. Millman (eds.), *Research Toward the Development of Management Thought* (San Francisco: Academy of Management, 1966), 124–36.

5. B. R. Clark, "Interorganizational Patterns in Education," *Administrative Science Quarterly*, X (September 1965), 224–37.

6. G. Strauss, "Tactics of Lateral Relationships," *Administrative Science Quarterly*, VII (1962), 161–87.

adjustment and preparation of the decision environment which necessarily precedes joint decision making. Depending upon the organizational setting in which the decision makers are embedded, interventions may take the form of legislation, exercise of statutory powers, coalition formation, contractual agreement, vertical integration, merger, co-optation, organization of a club or clique, revision of goals, revision of the current reward-penalty system, publication of guidelines, or advice and exhortations of various kinds to bring about behavioral adjustments.[7]

The forms listed suggest that intervention may be initiated by one, or a few, of the decision makers involved, by all simultaneously, or by an outside party who may or may not be in a position of authority relative to the decision makers. Selection of a suitable intervention varies, depending upon whether the decision makers are in different organizations, different divisions, or different departments, only to the extent that these organizational settings present dissimilar problems in arranging coordination among the decision makers.

There is no suggestion here that the objectives of joint decision making differ between organizational settings. A joint optimum is the common goal. The only difference is in the means of achieving agreement to engage in joint decision making. Once coordinated action has been arranged, we are prepared to argue that the same options with regard to decision technologies are available irrespective of organizational setting. This latter point explains the separation of the facilitation step from the selection of a decision technology in analyzing the steps in the joint decision process.

Two general comments are necessary before turning to a discussion of specific alternatives for bringing about agreement to engage in coordinated decision making.

First, bargaining, learning, and adaptation will generally precede and/or accompany determination of the method of intervention in the decision necessary to bring about joint decision making. (Bargaining will also remain as an alternative decision technology and a very important one, e.g., union-management decisions.) Perhaps the principal reason that bargaining may be required prior to the agreement to coordinate decision making is the sensitive question of distribution of the collective rewards envisioned to result from coordination.

Second, arrangements for sharing the collective rewards earned by co-ordinated action may either be implicit in the agreement to engage in joint decision making or in the joint decision technology chosen. If, for instance, a revised set of goals (or a new reward-penalty system) was the intervention which brought about agreement to engage in joint decision making, then the arrangements for sharing the collective reward are contained therein regardless of the decision technology used. (Think of this in terms of a new

7. J. Stringer, "Operational Research for Multi-Organizations," *Operational Research Quarterly*, XVIII (June 1967), 105–20.

reward-penalty system for the purchasing agents and engineers discussed earlier. Implicit in this system would be a means of crediting each department with a share of the savings derived from coordinated decision making. The specific technology chosen for coordinating their decisions might affect the size of the collective reward but not the proportions in which they share it.) As an interorganizational example, consider a situation in which legislation requiring joint decision making was the intervention used, and in which bargaining was subsequently chosen as the decision technology. Here the arrangements for sharing the collective rewards are implicit in the choice of the decision technology rather than in the agreement to engage in joint decision making. (Think here in terms of joint decision making between union and management bargaining teams.)

FACILITATING THE CONSIDERATION OF INTERDEPENDENCIES AT THE INTERORGANIZATIONAL LEVEL

A basic difference in the alternative means available in an interorganizational setting for bringing about agreement to engage in joint decision making when compared with an intraorganizational setting is the absence of a natural authority relationship between the decision units.

When the general public or a substantial segment of the public constitutes one of the parties with overlapping interests, legislation can create an authority structure by imposition. An enforcement agency can then be directed to tax or collect subsidies, or just check on compliance and levy fines, where appropriate. An alternative to legislating a direct authority overlay is the legislation of decision guidelines. The establishment of zoning constraints or the codification of pure food and drug standards are examples of means of channeling decision making where the decisions of one party might inflict external diseconomies on others. These guidelines at least restrict the range of externalities which are legally acceptable.[8]

Exhortations and "recommended" guidelines may fail to be successful interventions in interorganizational settings because of the absence of an authority structure. An example of lack of success would be the case of President Johnson's wage-price guidelines. On the other hand, the government has had limited success in getting firms to participate in job training and some civil rights activities. In the latter instance motivation may have been provided by the desire to avoid an externality – riots.

Another means of creating an authority structure in interorganizational decision situations is by contractual agreement. In the aerospace field the role of project manager has been developed to coordinate the interaction of a number of autonomous organizations. The project manager negotiates contracts with the various contractors who will contribute to the achieve-

---

8. O. Davis and A. Whinston, "On Externalities, Information and the Government-Assisted Invisible Hand," *Economica*, XXXIII (August 1966), 304.

ment of a project. By assuming the coordination function, "the number of contact points is reduced, and a central office can insure that all systems are consonant with total system objectives."[9]

A less formal authority structure is brought into existence by the formation of a coalition. Community decision organizations, a concept introduced by Warren, such as community welfare councils, antipoverty organizations, chambers of commerce, and federations of churches, would seem to fit this category. Such coalitions "constitute the means through which the community attempts to concert certain decisions and activities."[10] A club or a clique is a form of coalition open to a group of individuals who wish to pursue related and interdependent objectives.

Clark observed leadership talent increasingly moving into such coordinating structures of the coalition type as "the interagency compact, the limited alliance, the consortium, the grants committee and the federation." He stresses the increasing importance of this approach to coordination which is not "bounded by the kind of structure usually designated as organization."[11]

At times it will be desirable to transfer the problem of arranging agreement on joint decision making from an interorganizational context to an intra-organizational context. This can be accomplished by vertical integration, merger, or co-optation. Vertical integration and merger are methods of absorbing externalities. Co-optation is the process of absorbing members of interacting organizations — for example, by placing them on one's board of directors. According to Thompson and McEwen, "to the extent that co-optation is effective it places the representative of an 'outsider' in a position to determine the occasion for a goal decision, to participate in analyzing the existing situation, to suggest alternatives, and to take part in the deliberation of consequences."[12]

Transferring the problem of arranging agreement on joint decision making to an intraorganizational setting leaves agreement still to be arranged, but under different circumstances. In the case of co-optation, for instance, it must be made "effective" in Thompson-McEwen terms before joint decision making can take place.

FACILITATING THE CONSIDERATION OF INTERDEPENDENCIES AT THE INTRAORGANIZATIONAL LEVEL

In an intraorganizational setting perhaps the key interventions take the form of revision of goals and revision of the current reward-penalty system. These

9. D. A. Wren, "Interface and Interorganizational Coordination," *Academy of Management Journal*, X (March 1967), 69–81.

10. R. L. Warren, "Interorganizational Field as a Focus for Investigation," *Administrative Science Quarterly*, XII (December 1967), 396–419.

11. Clark, *op. cit.*, 237

12. James D. Thompson and William J. McEwen, "Organizational Goals and Environment," in Amitai Etzioni (ed.), *Complex Organizations* (New York: Holt, Rinehart, & Winston, Inc., 1961), 184.

interventions parallel legislation in the case of an interorganizational setting and are possible because an authority structure already exists. Assuming that decision makers react essentially in their own best interests, the establishment of individual subgoals whose accomplishment optimizes corporate goals is the most effective means of achieving desired joint decision making behavior.

There is an interesting overlap here between interventions and the choice of a decision technology. On the one hand it may be possible to establish new subgoals for units within a firm as an integral part of the intervention by which agreement to engage in joint decision making is arranged. This is illustrated by the purchasing-agent example. On the other hand there is a decision technology by which adjustments in individual subgoals are made in an iterative fashion until the accomplishment of the subgoals results in a joint optimum. This is referred to as "coherent decentralization" in the section on decision technologies.

Between divisions of a firm, among agencies operating under the influence of a single governmental authority (e.g., Congress) and in numerous other circumstances, the control of funds by the central authority provides a powerful intervention by which cooperative decision behavior can be encouraged. (The requirement of interagency coordination as a precondition to the dispersal of Model Cities funds is an example). The publication of formal decision guidelines (contrasted to exhortations) is another bureaucratic alternative for achieving cooperative behavior. The extreme form of bureaucratic intervention is, of course, simply to order the subunits involved to coordinate their decisions.

A form of co-optation can be achieved in interdepartmental decision making if two functional departments, such as production and marketing, cooperate in deciding values for their respective choice variables through the use of a joint decision model. Tuite illustrated this form of intervention in a recent paper in which the demand-smoothing activities to be engaged in by marketing were simultaneously determined with the production-smoothing activities of production, in order to achieve a joint optimum.[13] In this case the decision function of marketing was co-opted by production.

Within an organization there are behavioral counterparts to the formation of coalitions between organizations. As suggested by Walton,[14] these take the following forms:

1. Initiating efforts to change the decision process that involves interacting subunits from a bargaining to a problem-solving orientation.
2. Changing the structure of interaction between decision makers from

13. Matthew F. Tuite, "Merging Marketing Strategy Selection and Production Scheduling: A Higher Order Optimum," *Journal of Industrial Engineering* (February 1968), 76–84.

14. Richard E. Walton, "Theory of Conflict in Lateral Organizational Relationships," in J. R. Lawrence (ed.), *Operational Research and the Social Sciences* (London: Tavistock Publications, 1966), 409–26.

one that is inflexible, formal, and closed, to one that is flexible, informal, and open.

3. Initiating efforts, where negative attitudes exist, to bring about a positive attitude between interacting decision makers.

These behavioral interventions may be more important when departments and functional units are involved than when subsidiaries are trying to arrange agreement on joint decision making. There is usually more personal interaction between units such as departments, but in all situations of interdependency there exists a tendency for issues such as status, power struggles, and professionalism versus nonprofessionalism to impede agreement.

Technologies for Joint Decision Making

The very nature of a decision situation involving interdependencies requires that information be exchanged between units or transmitted to a central unit in order to achieve coordination. The joint decision making technology is basically the format within which this information exchange takes place. But there are, in fact, three major facets of a decision making technology to be considered: first, whether authority for the joint decision will be centralized or decentralized; second, whether there will be informational centralization or decentralization; and third, whether information will be made freely available or be rationed.

Baumol and Fabian[15] suggest that centralization of authority can be coupled to informational decentralization. Their linear decomposition model meets Hurwicz's basic criterion that "in a decentralized allocative process there should not be transmission of detailed information concerning one unit (cost functions, production functions) from that unit to another unit whether the latter be a firm or some third party."[16] Charnes, Clower, and Kortanek claim for the Baumol-Fabian (Dantzig-Wolfe[17]) model the attribute of "division of information ... since each unit uses only its 'special' technology and imputed prices, while the control unit uses only the overall linking information and results of computations of individual units."[18] Yet, Baumol and Fabian note that at times "division managers *must be told by the company* what weights they are to employ, i.e., what combination of their proposals the company desires them to produce. There is not necessarily an automatic motivation mechanism which will lead division managers to arrive at such a combination of outputs of their own volition. In such cases,

15. W. J. Baumol and Tibor Fabian, "Decomposition, Pricing for Decentralization and External Economies," *Management Science*, XI (September 1964).

16. Leonid Hurwicz, "On the Concept and Possibility of Informational Decentralization," *American Economic Review*, LIX (May 1969), 513–24.

17. G. B. Dantzig and P. Wolfe, "Decomposition Principle for Linear Programs," *Operations Research*, VIII (1960), 101–11.

18. A. Charnes, R. W. Clower, and K. O. Kortanek, "Effective Control Through Coherent Decentralization with Preemptive Goals," *Econometrica*, XXXV (April 1967), 296.

the decentralization of authority permitted by decomposition breaks down completely."[19] Thus it would seem that the Baumol-Fabian decision technology sometimes combines informational decentralization with centralization of authority.

Charnes, Clower, and Kortanek have defined coherent (or optimal) decentralization of authority as existing when the total joint decision problem can be decomposed into subproblems such that the optimization of the subproblems leads to optimization of the total problem. They further define levels of coherency in terms of the amount of information which must be exchanged between subunits and the central unit in achieving optimization. The highest level of coherency requires the transmission of price information to the subunits and of subunit solutions back to the central unit until optimization occurs. Lower levels of coherency require the transmission of other information in addition to prices to the subunits.[20]

With an increasing "quantity" of information transmitted to subunits at lower levels of coherency, the question of centralization or decentralization of authority arises again. Combined with this is the unresolved issue of the "quantity" of information which can be transmitted from subunit to subunit or to a central unit while retaining "informational decentralization."

Returning to the Baumol-Fabian model again, if the information transmitted from a central unit to the subunits or from one subunit to the other or others includes the exact level at which their variables are to be set, it must be assumed that authority has been centralized.

As to the availability of information between units, Walton[21] distinguishes a problem-solving orientation between units as opposed to a bargaining orientation. Rationing of information is identified with a bargaining orientation, while a free exchange of information, accurately presented, characterizes a problem-solving orientation.

Most joint decisions are not made in conformity with the normative models just cited, nor are they made with assurance that the decision reached will be optimal. The information exchange for coordination of interdependencies in the bulk of cases ranges in formality and quantity from full disclosure, to the publication of plans and estimates (PPBS), to PERT, to agreement on guidelines, to suggestions and conversational exchange. In terms of authority the range is from complete domination by a central coordinator, to committees whose members share authority, to complete decentralization of authority. Agreement on the level at which variables are to be set in a joint decision can be by fiat, by vote, by bargaining, or by mutual adjustment.

Conclusion

The full development of a theory of joint decision making will permit better understanding of the nature of joint decision problems, the prediction

19. Baumol and Fabian, *op. cit.*, 14.

of outcomes in various situations involving externalities, and, on the normative level, the improvement of joint decision making.

At the descriptive level, Whinston[22] has observed that organizational structures and problem complexity are often of such character that no one person can assemble all the required information or form a plan of action in a situation where interdependencies exist. This in itself may rule out centralization of both authority and information. At the normative level organization theorists and behavioral scientists devise means of easing the flow of information, and they continue to search for optimal organizational and authority structures for joint decision making. Economists and operations researchers consider various optimality conditions for idealized organizations. This synthesis has tried to emphasize the fact that the work of organization theorists and behavioral scientists cannot be isolated from the work of economists and operations researchers in building a theory of joint decision making.

20. Charnes, Clower and Kortanek, *op. cit.*, 296.

21. Walton, *op. cit.*, 413.

22. A. Whinston, "Theoretical and Computational Problems in Organizational Decision-making," in J. R. Lawrence (ed.), *Operational Research and the Social Sciences* (London: Tavistock Publications, 1966), 191.

2

The Concerting of Decisions as a Variable in Organizational Interaction

ROLAND L. WARREN

It is important to attempt, at least, to find conceptual rubrics under which the wide variety of interorganizational decision-making contexts and processes can be ordered. As will be mentioned later, the conceptualization in this paper has arisen in connection with a study of interaction among organizations of a specific type, but the formulation has been kept as broad as possible, with the idea that it may apply equally to all formal organizations of whatever type. We are not sure that this is the case, and we welcome this opportunity to present some of our observations — for they can hardly be called more than that — for testing and criticism.

What, specifically, is meant by the concept "interorganizational decision making"? Under what circumstances do organizational units engage in this process? How does interorganizational decision making vary according to the contexts in which it occurs, and on what important dimensions does such variation take place?

The wording of the title to this chapter suggests two underlying theses as a basis for exploring these questions. First,[1] *interorganizational decision making is fruitfully approached through utilization of the concept of concerted decision making.* Second, *interorganizational decision making is only one type of organizational interaction.*

Let us begin, then, by differentiating concerted decision making from other processes of organizational interaction. At the most elementary level, the activities of one organization may affect another organization even though such an effect was not intended and even though the first organization is quite oblivious to the very existence of the other organization. When this

The author's work is supported by a Public Health Service research career program award (1-KO5-MH-21, 869), from the National Institute of Mental Health.

1. Twenty different insertions constitute the framework for the development of this paper. As they occur, they are italicized for ready reference.

relationship is reciprocal, one can speak of interaction, but not social interaction in the strict sense of the term. We need not quibble over terms here; the point is that much of the impact of any one organization on others is of this inadvertent type, though such impact may be crucial at times.

Beyond this level of unintentional one-sided or reciprocal impact are those actions in which two or more parties deliberately relate their behavior to each other. It is this deliberate relating of one's behavior to that of another that Max Weber takes, incidentally, as the criterion of *social* behavior.[2] When it is engaged in by two or more organizations, we can quite appropriately speak of organizational interaction in the sociological sense. Such organizational interaction constitutes a broad field for study and research.

Within the broad field of organizational interaction is a much narrower field in which the interactional process is not left as a series of mutual adaptations made by each organization to the behavior of the other(s). This narrower field of interorganizational decision making can be conceptualized as a part of the general concept of concerted decision making. *Concerted decision making is a process in which the individual decisions of two or more units are made on a more inclusive systemic level which includes these units.* The rationale underlying the concerted decision making is that the process will produce a more satisfactory outcome if concerted than if the units are left to make their own decisions independently.[3] In this paper the concept of concerted decision making will be used as the basis for analysis of inter-organizational decision making.

A number of questions immediately arise from such a formulation. What is a "more satisfactory" outcome? For whom is the outcome presumed to be more satisfactory?

A number of additional questions concern themselves with the circumstances under which the process occurs: Must the presumed greater satisfaction apply to all the participating organizational units, in a Pareto-optimal sense? What is the role played by coercion in this process, and how do voluntarily negotiated decisions compare with those which are coerced by third parties or by authority within a more inclusive organizational context? Do units always concert their decision making when the potential payoff appears greater; and if not, under what circumstances do they concert their decisions and under what circumstances do they make them individually? How inclusive is the *scope* of decisions which are concerted by a given number of organizational units as contrasted with the decisions which are made at the unit level? What differences are there in the contexts within which

2. Max Weber, *Wirtschaft und Gesellschaft*, Vol. 1, Johannes Winckelmann (ed.) (Köln-Berlin: Kiepenheuer & Witsch, 1964), p. 3 and chap. 1 *passim*.

3. The concept of concerted decision making is elaborated in the author's "Concerted Decision-Making in the Community," in *The Social Welfare Forum, 1965* (New York: Columbia University Press, 1965).

organizational units concert their decisions, and what implications do these differences in context have for some of the above questions?

Such questions can be approached through considering some important dimensions of concerted decision making among organizations. Let us start with the question of organizational domain. In a current research project on interorganizational behavior, we have found it helpful to conceptualize domain in terms of an organization's access to necessary resources. In this conception, organizational domain is the organization's locus in the inter-organizational network, including its legitimated "right" to operate in specific geographic and functional areas and its channels of access to task and maintenance resources. The two important components here are the organization's right to do something, and its access to the resources it needs in order to do it. This conception includes the organization's access to both input and output resources, and as such approximates Thompson's definition.[4] It is broader than Thompson's, in that it includes not only those resources needed for task performance, which Thompson emphasizes, but also those needed for maintenance of the organization itself, such as legitimation, investment capital, personnel, and long range "supporters." We see continued access to such necessary maintenance resources as also constituting an important part of an organization's domain. In short, an organization's domain consists of access to those resources which it needs to perform its task functions and to remain viable as an actor.[5]

I do not believe that any of the subsequent analysis stands or falls on this particular conception of domain. The term has been elaborated only to indicate how it is used in the assertions to follow. The next such assertion, which we take as axiomatic, at least for purposes of the present analysis, is as follows: *In its interaction with other organizations, an organization acts to preserve or expand its domain.* This proposition will be of help as we examine the circumstances under which concerted decision making takes place; but first, two brief comments: The question arises whether the proposition is an assertion about the way organizations behave in reality or about the way they would behave if they were completely rational. Actually, the latter is the case here, but I believe that the presumed rational behavior in this respect corresponds so closely to actual behavior in most interorganizational situations that the statement can be taken for our purposes as applicable to most organizational interaction. The same applies to the next assertion as well,

4. Cf. James D. Thompson, *Organizations in Action: Social Science Bases of Administrative Theory* (New York: McGraw-Hill Book Co., 1967), 22 ff.

5. Importance of the viability of the organization as a system, in contrast to the importance of merely one aspect of its functions—task performance—has been emphasized recently by Ephraim Yuchtman and Stanley E. Seashore in "A System Resource Approach to Organizational Effectiveness," *American Sociological Review*, XXXII (December 1967), and in an earlier article by Amitai Etzioni, "Two Approaches to Organizational Analysis: A Critique and a Suggestion," *Administrative Science Quarterly*, V (September 1960).

to which we will come shortly. The second comment has to do with the circumstance that in some instances, in order to remain viable, an organization must reduce its domain. For example, an organization which has sought to diversify through producing a particular line of merchandise may discover that its venture is not profitable and may decide to withdraw from this activity, thus reducing part of its domain in order to preserve or enhance the remainder and thus assure its continued viability.

The Dimension of Voluntarism/Coercion

We can now begin our analysis of a number of dimensions affecting interorganizational decision making. If our preceding assertions are valid, then it follows that *organizations enter voluntarily into concerted decision making processes only under those circumstances which are conducive to a preservation or expansion of their respective domains.* Where this situation does not exist, some degree of inducement or coercion is necessary to ensure the participation of those organizations which see a net threat to their own domains in the concerted decision making. The inducement may be some form of compensation to equalize the presumed loss to the organization in some aspect of its domain. If such inducements are not possible, then coercion must be exercised to secure participation. Such coercion may be divided for purposes of analysis into three forms: (1) Coercion exercised by one of the organizations involved over one of the other organizations involved. (2) Coercion exercised by a third party over one of the organizations involved. (3) Coercion arising from authority flow within the same hierarchically structured organization.

The question of the relevance of coercion to the possibility of concerting certain orders of decisions among particular organizations is a crucial one. On the one hand, it is sometimes erroneously asserted that coercive power must always be present to assure that decisions are concerted and that the concerted decisions will be carried out; and on the other hand, unrealistic assumptions are sometimes made about the likelihood of persuading organizations to operate in the alleged public interest when there is neither coercive power nor a condition where each organization can have reasonable assurance of domain preservation in the concerting process. To sum up, concerted decision making can take place where there is no coercive power, but it will take place only among those organizations which see no threat to their respective domains and only on those issues in which the organizations find this to be the case. In other instances, *concerted decision making is possible only if trade-off inducements can be offered to ensure voluntary participation or if coercive power can be exercised to bring it about. Such coercive power may be exercised by one or more of the parties over the other(s), or by a third party, or by legitimated authority within a hierarchical structure of which the organizations are an integral part.*

The Dimension of Decision Making Context

In the preceding paragraphs, an important consideration has been temporarily ignored – the organizational context *within which* one is considering the concerting of decisions by organizational units. At the one extreme, we may be talking about the concerting of decisions among virtually autonomous and mutually independent organizations. But on the other hand we must acknowledge that organizations often join together not merely around a single issue, but in more lasting frameworks through which certain types of decision making are more or less regularly concerted. And organizational units may be combined in various types of organizational framework in which they are not so much independent organizations joined loosely for decision making, as subunits of a single formal organization, hierarchically organized for decision making. Concerted decision making is applicable to all these contexts, and it varies with them on several dimensions to be considered below. *Since the concerting of decisions among organizational units may take place at various levels, it is important to identify the level at which the decisions are being concerted, and the context in which they are being concerted at that level.*

Four different types of context have been differentiated and described, and a recognition of the types forms a useful analytical tool for a consideration of decision making contexts. *Decision making contexts vary from the "social choice" context through the "coalitional" and the "federative" to the "unitary" context.*[6] These types vary as to the structure of the context in which interorganizational decisions are concerted, from a nonexistent structure at one extreme to a tightly integrated structure at the other. Specific dimensions of variation in these decision making contexts include (1) the relation of the organizational units to an inclusive goal, (2) locus of inclusive decision making, (3) locus of authority, (4) structural provision for division of labor, (5) commitment to a leadership subsystem, and (6) prescribed collectivity-orientation of the organizational units.

The decision making contexts range from the social-choice context at one extreme, with these six dimensions close to the zero point, through coalitional and federative, to unitary contexts where each of these dimensions has the greatest magnitude.

Organizations interacting in a social-choice context, where there is no concerting of decisions, may agree that they have mutual interests in concerting decisions around some particular issue; or, as in the analysis above, a third party may attempt to induce them to concert their decisions around some issue or project in the interests of a more inclusive system.

Insofar as they concert their decisions voluntarily, they may enter into a coalition, under which they retain their autonomy but make decisions and

6. For an elaboration of this typology, see the author's "The Interorganizational Field As a Focus for Investigation," *Administrative Science Quarterly*, XII (December 1967).

act in concert only insofar as they see such behavior as preserving or enhancing their respective domains. There is little permanent structure, little sense of loyalty to a more inclusive decision making unit, and no authority which the joint venture can exercise over its participants. The concerted decision making lasts only until the issue is resolved or until for some other reason one or more of the parties no longer finds it desirable to maintain the decision making interaction. An example is the campaign waged by a number of local industrial organizations to influence the official action of the city government.

Compared with the coalitional context for concerting decisions, the federation is stronger on all of the dimensions mentioned above. Here there is not only a partial concerting of decisions through ad hoc interaction but also a special organization set up for such concerted decision making, involving strictly delimited parts of the total decision making scope of the organizational units involved. And the occasion for the concerted decision making is less likely to be an ad hoc, episodic issue than to be a continuous interaction around certain issue areas over an extended period of time. But the individual organizational units maintain their autonomy except in the strictly delimited area in which they agree to concert their decisions and actions. An example is the trade association.

In the unitary context, on the other hand, the organizational units are not autonomous but are part of a single hierarchical decision making structure which orders their interaction, including the concerting of decisions.

The fourfold typology consists of four "ideal types" in the Weberian sense. It is not asserted that organizations in reality always fall neatly into one of these discrete types. They represent merely points on the continuum of each of the six dimensions listed. The typology is useful for analytical purposes, so long as this reservation is kept in mind.

To return for a moment to the dimension of voluntarism or coercion in concerted decision making among organizational units: it is readily apparent that the concerting of decisions among relatively autonomous units involves the question of whether such units, operating in an otherwise social-choice context, wish to enter into a coalitional or federative context for purposes of concerted decision making. Unless there is coercion, what we have said about the constraints of domain preservation applies. The coercive power which comes from authority flow within a legitimated hierarchically structured organization represents, of course, the unitary context.

The Dimension of Issue-Outcome Interest

A group of banking companies may get together to raise investment capital for a specific venture; a number of community agencies may get together to plan an application for a federal grant-in-aid program for their city; a number of organizations may concert their activity in opposition to a certain piece of proposed legislation. The examples given involve converging interests of two or more organizations on an ad hoc issue.

It is also possible for organizations to engage in concerted decision making where their interests around the specific issue are opposed to each other. This type of occasion is sometimes overlooked when interorganizational decision making is discussed. But it is apparent that organizations may make concerted decisions in areas where their interests do not coincide, and even where they directly conflict. In such cases, the parties wish a different outcome for the issue involved. They may negotiate as the principal parties to the issue. Or a third party may intervene as mediator, conciliator, or arbitrator; or the third party may be a unit or an official in a superordinate position within a formal organizational hierarchy, as where a dispute between department heads is resolved by the general manager. (This latter, the unitary context, is admittedly a limiting case, for some may argue that the concept of interorganizational decision making should not be carried over into the subunits of a single organization. But our approach to decision making contexts makes this possible, though not necessary, and it is useful to pursue it, if only to indicate its applicability for those theoretical conceptions which consider even a so-called unitary organization to be in essence a coalition of subunits.)[7]

To resume the main thread of the discussion: *Any issue may become the occasion for concerted decision making.* An important dimension of concerted decision making among organizational units concerns their respective positions with regard to the substantive issue of the decision making. From the analysis so far, it is apparent that *organizations enter into concerted decision making in order to resolve issues in a way that will preserve or if possible enhance their respective domains.* This consideration will determine the interest of each organization in the outcome of any specific issue on which ad hoc interorganizational decision making occurs.

On any given issue, each organization can be regarded as having an issue-outcome interest, namely, an interest in seeking that particular outcome for the issue which would be most advantageous to it in terms of the anticipated impact on its resource domain.

On any particular issue, any two organizations may have the same issue-outcome interest, or divergent issue-outcome interests. It is important to note that *concerted decision making may occur under situations of issue-outcome interest convergence or divergence. Where issue-outcome interests of two or more organizations converge, their concerted decision making is likely to be characterized by cooperative processes in the decision making itself and in seeking to assure the mutually desired issue-outcome.* Examples of such a mutually desired outcome would be the setting up of an industrial develop-

7. Cf. Richard M. Cyert *et al., A Behavioral Theory of the Firm* (Englewood Cliffs, N. J.: Prentice-Hall, 1963), 27 ff.

ment corporation; the pooling of efforts in obtaining a government contract involving anticipated profits for the respective firms, or the passage of a particular bill before the state legislature. As can be seen from these examples, convergence of issue-outcome interests does not necessarily imply agreement about all the values or goals involved in the issue, but merely that the organizations want the same outcome in the specific issue. They may desire this for the most varied and apparently contradictory sets of reasons. The criterion here is that they want the issue resolved in the same way.[8]

Where issue-outcome interests of two or more organizations diverge, their concerted decision making is likely to be characterized by contest processes in the decision making itself and in seeking to assure the mutually exclusive desired issue outcomes. The decision making regarding the disputed issue may or may not involve the intervention of third parties. In the above, for purposes of simplification, no consideration has been given to the frequent cases where organizations have similar issue-outcome interests in some respects but different interests in other respects. Thus, two or more organizations may have similar interests in forming a consortium to obtain a large government contract, but different interests with respect to the resources to be contributed to the venture and the share of the profits to be extracted from it by each organization. For our analytical purposes, these can be considered separate issues, for as Walton points out, the quality of the interaction between the same organizational units differs as one or the other issue comes to the forefront.[9]

The Dimension of Salience

In what has just been said, the nature of the concerted decision making has been related to the respective issue-outcome interests of the participating organizations. For purposes of simplicity we have assumed that concerted decision making is taking place. However, *whether the situation is one of issue-outcome interest convergence or divergence, concerted decision making is not assured, but depends on a number of variables which can be subsumed under the concept of salience.*

Let us consider first the case of similar issue-outcome interests on the part of two organizations. One might expect that if they have similar interests in the outcome of a particular issue, say the passage of a particular piece of legislation, they will concert their decision making regarding how they might respectively work to bring about the desired outcome. But in fact, they may or may not act in this way. What are the important variables here? Let us

---

8. For an analysis of the relationship between issue-outcome interests and action strategies, see the author's "Types of Purposive Social Change at the Community Level," *Brandeis University Papers in Social Welfare, No. 11* (Waltham, Mass.: Brandeis University, 1965).

9. Richard E. Walton and Robert B. McKersie, "Behavioral Dilemmas in Mixed-Motive Decision Making," *Behavioral Science,* XI (September 1966).

stick to the example of the proposed legislation, and let us consider the situation from the standpoint of one of the organizations, Organization A.

First, Organization A may not know that Organization B is also interested in the passage of the legislation. Thus, it is apparent that the procedures for scanning the interorganizational field in respect to possibilities for enhancement of resource domain are relevant to whether the process of concerted decision making takes place.

Second, even if one assumes awareness of Organization B's similar issue-outcome interest, Organization A may determine that the benefits offered by concerting decisions with Organization B regarding their respective action to support the legislation may not outweigh the resources which would have to be expended in the process. The issue itself—in this case, the passage of the legislation—may not be important enough to merit the investment of executive time in interorganizational conferences, strategy planning, and so on; and the resources in terms of influence over the legislature, whatever these may be, could be excessive when compared with the prospective benefits.

Third, it may be that Organization A is simply unable to mobilize its resources to bring them to bear on the issue, even though it may consider the issue important. Because of the press of other matters, or because of its own incapacity to move rapidly and fluidly to enhance its own interests, it misses an opportunity to benefit through concerted decision making.

Fourth, regardless of how important it may consider the issue, or how capable it may be to muster resources for it, Organization A may feel that the impact of concerting decisions with Organization B will not affect the issue outcome. This may be either because it believes that both organizations are presently working as effectively without concerting their decisions as they might be expected to work if they concerted them, or because it believes that the fate of the legislation is pretty well decided in any case, and any additional impact which might be gained through concerted decision making would not affect it.

Fifth, there may be a spillover to this issue from other episodes of cooperation or contest between the two organizations. The fact that the two organizations have recently collaborated successfully on a similar matter may predispose them to take advantage of this new opportunity as well. On the other hand, recent interaction episodes in which their interests were opposed may make it less likely that the organizations will seize a given opportunity to collaborate to their mutual advantage.

Sixth, inducements may play a role in the decision to engage in interorganizational decision making. Such inducements may be positive or negative, and may be offered either by the parties who would be directly involved in the concerted decision making or by third parties.

In sum, given similar issue-outcome interests, organizations may or may not engage in joint decision making to promote these interests, and in doing so they will be influenced by such considerations as the above. These considerations apply especially to the voluntary development of coalitions or federations from within the social-choice context. Organizational units within a unitary context are subject in addition to authoritative orders from a superior hierarchical level to concert their decisions, even where they might not otherwise care to do so. Yet even in these unitary contexts, the factor of issue-outcome interest and the six different circumstances outlined above may also be applicable.

What is less apparent is the circumstance, mentioned earlier, that concerted decision making may occur not only in situations of convergence of issue-outcome interest but also in situations of divergence. In situations of issue-outcome interest divergence, it is likewise problematic whether or not concerted decision making will take place. The scanning process is relevant in these situations as well, for there are numerous situations in which issue-outcome interests differ and where there might be a potential payoff for one or more of the organizations involved to enter into concerted decision-making, on the assumption that through such a process the issue will be resolved more favorably from its point of view than it would otherwise. Aggregately, this is a logical possibility in all but zero-sum situations: and even in zero-sum situations any given organization, or even a combination of organizations, may consider it in its own respective interest to concert the decisions in attempting to resolve the issue.

Thus, in issue-outcome difference situations, organizations may or may not concert their decisions, and whether they do depends on much the same considerations as those already given for situations of issue-outcome interest convergence.

These considerations have been discussed under the general rubric of salience, which term is subject to ambiguity. As can be seen, it is used here only in the general sense of suggesting that the decision to concert decisions does not occur automatically, but is contingent upon the relative importance of the issue, the possible effect of the joint decision making on the issue outcome, and so on.

The Dimension of Inclusiveness of Organizational Involvement

On most issues, organizational interaction involves only a part of the personnel, interests, domain sectors, and resources of the respective organizations. Only parts of the organizations may be interacting, with most of the respective organizations possibly even oblivious to the very existence of the other organization(s) with which their own is presumably interacting. Likewise, the same two organizations may be interacting in a competitive fashion with respect to certain aspects of their domains, and in a cooperative fashion with respect to other aspects, and not at all with respect to still other aspects of their domain.

Thus, if we are to do justice to the complexity of interorganizational decision making, we must recognize the importance of the dimension of inclusiveness of organizational involvement in interaction in general and in concerted decision making in particular. There is time here to explore only some of the aspects of the fact that interorganizational decision making usually involves only parts of the organizations in only parts of their total domains.

We have already touched upon one of these aspects in referring to previous episodes of successful concerted decision making as a factor in the decision to concert decisions. A successfully concluded and mutually advantageous business transaction between two organizations may become the basis for additional transactions which spread to other types of goods or services. The basis for the interorganizational decision making may be more than an individual transaction, however. For example, they may take the form of a more permanent collaborative relationship of some sort (as where two governments agree to consult each other before taking action in certain areas), or the organizations may set up even more formal and permanent machinery for concerted decision making in certain aspects of their domains, as in a trade association.

As can be seen, the dimension of the decision making context is definitely relevant to that of organizational involvement. *Generally, the extent of an organization's involvement in concerted decision making around a specific issue is small or nonexistent in the social-choice context, larger in the coalitional, still larger in the federative, and largest in the unitary context.*

In another vein, just as concerted decision making applies both to similar and to different issue-outcome interests, the degree of organizational involvement in concerted decision making may either grow or diminish, in either type of issue-outcome interest. This increasing involvement in the interaction is what is implied in the concept of conflict escalation. On various levels of social organization, including the formal organizational level, what begins as a relatively minor controversy may escalate to one of major proportions. Part of this process of escalation is the involvement of more and more of the personnel, resources, and domain activity of the respective organizations in the conflict process. Thus, the conflict may spread to involve a larger part of the organizations, and a larger number of issue areas. It may also spread to involve the search for allies, the involvement of third parties in the conflict.[10] Parenthetically, conflict episodes are resolved through victory of one of the parties, through compromise, through the coercion of third parties, and so on. The resolution of the conflict involves a rapid or slow de-escalation which in our terms can be seen in a lesser organizational involvement in the conflict interaction.

All this is widely recognized. What is not so widely recognized is the fact

10. Coleman has documented the process for community conflicts. See James S. Coleman, *Community Conflict* (Glencoe, Ill.: The Free Press, 1957), 9–14.

that cooperation, also, may escalate, may involve more of the personnel, resources, and domain areas of the respective organizations, may involve third parties being drawn into the cooperative process, may eventually reach a peak and then de-escalate, as various of these aspects are no longer involved or become involved less intensively. Thus, *the escalation and de-escalation of either cooperative or contest processes is associated with the degree of organizational involvement in interaction on the issue.*

Thus, the extent of organizational involvement in concerted decision making is a variable; and it will be great or little, whether in issue-outcome divergence or convergence situations, depending on the anticipated effect of the interaction on each individual organization's resource domain and on the considerations of salience discussed earlier. Escalation and de-escalation of the interaction process, whether of a cooperative or of a contest nature, can be analyzed in terms of the scope of respective organizational involvement in such aspects as personnel, other resources, and the breadth of the domain sector involved.

Two organizations may engage simultaneously in different types of cooperative or contest interaction focused on different issues and involving different configurations of personnel, interests, domain sectors, and types of resources applied to the issues.

The complexity of these situations can be accommodated conceptually as long as we recognize the importance of specific issues or issue areas as foci of organizational interaction, and as long as we recognize that organizations seldom act totally on any issue.

This analysis of concerted decision making among organizations has emerged in the application of some earlier considerations to a current interorganizational research project in which we are examining the interaction of a specific number of so-called "community decision organizations," or CDOs, with each other in nine different American cities. The CDOs under study are the Board of Education, the local urban renewal agency, the poverty agency, the health and welfare council, and the mental health planning agency if there is one. The purpose of this research is to gain more knowledge of the way in which the interaction of these organizations (and others with similar characteristics) affects the outcome of decisions at the community level. In devising a model of CDO interaction which guided the development of our methodology, we found it helpful to make certain interrelated assertions about interorganizational behavior which could then be either precisely or roughly "tested" in our research. We tried insofar as possible to formulate our assertions about the interaction of these community decision organizations in a way which would be applicable to other types of organizations as well, such as, for example, business firms, trade unions, or national governments. Whether or not they can be so broadly applied is problematic. Indeed, we are not even sure that they apply to the community decision organizations we are studying. We feel sure there will be many revisions as a result of our research. Meantime, we have found them helpful, and it has been helpful also to apply some of them to the topic of the concerting of decisions as a variable in organizational interaction. Suggestions are welcome, particularly regarding pertinent areas of inter-organizational decision making to which this type of analysis seems less applicable or relevant.

II

A Framework for Solving Joint Decision Problems: Introduction

Progress in the resolution of interorganizational decision problems awaits the design of organizational arrangements which will facilitate optimal joint decision making. These organizational arrangements correspond to the "interventions" which were discussed in Part I. The designer of organizational arrangements, however, needs more than a specification of interventions to be made. He needs criteria by which he can judge the likelihood that his particular design will be effective in facilitating joint decision making. In this section Leonid Hurwicz provides some necessary criteria. But the designer needs even more than criteria. He needs suggestions as to specific structural and behavioral elements which are likely to meet the imposed criteria. Thomas, Walton, and Dutton provide such suggestions. Finally, he needs direction in the selection of an information and decision technology compatible with the design criteria. Kortanek's survey of coherent decentralization models outlines this direction.

The Hurwicz, Thomas *et al.*, and Kortanek papers represent a framework for solving joint decision problems. These authors examine control variables and decision processes which could be manipulated to achieve optimization if one were free to design the interorganizational structure from the beginning or to alter existing organizations in any way desired. In Part III this framework is further refined. There, papers by Reiter, Walton, and Hass complement the efforts of Hurwicz, Thomas *et al.*, and Kortanek, respectively.

In Part II, Hurwicz examines structural variables from the designer's point of view. In designing an organizational structure for optimal joint decisions certain design criteria are essential. His criteria are "desirability" and "feasibility."

A desirable organizational structure would, for instance, not favor any one decision maker. It would be unbiased in terms of outcomes capable of occurring. (All Pareto-optimal outcomes, in which each decision maker is as well or better off than before, would be capable of occurring. Marketing

33

values would not be served to the exclusion of production, or vice versa.) Another desirable feature is absence of waste. For a given environment a desirable organizational structure would be nonwasteful in terms of outcome. This characteristic refers to the joint outcome and includes all those factors which lead to mutual agreement of a joint optimal or near-optimal solution by the subunits involved.

In discussing the feasibility criterion, Hurwicz divides this characteristic of an organizational structure into "behavioral" and "material" feasibility. Behavioral feasibility is exhibited when neither the individual decision maker nor the group is expected to act in a way that is disadvantageous from his or its point of view. Material feasibility refers to the availability within the organization of the material resources and technological know-how to carry out the organizational design. This raises the very practical problem of implementation. If the decision model, including the information system requirements, is too complex or too costly for the organization involved, it cannot be implemented. This factor must be realistically evaluated in the development of an interorganizational decision model.

As is readily apparent from the description of the Hurwicz paper, any attempt to subdivide the interorganizational decision making problem will suffer a certain lack of clarity or crispness. The criteria employed by Hurwicz would apply equally well to behavioral models or to the decision technology. Yet the thrust of Hurwicz's remarks was toward the structural problem, and so it was categorized. In each of the papers to follow, it is the importance of the main theme of that paper which served as the classification criterion. Thus, the behavioral paper will differ only in degree from the structural paper, and the first tentative steps toward interdisciplinary research are taken.

In the behavioral subdivision, emphasis is placed on variables recognized as specific determinants of the decision making behavior of participants. The key people, whose behavior is analyzed, are the boundary personnel. The behavioral variables are closely related to the specific organizational structure within which joint decisions are to be made. The response of boundary personnel to the possibility of coordination with their interface counterparts can tend toward conflict or collaboration.

Where along the conflict-collaboration continuum the response of the boundary personnel will lie depends in part on structural characteristics and in part on behavioral variables. The directly structural elements which may affect their response are organizational differentiation (including the effect of differences in organizational culture and norms on boundary personnel attitudes and orientation), performance criteria and rewards, mutual task dependence among units, task-related asymmetries, dependence on common resources, communication obstacles, and role ambiguities. A mixed personal-structural element is the assertion that an individual's personal skills and personality traits will affect his functioning at organizational interfaces. The organizational functions of selection and training of personnel tends to place even these personal elements within the range of organizational design considerations.

In Chapter 4, some of these behavioral variables are examined by Thomas, Walton, and Dutton in their paper in which they develop a theory of inter-departmental conflict as a function of a number of behavioral variables. Their list of behavioral variables contains the salience of interdepartmental relationship, competition incentives, jurisdictional ambiguities, factors inhibiting communications, sources of friction and frustration, and scarcities within a department. They also deal with a number of personal factors, such as age.

Thomas *et al.* make the interesting and practical suggestion that after estimating the sensitivity of interunit conflict to a given variable, analysis should then be undertaken to compare the costs of manipulating the variable with the resulting reduction in conflict. This certainly suggests a promising beginning to the quantification and optimization of variable settings in an organizational design context.

The final subdivision of variables affecting interorganizational decision making is in terms of the information and decision technology which guides the decision makers. The requirements of the decision technology depend primarily on the organization structure adopted. The effectiveness of the technology will depend in part on the motivation of the decision makers if it is decentralized or on the supervisory skill of management if it is centralized. Implementation difficulties may particularly arise when decision making is centralized or when "guidelines" are imposed on the decision units from "above."

Implementation and other problems of decentralized decision making are discussed more fully by David Baron in his paper in Part IV to follow. In the present part, Kenneth Kortanek reviews the decision models for de-centralized decision structures. The decision technologies which Kortanek examines are capable of providing optimal solutions for subunits in terms of some joint goal. They assume full adherence by all parties to this joint goal. These decision technologies, which are labeled coherent decentralization, specify an information structure and decision process within which each decision unit, as it optimizes its subprogram, automatically contributes to the optimization of the joint goal.

By developing organizational design criteria which are conducive to coordinated decision making, by exploring behavioral determinants which lead to problem solving rather than bargaining behavior by decision partici-pants, and by creating decision technologies which minimize information requirements and costs and protect participant motivation, the theory of optimal interorganizational decision making deals with the basic problems which threaten the achievement of joint optimum solutions.

3

Organizational Structures for Joint Decision Making: A Designer's Point of View

LEONID HURWICZ

My purpose here is to examine organizational structures from the point of view of a designer of such structures. It is, of course, very worthwhile to study organizations in the spirit of positive (as distinct from normative) science, taking the existing structure as given; thus in economics a great deal of attention is paid to oligopolistic market phenomena, not because one favors oligopoly but simply because it is believed to exist. But economists are not always willing to confine themselves to the analysis of what exists, because they regard the economic structure as subject to conscious modification, by legislation as well as other techniques. If one is willing to consider such modifications, one must study their *feasibility*, and it becomes natural to develop a set of criteria by which to judge their *desirability*. In what follows we shall discuss such criteria. Although much of our analysis is inspired by problems arising in connection with economic organizations, our formulation is intended to be of sufficient generality to apply in other fields as well.

To delimit the area of our primary interest further, it is necessary to distinguish between two types of normative analysis. On the one hand, one may take the organizational structure as given while considering alternative policies admissible within such a structure. In economics, the problem of choosing income tax rates might be an example of such policy choice within the existing structure. On the other hand, the choice between a free market and one subject to price controls and quantity allocations would exemplify a situation in which the economic structure itself becomes the variable of the problem. It is the latter type of choice that involves what we have called "the designer's point of view," in the sense that in making the choice one is in the position of someone designing the economic organizational structure.

The designer's point of view is not a rarity in the field of social organization. Much legislation has considerable impact on the society's organizational

Research partly supported by National Science Foundation Grants G24027 and GS2077.

structure, and those who write laws are often very conscious of this. An outstanding example of this is the writing of a new country's constitution, a field in which the United States pioneered and in which scores of nations have since been engaged. In fact, the designer's point of view has antecedents in the economic area as well, whether it be advocacy of laissez-faire, or centralized controls and planning. Utopias, when taken seriously, are classic examples of conscious design of social organizational structures.

If one is willing to bypass the issue of "salability" of an organizational structure, the two major issues are feasibility and desirability. We shall find it convenient to reverse what might be a more realistic order and consider first the criterion of desirability.

Desirability of Organizational Structures

Goals are typically formulated in terms of the *outcomes* produced by the functioning of an organization. Thus, in economics, goals are basically formulated in terms of human satisfaction generated by goods that are produced and distributed by the economy. When one is comparing *policies*, it is often possible to ascribe specific outcomes to the alternative policies and compare these outcomes on some welfare ordering scale. A widely used ordering of this type is the Pareto-ordering according to which outcome $0'$ is Pareto-superior to outcome $0''$ if and only if no member of the group in question is (in terms of his preferences) any worse off under $0'$ and at least one is better off; an outcome is called Pareto-optimal if it is feasible and if no feasible outcome is Pareto-superior to it. Economists frequently confine themselves to Pareto-ordering type comparisons and refrain from judgments as to the comparative merits of two different Pareto-optimal outcomes. In judging alternative forms of economic organization it then becomes natural to ask whether the outcomes produced by the given structure are or are not Pareto-optimal and let it go at that. The best known example of such analysis is the theorem of welfare economics stating that, for a certain category of environments which we shall call "classical," the perfectly competitive mechanism produces Pareto-optimal equilibria. ("Mechanism" is here a synonym for "organizational structure.") Such a mechanism may be said to be *non-wasteful* for classical environments. (The economic *environment* is characterized by its initial resource distribution, technology, and preferences or wants; "classical" environments are characterized by absence of external economies and diseconomies of scale, perfect divisibility of goods, convexity of the relevant sets and functions describing preferences and technology, and certain other mathematical features.)

When all members of the group share their goals, values, or desires, as in a *team*, nonwastefulness (or some other concept of efficiency) may be an adequate criterion of desirability. But the team in such a pure sense is a rarity at best, or perhaps is primarily a convenient analytical abstraction. Normally, there will be conflict, and different Pareto-optimal outcomes will favor different members of the group. Just as one might object to a political constitution that determines in advance which party will win elections, so one may be interested in organizational structures that do not prejudge which of the optimal outcomes will come to prevail. For instance, one may require that all Pareto-optimal outcomes be capable of occurring; such a mechanism may be said to be *unbiased*. In welfare economics it is shown that, again for classical environments, the perfectly competitive mechanism (when combined with income or wealth transfers) has this property of unbiasedness.

It is not my intention to argue that the Pareto-ordering has special merit as a welfare criterion. Rather, I use it because its implications, unlike those of possible other criteria, have been studied in considerable detail. For this reason, it is helpful in illustrating the considerations that may be of importance to the designer of organizational structures. The attribute of unbiasedness as a counterweight to nonwastefulness is one illustration of such considerations. Another important aspect of the problem that becomes apparent from the preceding discussion is that properties of interest to the designer, whether it be nonwastefulness or unbiasedness, are relative to the class of environments in which they are assumed to operate. Thus perfect competition is nonwasteful in the absence of external diseconomies, but (as stressed by those concerned with the ecological consequences of pollution) not necessarily otherwise. The welfare economics theory "guarantees" nonwastefulness and unbiasedness over the category of classical environments, but not for broader classes of environments, just as an automobile of particular design may be excellent for high-speed travel on freeways and quite inadequate for driving over mountainous country roads. It is the need for economic mechanisms that would be satisfactory (in the sense of nonwastefulness and unbiasedness) over a class of environments significantly broader than the classical ones that has led some economists to explore such alternatives as tax-subsidy schemes, marginal cost pricing, centralized planning, etc.

As we proceed to develop suitable categories for analyzing organizational structures, it is well to note that such analysis is based on a fundamental, and yet subjective, distinction. In our terminology, it is the distinction between the environment and the mechanism. In the preceding discussion, the two concepts were illustrated by their usage in economics, but the underlying distinction is based on what the designer considers as given (this is, in general, called environment) and what he regards as something he can tinker with (this is what, in general, we call the mechanism). Whether a specific feature of reality (e.g., a set of laws) is to be considered in the category of givens or subject to modification by the designer is, of course, subjective. Depending on where the line is drawn, different normative theories of organizational structure will result.

Feasibility of Organizational Structures

Among the ways of classifying the various aspects of feasibility, one has emerged rather naturally in the context of economic planning structures. Since there does not seem to exist an accepted terminology in this area, we shall adopt, as somewhat arbitrary labels, the terms "material" and "behavioral."

Behavioral feasibility has to do with human motivation and incentive structures. Whenever it is ignored, finely drawn organizational schemes turn out to be inoperable. Perhaps the simplest aspect of behavioral feasibility is *individual-incentive compatibility*. Here the issue is whether the behavioral rules postulated for a given individual under a specified organizational structure are consistent with the behavior pattern that this individual would find most advantageous from his own point of view. Analytically, this can be expressed through the concept of Nash equilibrium in a noncooperative game, since such an equilibrium, by definition, prevails when no player has an incentive to modify his strategy given that others retain theirs. (Certain forms of speculative behavior illustrate the possibility of departing from prescribed rules.) But there is no reason to confine oneself to individual incentives. To the extent that groups can and are permitted to communicate, they may collectively upset organizational rules or structures that might be individual-incentive compatible. (When disapproved of, such forms of behavior are known as collusions.) The question of behavior patterns that would be *group-incentive compatible*, as well as individual-incentive compatible, has been studied in the theory of cooperative games; in particular, the core of a game (and, earlier, the von Neumann–Morgenstern "solution") have been proposed as exhibiting such behavioral viability. When not all groups are able to interact, more specialized concepts — for example, psi-stability proposed by Luce and Raiffa[1] — become appropriate.

Thus it is seen that behavioral feasibility can be analyzed within the framework of the theory of games of strategy; those with experience in organizational problems have long faced this fact.

Material feasibility involves, as in other economic processes, resource availability and technological knowledge. To the extent that organizational structure requires specialized *resources* (skilled personnel, computing machines, telecommunication equipment), its material feasibility depends on the existence of such resources. (Moreover, resources may exist in the economy and yet not be available for use by the organizational structure.) In a market economy, traders, accountants, and marketing and management experts have to be counted among the resources required to operate the mechanism; in a planned (or mixed) economy, various planning officials, and regulatory-agency employees are in the same category.

---

1. R. D. Luce and H. Raiffa, *Games and Decisions* (New York: John Wiley & Sons, Inc., 1957), chap. 10.

Technological knowledge that is of special relevance in this context is the knowledge involved in designing tables of organization, prescribing paths of communication, choosing procedures for decision making, and structure of authority, as well as the more obvious requirements of the physical communication and accounting and computational procedures.

Of particular interest are feasibility restrictions due to the dispersion of information and the limitations on the information processing capacities of the various members of the organization. By *dispersion* of information we mean the fact that at any given time different agents (persons, committees, data banks) have information that pertains only to a relatively limited aspect of the total environment. The typical assumption made in economic analysis is that initially an agent only has information concerning his own circumstances (technology, resources, preferences). Since optimal decisions cannot, in general, be made when such dispersion prevails, nonwastefulness (as well as unbiasedness) requires that some information be transmitted from agent to agent. Market bidding processes constitute an example of such transmission. Now transmission of information is subject to capacity limitations involving the "amount" of information, as well as time and degree of accuracy. These limitations are functions of both the resources that are available and the existing technology of information transmittal.

The awareness of such limitations has led to the development of concepts of informational efficiency and informational decentralization. Informational efficiency is the more general of the two concepts. Given two (information processing) mechanisms M' and M'', the mechanism M' is said to be informationally more efficient than M'' if, other things being equal, it requires fewer resources or less effort in processing information. Thus if the only difference between the two is that M'' requires that two numbers, say x_1 and x_2, be transmitted and perceived whereas M' requires only that their sum $y = x_1 + x_2$ be transmitted and perceived, then M' would be informationally more efficient. This concept of efficiency is related to feasibility, since it is conceivable that, given the existing resource limitations, only the more efficient of two mechanisms would be feasible. However, even when both are feasible, there is an obvious advantage in using a mechanism that requires fewer resources; this aspect will be discussed under the rubric of *cost* of operating the mechanism (below).

Informational decentralization (the adjective is intended to distinguish it from decentralization of authority) is a characteristic (of a mechanism) related partly to the dispersion of information and partly to the feasibility (and cost) of information transmission. Although there is no agreement on what constitutes a universal concept of informational decentralization, a basic feature of an informationally decentralized mechanism is that at no time in its decision making process is complete information concerning the environment (including all other agents' circumstances) and prospective actions of all parties available to any one agent. Now if one assumes the initial dispersion of information, it is clear that such concentration of information in one agent could occur only under essentially unlimited transmission and perception conditions. Thus informational decentralization will necessarily occur (to a greater or lesser extent) if limits are put on the feasible (or permissible) transmission facilities. (We ignore the related computational and problem-solving limitations.) Such limits may involve memory restrictions (e.g., one-period memory), the number of variables (i.e., the dimensionality of the message together with certain continuity properties of the response functions and of the decision functions), the aggregativeness of the process, etc. (These limitations were formulated by the writer[2]; alternative formulations have been proposed by Camacho[3], Radner[4], and Reiter[5].

"Costs" Associated with the Operation of the Organizational Structure

It has become evident from the preceding discussion of feasibility that feasible mechanisms may differ greatly in the extent to which they absorb resources. Oversimplifying, let the organization's resources be denoted by a, a vector of which the different types of resources (personnel, machines, etc.) are components. Denote by $b(M)$ the resources required for the operation of the mechanism M, and let $f(x, M)$ denote a functional relation which specifies a measure (possibly vectorial) w of welfare attainable when mechanism M is used and resources x remain available for purposes other than operating the system. Now the efficiency of different mechanisms may differ in two respects: first $b(M')$ may be less than $b(M'')$, i.e., M' requires fewer resources (perhaps in the vectorial ordering sense) than M''; second, $f(x, M')$ may be higher than $f(x, M'')$, i.e., M' may be capable of producing (vectorially) more welfare than would M'' from the same resources available for purposes other than operating the mechanism itself. It may happen that these two criteria may yield opposite orderings: for example, the mechanism M^* may require greater resources than M^{**} to operate, but, on the other hand, $f(x, M^*)$ may be higher than $f(x, M^{**})$, Now the relevant comparison will be the net one, viz., that of the two magnitudes

$$f[a - b(M^*), M^*] \text{ and } f[a - b(M^{**}), M^{**}];$$

2. Leonid Hurwicz, "Optimality and Informational Efficiency in Resource Allocation Processes," *Mathematical Methods in the Social Sciences,* K. J. Arrow, S. Karlin, and P. C. Suppes (eds.) (Palo Alto: Stanford University Press, 1960), 27–46; and "On the Concept and Possibility of Informational Decentralization," *American Economic Review,* LIX (May 1969), 513–24.

3. Antonio Camacho, "Centralization and Decentralization of Decision Making Mechanisms: A General Model," Northwestern University Graduate School of Management, May 1970.

4. Roy Radner, "The Evaluation of Information in Organizations," *Proceedings of the Fourth Berkeley Symposium on Mathematical Statistics and Probability,* J. Neyman (ed) (Berkeley: University of California Press, 1961) I, 491–530.

5. Stanley Reiter, "Informational Efficiency of Resource Allocation Processes," presented at the World Econometric Congress, Cambridge, 1970.

i.e., we would be comparing the "*net*" amount of welfare the two systems produce after one has deducted the resource amounts required to operate the respective mechanisms. Although this way of looking at it is obvious to the point of triviality, it is often overlooked in assessments of comparative merits of alternative systems.

The exposition of the preceding paragraph was purposely simplified to focus on the point being made. Actually, formidable technical questions arise in trying to effect the "net" comparisons when complex welfare criteria, including distributive aspects, are taken into account.

Also, one should not overlook the fact that there are aspects akin to resource costs that must enter such comparisons. Some of these could be classified as ideological or psychological. They involve the amount of freedom of decision making left to the members of the organization, the degree of privacy, etc. In some sense these "side effects" of the various mechanisms should be added to (or subtracted from) the welfare indicators obtained along the lines of the previous discussion. Insofar as distributive justice is valued by group members, its presence or absence would be among the factors entering this calculation. Similarly, the degree of centralization of authority, in addition to the direct effect it has on the "material" performance of the system, will also have to be assessed for its psychological or ideological costs. Resorting again to extreme simplification for expository purposes, one might write a formula for "net welfare" taking into account the psychological and ideological cost $c(M)$ associated with the mechanism M, viz.,

$$f[a - b(M), M] - c(M).$$

(Of course, expressions more sophisticated than a difference of the two terms could be introduced: they would be of the form $g\{f[a - b(M), M], M\}$.)

"Imperfect" Outcomes

So far the discussion has proceeded without devoting explicit recognition to two aspects of outcome that are of crucial importance in the comparative evaluation of organizational structures viewed as problem-solving systems: the speed with which information is produced and the accuracy of such information. A simple formulation of these aspects may be obtained by postulating the existence of a function, say ϕ, which associates the degree of accuracy of the "solutions" obtained by the mechanism with the passage of time. Thus if the accuracy is denoted by θ (say the reciprocal of the variance of the "solution" about the "correct" value), we would write

$$\theta = \phi(T; M),$$

where T is the elapsed time, θ the accuracy, and M the mechanism used. Again, there are serious difficulties in relating the concept of "correct" value as used here to the welfare criteria introduced earlier. Technically, a bridge may be built by defining the mechanism as an adjustment process[6] but with stochastic response (and perhaps also outcome) functions.[7]

The stochastic element can enter in several ways. The more obvious is the inaccuracy characterizing the process due to erroneous information held by agents, imperfect transmission procedures, imperfect computations, etc. Another, however, is related to what one might call the reliability of the mechanism, i.e., the probability that for either material or behavioral reasons it would break down, so that its normal procedures could not or would not be followed.

Deductive Analysis

Model construction for organizational analysis is, of course, only a first step, although possibly helpful in organizing one's thinking. As in other areas, one is interested in the possibility of deductive results that are not immediately obvious from definitions and assumptions. In fact, there are a few such results now available. Of those that are particularly close to my own focus of interest, theorems have been obtained on the existence of mechanisms that are informationally decentralized and also nonwasteful and unbiased over broad classes of economic environments (e.g., all those that are free of external economies and diseconomies); also, there are examples of nonexistence of such mechanisms when externalities are present. But a vast area remains hardly touched. As an example, there are relationships between the structure of information processing and the structure of authority; e.g., authority can hardly be centralized when information and commands cannot be effectively transmitted. A systematic investigation of these relationships seems already overdue.

6. Hurwicz, "Optimality . . .," *op. cit.*
7. Hurwicz, "On the Concept . . .," *op. cit.*

4

Determinants of Interdepartmental Conflict

KENNETH W. THOMAS, RICHARD E. WALTON,
AND JOHN M. DUTTON

The present study is part of an investigation testing a general model of inter-departmental conflict and its management.[1] This paper identifies some causes of interdepartmental conflict in organizations and attempts to extrapolate the findings to interorganizational conflict as well.

In general, the authors feel that much of the literature on interdepartmental relations can be used to advantage by interorganizational theorists. The dividing line between interorganizational relations and interdepartmental relations is a blurry one. In Evan's words, "The phenomena and problems of interorganizational relations are part of the general class of boundary relations problems confronting all types of social systems.[2]" We shall return to the issues involved in extrapolating our findings to interorganizational decision making when we discuss the implications of our findings.

The Organization Studied

The present study involved lower and middle management levels in a telephone company. The company is organized by exchanges. Within a modal exchange there are six interdependent departments, each performing a specialized function (see Figure 4.1). The Commercial department receives residential orders, collects money, and handles community relations. The

This research was supported primarily by McKinsey Foundation for Management Research, Inc., with supplemental support from the Division of Research, Harvard Graduate School of Business Administration, and Krannert Graduate School of Industrial Administration, Purdue University.

1. R. E. Walton and J. M. Dutton, "Interdepartmental Conflict and Its Management: General Model and Review," *Administrative Science Quarterly*, XIV (Winter 1969), 73.
2. W. M. Evan, "The Organization Set: Toward a Theory of Interorganizational Relations," In J. D. Thompson (Ed.), *Approaches to Organizational Design* (Pittsburgh: University of Pittsburgh Press, 1966), 175.

Plant department installs telephones and other equipment, and maintains and services the outside and central office equipment. The Traffic department is composed primarily of the operators who handle calls. The Marketing department handles sales of equipment to businesses. The Engineering department plans the installation of poles, cable, and other operating facilities. The Construction department installs poles and cables. The superordinate goals that require effective joint decision making and coordination are customer service and profit.

With regard to division of labor and formal goals, the telephone departments resemble stereotyped departments within a single organization. However, with respect to autonomy and commitment, the departments operate somewhat like a federation of separate organizations. This is due mainly to organizational structure (see Figure 4.2 for a partial organization chart). The departmental separation begins below the vice presidential level, extending through department heads, division managers, district managers, occasional second-level supervisors, and first-level supervisors. So although authority rests in a common supervisor, the hierarchical distance from exchange managers to vice president requires all but a few interdepartmental issues to be resolved jointly at lower levels by coordinates in different departments. Interdepartmental committees at the exchange level are a company policy. Joint decisions can be made in these committees, but the committee lacks formal authority over the individual exchange managers.

Informal coalitional decision making also occurs between subsets of departments, to resolve specific interdepartmental problems. The six departments are all interdependent to some extent in achieving organizational goals, but work flow makes some relationships more critical than others. For example, Plant is dependent upon Commercial for swift, accurate processing of new installation orders. Slow or inaccurate transmission of orders to Plant interferes with Plant's scheduling with consequent increases in overtime and missed orders, both of which are involved in Plant's performance criteria. Traffic is highly dependent upon Plant to repair malfunctioning equipment before its level of performance drops, although

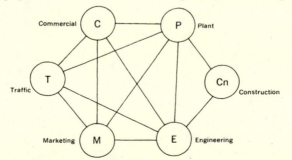

Figure 4.1. Interrelations between Departments in an Exchange

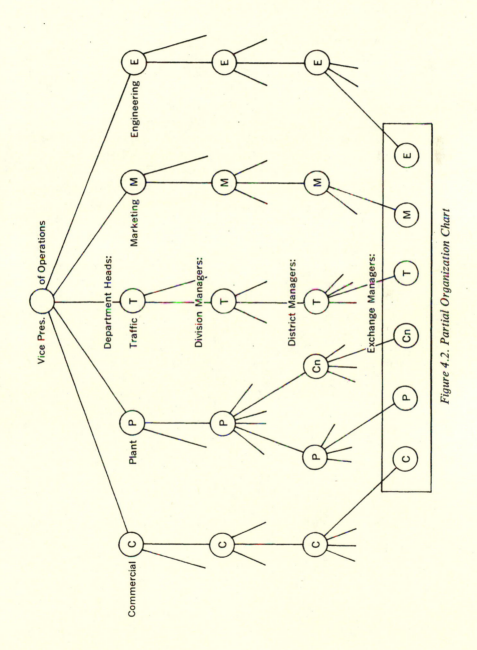

Figure 4.2. Partial Organization Chart

Plant's level of performance is relatively independent of Traffic. All departments are to a large degree dependent upon Plant's work to meet their own goals, both in terms of everyday work and occasional crises. Construction is relatively isolated in terms of dependence, interacting on the whole with only Plant and Engineering.

Elaborate indices of performance play a large role in managerial control and in promotions and merit raises, intensifying the subgoal orientation of the departments. For example, all Commercial offices are scored on billing errors, bad debts, sales, and several other measures. In addition, calls from customers are monitored in larger Commercial offices, and the department is rated according to the accuracy of the information given the customer and such things as the politeness and helpfulness of the Commercial personnel. Individual indices are weighted and combined into overall indices to yield one or two numbers, so that the performance of Commercial exchange departments throughout the state can be easily compared. The same condition exists for Plant, Traffic, and Construction, while Marketing and Engineering managers are evaluated according to less explicit criteria.

On the whole, then, other exchange departments within the same department serve as reference organizations for evaluating performance. The relationship of departments within an exchange is similar to relationships between "corporate" public service organizations on the local level – those that delegate authority downward from the national or state level to the local.[3]

Behavioral norms, on the other hand, are influenced by top management, department, and local coordinates, so that commitment is divided between organizational goals, departmental goals (indices), and any joint goals of the local managers. The elaborate performance indices serve both to intensify the importance of coordination – since high indices necessitate consideration from other departments – and to make coordination difficult – since giving consideration to another department's problems is often done at the expense of one's own indices. In short, coordination is a mixed-motive game.

Levine and White describe similar obstacles to cooperation engendered by local public service organizations' "dependence upon a system outside the community" for resources and evaluation.[4] In an attempt to overcome these obstacles within the present organization, some integrative devices were devised for use throughout the state. On the whole, districts were identical for the six departments, and the six district managers were located in the same city, usually in the same building. The same held true at the division level. Weekly interdepartmental meetings at the local levels were an official policy. Annual tours of inspection of exchanges were conducted jointly by coordinates at the district level, and employee evaluations by district managers involved district managers from other departments.

3. D. L. Sills, *The Volunteers: Means and Ends in a National Organization* (Glencoe, Ill.: The Free Press, 1957).
4. S. Levine and P. E. White, "Exchange as a Conceptual Framework for the Study of Interorganizational Relationships," *Administrative Science Quarterly*, V (March 1961) 590–592.

Other integrative devices were the result of policies established between individual coordinates at lower levels. For example, weekly meetings occurred in some exchanges between Marketing salesmen and Plant installation foremen at which issues relevant to coordination were discussed. Other exchanges held joint social gatherings for the craft personnel of two departments. Joint rules or agreements between departments were also adopted in various exchanges to govern activities which were crucial to coordination. For example, in some exchanges Commercial was not allowed to accept service orders for the following day after a certain hour so that Plant could complete the scheduling of those installations before quitting time.

Procedure

QUESTIONNAIRES

On the basis of interviews and existent theory, a questionnaire was designed as our primary data-gathering device. The questionnaire included many questions concerning the respondent and his department, as well as questions designed to measure various aspects of his relationship with each of the other five departments.

To some extent, the wording of questions was tailored to individual departments and managerial levels, but questions were essentially the same for all respondents. A pilot study tested the clarity of the questions.

The questionnaire method of data collection is in some ways less desirable than more objective measurement of behavior and conditions. It introduces the possibility of systematic bias and inflated correlations due to selective perception and the halo effect. Nevertheless, it was felt to be the superior method for the present study because some of our variables concerned sentiments, and because of the time costs and random sampling errors which would have been introduced by more objective observational measures. In general, questionnaire items measuring the independent variables were decided upon as a balance between two goals. The first goal was to ask questions broad and abstract enough to adequately tap the variable in question. The second goal was to ask questions objective and specific enough to avoid tapping general sentiments. When possible, several more specific questions were asked instead of one more general question. The danger is that the category may not be fully measured, but the advantages are that responses are hopefully less distorted and that the researcher has a more concrete understanding of the dynamics. Thus we did not ask managers how much conflict existed between departments. Instead, we asked more specific questions about behavioral patterns or attitudes which we considered integral components of conflict in this organization.

SAMPLING

Managers were selected as respondents in thirty-two exchanges throughout the state. These exchanges were selected to provide a range of department sizes and urban-rural locations.

All six departments were not physically housed in every exchange. Virtually every exchange contained Commercial and Plant departments. The remaining departments sometimes operated out of larger exchanges to service smaller nearby exchanges. But despite the lack of resident managers in some departments, technology usually forced managers who were stationed in these exchanges to interact with coordinates in the absent departments.

Managers in five of the six departments were questioned about their relationship with counterparts in each of the other five departments. Managers in Construction were not sampled because of their relative lack of interaction with most other departments. All district managers in the five sampled departments were selected as respondents. Of the lower (first and second level) managers, some less interdepartmentally critical jobs were not sampled. Where there was duplication of job titles within an exchange department, some further elimination was done.

In all, 330 questionnaires were mailed to sampled managers, and 310 were returned — 94 percent. Since each manager was asked about his relationships with five other departments, this represented 1,550 potential views of an interdepartmental relationship. Of these, 360 were eliminated because respondents indicated that no relationship existed, leaving 1,190 sets of data. Most of the eliminated cases involved the Construction department.

OPERATIONAL APPROACH TO INTERDEPARTMENTAL RELATIONS

The study set out to investigate the determinants of conflict in interdepartmental relations. Three operational approaches seemed possible: studying conflict between individual pairs of managers in two departments, studying central tendencies in the relationship of all managers in one department with all managers in another department, or studying the relationship of one manager with his coordinate(s) in another department. The present study made use of the third approach for theoretical reasons and for operational convenience.

All three approaches yield the same results when there is only one manager in each department, for then the interactions of two managers are the interactions of two departments. In larger departments, however, there are a number of managers, each interacting with different subsets of the managers in another department. And the nature of these interactions may be quite different: because larger departments subsume more specialized positions, the managers of one department may interact with managers in another department over different issues, with different frequencies, and with different power positions. Each relationship between two individuals may be characterized by its own dynamics and its own level of conflict. The most information would be gained through the first approach mentioned above, that is, studying each pairwise relationship between managers in different departments. However, this approach would have had some operational disadvantages. It was often difficult to identify coordinates. Where relationships existed between departments, respondents indicated an average of 3.86 coordinates in each other department. The standard deviation on this measure was 3.54, indicating that many managers had considerably more than four coordinates in some departments. To ask respondents the requisite questions about all these relationships would have been impractical. Some further sampling would have been required. Finally, the field interviews suggested some reluctance on the part of interviewees to give candid ratings of their coordinates individually.

The pilot questionnaire revealed that individual managers could generalize about the nature of their relationship to a given other department. Even though a manager had relationships with individual managers in another department and each of those relationships may have been different from the other, that manager was apparently able to express generalized sentiments toward the other department and to state generalized perceptions concerning the behavior patterns of that department. Our dependent variables and several independent variables were therefore obtained in this way.

This method of data collection had some disadvantages. Each set of data was almost entirely from one manager's questionnaire. Because pairwise relationships were not investigated, it was not possible to get an independent reading on items such as the coordinate's interpersonal skill and the coordinate's tendency to overstate his requirements. It was also impossible to achieve measures that combine the responses of managers in both departments, such as mutual dependence, status incongruities, and asymmetric knowledge of the other department. Managers *did* rate the asymmetry of initiation between themselves and the other department, however, so that the effects of this variable could be assessed. Another paper in progress will make use of aggregate measures over the managers in each exchange department so that aggregate asymmetries and incongruities between exchange departments can be assessed and related to the average level of interdepartmental conflict.

Measures of Conflict

"Conflict" is a vague concept. Pondy indicates four alternative denotations of the word "conflict": as antecedent, conflict-promoting conditions; as affective states of the individuals involved; as cognitive states of the individuals — the awareness of conflictful conditions; as conflictful behavior of the participants.[5]

The purpose of the study was to identify the antecedent, conflict-promoting conditions. Our measures of conflict concerned affective states and conflictful behavior. Three measures of conflict were used: (1) the respondent's feeling of distrust toward the department in question; (2) his rating of the lack of consideration shown to him and to his needs by the actions

5. L. R. Pondy, "Organizational Conflict: Concepts and Models." *Administrative Science Quarterly*, XII (September 1967) 298.

of the department in question; and (3) his rating of the other department's tendency to overstate its needs in attempting to influence him.[6]

Distrust, then is a measure of the respondent's affect. Lack of consideration pertains to a general characteristic of the other department's actions with regard to the respondent. And overstatement is a particular tactic characteristic of conflict bargaining, whereas accurate information exchange is instrumental for problem solving. Respondents were asked to rate these variables on the basis of averages over the previous six months.

These measures of conflict were important to the organization. It was the belief of the top management that bargaining activities were too common, at the expense of problem-solving activities. Problem solving consists of defining the problem, finding alternatives, tracing the probable outcomes of the alternatives, and selecting the alternative whose outcome is optimal in terms of the joint needs of the participants. Distrust, overstatement of departmental needs, and lack of consideration of another department's needs are more characteristic of a bargaining orientation. Hence, top management believed that reducing the levels of all three conflict variables would increase problem-solving behavior.

Figure 4.3. Payoff Matrix for Interdepartmental Decision Making*

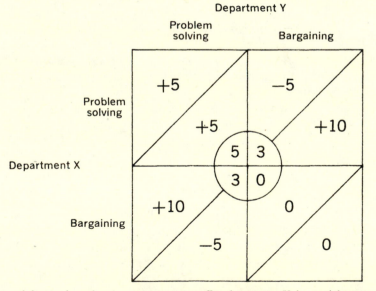

* Upper left entry in each square represents payoff to department X, lower right entry payoff to department Y. Organizational payoffs are within center circle.

6. Throughout this paper variables are labeled according to that pole of the dimension associated with conflict or hypothesized to produce conflict, such as "distrust" and "ignorance of the other department." However, some of the questionnaire items were phrased in terms of the opposite pole: "How much trust do you have . . ." and "How much knowledge do you have . . ."

In many ways, interdepartmental decision making resembled an iterated prisoner's dilemma game, with bargaining and problem solving as alternative strategies (see Figure 4.3 for a hypothetical payoff matrix which represents the agenda characteristic of the interunit relations studied). On individual decisions, joint problem solving was believed to result in highest organizational utility, unilateral problem solving in a decision of moderate utility to the organization, and joint bargaining in a lower utility decision. On the other hand, a manager would increase his own *departmental* utility on any one decision through a bargaining approach (e.g., distorting or concealing information), regardless of his coordinate's orientation, so that there was some pressure toward the low-joint-payoff, low-organizational-utility corner of the prisoner's dilemma matrix.

Based on an earlier study, we expected that distrust, lack of consideration, and overstatement of needs would be positively correlated with each other.[7] Conceptually we regarded each as an aspect of a conflictful bargaining syndrome. As expected, distrust and lack of consideration were significantly correlated with each other ($r = .45$) and with overstatement of needs ($r = .45$ and $r = .41$, respectively), giving some support to the syndrome model. However, these correlations were not as large as was expected, each variable accounting for less than 20 per cent of the variation in the others. The various measures of conflict, although intercorrelated, exhibited a sufficient degree of independent variation to underscore the idea that conflict itself is a complex relationship of variables. Using one measure of conflict as an operational definition would appear to be unwise; an aggregate measure incorporating several individual measures would yield stronger results.

The Independent Variables and Their Effects

Walton and Dutton[8] list nine categories of antecedent conditions affecting conflict: mutual dependence, asymmetries, rewards, organizational differentiation, role dissatisfaction, ambiguities, common resource pools, communication obstacles, and personal skills and traits. However, a different categorization evolved for this study. Six categories were used: the salience of an interdepartmental relationship, competition incentives, jurisdictional ambiguities, factors inhibiting communication, sources of friction and frustration, and scarcities within a department.

In all correlations for over thirty individual variables from these categories were run with the three conflict measures. The results are shown in Table 4.1.

The large majority of hypothesized relationships were found to hold. For example, distrust was correlated at the .01 level of significance with twenty

7. R. E. Walton, J. M. Dutton, and H. G. Fitch, "A Study of Conflict in the Process, Structure, and Attitudes of Lateral Relationships," *Some Theories of Organization,* Haberstroh and Rubenstein (eds.) (Homewood, Ill.: Richard D. Irwin, Inc., 1966) 444–465.

8. Walton and Dutton, *op. cit.*

Table 4.1. Correlations of independent variables to conflict measures (N = 1190)

Independent Variables	Conflict Measures		
	Distrust	Perceived lack of con- sideration	Perceived overstate- ment of needs
Salience:†			
1. Normal dependence	NS	NS	.12*
2. Crisis dependence	NS	−.06	NS
3. Number of coordinates (√)	NS	NS	.16*
4. Frequency of contacts (√)	NS	−.07	.11*
Competition incentives:			
5. Supervisor's deemphasizing cooperation	.16*	.10*	.10*
6. Supervisor's failure to reward consideration	.09*	.12*	.07*
7. Opposing expectations	.35*	.27*	.37*
Jurisdictional ambiguity:			
8. Jurisdictional ambiguity	.31*	.19*	.35*
Intradepartmental scarcities:			
9. Money limitations	.14*	.11*	.11*
10. District Manager's difficulty in obtaining facilities	.13*	.09*	.12*
11. Subordinates' unresponsiveness	.15*	.16*	.19*
12. Craft unresponsiveness	.11*	.15*	.17*
13. Craft unskillfulness	.17*	.13*	.16*
14. Craft shortages	.16*	.14*	..12*
Sources of friction, frustration:			
15. Asymmetry of initiation	NS	NS	.15*
16. Difficulty of task	.13*	.08*	.13*
17. Technological change	NS	NS	NS
18. Closeness of supervision	NS	NS	NS
19. Supervisor's unresponsiveness	.16*	.13*	.12*
20. Supervisory distrust	.13*	.12*	.12*
21. Technical focus of supervision	NS	NS	NS
22. Supervisor's policing	.12*	.12*	.07*
23. Dissatisfaction with supervisor's style	.17*	.14*	.16*
Communication-inhibiting factors:			
24. Physical communication obstacles	.35*	.25*	.23*
25. Own interpersonal difficulty	.07	.09*	.05
26. Coordinate's verbal difficulty	.33*	.27*	.29*
27. Coordinate's interpersonal difficulties	.32*	.25*	.21*
28. Ignorance of other department	NS	.09*	−.09*
29. Craft unacquaintance	.10*	.13*	NS
30. Brevity of time known coordinate	.05	NS	.08*
31. Newness to position (√)	.15*	.07	.14*

Table 4.1. *(continued)*

Independent Variables	Conflict Measures		
	Distrust	Perceived lack of consideration	Perceived overstatement of needs
Miscellaneous†			
32. Age (√)	−.16*	−.13*	−.21*
33. Education	NS	.07	NS
34. Managerial level	−.10*	.08*	NS
35. Promotability	.06	NS	.06

NS Indicates not significant at $p = .05$.
* Significant at $p = .01$ or better
† These variables were given two-tailed tests of significance.

of the twenty-seven factors in the categories of competitive incentives, ambiguity, scarcities, frustrators, communication inhibitors, where we had clear-cut hypotheses. There were no predictions for the salience and miscellaneous factors, although two factors did correlate significantly (.01 level) with trust. Similar results obtained for the other two indices of conflict, namely, perceived lack of consideration and perceived overstatement of needs. The failures of certain independent variables to relate significantly to one or more of the three conflict measures are interesting because in each case some persuasive or generally accepted hypothesis was involved. In one case, the results were opposite to those predicted. The relatively strong correlations, as well as the instances where predictions failed or were reversed, will be discussed further. However, it should be noted that on this relatively large sample of 1190 sets of data, the significant correlations were modest, ranging from .07 to .37. Thus, while many independent variables are related to lateral conflict, no single factor accounted for more than 14 percent of the variation in any one conflict variable.

In addition to correlation analysis, regressions were used to learn how much of the variance in the conflict measures could be explained by the cumulative effect of independent variables.

Because there were intercorrelations among the independent variables, their effects upon the conflict measures were not additive and there was some duplication of information in the variables. In some cases, independent variables with significant correlations to conflict measures made no contribution to conflict prediction after the effects of other variables had been calculated; that is, the variance in conflict for which the superfluous variable could account had already been accounted for by other variables correlated with it. To simplify presentation, such variables were eliminated from further data analysis as a result of preliminary data runs. Only those variables were retained in the final analysis which were found to make a significant contribution (by F-test at $p = .05$) to the prediction of at least one of the conflict measures after all remaining variables had been loaded into the regression equation.

The remaining twenty-four variables were then loaded into regressions on each of the three conflict measures. Figure 4.4 shows the correlations of the individual variables with the three conflict measures (r), the multiple correlation of the variables within a category with each measure (category R), and the overall multiple correlation for each measure (overall R).

The reactions of the three conflict measures to the categories of variables are quite similar on the whole. The differences which do appear in Figure 4.4 will be discussed later in the paper. However, in view of their generally similar response to the independent variable, their intercorrelation, and the fact that they are conceptually treated as aspects of conflict, the three conflict variables were added to obtain an aggregate measure of generalized conflict. Regressions were run on this aggregate measure by using the same independent variables. The results are shown in Figure 4.5.

The correlations of the independent variables are generally higher with generalized conflict than with the individual conflict measures, and the multiple correlation of .61 now accounts for 42 percent of the variation in generalized conflict. Random errors due to unreliability in the three measures would tend to cancel each other out, making the aggregate measure more reliable. Also, if the three conflict measures are viewed as factors which tend to vary together but sometimes do not because they are affected individually by incidental factors unrelated to the independent variables, then the effects of these incidental factors would partially cancel each other out in the aggregated measure.

Within this organization and given the variables tested, communication-inhibiting factors and competition incentives were the most strongly related to generalized conflict, both exceeding a multiple correlation of .4. Next in order were jurisdictional ambiguity and intradepartmental scarcities which exceeded a multiple correlation of .3. Sources of frustration correlated better than .2. The salience variables yielded a multiple correlation slightly better than .1.

SALIENCE

Briefly, salience involved the amount of dependence upon another department and contact with it. The four variables used as measures of salience were (1) the manager's day-to-day dependence upon the department in question, (2) his dependence during operating crises, (3) the number of people in that department with whom he interacted, and (4) the average frequency of contact with his most frequently contacted coordinate in that department. If we had had measures of the other department's dependence upon the

Figure 4.4. Regressions of Independent Variables on Conflict Measures (N = 1190)

	Distrust			Perceived Lack of Consideration			Perceived Overstatement of Needs		
	r	Category Overall R	R	r	Category Overall R	R	r	Category Overall R	R
Salience:									
1. Normal dependence	.05			−.05			.12*		
2. Crisis dependence	−.05			−.06			.01		
3. Number of coordinates (√)	.03	.11		−.06	.09		.16*	.21*	
4. Frequency of contact (√√)	−.01			−.07			.11*		
Competition incentives:									
5. Supervisor's deemphasizing cooperation	.16*			.10*			.10*		
6. Supervisor's failure to reward consideration	.09*	.38*		.12*	.29*		.07*	.37*	
7. Opposing expectations	.35*			.27*			.37*		
Jurisdictional ambiguity:									
8. Jurisdictional ambiguity		.31*			.19*			.35*	
Intradepartmental scarcities:									
10. District manager's difficulty in obtaining facilities	.13*			.09*			.12*		
11. Subordinates' unresponsiveness	.15*	.25*	.59*	.16*	.22*	.48*	.19*	.26*	.57*
13. Craft unskillfulness	.17*			.13*			.16*		
14. Craft shortages	.16*			.14*			.12*		

Figure 4.4. (continued)

	Distrust			Perceived Lack of Consideration			Perceived Overstatement of Needs		
	r	Category R	Overall R	r	Category R	Overall R	r	Category R	Overall R
Sources of friction, frustration:									
15. Asymmetry of initiation	.02			−.01			.15*		
16. Difficulty of task	.13*	⎫		.08*	⎫		.13*	⎫	
22. Supervisor's policing	.12*	.22*		.12*	.18*		.07*	.24*	
23. Dissatisfaction with supervisor's, style	.17*	⎭		.14*	⎭		.16*	⎭	
Communication-inhibiting factors:									
24. Physical communication obstacles	.35*	⎫		.25*	⎫		.23*	⎫	
26. Coordinate's verbal difficulty	.33*			.27*			.29*		
27. Coordinate's interpersonal difficulties	.32*	.46*		.25*	.37*		.21*	.34*	
28. Ignorance of other department	−.04			.09*			−.09*		
29. Craft unacquaintance	.10*	⎭		.13*	⎭		.0	⎭	
Miscellaneous:									
32. Age (√)		−.16*			−.13*			−.21*	
34. Managerial level		−.10*			.08			−.0	
35. Promotability		.06			−.02			.06	

* Indicates correlation or regression coefficient is significant at $p = .01$ or better.

Figure 4.5. Correlations and Regressions of the Independent Variables with Generalized Conflict (N = 1190)

	r	category R	overall R
Salience†			
1. Normal dependence	NS		
2. Crisis dependence	NS	.11	
3. Number of coordinates (√)	NS		
4. Frequency of contact (√)	NS		
Competition incentives:			
5. Supervisor's deemphasizing cooperation	.15*		
6. Supervisor's failure to reward consideration	.12*	.44*	
7. Opposing expectations	.42*		
Jurisdictional ambiguity:			
8. Jurisdictional ambiguity		.36*	
Intradepartmental scarcities:			
10. District Manager's difficulty in obtaining facilities	.15*		
11. Subordinates' unresponsiveness	.21*	.31*	
13. Craft unskillfulness	.19*		.61*
14. Craft shortages	.17*		
Sources of friction, frustration:			
15. Asymmetry of initiation	.07		
16. Difficulty of task	.15*	.25*	
22. Supervisor's policing	.13*		
23. Dissatisfaction with supervisor's style	.20*		
Communication-inhibiting factors:			
24. Physical communication obstacles	.35*		
26. Coordinate's verbal difficulty	.37*		
27. Coordinate's interpersonal difficulties	.33*	.48*	
28. Ignorance of other department	NS		
29. Craft unacquaintance	.10*		
Miscellaneous†			
32. Age (√)		−.21*	
34. Managerial level		NS	
35. Promotability		NS	

NS indicates not significant at $p = .05$.

* Significant at $p = .01$ or better.

† These variables were given two-tailed tests of significance.

manager in question, the degree of mutual dependence would also have been included in this category. Salience was believed to have mixed potential in influencing conflict. Dependency was assumed to provide incentive for developing trusting, problem-solving relationships. Similarly, increased contact was believed to reduce conflict potential by increasing familiarity and preventing the formation of unfavorable stereotypes. However, both contact and dependency were also believed to intensify any existent conflict generated from other factors. Hence, no specific hypotheses were formulated concerning the overall effects of the salience measures by themselves.

Taken together, the four salience measures yielded a significant multiple correlation coefficient ($R = .11$, at the $.05$ level of significance) with the generalized conflict measure. Individually, however, the salience variables were not significantly correlated to distrust. Two of them, crisis dependence and frequency of contact, had small but significant (at $.05$) negative correlations to lack of consideration. All but crisis dependence were positively correlated to perceived overstatement of needs at $p < .01$.

The failure of salience to correlate significantly with distrust and the low and mixed positive-negative correlations of the other conflict indices were not surprising, given the mixed potential predicted on theoretical grounds. In short, our measures of the significance of the relationship are not highly or consistently related to the cooperation-conflict quality of the relationship. The relationships which did emerge show salience to be related to conflict measures in much the same way as knowledge of the other department. Indeed, ignorance of the other department was found to be negatively correlated to all four salience measures at well above $p = .01$. Salience of a relationship apparently affects the knowledge one gains about the other party in a relationship. Below we offer an explanation for the relationships between knowledge of other department and the three conflict measures.

COMPETITION INCENTIVES

Competition incentives include those aspects of the reward structure which encourage attending to departmental goals at the expense of other departments. The three measures of competition incentives were (1) the supervisor's lack of emphasis on cooperation, (2) the supervisor's failure to reward his subordinate for giving consideration to another department's problems, and (3) the degree of opposition between what is expected of the two departments, respectively. It was hypothesized that competition incentives would correlate positively with conflict. Common resource pools have also been hypothesized to generate conflict among departments, but our field study did not reveal any common resource pool at the exchange level of the organization.

As a category, competition incentives were relatively strongly related to generalized conflict ($R = .44$). The dominant factor ($r = .42$) was a generalized perception that the respondent was operating under task expectations that were opposed to the expectations bearing on his coordinate in the other department. The more specific questions dealing with whether his supervisor emphasizes cooperation and rewards him for engaging in cooperative acts yielded more modest correlations with the overall conflict-cooperation measure ($r = .15$ and $.12$, respectively). Thus, it is suggested that such factors as the formal and informal basic job requirements, the formal and standardized indexes, and the more general reward system combine to present substantially stronger signals than his immediate supervisor can about what mixture of effectively competitive versus cooperative acts are expected of him. Given these signals, supervision's explicit attention to this dimension has relatively small, but nevertheless significant, positive leverage on the co-operativeness of the lateral relationship of immediate subordinates.

It should be kept in mind that in the organization studied, the two co-ordinates in a lateral relationship reported to different superiors. It seems reasonable that where both persons report to a common superior, the superior's emphasis and rewards for cooperation would have more leverage.

JURISDICTIONAL AMBIGUITY

Jurisdictional ambiguity, that is, a lack of clarity about which of the two departments has responsibility for particular decisions or actions, was hypothesized to be a source of conflict. The reasoning is that where there is ambiguity, the parties will try to resolve the jurisdictional question according to their own respective preferences, which will at least sometimes be opposed —each will want the other to perform the task or each will want to claim the responsibility himself.

The category and single item assessing the ambiguity about division of responsibilities between two interdependent departments correlated $r = .36$ with generalized conflict. The direction and strength of the relationship was about as expected on theoretical grounds. It is interesting that the field interviews revealed that jurisdictional disputes involved joint attempts to *avoid* responsibility for tasks which required time and men. Strauss's purchasing agents, operating under a less demanding system of time constraints and performance criteria, used jurisdictional ambiguities to expand their activities.[9]

INTRADEPARTMENTAL SCARCITIES

Intradepartmental scarcities included shortages of those resources which would increase the manager's ability to perform his job adequately and respond to coordinates' requests. March and Simon use the term "organizational slack" to refer to the relative abundance of such resources.[10] The original group comprises six factors, each assessing the perceived scarcity of

9. G. Strauss, "Tactics of Lateral Relationship: The Purchasing Agent," *Administrative Science Quarterly*, VII (September 1962).
10. J. G. March and H. A. Simon, *Organizations* (New York: John Wiley & Sons, Inc., 1958) 126.

a particular type of resource upon which respondents typically depended to accomplish their task. The six measures of intradepartmental scarcities were: (1) the manager's reported money limitations, (2) the difficulty in obtaining facilities reported by his superior, (3) the unresponsiveness of his direct subordinates, (4) the unresponsiveness of the craft people in his unit, (5) the inadequacy of the skills among his craft people, and (6) the inadequacy of numbers of craft people. An effort was made to be as comprehensive as possible in assessing the scarcity of financial, material, and human resources; and with respect to human resources, their quality, quantity, and responsiveness in attitude were all considered. However, with such concepts as scarcities one can never be confident that he has included all of the relevant operations. Scarcities were hypothesized to be positively correlated to interdepartmental conflict.

As a group, intradepartmental scarcities correlated $R = .31$ with generalized conflict. The correlations of these six scarcity factors with the three aspects of conflict shown in Table 4.1 show a striking uniformity. All eighteen correlations were significant at the .01 level. All fell between $r = .09$ and .19. Simply, emergent distrust, lack of consideration, and overstatement tactics in lateral relationships are reliably but only slightly increased by each of a variety of scarcities or limitations bearing on one of the two parties. Considered together, scarcities are a more significant determinant.

Two of the scarcity factors in Table 4.1 are not included in the regression analysis reported in Figures 4.4 and 4.5 because they failed to account for additional variance not already explained by the other four. Respondents' ratings of money limitations were superfluous because of high correlations with inadequacy of numbers of craft personnel ($r = .42$) and with the district manager's rating of difficulty in obtaining facilities ($r = .34$). Craft unresponsiveness was likewise correlated with subordinates' unresponsiveness ($r = .48$), inadequacy of craft skills ($r = .26$), and to a lesser extent with other variables.

SOURCES OF IRRITATION AND FRUSTRATION

Sources of irritation and frustration refer to various conditions within the respondent's department which might be expected to affect a manager's frustration level and in turn his tendency to develop conflictful relations with his peers. The nine items used in this category were: (1) asymmetry of initiation between the respondent manager and the other department, (2) the difficulty of the task faced by the respondent's department, (3) the amount of technological change, (4) closeness of supervision by the manager's supervisor, (5) the supervisor's lack of responsiveness to the manager's requests, (6) the lack of trust in subordinates displayed by the respondent's supervisor, (7) the technical, as opposed to human, focus of the supervisor, (8) the supervisor's use of information for policing or punishment, and (9) the manager's dissatisfaction with his supervisor's leadership style. These variables were hypothesized to be generalized sources of irritation and frustration and to contribute to friction in interdepartmental relations. Other variables inducing tension could have been included in this category, such as the respondent's job dissatisfaction, the lack of departmental cohesion, and ambiguity regarding evaluation criteria. The concept would have been extended to include extraorganizational factors impinging on the individual manager as well, if this information had been available.

Altogether, the irritation and frustration variables had a multiple correlation of only .25 with generalized conflict. Individual correlations tended to be small; and some hypothesized relationships failed to be supported.

Six of the nine variables concerned aspects of the supervisory style under which the respondent worked. Four of the six supervision variables were slightly but significantly related to the three measures of lateral conflict: the supervisor's unresponsiveness to the manager's requests, the lack of trust in subordinates reflected in his style, his policing, and the manager's general dissatisfaction with the supervisor's leadership. These correlations ranged from .07 to .17.

However, two of the supervisory variables were not found to be correlated to any of the three conflict measures: the technical (as opposed to human-relations) focus of the supervisor, and the closeness of his supervision. Thus, in our sample of over 1,000 sets of data about lateral relationships, we failed to find any support for the widespread beliefs that closeness of supervision will promote conflict among subordinates and that a human-relations focus of supervision will promote a cooperative climate.

Difficulty of task and technological change were two aspects of the manager's work that were assumed to be sources of frustration and, in turn, to increase the likelihood that he would be engaged in conflictful lateral relations. The hypothesis was confirmed for difficulty of task. However, technological change had no effect on interdepartmental conflict, thus failing to support the popular assumption that change creates conflict. The field interviews revealed that some managers believed that technological changes, especially major projects, often resulted in increased cooperation. The completion of these changes represented a superordinate goal in some cases and hence tended to be an integrating force.

The remaining variable in this category, asymmetry of initiation, was defined as the proportion of contacts initiated by the other department minus the proportion initiated by the respondent, so that high values represented high relative initiation by the other department. Whyte's classic study of human relations in the restaurant industry and other studies indicate that when the rate of initiation between two positions is unbalanced, there is a tendency for a low initiator to become irritated and resentful.[11] This tendency is believed to lessen to the extent that the high initiator has more

11. W. F. Whyte, *Human Relations in the Restaurant Industry* (New York: McGraw-Hill Book Co., 1948).

status, thus legitimating the imbalance. In this study the latter condition was not controlled for, and we therefore expected some significant impact on all three conflict measures. Nevertheless, asymmetry of initiation proved to be uncorrelated to either distrust or lack of consideration. Asymmetry of initiation did correlate ($r = .15$) with the manager's rating of the other department's overstatement of needs, but this correlation may only mean that people who overstate their needs initiate more contacts than others. It is interesting to note that respondents tended to perceive themselves as initiating a majority of contacts—approximately 57 percent.

Five of the frustration variables were excluded from the regression results presented in Figures 4.4 and 4.5. The five excluded variables comprised the three which failed to correlate with any conflict measure and two supervisory variables—supervisory distrust and supervisor's unresponsiveness. The latter variables were highly intercorrelated with the two supervisory variables which were included—supervisor's policing, and general dissatisfaction with the supervisor's leadership.

COMMUNICATION-INHIBITING FACTORS

Communication-inhibiting factors included variables believed to make problem-solving and conflict-managing dialogue more difficult. The category contained very different types of communication inhibitors, including physical obstacles, lack of shared task knowledge, lack of familiarity between coordinates, and lack of interaction skills. The eight specific measures used were: (1) physical communication obstacles, (2) the manager's rating of his own lack of interpersonal skill, (3) the lack of verbal skill on the part of his primary coordinate in the other department, (4) the lack of interpersonal skill on the part of his coordinate, (5) the manager's ignorance of the problems and procedures of the other department, (6) the lack of acquaintance of the craft people across the two departments, (7) the briefness of time the manager had known his primary coordinate in the other department, and (8) the brevity of the manager's tenure in his position. Past job experience in another department was believed to facilitate communication and problem solving, but this variable was not included here because only a small minority of managers had had such experience. Communication-inhibiting factors were hypothesized to be positively correlated to conflict.

As a category, communication inhibitors were relatively strongly related to generalized conflict ($R = .48$). Communication inhibitors were more highly related to trust ($R = .46$) than to consideration ($R = .37$) or overstatement ($R = .34$), a finding which suggests that the effect of faulty communication is somewhat more apparent in interdepartmental feelings than behavior patterns.

Physical obstacles to communication was related to distrust ($r = .35$), perceived lack of consideration ($r = .25$), and perceived overstatement of needs ($r = .23$), as predicted.

We assumed that more knowledge about the work situation of another department would generally facilitate communication, would make the knowledgeable manager more responsive to the other's requests and more considerate of him, and would, through reciprocal processes, cause greater mutual cooperation to develop. We believe such knowledge is an essential part of being able to take the role of the other – a concept which figures importantly in many social psychological approaches to conflict resolution. The concept is also an important part of management's rationale for rotating personnel through positions which affect or are affected by the man's primary functional area of responsibility. Thus, we predicted that ignorance of the other department would be positively correlated with all three indices of conflict. The results were mixed: trust level was not related, perceived lack of consideration was positively related, and perceived overstatement of needs was negatively related. Both significant correlations were low($r = .09$). Our ad hoc interpretation of these correlations is that knowledge of another department enables one to better recognize both instances of overstatement and consideration when they do occur. Knowledge of the other department may still have resulted in increased consideration *by the respondent* toward his coordinate, but we were unable to test this hypothesis. In any event, we were surprised that knowledge was not a stronger factor influencing lateral cooperation.

As a group, the three unfamiliarity measures – lack of craft acquaintance, brevity of time known coordinate, and brevity of time in current position – correlated as predicted with the three indices of conflict. Of the nine relationships, five were significant at the $p = .01$ level (ranging from .08 to .15), and two were significant at the .05 level. Thus, the findings support the idea that as two coordinates work with each other the relationship will be marked by increased trust and by some increase in the ratio of cooperative to competitive acts. They also imply that high turnover of personnel in liaison positions can be a factor affecting the amount of lateral cooperation. (Because of promotions, a manager's experience in his current job in this organization tended to be rather low, averaging three years.) Still, the correlations were low and suggest that *as a generalization*, steps taken that increase a man's familiarity with his own job and with his coordinate will not provide much leverage in moving a conflictful relationship toward more cooperation.

The three interaction-skill factors were the respondent's assessment of his own interpersonal skill, his coordinate's interpersonal skill, and the latter's verbal skills. The probable biases in these responses are obvious: the respondent would tend to overestimate his own interpersonal effectiveness, to underestimate his coordinate's skills when the relationship is conflictful, and to overestimate them when the relationship is cooperative. In any event, own interpersonal difficulty showed low correlations with the conflict measures – in one case (consideration) at the .01 level and in the other two cases at the .05 level. This factor was dropped in the regressions. Interestingly, it was intercorrelated with age ($r = .18$), supervisory unresponsiveness ($r = .17$), subordinates' unresponsiveness ($r = .27$), craft unresponsiveness ($r = .16$), and the district manager's difficulty in obtaining facilities ($r = .17$). Coordinate's interpersonal difficulty and coordinate's verbal difficulty were both relatively highly correlated to all three conflict measures.

MISCELLANEOUS VARIABLES

Also included in the analysis were four miscellaneous variables which were felt to be of potential relevance but whose net effects upon conflict could not be specified: (1) the manager's age, (2) his educational experience, (3) his managerial level, and (4) the promotability of the chief exchange department manager in the manager's exchange as rated by his supervisor.

Age was found to be correlated negatively to all three indices of conflict. We did not have an a priori prediction based on theoretical grounds. Older managers may receive better treatment because of their age and experience, or they may be less aggressive and thus generate less conflict. (Age correlates $-.08$ with initiations by self, and $.11$ with initiations by coordinates.) And, finally, older managers may be less critical in their ratings. (Age correlates $-.18$ with ratings of coordinate's verbal difficulty.)

March and Simon predicted more intergroup conflict at higher organizational levels than at lower levels, based upon two more basic propositions: first, that with lesser operationality of goals there will be more goal conflict; second, that the operationality of goals declines as one moves up the hierarchy.[12] Our results confirm less consideration at higher levels of the range of managers sampled, but they also confirm greater trust. Overstatement of needs was not affected.

There were no significant correlations between educational experience and the conflict measures that could not be discounted in view of their mutual relationships with age and managerial level.

The promotability of the head manager in an exchange department (as rated by his district manager) was found to have significant but low positive correlations to distrust and overstatement of needs ($p < .05$).

Discussion

IMPLICATIONS FOR THEORY

Two general implications of the study are that (1) conflict is a complex relationship of factors, and (2) conflict appears to be influenced through a complexity of factors, instead of being almost entirely determined by a few variables.

One striking aspect of the results was the modest size of the multiple correlation coefficients. This modest size was partially due to technical factors such as the limited reliability of questions, unmeasured interaction

12. March and Simon, *op. cit.* 126.

affects, and nonlinearities, and to the fact that the dependent variables were measured by a few discrete response categories, rather than a continuous measure. Nevertheless, a great deal of the unexplained variation appeared to be due to the incompleteness of the variables used.

Some increase in predictability would be obtained by adding the effects of the variables which were mentioned above and in Walton and Dutton[13] but have not as yet been tested. Interviews conducted prior to and following the collection of data by questionnaire suggested the particular importance of several variables. Status incongruities appeared important, as did the compatibility of coordinates' personalities. Incongruity of status and initiation was a factor whose effects were apparent in the Traffic-Plant relationship, where women Group Chief Operators were forced to request services from male Plant foremen of higher managerial rank. Asymmetric dependence was also a factor in this relationship, since the Group Chief Operators performed very few services for the foremen who repaired and maintained their equipment. Incongruity of status and dependence was a factor in district-level relations of Plant and Engineering, where the district engineer was ranked as second-level management but controlled expenditures vital to the third-level district plant manager. Special interdepartmental mechanisms such as meetings appeared helpful in some exchanges. Another factor was tradition — some exchanges had state-wide reputations for co-operative and productive interdepartmental relations of which they were proud and which they strived to maintain.

PRACTICAL IMPLICATIONS FOR INTERDEPARTMENTAL RELATIONS

One interpretation of the specific correlations obtained is that organizations should assign interdepartmental relations to older, articulate, interpersonally skilled men who are easily reachable, with adequate numbers of skilled, responsive personnel who have clear-cut and nonopposed responsibilities and jobs which are not too difficult, and with satisfactory supervisors who emphasize cooperation. This interpretation would incorporate the dozen variables having the greatest impact on interdepartmental conflict, but would not be of much use to a real-world administrator.

In practice, most of these variables *can* be manipulated by an organization through recruiting, training programs, and structural changes, but they have costs associated with them which may be prohibitive. Generally, interdepartmental bargaining is relatively easy to obtain, but it has opportunity costs for the organization in the form of suboptimal decisions. Interdepartmental problem solving produces higher-quality decisions but is more expensive to promote.

The optimal approach to conflict reduction would appear to be estimating the sensitivity of conflict to a given variable and then comparing the costs of

13. Walton and Dutton, *op. cit.*

manipulating the independent variable with the value of the resulting decrease in conflict. The present study verifies the sensitivity of conflict to several groups of variables which vary in cost of manipulation. Supervisory style and jurisdictional ambiguity could be manipulated at relatively low cost to the organization. Several aspects of supervisory style influence interdepartmental conflict: lack of emphasis on cooperation, failure to reward consideration, policing, and the general satisfactoriness of supervisory style. (The unresponsiveness of subordinates is also largely a function of supervisory style, of course.) Supervisors were occasionally sent to managerial-development sessions which examined supervision and coordination styles, although no systematic program was involved. Top management continually stressed the value of interdepartmental cooperation.

Because the environment was relatively predictable, jurisdictional ambiguities were reduced through elaborate job descriptions and procedural policies. This approach would be less effective, or more costly, in organizations with less predictable environments, where elaboration of structure would impede adjustments to environmental changes.

Some physical communication obstacles were also relatively inexpensive to remove. Physical communication obstacles were reduced by physical proximity when practical. District managers in different departments were usually located on the same floor of one building. First- and second-level supervisors in different departments were frequently located in a common building, and some exchanges had a common coffee lounge for several departments. But proximity was impractical in many cases. Construction supervisors and some Plant supervisors operated out of garages in various parts of the city more central to their geographic areas of responsibility. Some exchanges were too small to justify separate Traffic, Marketing, or Engineering departments, so that local managers had to deal with coordinates in larger nearby exchanges. Furthermore, job requirements kept many managers away from their desks, so that they were out of reach during much of the day, although mobile phones reduced this problem to some extent.

Other variables affecting conflict involved high costs. Craft skills and managerial verbal and interpersonal skills might have been improved through recruiting, but the money costs would have been high. And some degree of craft shortages, difficulty in obtaining facilities, and task difficulty may be inevitable, given the costs of manpower and equipment. Furthermore, specialization (and therefore somewhat differentiated goals), together with interdependence and scarcities, may well make some degree of opposing expectations inevitable. Nevertheless, the effects of these variables upon interdepartmental conflict may justify reevaluation of current organizational procedures.

While the costs of implementing changes in many of these variables on a company-wide basis is prohibitive, the expense of such changes in individual "problem" locations might be justified. For example, more articular, interpersonally skilled managers could be hired or transferred to troublesome areas, along with more highly skilled craft. Work loads might be temporarily lightened and other difficulties lessened. With improved interdepartmental decision making, work load and other variables could then be gradually restored to more normal levels.

IMPLICATIONS FOR INTERORGANIZATIONAL DECISION MAKING

The five variables affecting interdepartmental conflict most strongly would also appear to influence interorganizational conflict: opposing expectations, jurisdictional ambiguity, physical communication obstacles, verbal difficulty, and interpersonal difficulty.

From the point to view of one organization, opposing expectations between organizations may be difficult to manipulate without very basic changes in organizational goals. Jurisdictional ambiguities, on the other hand, may be diminished through interorganizational decision making, where this is legal.

Generally speaking, interorganizational decision making differs from the interdepartmental decision making in our study in that a smaller proportion of organizational personnel serve as coordinators. Therefore, it becomes economically more feasible to manipulate variables which pertain to these coordinators. Coordinators of higher verbal and interpersonal skill can be hired, or present coordinators can be more extensively trained. Since younger men appear to stimulate bargaining behavior, more experienced men may be assigned to coordination positions. Where relations are critical, work load and other aspects of task difficulty for the coordinator may be reduced. Close, controlling supervision may be relaxed, and adequate staff provided. The impact of physical communications obstacles suggests that coordinators be made easily reachable. In critical relationships, coordinators may even be physically relocated to be near another organization.

5

Effective Control Through Coherent Decentralization in Separably and Non-Separably Structured Organizations

K. O. KORTANEK

Introduction: Decentralization and Economic Market Mechanisms

It is generally agreed that a decentralized decision making system accrues certain benefits for the entire system as a whole. Following Koopman's exposition, for example, "decentralization utilizes incentives that are naturally operative in the market system" as well as providing an economy of information which in many situations is secured free of charge; that is, no loss of total profit or in satisfaction level results from decentralization.[1] It is natural then to ask whether a price mechanism can be found which will reconcile the freedom of action of individual units with the balancing out of supply and demand in the long run — or, stated differently, for the optimization of the total system.

Koopmans reveals the nature of this question in his discussion of the classical Robinson Crusoe example, a case in which production and consumption decisions are made in combination, and shows in simple terms how, under certain well-accepted assumptions, a set of prices exists such that the decision making functions of consumption and production can be decentralized in a compatible manner for the "total" Robinson.[2] However, Koopmans

The intrinsic part of this paper depends crucially on the joint work of A. Charnes, R. W. Clower, and K. O. Kortanek as set forth in *Systems Research Memorandum No. 88*, August, 1964, Northwestern University, and subsequent extensions and revisions appearing in *Econometrica*, 1967 and *Management Science Applications*, 1968. A related presentation by A. Charnes and K. O. Kortanek entitled "Mathematical Theory and Applications of Effective Control Through Coherent Decentralization with Preemptive Goals" was accepted by the *International Congress of Mathematicians*, Moscow University, Moscow, USSR, August 1966.

1. T. C. Koopmans, *Three Essays on the State of Economic Science* (New York: McGraw-Hill Book Co., Inc., 1957) 22–23.
   2. *Ibid*. p. 17–34.

points out that in a situation where either for Robinson the supplier or for Robinson the consumer there is more than one point which maximizes the revenue (i.e., alternate optima are present), then no price system can by itself provide a complete decentralization of decisions. Koopmans expresses the need for further investigation and research as follows: "It is conceivable that these difficulties could be overcome by further refinement of the concept of strict convexity as applied to the consumption set, permitting us to state conditions that insure decentralization through unique and compatible response to incentives defined or circumscribed by suitable prices. Present appearances are however, that if this is at all possible it would require technicalities of reasoning transcending the expository purpose of the present essay.[3]

Professor Koopmans' doubts and reservations are indeed well taken. In examining even the simplest cases of a real nature involving managerial control through profit performance incentives of divisions of an enterprise, it is apparent that couplings between various divisions will almost always exist which will destroy the unique optimum characteristic, that is, which a fortiori vitiate the possibility of strict convexity in the mathematical description of the system.

In the planning phase of the economic system the selection of control parameters such as prices has been prescribed in the economic literature. This concept has roots going back to English classical economists, but it first received recognition with respect to simultaneous successive approximations to all prices in the concept of tatônnement of Walras: a view of the competitive process achieving decentralization. From the limiting case of independent individual action to more complicated decision units, the viewpoint is that through the workings of a dynamic, converging, and adjusting price mechanism, production plans of individual units will be brought into the optimal relationship from the point of view of the overall system. In recent years there have been studies on how such price selection can be achieved by the role played by a central agency which adjusts prices successively so that in the long run supply and demand are in balance. At this level of decentralization the central agency does not have to do detailed calculations for individual demands but needs only to aggregate total demands and total supply and effect price adjustments in a direction to affect a balance.

"At each stage in the market's process of successive approximations, any individual firm adjusts its tentative production plans making use of information only about the current tentative prices and its own technology (decentralization enters here). The adjustment of tentative prices, at the same time, depend only on the aggregate demands and supplies. These are simply a sum of the tentative production plans of the individual firms plus the originally existing supplies of basic resources. Thus the information needed by firms consists solely of their technologies plus prices, while the adjustment of

3. *Ibid.* p. 34.

prices is based only on the aggregate of individuals' decisions. It is the minimization of information requirements for each participant in the economy which constitutes the virtue of decentralization"[4]

The tatônnement process of finding prices is a virtual one, one which occurs before any trading takes place and which involves an interchange of information between individual units and the central agency. (We point out that in the Robinson Crusoe example the third person, Robinson the price setter, is always present.) In the tatônnement process itself there is no criterion function such as utility or overall profit. The coupling conditions are the balancing conditions of demand and supply, and other constraints appear in the form of individual technological constraints. In this sense the system differs from a single firm where such a criterion functional is present.

Decentralization for Planning and Computational Methods in Linear Systems

It is the tatônnement market mechanism that economists have in mind when they refer to special computational methods and make the interpretation of market dynamics with respect to these methods. T. Marshak at an early date drew an analogy between the workings of the simplex method and market mechanisms.[5] Later methods, such as the decomposition of Dantzig-Wolfe,[6] the mixing routines of Charnes-Cooper,[7] and the multipage method of Charnes-Lemke,[8] were developed to take advantage computationally of the separable structure of many models in the planning of optimal programs. All of these methods are iterative, and on problems of modest size they involve many iterations. In the particular instance of the decomposition principle, the divisions of the organization work independently, putting forward plans (solutions of their transfer-priced subproblems) using a vector of imputed prices π_k^T at iteration k. Upon receipt of these solutions from divisions, the central unit revises the prices from, say, π_k^T to π_{k+1}^T in an effort to induce divisions to resolve their divisional problems with these adjustments in an effort to clear the market. During the iterative process each division usually generates many extreme point solutions of its divisional-constraint set. At the conclusion of the process each must receive

4. Kenneth J. Arrow and A. C. Enthoven, "Quasi-Concave Programming," *Econometrica*, XXIX (October 1961) 36.

5. T. Marschak, "Centralization and Decentralization in Economic Organizations," *Econometrica*, XXVII (July 1959). See also T. C. Koopmans (ed.), *Activity Analysis of Production and Allocation* (Cowles Commission Monograph 13, chapter 3; New York: John Wiley & Sons, Inc., 1951).

6. George B. Dantzig and P. Wolfe, "Decomposition Principle for Linear Programs," *Operations Research*, VIII (February 1960).

7. A. Charnes and W. W. Cooper, *Management Models and Industrial Applications of Linear Programming* (Vols. I and II; New York: John Wiley & Sons, Inc., 1961).

8. A Charnes and C. E. Lemke, *Multi-Copy Generalized Networks and Multi-Page Programs* (RPI Mathematics Report No. 41, December 23, 1960).

a set of weights with which to combine its previously designated extreme points in order to achieve a divisional optimal solution. Thus, in a meaningful way, the central staff must ultimately give explicit directions to the divisions. This point is emphatically emphasized in Baumol-Fabian, where we quote the following sentences: "It is to be emphasized that now division managers *must be told by the company* . . . what combination of their proposals the company desires them to produce. There is no automatic motivation mechanism which will lead division managers to arrive at such a combination of outputs of their own volition. In this way the decentralization permitted by decomposition breaks down completely at this point."[9]

It is important to observe the precise state of economic affairs of the firm during the course of computation. At any step in the iteration, imputed prices are computed and delegated to the divisions. *Not all divisions may even take action with respect to these prices.* In other words, it is possible for 99 of the 100 divisions to be economically idle while for just division 1 the iterations will proceed into a sequence of imputed prices π_1^T, π_2^T . . . . At each step all firms face the same imputed cost vector, say π_i^T, but most of them may very well be idle while all the action centers on bringing one firm to an optimal position. In reality, or in any economic sense, each firm must transact or react at any given time, such as meeting a payroll, and cannot or does not exist in an inactive state. All iterations take place in a virtual sense without commitment of resources. For a realistic or "unsurprising" problem, solution techniques of the type described above may involve thousands of iterations, which in terms of real-life message times may involve considerable time in a state of inactivity for certain firms. For valid models of these systems the time and expense involved even for planning through such computational methods requires a very efficient truncation, which can give disastrous results. (This can be easily seen if one tries to truncate the simplex procedure on a large problem after a few steps.) Thus decentralization models, as meaningful economic models, must use an efficient method of truncation so that the system can interact.

The natural approach is through the price system again where computational efficiencies can be had. "The problem is to assign shadow prices to be paid by the central office to the departments and to impute the remaining profit."[10] Once these shadow prices have been imputed, decisions are made immediately (divisional extremal problems are solved with these imputations) and resources are committed. There is a variety of ways to assign the proceeds of a joint profit. The most well known is the imputation derived from the dual evaluators or Lagrangians of the total firm problem. Another method

9. William J. Baumol and T. Fabian, "Decomposition, Pricing for Decentralization and External Economies," *Management Science,* XI (September 1964) 14.

10. Martin Shubik, *Incentives, Decentralized Control, the Assignment of Joint Costs and Internal Pricing* (Cowles Foundation Paper No. 178; New Haven: Yale University Press, 1962), 332.

described by Shubik involves detailing five axioms for a good assignment for the imputation of joint costs, internal prices, and revenues to different decision centers of a firm.[11] Shapley has proved that these five axioms lead to a unique formula based on the characteristic function which assigns a share of the joint profits to each center and which can be used to calculate shadow prices or awards that are consistent with the optimal production under current technology and that also provide an incentive for improvement.[12]

It should be mentioned that in the special case of a strictly convex objective function, certain nonlinear versions of decomposition appear to converge much quicker than for linear objectives. Whinston[13] and Hass[14] have applied nonlinear versions of decomposition to obtain, in relatively few iterations, sets of transfer prices provided that the structure is separable. Roughly speaking, strict convexity usually carries with it uniqueness of solutions, and the computationally difficult portion of eliminating alternate optima for the divisionally priced problems is eliminated. In general, however, no results have been obtained on truncated procedures even in these cases.

Centralization and Decentralization from the Viewpoint of Operations and Control

The Charnes-Clower-Kortanek paper was the first instance in which the theory of economic models of decentralization was developed from a point of view quite different from the virtual planning phases of economic systems as displayed by market-mechanism type procedures. The central unit transmits appropriate information to each divisional unit, which then acts (commits resources) according to optimization with respect to variables under its control. The following definitions were introduced in order to emphasize the operation and control viewpoint of the system, a viewpoint which is quite different from the planning function to which economists have devoted most of their efforts.[15] The operation and control functions have not been emphasized.

Complete *centralization* of a business or economic system requires that the central office be completely informed and merely use the remainder of the organization as an instrument for execution and information gathering.

11. *Ibid.*

12. L. S. Shapley, "The Value of an N-Person Game." *Contributions to the Theory of Games,* H. W. Kuhn and A. W. Tucker (eds.) (Princeton, N.J.: Princeton University Press, 1953), II, 307–17.

13. Andrew Whinston, *Price Coordination in Decentralized Systems* (O. N. R. Research Memo 99; Pittsburgh: Carnegie Institute of Technology, June 1962); and "Price Guides in Decentralized Organizations," *New Perspectives in Organization Research*, W. W. Cooper, H. J. Leavitt, and M. W. Shelley, II (eds.) (New York: John Wiley & Sons, Inc., 1964).

14. Jerome E. Hass, "Transfer Pricing in a Decentralized Firm," *Management Science Applications* XIV (February 1968).

15. Charnes, Clower, and Kortanek, *op. cit.*

Assume that the firm faces the following extremal problem, which we term linear division separable:

$$
\begin{aligned}
&\text{minimize } u_1^T c^{(1)} + u_2^T c^{(2)} + \cdots + u_n^T c^{(n)} \\
&\text{subject to } u_1^T B_1 \qquad\qquad\qquad\qquad \geqq b^{(1)T} \\
&\qquad\qquad\quad u_2^T B_2 \qquad\qquad\qquad\quad \geqq b^{(2)T} \\
&\qquad\qquad\qquad\qquad \ddots \\
&\qquad\qquad\qquad\qquad\quad u_n^T B_n \geqq b^{(n)T} \\
&\quad u_1^T C_1 + u_2 C_2 + \cdots \quad u_n^T C_n = d^T \\
&\qquad\quad u_1, \cdots, u_n \geqq 0,
\end{aligned}
$$

(T)

where u_i^T is the production level for the ith division, B_i is the ith division's technology matrix, and the C_i matrices represent the linking or coupling of all divisions through known interdependencies. Centralized action is characterized by solving the total problem for optimal divisional production levels, $u^*_1, u^*_2, \cdots, u^*_n$, and simply directing the divisions to execute these decisions.

By *decentralization* we mean the ability to delegate all technical decisions to individual units with the behavior of each unit described by optimization with respect to variables under its control. Thus, the concept of decentralization deals with delegating decision making to more than one location. Broadly speaking, we shall take the view of the concept of an organization as a series of arrangements between individuals with possibly differing goals, rather than as a team expressed in terms of centralization. "A good decentralized system should have the property that each decision center will make a decision which is optimal for the whole with a minimum of cost for coordination and information and message costs."[16] "An optimally decentralized system will have the property that the net effect of all individual actions will be more favorable to the firm as a whole than the actions selected by any other array of decision centers. The limiting case for the possibilities of decentralization is the situation where all decision centers are independent."[17] In this case the C_i matrices in the model are all zero, reflecting the fact that no interdependencies exist. This is merely another way of saying that an action by any one unit has no effect on any other unit — for example, a purely competitive market, which may be viewed as a decentralized organization.

By "coherent decentralization" we mean that the system has the property that either by prices alone or with additional information it is possible to effect proper decentralized behavior. Thus any coherent system must require at least price information to be delegated to individual units. There are different levels of coherency; for example, one type of coherency arises from strict convexity with linear constraints while another is the more common linear functional with linear constraints. Each level of the natural hierarchy

16. Shubik, *op. cit.*, 331.
17. *Ibid.*, 329.

of coherently decentralized systems will require different amounts of information which is to be delegated to individual units for proper decentralized decision making.

Decentralization by Prices and Strictly Convex Division Separability

Let us consider a more general version of the decentralization model than presented in the previous section:

$$\text{Minimize } \phi_1(u_1) + \phi(u_2) + \cdots + \phi_m(u_m)$$

(T)

$$
\begin{aligned}
\text{subject to } & b_1 - B_1(u_1) && \geqq 0 \\
& b_2 \qquad\quad - B_2(u_2) && \geqq 0 \\
& \quad\vdots && \vdots \\
& b_m \qquad\qquad\qquad\quad - B_m(u_m) && \geqq 0 \\
& C_1(u_1) + C_2(u_2) + \cdots + C_m(u_m) \geqq 0,
\end{aligned}
$$

where $\phi_k(u_k)$ is a convex function of the vector u_k and all constraint functions are concave. Let λ^* be a vector of transfer prices (or Lagrangians) associated with coupling constraints. The kth associated subproblem is defined as

(T_k)
$$\text{Minimize } \phi_k(u_k) - C_k(u_k)^T \lambda^*$$
$$\text{subject to } B_k(u_k) \leq b_k.$$

THEOREM 1.[18] Assume that an optimal solution exists for the total problem (T) and that ϕ_k is strictly convex for each k and all constraint functions are linear, i.e., $C_k(u_k) = u_k^T C_k$, $B_k(u_k) = u_k^T B_k$. Then there exists a price vector λ^* such that each subproblem (T_k) has a unique solution which, when taken together, form an optimum for (T).

A Simple Linear Example

Charnes, Clower and Kortanek present one of the classic cases in business economics, namely, the Birch Paper Company case, which is used to establish the inadequacy of prices alone in the linear case.[19]

As a very simple example of what may happen if firms are immediately charged optimal equilibrium prices we present here exercise (20) from D. Gale's book, "where the economy consists of two firms and two goods with each firm operating one activity given respectively by $a_1^T = (2, 1)$, $a_2^T = (2, 3)$

18. Charnes, Clower, and Kortanek, *op. cit.*, 304.
19. *Ibid.*

with the respective rates of return $\gamma_1 = 3$, $\gamma_2 = 4$ and the available resources are $s_1 = 3$, $s_2 = 4$. Because of limitations of plant capacity the activities are to operate at maximum intensities of one unit."[20] Thus we have

$$\text{maximize } 3x_1 + 4x_2$$
$$\text{subject to } x_1 \leqq 1, x_2 \leqq 1$$
$$\binom{2}{1}x_1 + \binom{2}{3}x_2 \leqq \binom{3}{4}, x_1, x_2 \geqq 0.$$

Here the unique optimal intensities are $x^*_1 = \frac{1}{2}$, $x^*_2 = 1$ with equilibrium price vector $p^T = (\frac{3}{2}, 0)$, and by duality (x, p) form a competitive equilibrium. Thus with these prices we determine the subproblem for each firm following the more general development of problems (T_k) from (T) in the previous section:

Firm 1

$$\text{maximize } [3 - (\tfrac{3}{2}, 0)^T\binom{2}{1}]x_1$$
$$\text{subject to } x_1 \leqq 1;$$
or
$$\text{maximize } 0 \cdot x_1$$
$$\text{subject to } x_1 \leqq 1.$$

Firm 2

$$\text{maximize } [4 - (\tfrac{3}{2}, 0)^T\binom{2}{3}]x_2$$
$$\text{subject to } x_2 \leqq 1;$$
or
$$\text{maximize } 1 \cdot x_2$$
$$\text{subject to } x_2 \leqq 1.$$

Hence firm 2 is led to correct action by this system of prices, but firm 1 is *indifferent* and depends on implicit orders from firm 2 or higher authority, orders which could take the form

$$p^T\left(s - \sum_{k=1}^{m} A_k x_k\right) = 0$$

inherent in the definition of competitive equilibrium.

Decentralization by Prices and Preemptive Goals: Linear Minimands[21]

PREEMPTIVE GOALS AND TRANSFER PRICES

Returning to the linear model presented earlier, problem (T_k) assumes the special form

(T_k):
$$\text{minimize } u_k^T(c^{(k)} - C_k \lambda^*)$$
$$\text{subject to } u_k^T B_k \geqq b_k^T, u_k^T \geqq 0,$$

20. D. Gale, *The Theory of Linear Economic Models* (New York: McGraw-Hill, 1960) 96.
21. Charnes, Clower, and Kortanek, *op. cit.*, 307–14.

where as usual λ^* represents optimal transfer prices. It may be proved that there exist goal vectors $\alpha_k{}^T$ for each division k so that upon solving problem

(T_k^c):   minimize $u_k{}^T(c^{(k)} - C_k\lambda^*)$
              subject to $u_k{}^T B_k \geqq b_k{}^T$, $u_k{}^T C_k = \alpha_k{}^T$, $u_k{}^T \geqq 0$,

the optimal solutions $\{u_k{}^T*\}$ when taken together form an optimal solution to the total problem (T). The economic value vectors $\alpha_k{}^T$ are called preemptive goals. More precisely, the notion of a goal is meant to be either a scalar or a vector together with a system of equations which relates activity levels within a divisional unit to the specified goal.[22] We say that the goal is attained when activity levels are such that the equality system is satisfied. Goals may be incorporated either in the constraints or in the functional.[23] Any set of goals may be well ordered, or equivalently assigned priorities according to the relative importance of individual goal fulfillment. If a given set of goals is so ordered, they are called preemptive goals, and they may be handled analytically by assigning penalty costs of different order to deviations from stated goals in accordance with the preemptive scheme.

In discussing methods of effecting correct decentralization, Baumol-Fabian emphasize the importance of optimal company solutions which occur at divisional corner points.[24] In this situation, only *one* value, a^*_k, need be delegated to each division k, and correspondingly only *one* equation, as stated in Theorem 5 of Charnes, Clower and Kortanek.

APPROXIMATE FULFILLMENT OF GOALS: ROBUSTNESS

Suppose now that the preemptive goals are not met exactly, i.e., our divisional solutions v^*_k are *infeasible* with respect to the goals. More specifically, assume that, in the first p divisions, value vectors are necessary and we have approximate solutions; that is,

$$\alpha_k{}^T = v^*_k{}^T C_k + \beta_k{}^T,$$

where $\| \beta_k^T \| < \delta$, for divisions $k = 1, 2, ..., p$. Here v^*_k is infeasible with respect to goal fulfillment but is technologically feasible for division k; to be specific, $\alpha_k{}^T = \alpha^*_k{}^T = u^*_k{}^T C_k$ (where, as throughout our discussion, u^*_k is the respective kth unit's part of a total (I) - optimal solution). Thus the $\alpha_k{}^T$'s are vector-value delegations. Assume further that value equations are sufficient for the remaining divisions, and that they are met approximately, i.e.,

$a^*_k = v^*_k{}^T Q^*_k + \delta_k$, where $|\delta_k|$ is small, and Q^*_k is an appropriate vector,

22. *Ibid.*, 309.
23. See also Charnes and Cooper, *op. cit.*, 215; Yuji Ijiri, *Management Goals and Accounting for Control* (Chicago: Rand McNally), chaps. 2, 3; and A. Stedry, *Budget Control and Cost Behavior* (Englewood Cliffs, N.J.: Prentice-Hall, 1960).
24. Baumol and Fabian, *op. cit.*

for divisions $k = p + 1, p + 2, ..., n$. The problem then is to find the error in total profit that occurs if the v^*_k's are taken as divisional solutions. In Charnes, Clower, and Kortanek this error term is expressed as a function of β_k^T and δ_k and is shown to be small when all β_k^T's and δ_k's are small.

Therefore, in the same manner that internal prices are delegated to divisional units, the partitions of d are also passed on, whether in vector form or in value form. If a partition is close to a coherent one, one which corresponds to a proper divisional alternate optimum, and if the divisions attain these preemptive delegations, then the effect on total profit is also small. Alternatively, if a coherent partition is designated, then we know explicitly the effect on profit if divisions meet these goals only approximately. Thus, the preemptive goal method is a *robust* one; small errors in assignment of preemptive goals result in small errors in total profit.

BEHAVIORAL AND MOTIVATIONAL IMPLICATIONS

Baumol-Fabian[25] and Whinston[26] point out that relative interior points of the divisional-constraint sets cannot be reached by pure price manipulation alone. We have seen that the trouble is not due to the interiority alone, for, as is shown by Charnes, Clower, and Kortanek, (by the development of the Birch Paper Company example), price manipulation by itself is not sufficient even if *all* divisional solutions occur at extreme points of their respective divisional constraint sets. Second, the "greatest behavioral hindrance," i.e., where optimality requires production within the relative interior of the divisional-constraint set, is handled in principle by the preemptive goal procedure, since in this situation additional equations may be adjoined to the divisional problems so that individual optimization by division managers does give appropriate optimal solutions for the total problem.[27] The preemptive scheme is applicable to both situations, where optimal solutions are either relative interior points or extreme point solutions of divisional-constraint sets.

Convex Approximants in Nonseparably Structured Organizations

In Charnes-Fiacco-Littlechild, significant extensions are obtained to the models (T) discussed in two earlier sections where now the concave constraint functions are nonlinear, the convex objective function is not necessarily separable, and there is also no necessity for interdivisional (coupling) constraints to be separable.[28] By application of the SUMT method, approxi-

25. *Ibid.*
26. Whinston. *op. cit.* (1964).
27. See Hass, *op. cit.,* Sect. V, par. B.
28. A. Charnes, A. V. Fiacco, and S. C. Littlechild, *Convex Approximants and Decentralization: A SUMT Approach* (Systems Research Memorandum No. 165, Evanston, Ill.: Northwestern University, December 1966).

mants are obtained which yield decentralization but which are within pre-
assigned amounts of deviation of the total overall optima. Their methods are
also made computationally feasible through the use of the SUMT programming techniques.[29] Under the SUMT formulation, divisional problems
automatically become strictly convex and therefore possess unique solutions
which will be as close to optimal of the total problem as desired. To be more
specific, the problem (T) now assumes the general form[30]

$$\text{minimize } f(x_1, x_2, \ldots, x_n)$$

(T)

$$\text{subject to } g^1_i(x_1) \qquad\qquad \geqq 0 \; (i = 1, 2, \ldots, m_1)$$

$$g_i^n(x_n) \geqq 0 \; (i = 1, 2, \ldots, m_n)$$
$$h_l(x_1, x_2, \ldots, x_n) \geqq 0 \; (l = 1, 2, \ldots, m),$$

where x_k is the *vector* of decision variables for division k, as in all of our models.
The corresponding P-function, inherent in the SUMT method, becomes

$$P(x, r) = f(x) + r \sum_{j=1}^{n} \sum_{i=1}^{m_j} \frac{1}{g_i^j(x_j)} + \sum_{l=1}^{m} \frac{1}{h_l(x)},$$

where $x = (x_1, x_2, \ldots, x_n)$. For $r > 0$, $P(x, r)$ has a unique minimum, $x^*(r) = \{x^*_1(r), x^*_2(r), \ldots, x^*_n(r)\}$. An important theorem of Charnes, Fiacco, and
Littlechild ensures that *regardless* of how the optimal solution $x^*(r)$ is
obtained, any set of divisional levels $\{x^*_1 \ldots, x^*_n\}$ can be attained by divisions
by setting each division a problem of the form

$$\text{minimize } f(x^*_1, \ldots, x^*_{k-1}, x_k, x^*_{k+1}, \ldots, x^*_n)$$

(T^*_k)

$$\text{subject to } g_i^{(k)}(x_k) \geqq g_i^{(k)}(x^*) \quad (i = 1, \ldots, m_k)$$
$$h_l(x^*_1, \ldots, x^*_{k-1}, x_k, x^*_{k+1}, \ldots, x^*_n) \geqq h_l(x^*), \quad (l = 1, \ldots, m),$$

provided that (T^*_k) has a unique minimum, which is usually the case under
strict convexity assumptions.

Although problem (T_k) is now much more complex than our earlier versions
under separability, nevertheless a subproblem is obtained for each division
k with a guiding criterion which will ensure that its program is uniquely
optimal from its own point of view and from that of the whole firm. Observe
that in each subproblem, Lagrangians or transfer prices as such do not
occur. In fact the exact form of T_k and its informational requirements "sans
prices" is precisely the breakthrough obtained by Charnes, Fiacco, and

29. See A. V. Fiacco and G. P. McCormick, "The Sequential Unconstrained Minimization
Technique for Non-Linear Programming: A Primal-Dual Method," *Management Science,* X
(January 1964); and A. V. Fiacco and G. P. McCormick, "Computational Algorithm for the
Sequential Unconstrained Minimization Technique for Nonlinear Programming," *Management
Science,* X (July 1964).

30. See Charnes, Fiacco, and Littlechild, *op. cit.*

Littlechild. Several writers such as Whinston showed that the *relaxation of separability* in the constraint and objective functions implies that "the price guides no longer give sufficient information to guide the individual decision makers in making correct decisions even on their own accounts, much less in terms of overall organizational goals and constraints."[31] Even earlier, Arrow and Hurwicz[32] showed that in the (slightly adapted) model

(T)   maximize $f(x_1, ..., x_n)$

subject to $\sum_j g_{ij}(x_j) \leq 0$ $(i = 1, ..., m)$, $x_j \geq 0$,

where f is concave but not necessarily separable, and the $g_{ij}(x_j)$ are convex, the internal prices can again be derived but again will not in general be adequate.

Observe further that except for nonuniqueness and local optima, essentially any problem can be decentralized by using the SUMT approach. In fact there are generalizations, called SLUMT,[33] which permit equality constraints. Both of these computational methods have had wide computational experience at Research Analysis Corporation, Bethesda, Maryland, even for nonconvex problems which are not separable.

Conclusions

One of the central themes is the marked difference in economic interpretation between decentralized planning through procedures of the virtual market mechanism type and the coherent decentralization for operations and control. In the *former* case, iterations proceed in a random fashion, via the invisible hand of Adam Smith, until all markets are cleared. Then only are resources assuredly committed. Analogies have been drawn between market processes and many computational methods – for example, simplex method and decomposition principles. Upon observing the actual sequence of iterations of these methods, one can see how random, albeit relatively efficient, these methods really are. It may be that during the course of iterations a single division gets all the attention for several moments, while all others are computationally idle. All divisions are idle in an economic sense until an optimum is reached. In fact, it may not be wise to cease iterations even within 5 percent of the optimal value (if it were known) because, in the case of decomposition, an extreme point of the total problem may not yet be on hand, and thereby there is no assurance of existence of marginal prices or dual evaluators. While no known truncation procedures yet exist, some people have reported excellent results on small numbers of iterations for

31. Whinston, *op. cit.* (1964) 429.

32. K. J. Arrow and L. Hurwicz, "Decentralization and Computation in Resource Allocation," in *Essays in Economics and Econometrics* (Chapel Hill: University of North Carolina, 1960), 77–78.

33. A. V. Fiacco and G. P. McCormick, "The Slacked Unconstrained Minimization Technique for Convex Programming," *SIAM*, XV (May 1967).

the situation in which the objective function is strictly convex.

With the emphasis on operations and control, the control unit transmits appropriate information to each division which then commits resources according to optimization with respect to variables under its control.[34] The amount of information depends on the structure of the divisional-constraint set and, for divisionally separable structure, takes the form of preemptive goals. The more general situation of nonseparability gives rise to new subproblems for cases in which transfer prices do not exist, but such that divisions may act as autonomously as possible.[35] Division managers are judged on the modified accounting system which these schemes imply. Motivationally there is no hindrance attached to one mathematical structure or another provided that it is possible to obtain reasonable approximations of goals for subproblems. Mathematically speaking, almost all substructures and goals are continuous, thereby affording the most flexibility in near-solutions even though slightly "infeasible."

In conclusion, we return to Koopmans[36] and state a theorem on the hierarchical structure of coherent decentralization for convex division-separable organizations.[37] The statements here are similar to those of Koopmans.[38] However we are not referring to the interchangeability of the operations of maximization of objective functions and summation of feasible sets; rather, we are summarizing main results developed for convex division-separable minimands subject to linear constraints.

THEOREM *Structure of Coherency:*[39]

a) If there exists no interaction between productive units, i.e., if all couplings between units are zero, then the maximization of aggregate profits is equivalent to maximization of individual profits.[40]

b) If each productive unit has a polyhedral convex constraint set and its profit function is strictly concave, then there exists a set of internal prices such that maximization of total profit is equivalent to maximization of individual profits.[41]

c) In the general case of concave profit functions — in particular, piecewise linear ones[42] — additional information beyond prices alone is necessary for proper coordinated action. Preemptive goals are sufficient to ensure proper decentralized coordination. Further, the preemptive goal procedure is a robust one, i.e., approximate fulfillment of preemptive goals results in small errors in profit.

34. Charnes, Clower, and Kortanek, *op. cit.*
35. Charnes, Fiacco, and Littlechild, *op. cit.*
36. Koopmans, *op. cit.* (1957).
37. Charnes, Clower and Kortanek, *op. cit.,* 317.
38. Koopmans, *op. cit.* (1957). 14.
39. See Charnes, Clower, and Kortanek, *op. cit.,* 317.
40. Koopmans, *op. cit.* (1957), 14.
41. *Ibid.,* 32–33.
42. *Ibid.,* 25.

III

A Framework for Solving Joint Decision Problems: Elaboration

As models of joint decision making become more specific and detailed, as they do in this part, it is harder to maintain an interdisciplinary perspective. At the point of greater detail, authors begin to define the problem differently. Reiter's paper, the first in this part, treats organization structure and information and decision processes while assuming agreement on a joint welfare function. Walton concentrates on motivation and behavior as it relates to the general decision technology choice between bargaining and problem solving. A key issue in joint decision problems is whether the incentive for subunits to act in accordance with a joint welfare function is automatically present. Hass, in the third paper of Part III, shows that a properly specified quadratic objective function in the decision model possesses an embedded incentive for the subunits. With such a quadratic decision function, as the subunits attempt to act in their self-interest they are in fact acting in conformity with the joint welfare function. Hass shows that this embedded incentive is not necessarily present in the case of a linear objective function.

The papers in Part III continue the theoretical development begun in Part II. The organization model in Reiter's paper consists of centers which observe the environment, communicate with each other until an optimal action with respect to some set of goals is agreed upon, and then carry out that action. His model specifies linkages, or communication arrangements, between centers; it specifies a response function which defines information reception, processing, and reply; and it specifies a decision function which translates "terminal" messages into actions. A "stopping" rule indicates the point at which communication ends and action begins. The action of the organization is determined by individual center actions.

Communication, in Reiter's model, can be restricted by placing limitations on messages each center can send and receive to and from other centers and from the environment. Linkages between individual centers may allow one-way or two-way communication, or no communication. Without communication, or with restricted communication, perceptions of the environment may be distorted and thus lead to inappropriate actions. Similarly, with restrictions on communication, the centers may lack the necessary degree of coordination for the attainment of organization goals. Restrictions may also be placed on actions available to individual centers. These restrictions may likewise frustrate the attainment of organization goals.

The restrictions on communication or on action in Reiter's formulation are physical restrictions. These restrictions reflect human limitations in terms of type and amount of energy output and in terms of information processing capabilities or they reflect cost considerations whereby the cost of information processing or of performing an action exceeds the benefits. Thus, Reiter deals with the material-feasibility criterion of organizational design suggested by Hurwicz.

Reiter's treatment of behavioral feasibility as an issue resolvable outside his model is consistent with the assumptions of other theory of teams formulations which represent a rigorous body of work on joint decision problems. As interdisciplinary work on joint decision problems develops, it should be possible to remove this separation of physical and behavioral variables in model formulation. Just as physical or material impediments to organizational performance can only be corrected at a cost, behavioral impediments are likewise adjustable. The cost of modifying the behavior of organization members in terms of incentives, training, or replacement can be weighed against the benefits in terms of organization goal attainment and the trade-offs possible here would seem to be every bit as real as those contemplated in removing physical impediments. One objective of a theory of inter-organizational decision making would be to merge material and behavioral constraints in a single model.

Walton's paper suggests that in the extreme, behavioral problems can take the form (to continue the use of Reiter's terminology) of an unwillingness on the part of centers to communicate with each other. This form of behavior is expected to be more common when the centers represent separate organizations, but effectively such behavior is not unknown within a single organization. Walton has observed "avoidance" of communication relevant to a joint decision problem occurring among government agencies. He cites reasons for their desire to retain independence in their choice of actions as including the facts that (a) the agencies' goals are interdependent only in the long run, (b) there are few direct costs to the individual agencies for failure to coordinate their decision making, (c) interagency efforts take more bureaucratic time and have a higher risk of failure, (d) interdependent ventures very seldom have symmetrical gains for the two or more participating agencies, (e) interdependent ventures increase the visibility of an agency's actions, and therefore increase the agency's vulnerability to attack and criticism, and (f) interagency actions tend to blur individual program indentity or status.

Alternative organizational structures can be developed to overcome communication blocks which are behavioral rather than physical in nature. Walton suggests redesigning the reward and penalty system to add costs for not cooperating; reducing identity competition by rearranging goals, altering task responsibilities, or reassigning personnel; or in the extreme by bringing about a merger. These are all costly decisions which have to be evaluated against the potential benefits of increased interunit communication.

There are many behavioral factors which interfere with the flow of information between centers short of completely blocking communication. Walton's paper deals extensively with one of these, identity conflict, as it relates to the choice that centers make between engaging in bargaining and engaging in problem solving. Inherent in the process of bargaining is a restrictive information flow. Not only is information restricted, it is also distorted. In problem solving, a free flow of information, without distortion, is assumed.

Hass, in his paper, develops an algorithm for a decentralized solution to a problem of river-basin pollution which has the behavioral advantage that the decentralized decision maker can arrive at his own optimal decision by using his cost of waste treatment and the tax rate provided by the taxing authority. The problem Hass tackles is to motivate each polluter along the river to perform sufficient in-plant treatment of waste water before discharging it into the river so that the established water standards of the river basin will be maintained. Costs of in-plant treatment are known only to individual polluters. The taxing authority establishes water standards and taxes each polluter at a rate in proportion to the waste material remaining in the water he discharges into the river. Using Hass's algorithm, it is possible to set a tax rate for each polluter, in an iterative manner, so that when, at the final interaction, each polluter minimizes his total cost (tax on waste discharged plus treatment cost before discharge), there will result a least-cost treatment scheme for the entire basin and the indicated water standard will have been met.

6

Formal Modeling of Organizations

STANLEY REITER

Organizations are the means by which man achieves purposes that exceed the capacity of one individual. In this statement we recognize that organizations are the creations of man, that they are to be viewed as instruments for the accomplishment of objectives or purposes, and that their component elements, including human beings, are of restricted capacity in relation to the accomplishment of those objectives or purposes.

To understand organizations means to understand the ways in which the efforts of many individual agents can be brought to bear on the tasks to be accomplished, taking account of the operative restrictions on performance proposed by the limited capacities of agents and by the techniques for co-ordinating them. More specifically, a theory of organization should provide means for the expression of objectives or purposes in relation to the given uncontrollable elements of the situation in which the organization is supposed to function. Such a theory should also provide means for representing the processes of functioning of the organization and for exhibiting the resulting performance of the organization evaluated in comparison to the stated objectives. Such a theory should also provide for the expression of the relationships between the capacities of individual components and the organizational possibilities.

From the point of view adopted here, we may liken organizations to machines; indeed, formally, an organization may be modeled as a "cybernetic machine."[1] The questions that would occur to one to ask about ordinary machines may also be asked about organizations. For example: Is this organization (machine) capable of a certain specified performance? Is there

The author's work on this paper was supported by National Science Foundation Research Grant No. GS 2061, Comparison and Analysis of Systems and Techniques of Economic Organization.

1. J. Klir, and M. Valach, *Cybernetic Modelling*, English translation, W. A. Ainsworth (ed.) (London: Iliffe Books, Ltd., 1967).

a member of this class of organizations capable of a specified performance? Among all organizations capable of a given performance, which of them have a stated property — for example, minimum number of components, minimum cost, etc.? And just as with other classes of machines, new types of organizations may be designed to meet specified criteria.

In this study the restricted capacity of individual components is an essential element of the problem. As our first sentence already indicates, if no task is beyond the grasp of one person, there is no need for organization. The question remains: Just which constraints on the performance of individuals should be incorporated into the theory? Constraints may be put into two classes; those arising from the existence of individual motivation, commonly called "behavioral" constraints, and those arising from "physical" facts which limit the amount and forms of human energy output and information processing capability. While either type of constraint may be important in a particular situation, the two types differ in their logical relationships to the rest of the organization theory. Where behavioral constraints are involved, it is logically possible to superimpose another system of rules or relationships with the aim of modifying behavior. This is not possible in the case of "physical" constraints. Thus, if in particular circumstances someone's behavior is not that which is desired, it is possible to provide additional incentives — rewards or punishments — to induce him to modify his behavior. If he is unable to read 50,000 words per minute, although he may be led to try, no inducements will lead him to do so; additional physical resources will be required, entailing additional problems of coordination of the type already recognized as an essential part of the problem of theory of organization.

Goals

We begin our theory of organization with a formulation which permits the goals of organization to be stated. We base this formulation on the theory of decision making.[2]

We focus interest on a certain set of tasks. All the factors which can influence significantly the outcome or performance of those tasks may be classified as being either to some extent under the control of the organization under consideration, or totally outside its control; the latter we regard as the "givens" and call them collectively "the environment." A complete description of an environment we will denote by e and the set of all (alternative) environments under consideration we denote by $\mathscr{E}$. Those factors under the control of the organization we call "joint actions" available to the organization and denote them as $a \in \mathscr{A}$, where $\mathscr{A}$ is the set of joint actions available to the organization. When the environment $e \in \mathscr{E}$ obtains and the joint action $a \in \mathscr{A}$ is taken, an "outcome" or "performance" is thereby determined. In

2. See, e.g., D. Blackwell and M. A. Girschick, *Theory of Games and Statistical Decisions* (New York: John Wiley & Son, Inc., 1954).

order to have a problem, there must be some system of evaluation that permits us to compare one possible outcome with another; otherwise there is nothing to choose. There are various ways to represent the valuation of outcomes. Most generally, we may suppose a partial preordering $\gtrsim$ on $\mathscr{E} \times \mathscr{A}$ such that $(e, a_1) \gtrsim (e, a_2)$ means that action a_1 is preferable to a_2 when the environment is e, $(e, a_1) \sim (e, a_2)$ means a_1 and a_2 are indifferent for environment e. Some environment-action pairs may be incomparable. Other more specialized representations of valuation are possible, corresponding to more detailed valuations – as, for example, in the case of a firm with a profit function which associates to each joint action in each environment the amount of profit resulting. This determines a total preordering on $\mathscr{E} \times \mathscr{A}$ such that $(e_1, a_1) \gtrsim (e_2, a_2)$ if the profit resulting from (e_1, a_1) is at least as large as that from (e_2, a_2). Whatever the nature of valuation of outcomes, we may suppose it to be sufficiently precise so that there is corresponding to each environment $e \in \mathscr{E}$, an ordering of the subsets of joint actions which indicates their relative desirability when e is the environment. We shall specialize further by assuming that there is a subset of joint actions which is most desirable for e and represent this by a mapping $D: \mathscr{E} \mapsto 2^{\mathscr{A}}$, where $D(e)$ is the subset consisting of joint actions the organization should take when the environment is e. This mapping $D: \mathscr{E} \mapsto 2^{\mathscr{A}}$ then expresses the *goals* of the organization in the sense that it tells us how the organization should act in each environment that might arise. If it were possible for an individual to determine which environment e obtains, to figure out the desirable actions $D(e)$, and to carry out one of them, there would be no need for organization and no organizational-theoretical problem. A problem of organization arises when one or another of these tasks exceeds the capacity of one person.

A Model of Organization

An *organization* consists of a finite number of *centers*, called 1, ..., *n*. A *center* may consist of more than one person, together with equipment. Just what we take to be a center depends on the fineness of the analysis and is to some extent arbitrary.

Each center is able to perceive some aspect of the environment. We represent this by mappings

$$h^i : \mathscr{E} \mapsto h^i(\mathscr{E}) \equiv \mathscr{E}^i \qquad (i = 1, \dots, n),$$

where h^i represents "measurements" or "observations" that the ith center is able to make on the environment. Some centers may be unable to observe the environment at all, in which case h^i would be constant for such a center.

The center i is supposed to have available to it a set B^i of *actions of center i*. The actions

$$b \in \underset{i=1}{\overset{n}{\times}} B^i, b = (b^1, \dots, b^n), b^i \in B_i \qquad (i = 1, \dots, n)$$

of each center together determine a joint action $a \in \mathscr{A}$ of the organization. Thus, there is given a function

$$G: \underset{i=1}{\overset{n}{\times}} B^i \mapsto \mathscr{A}.$$

Here $G(b) \in \mathscr{A}$ is the joint action taken by the organization when the centers take the actions $(b^1, \ldots, b^n) = b$.

What we have so far defined almost suffices to study a particularly primitive type of organization, that of uncoordinated decision making. We consider two examples.

Let $\bar{g}^i: \mathscr{E}^i \mapsto B^i$, $i = 1, 2$, be functions selecting an action $\bar{g}^i(e^i) \in B^i$ corresponding to each observed environment $e^i \in \mathscr{E}^i$.

Example 1. $\mathscr{E} \equiv \mathscr{A} = R^2$ (Euclidean 2-space):

$$N = 2, h^1(e) = e_1, h^2(e) = e_2,$$
$$D(e_1, e_2) = \{(e_1, 2e_1)\}, B = B^1 \times B^2 = \mathscr{A}, G = I_B \text{ (the identity function on } B).$$

We see that $\bar{g}^2$ must be a function of e_2 alone, but the optimal action requires

$$G(\bar{g}^1(h^1(e)), \bar{g}^2(h^2(e))) = D(e) = \{(e_1, 2e_1)\},$$

so that in general there is no function $\bar{g}^2$ which guarantees optimal joint action. This organization is incapable of realizing the goals expressed by the mapping D in the environments $\mathscr{E}$.

Example 2. $\mathscr{E} = \mathscr{A} = R^2$. Here D is a 1 to 1 function from $\mathscr{E}$ to $\mathscr{A}$, $N = 2$:

$$h^1(e) = \alpha e_1 + \beta e_2, h^2(e) = e_1 \cdot e_2, B = \mathscr{A}, G = I_B.$$

We see that any function $\bar{g}^1$ will be constant on the sets $\{e \in \mathscr{E} \mid \alpha e_1 + \beta e_2 = c$ (constant)$\} = \mathscr{C}$. Similarly, $\bar{g}^2$ must be constant on sets of the form $\{e \in \mathscr{E} \mid e_1 \cdot e_2 = d\} = \mathscr{D}$. Sets of the form $\mathscr{C} \cap \mathscr{D}$ in general consist of two points. Since D is 1 to 1, there is in general no pair of functions $(\bar{g}^1, \bar{g}^2)$ which can lead to the desired decisions $D(e)$ for $e \in \mathscr{E}$. There is, however, an interesting difference between these two examples. In Example 1, it is possible for center 1 to communicate its observation e_1 of the environment (e_1, e_2) to center 2, thereby providing information which would allow center 2 to make the desired decision. In Example 2, exchange of messages will not help, for messages must be constant on sets of the form $\{e \in \mathscr{E} \mid h^1(e) = c\} = \mathscr{C}$ and $\{e \in \mathscr{E} \mid h^2(e) = d\} = \mathscr{D}$ and so cannot distinguish between the (generally) two points in $\mathscr{C} \cap \mathscr{D}$. In Example 2 there is not enough information in the organization, even when all information is pooled, to permit the desired performance to be achieved.

However, in nontrivial organizations, as in Example 1, communication is an important element. Let $t = 1, 2, \ldots,$ denote iteration number. We may think of it as internal time governing internal organizational processes, rather like the internal clock in a computer. Communication takes place by way of rounds of messages at successive points of time. Let center i have available to it a set S^i of messages it can recognize, its input signals, and a set M^i of messages it is capable of sending. These sets are subsets of a "language," $\mathcal{M}$.

We define *linkage functions*

$$L^i: \underset{j=1}{\overset{n}{\LARGE\ast}} M^j \to S^i \qquad (i = 1, \ldots, n)$$

representing communication linkages among the organization's centers. For example,

$$L^1(m^1, m^2) = m^2, \; L^2(m^1, m^2) = \phi,$$

so that center 1 receives the message sent by center 2 and center 2 receives nothing from center 1.

We define *response rules* f^i

$$f^i: \mathcal{E}^i \times S^i \to M^i \qquad (i = 1, \ldots, n).$$

These functions together determine a communication process as follows. The observations $(h^i(e), \ldots, h^n(e)) = h(e)$ are made. Initial messages $(f^i(\phi, h^i(e)), \ldots, f^n(\phi, h^n(e)))$ are emitted. Signals $L^i(m_0{}^1, \ldots, m_0{}^n)$ $(i = 1, \ldots, n)$ are received, and responses $(f^1(h^1(m_0{}^1, \ldots, m_0{}^n), h^1(e)), \ldots, f^n(h^n(m_0{}^1, \ldots, m_0{}^n); h^n(e))) = (m^1, \ldots, m^n)$ are made. The communication process continues until an agreement on action is reached, expressed by the condition

$$(m_t{}^1, \ldots, m_t{}^n, h^1(e), \ldots, h^n(e)) \in \overline{\left(\underset{i=1}{\overset{n}{\LARGE\ast}} M^i \right) \times \left(\underset{i=1}{\overset{n}{\LARGE\ast}} \mathcal{E}^i \right)}.$$

At that point the communication process terminates and actions are taken, i.e., the function g^i maps terminal messages into actions,

$$g^i: \overline{\left(\underset{i=1}{\overset{n}{\LARGE\ast}} M^i \right) \times \left(\underset{i=1}{\overset{n}{\LARGE\ast}} \mathcal{E}^i \right)} \mapsto B^i.$$

One example of such a stopping rule is given by *message equilibrium*

$$\bar{M}_e = \left\{ m \in \underset{i=1}{\overset{n}{\LARGE\ast}} M^i \mid f^i(\bar{m}, h^i(e)) = \bar{m}^i \qquad (i = 1, \ldots, n) \right\}.$$

Hence

$$\bar{M}_e \times \left(\underset{i=1}{\overset{n}{\LARGE\ast}} \mathcal{E}^i \right) = \overline{\left(\underset{i=1}{\overset{n}{\LARGE\ast}} M^i \right) \times \left(\underset{i=1}{\overset{n}{\LARGE\ast}} \mathcal{E}^i \right)}.$$

This setup follows that of Hurwicz[3] in certain basic respects, particularly the introduction of a formal language and response function. However, the explicit introduction of the linkage functions, which do not appear in Hurwicz's model,[4] permits more convenient representation of certain features

3. Leonid Hurwicz, *Optimality and Informational Efficiency in Resource Allocation Processes*, Mathematical Methods in the Social Sciences, Kenneth J. Arrow, Samuel Karlin, and Patrick Suppes (eds.) (Stanford: Stanford University Press, 1959).
4. In Hurwicz's formulation, the linkages are implicit in the response rules. These may be regarded as compositions of our response rules and linkage functions. There is therefore no gain in generality here as compared to the Hurwicz model.

of organizations, and particularly facilitates the study of information systems with differentiated information flows.

We may identify the centers with the basic organizational subunits chosen for the analysis of an organization; and we may identify the response rules and linkage functions with the systems and procedures manual and, at higher levels, together with the functions g^i, with the decision making functions of managers. The linkages describe "who reports what to whom." The functions h^i describe what information about the environment is directly perceived by each center, the set S^i of input signals describes the capability of the ith center to receive information from other parts of the organization, the information processing performed by each center is associated with the response functions f^i, and these things together determine what information is available at each center. The functions g^i may be associated with operating decisions or procedures.

We have referred several times to the restricted capacity of individuals and hence of centers as an important fact about organizations and therefore a central element of the theory of organizations. Without such restrictions, the problem of organization is trivial. To see just where restrictions on capacities enter the model, the following summary diagram will be helpful.

We have seen that the communication process represented by the response rules f^i and linkage functions L^i, $i = 1, \ldots, n$, lead from observations of the environment to agreed action. We may therefore define a communication process by a pair $(F, M) \equiv \mathscr{F}$, where

$$F = h(\mathscr{E}) \to \bar{V}$$

with

$$h(\mathscr{E}) = \underset{i=1}{\overset{n}{\ast}} h^i(\mathscr{E})$$

and

$$\bar{V} = \overline{\left(\underset{i=1}{\overset{n}{\ast}} S^i \right) \times \left(\underset{i=1}{\overset{n}{\ast}} h^i(e) \right) \times \left(\underset{i=1}{\overset{n}{\ast}} M^i \right)},$$

where the function F is defined by

$$F(h(e)) = v \in \bar{V} \Leftrightarrow f^1(L^1(m)h^i(e)), \ldots, f^n(L^n(m)h^n(e)) = v \in \bar{V}.$$

These mappings are depicted in Figure 6.1. (Here the language $\mathscr{M}$ is implicit in the definition of F.) In this diagram an organization is represented by the arrows labeled h, F, g, G, and the sets $\underset{i=1}{\overset{n}{\ast}} h^i(\mathscr{E})$, $\bar{V}$, $\underset{i=1}{\overset{n}{\ast}} B^i$. We may think of an organization as a way of "computing" the mapping D. Without restrictions, one way of performing this "computation" is to make $h^1(\mathscr{E})$ the identity mapping on $\mathscr{E}$, and $h^2, \ldots, h^n$ constant mappings, to make $B^1 = 2^{\mathscr{A}}$, $B^2, \ldots, B^n$ empty, to make G the identity on B, and to compute D by choosing f^1 and g^1 and $\bar{V}$ such that $g^1 \circ f^1 = D$. These choices represent an

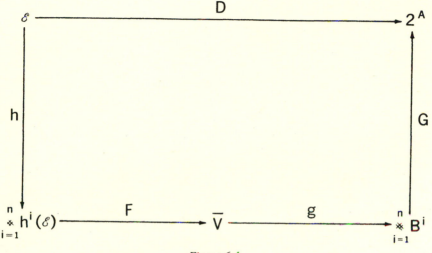

Figure 6.1.

organization that consists of one center which perceives the environment as it is, is able to carry out by itself any joint action $\mathscr{A}$, and computes directly which actions it should take. Without further specifications regarding capacities, this organization is feasible and cannot be compared unfavorably with any other.

We may distinguish two approaches to incorporating restrictions on information processing capabilities, although one may be regarded as a special case of the other. The first is to distinguish *admissible* from *inadmissible* observations, individual actions, and communication processes. This concept may be expressed by means of subsets of mappings h^i, F and g representing the admissible mappings.

The second approach is to attach "costs," measured in some way, to the mappings h^i, f^i, g^i. The definition of such "costs" constitutes a problem, especially in the case of costs to be associated with information processing, i.e., with the mappings f^i. Several approaches to this problem, a central one for the theory of organization, have been attempted (Marschak, Hurwicz), but the basic issues have not yet been resolved. The main point here is that "costliness" of operating the organization (cost of information processing) is itself a component of performance. Such "costs" may make certain (desired) outcomes unattainable, or in general create a "trade off" between organizational costs and performance vis-à-vis the environment.

In summary, the model presented here, as illustrated in Figure 6.1, provides categories and concepts in terms of which organizations may be represented, and internal functioning studied, in relation to different environments and different technologies of information processing. By these means we may study and analyze organizations as we study other types of "machines" with a view to being able to relate design features to performance criteria.

7

Interorganizational Decision Making and Identity Conflict

RICHARD E. WALTON

This paper is intended to contribute to the explanation and prediction of behavior in interunit decision making and the relative quality of decision outcomes under varying conditions. It focuses on the interaction processes which occur in joint decision making settings. It is first descriptive, but with prescriptive implications for how one structures the decision making situation. Two purposive *decision* processes, problem solving and bargaining, are instrumental to the formal purposes of the interunit relations. Two purposive *social* processes, identity reinforcement and identity conflict, are expressive of the way parties view themselves, compared with how they are viewed by each other.

This paper offers a conceptual space which helps one visualize different interaction systems with various mixtures of these four processes and helps one distinguish among several approaches to reducing conflict in the interunit system where that is desirable. It also postulates a system of propositions regarding the effect of each process on each of the other three processes, frequently indicating what steps or conditions will minimize the general tendency effects which involve deterioration of the interunit system.

Primary reliance is placed upon anecdotes both to illustrate general theoretical points and simultaneously to show their relevance to interorganizational decision making. In many places both the theoretical reasoning and empirical support could be (and in some future effort will be) strengthened by more extensive references to the relevant literature.

Interorganizational Situations Contemplated by the Theory

The most salient empirical reference for this discussion is the interorganizational decision making among foreign affairs agencies and among

This research was supported by the Advanced Research Projects Agency of the Department of Defense and monitored by the Air Force Office of Scientific Research under Contract No. F44620-69-C-0040.

urban agencies. In the recent past, I have consulted in these two inter-organizational fields and conducted research on numerous specific efforts to achieve more integration of the efforts of Federal agencies concerned with highly interrelated problems. Most of the illustrative material presented here is drawn from the unpublished case histories which I have developed on such efforts, and includes the following situations:

1. The regularized patterns of interagency decision making in a large overseas mission of the United States, involving the Ambassador and his office staff, and members of the Country Team including AID, USIS, the several military services, Agriculture, Treasury, Commerce, Labor, Peace Corps, and intelligence groups.

2. The functioning of an interagency working group charged with proposing a long-term foreign policy toward Country X. The group was chaired by a senior Foreign Service Officer on the Policy Planning Council of the Department of State and comprised officials from all foreign affairs agencies. Typically, each agency's representative to the group was the official most concerned with that agency's activities in Country X. The task of the group was to pool and synthesize their specialized information, examine their diverse interests and differing policy concerns, and then, in the context of some understanding of broad U.S. goals vis-à-vis nations such as Country X, develop a long-term policy statement which could be recommended ultimately to the top U.S. foreign policy makers.

3. The functioning of a Federal management system for the Neighborhood Centers Pilot Program (NCPP), an interagency program launched in August 1966 which has established or is in the process of developing viable pilot centers in each of fourteen cities. Like the Model Cities program, which was launched somewhat later, the NCPP is interorganizational in at least three significant respects. First, it is interagency, involving Housing and Urban Development (HUD) in a lead role, the Bureau of the Budget (BOB) in both initiating and evaluation roles, and the Office of Economic Opportunity (OEO), Health, Education, and Welfare (HEW), and the Labor Department (DOL) as participating program agencies. Second, it is intergovernmental, involving Federal, state, and city governments. Third, it involved as separate entities neighborhood resident-based organizations. The basic concepts of the NCPP are to develop multipurpose service centers concerting, inter-relating, and integrating the many Federal, state, and local services intended to cure the ills of city ghettos; and to develop capacities for residents to influence or control the center and thereby ensure that service programs are responsive to the needs of residents and are maximally available to them.

Stakes in the Situation: Two Types of Conflict and Integrative Potential

Interorganizational interactions have both instrumental and expressive meanings for the participants.

INSTRUMENTAL STAKES AND PROCESSES

Instrumental stakes will refer to the implications which joint decision making has for the goal achievement of participating organizations. The following are illustrative of the instrumental stakes in the interagency settings studied:

Policy commitments – In interagency plans, how much emphasis will be given the programs and philosophies of each participating agency?

Contributions – How much of each agency's scarce resources – in terms of funds and manpower – will be committed to an interagency venture?

Operational initiative and control – How much control will any particular agency be able to exercise over the operation of interdependent activities between agencies?

Bureaucratic procedures – Which agency's normal procedures will be utilized in an interagency effort when the participating agencies each use different procedures normally?

Credit and blame – How much credit will each agency receive from apparent successes in interagency ventures, and how much blame will each agency receive in the event of failures?

The preferences of two parties respectively regarding the instrumental stakes can be basically compatible and contain integrative potential. Alternatively, they can be fundamentally incompatible and contain conflict potential. In joint decision making settings, integrative potential is realized via problem solving, and conflict potential leads to a bargaining-type decision process.

The *problem-solving* type of decision making appropriately occurs when and to the extent that the joint gain available to the parties is variable, not fixed. Thus, under problem solving, total payoffs vary as a function of participants' abilities to discover how their basic interests are complementary or coincidental as well as their abilities to invent mechanisms for exploiting this integrative potential.

The process involves the following activities: First, the parties identify and define agenda items or areas of mutual concern in terms of the fundamental needs involved. There is a collaborative effort to reality test – that is, to test assumptions about the motives, needs, and preferences of others, and about the present state of the situation. Reality testing includes accurate assessment of the current dissatisfactions being experienced by either or both parties. A second activity involves searching for alternative courses of action and jointly assessing all of the consequences that might follow from each alternative. Potential solutions that would increase the joint gain are usually not immediately apparent, but have to be discovered or invented. Similarly, the full consequences of a given course of action are not obvious, but have to be inferred from all of the facts which can be made available. The effectiveness of this step depends upon a thorough, accurate exchange and pooling of information about alternatives and their consequences. The third activity entails the identification of the largest sum of values possible, given the alternatives. The parties must be as clear as possible about their respective preference functions.

The *bargaining* type of decision making appropriately occurs when and to the extent that the joint gain available to the parties is a fixed sum and their relative shares are not yet determined. Behaviorally, bargaining involves the following types of predecision activities on the part of both parties: for example, one party attempts to modify the second's perceptions of the utilities asociated with various courses of action in such a way that the second party will provide less resistance to decisions the first party favors. Also, the first party attempts to structure the second's expectations about what outcomes would be minimally acceptable to the first. Essential to bargaining are commitment tactics which involve the taking of bargaining positions and communication of threats, preventing one's opponent from implementing the same operations, and rationalizing away earlier commitments by either party which become untenable. In taking a bargaining position, the verbal or tacit communication is important: How much finality is implied? How specifically is the position indicated? And what consequences seem to be associated with a failure to reach agreement? Each of these considerations requires deliberateness in communicating with the other. However, equally important are the tactics which lend credibility to these communications: presenting one's proposal first, reducing it to writing and persistence in discussing it; arousing one's organization in support of a position; taking a stand publicly; behaving belligerently, to mention but a few possibilities.

EXPRESSIVE STAKES AND RELATED PROCESSES

Expressive behaviors include a participant's behavior that expresses who the person and the group he represents wants to be in the situation and that expresses how he perceives and feels about other participants and the group they represent. Individuals have certain characteristic personal identity needs which can become activated in the situation, a phenomenon well documented in the sociology and psychological literature, where self-concepts have often been viewed as meta-valued.[1] Similarly, we believe that institutions have identities, statues, or images which their members want to establish or maintain. The identity attributes which may be at stake are innumerable. A party to joint decision making may want to be seen, for example, as superior

1. W. G. Bennis, E. H. Schein, D. E. Berlew, and F. I. Steele, *Interpersonal Dynamics* (Homewood, Ill.: The Dorsey Press, 1964) 207–25; N. T. Fouriezos, M. L. Hutt, and H. Guetzkow, "Measurement of Self-Oriented Needs in Discussion Groups," *Journal of Abnormal and Social Psychology*, XXXXV (1950) 682–90; Erving Goffman, "On Face Work: An Analysis of Ritual Elements in Social Interaction," *Psychiatry*, XVIII (August 1955) 213–31; and C. Gordon and K. J. Gergen (eds.), *The Self in Social Interaction* (New York: John Wiley & Sons, Inc., 1968), 461.

or inferior or equal to the other party, as similar to or different from the other party, as aloof or committed, as confident or tentative, as knowledgeable or inexperienced, as a generalist or a specialist, as loyal or independent, as tough, as reasonable, as sophisticated, as approachable, as likable, as a member of a particular social class or profession, etc.

If the identity needs of the two parties which are stimulated in the inter-action setting are reciprocal or congruent with each other, this compatibility leads to *identity reinforcement:* one's identity bids are confirmed by the other.

When the salient expressive needs are not compatible, the result is *identity conflict*: assertions of identity by one participant are frustrated by identity-denying actions by the other who consciously or unconsciously refuses to accept the first's image of himself or of his organization. Initiatives to assert one's identity include self-references, posturing, and telling anecdotes about past experiences that lay claim to the preferred attributes. Identity initiatives also include manipulating the agenda or discussion format in order to facilitate a participant's efforts to do any of the above, as well as choosing physical aspects of the setting for the meeting, for example, the location, the type of conveniences available, etc., which tend to create the appropriate identity.

Identity-denying responses can involve passively ignoring the other's identity bids, continuing to treat him as initially perceived; or more deliberately undermining the other's efforts to establish his preferred identity. Until an official has some reason to believe that he and the organization he represents are seen in a way that he regards as minimally satisfactory, his main agendum in a newly formed joint decision making group is to present himself and his organization to other participants in the preferred way.

The following is an example of identity conflict in interorganizational settings: Officials of a large city in the southern part of the country and regional officials of the Federal government were negotiating toward the city's participation in the Federally funded NCPP. There were many substantive issues — reorganization, contributions, authority, etc. — containing potential for both problem solving and bargaining, but much of the behavior of the two groups in this interaction setting was attuned to the relationship between the identities claimed by the parties. Each preferred to see itself and to be recognized as having taken the initiative. The city was very sensitive about participating in Federal programs. Federal officials for their part were not willing to be seen as merely reactive. Each tended to violate the other's preferred identity. Of course, very similar identity problems exist between the governments of the United States and an underdeveloped country the U.S. is trying to help.

The following situation illustrates initial identity conflict giving way to identity reinforcement: The Peace Corps in an overseas mission had a deeply felt preference to be differentiated from other U.S. agencies in that country. This identity issue was mildly activated in any joint deliberations between the Peace Corps, AID, or State, and strongly activated in discussions involving the Military Assistance Groups and the CIA. Expressive behaviors, in the sense used here, were those actions by the Peace Corps officials in meetings which tended to preserve the Peace Corps's preferred identity. These behaviors took the form of passive or active resistance to ideas voiced by other representatives, and using styles of posture and presentation that reflected but also exaggerated the differences between the operating patterns of the various agencies. The bids to establish the preferred identity of the Peace Corps — in particular, to be highly differentiated — were at first opposed and then eventually accepted by the representatives of other agencies. Accordingly, the behavior of the Peace Corps representatives geared to this aspect of the interaction eventually decreased both in quantity and in their disruptiveness to decision making. The situation moved from identity conflict to identity reinforcement.

If the preferred identities of each party are denied by the other, the identity competition is symmetrical. While the magnitude of identity conflict is increased, the symmetrical condition is often easier to resolve because it creates mutual and balanced motivation to work through or otherwise accommodate on the identity issues.

The following did not occur in the interagency situations studied here, but sometimes in situations that ostensibly are subject to decision making the substantive issues and their associated processes are not really important — the real purpose for one or both parties being to achieve a desired identity for itself and/or reveal or manipulate the image of the other. Often "establishment groups" will endeavor to negotiate with "rebel groups" who have somehow developed bargaining power (e.g., at Brandeis, Berkeley, Columbia, San Francisco State), when in fact the dominant process is identity conflict. The fight, the conflict itself, may be gratifying for the rebel group. It is valued in and of itself because it confirms the group's preferred identity. Or the behavior of the rebel group may be designed to force the establishment into acting in ways that fit the rebel group's stereotype of the establishment group, namely, to use force and violence against the rebel group.

Mixed Interaction Systems: A Conceptual Space

Figure 7.1 presents a conceptual space showing the four processes and the conditions which produce them. Most interaction systems contain all four processes.

However, the relative prevalence of each of the four processes differs from one setting to another and can change over time. The composition of a particular setting can be visualized within the space. Figure 7.2a contains a predominantly competitive setting in which there is mixed decision making, but more bargaining than problem solving, and in which there is a mixture of identity confirmation and denial activities, but this social interchange also

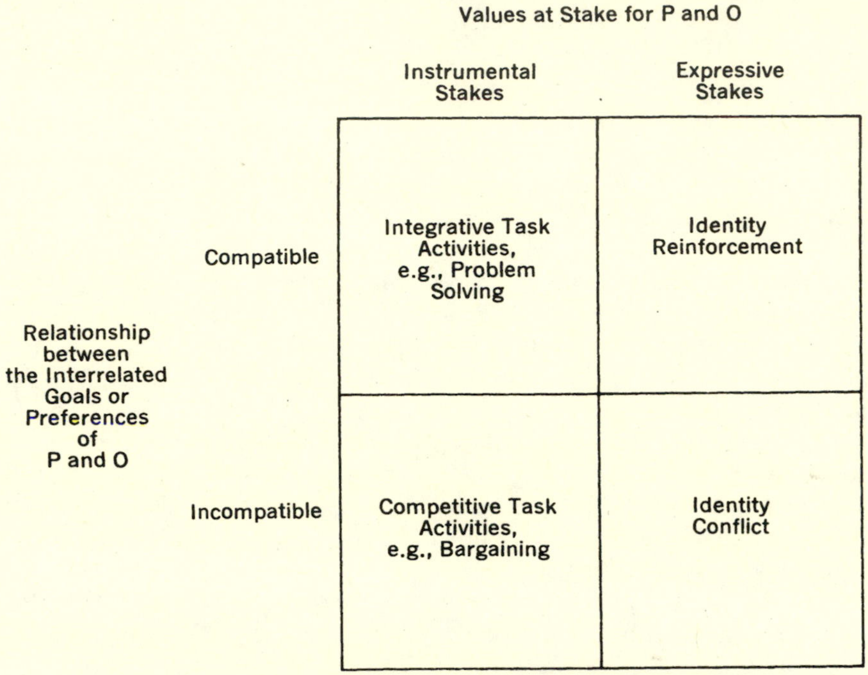

Values at Stake for P and O

		Instrumental Stakes	Expressive Stakes
Relationship between the Interrelated Goals or Preferences of P and O	Compatible	Integrative Task Activities, e.g., Problem Solving	Identity Reinforcement
	Incompatible	Competitive Task Activities, e.g., Bargaining	Identity Conflict

Figure 7.1. A Conceptual Space for Interaction Processes

is more competitive than cooperative. Systems that might be characterized by the 2*a* example include many current racial situations and labor-management negotiations during the first few years after unionization.

Figure 7.2*b* depicts a negotiation almost exclusively attendant to the substantive issues, with only a minimal concern for organizational or personal identities. Commercial negotiations between government and industrial firms and their suppliers often fit this pattern. However, negotiations leading to mergers of churches, industrial firms, or labor unions would typically involve more status conflict than shown in Figure 7.2*b*, as did the interagency decision making which I observed in both the foreign affairs and urban affairs communities.

Relationships Among the Four Processes

These processes do *not* occur in parallel without affecting each other. Identity conflict and reinforcement — which we all readily concede are factors in most human encounters — *are more than noise* in the interorganizational decision making situation. These affect-laden processes interact with the two decision making processes in ways that are systematic and predictable. The effect of one process on another will predictably facilitate,

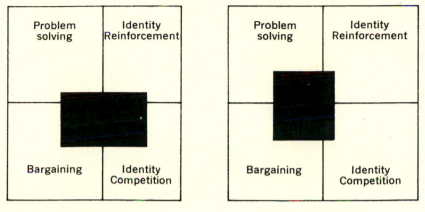

Problem solving	Identity Reinforcement
Bargaining	Identity Competition

Figure 7.2a.

Problem solving	Identity Reinforcement
Bargaining	Identity Competition

Figure 7.2b.

interfere, complicate, intensify, or exacerbate another process. Fundamental to any behavioral theory of joint decision making is a systematic understanding of how these four processes impact on each other. The following general propositions are offered (also see Figure 7.3):

Problem solving interferes with bargaining.
Bargaining interferes with problem solving.
Identity conflict interferes with problem solving, whereas identity reinforcement facilitates problem solving.
Problem solving promotes identity reinforcement and diminishes identity conflict.
Identity conflict and reinforcement both have varied and mixed effects on bargaining.
Bargaining promotes identity competition and diminishes identity reinforcement.

Problem solving and bargaining: mutually interfering. — A cornerstone factor in the present effort to develop a theory of joint decision making is the mutually interfering nature of bargaining and problem solving when they occur in the same interaction system, a relationship which we have analyzed in detail elsewhere.[2] A point-by-point analysis of the two joint decision processes (see Table 7.1) reveals many contrasting and contradictory elements which underlie their mutually interfering effects. The elements listed under each column heading are sometimes, if not always, instrumental behaviors or tendencies for the type of process identified in the column heading.

The contradictory orientations and tactical requirements of the two processes provide dilemmas for decision makers in mixed-motive situations:

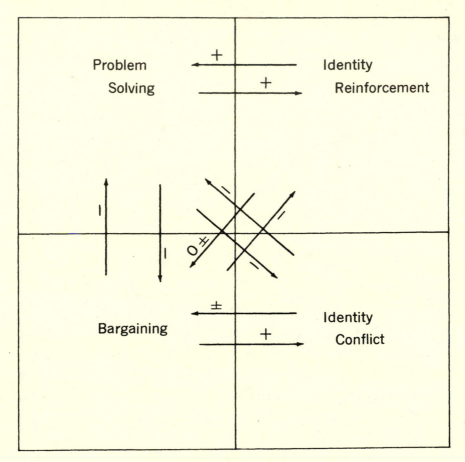

Figure 7.3. Interprocess Effects: Propositions

Keys: + indicates facilitating or promoting effect of one process on the other, − indicates an interfering or diminishing effect; 0 indicates that one process is relatively neutral with respect to the second process; ± indicates the significant possibility of both facilitating and interfering effects.

Table 7.1.

Bargaining	*Problem Solving*
Overstatement of own goals and preferences	Accurate statement of goals and preferences
Disguise of needs, anxieties, concerns that indicate weaknesses or vulnerabilities	Mutual understanding of needs, anxieties, concerns that are relevant to the agenda item under consideration
Tendency to include pseudo issues or low priority objectives as "trading horses"	Parties conscientiously include only genuine issues

Bargaining	Problem Solving
Tendency to state the agenda issue in terms of alternate solutions	Tendency to state the agenda issue in terms of underlying problems, needs, concerns, objectives
Tendency to define the issue or problem in a way which "points" to the solution presently preferred by the party	Tendency to define the agenda issue item in a way which increases the likelihood that new solutions will be invented or discovered
Tendency for discussion to center only on alternative solutions presently favored by one party or the other, and each alternative is discussed only at the insistence of that party	Emphasis is on generating many alternatives and genuine discussion is devoted to alternatives before either party has judged it to be minimally acceptable to itself
A firm statement of position is made as early in the process as possible	Judgment about alternatives is withheld as long as possible
Search behavior is devoted to finding ways of appearing to become committed to a position; logical, nonrational, and irrational arguments alike may serve this purpose	Search behavior is devoted to finding solutions to problems, utilizing logical and innovative processes
The following behaviors are often used to communicate tactical commitment: linking preferred solution to a principle; use of pre-planned speeches; reducing preferred solution to writing, etc.	Solutions are considered in terms of their specific implications rather than tied to principles; emphasis is upon spontaneous response
Occasionally moves are instrumental which threaten, surprise, and confuse the other; or which capitalize upon some misstatement of his	Threats, surprise and confusion are always disruptive
Sometimes it is instrumental to ignore or misconstrue other's arguments or his commitments	Emphasis is on common signification
Sometimes it is instrumental to interpose an obstacle to communication in order to prevent the other from making a commitment	Emphasis is on removing barriers to interparty communication
Tendency for interunit contacts to be channeled, i.e., confined to few persons; this controls information made available to the other	More rather than fewer persons from two units are involved; this increases the availability of information and the diversity of viewpoints
Sometimes tactical for participant to have limited authority to make decisions; this frustrates commitments and some other influence attempts of the other	Usually will involve participants who have knowledge and authority to reach decisions

Should a party make a relatively complete investment in the problem-solving activity and thus tend to increase the positive values available to the two parties, but increase his own vulnerability in the interparty bargaining process? Or should the party engage in relatively less problem solving, in effect accepting whatever joint positive values are already available, and thus minimize his vulnerability in bargaining? The essential bind is that among other things problem solving requires the party to identify his true needs, and this requirement makes it extremely difficult for him to engage subsequently in hard bargaining since the latter involves misrepresentation of his needs. On the other hand, strategies which do not involve the accurate identification of needs will result in lower joint utilities. The second party to the mixed decision processes faces exactly the same dilemmas.

Thus, problem solving and bargaining are not merely contrasting alternatives, but mutually interfering when mixed.

Problem-solving tactics often weaken one's bargaining position and preclude certain advantageous bargaining tactics. Conversely, many bargaining tactics limit the extent to which the parties can discover and exploit the integrative potential. Thus, in mixed process situations, either one or both processes will be relatively less *effectively* executed. Also, the mixed process, compared with either process in pure form, is probably less *efficient* in the sense that it would consume relatively more social and psychological energy.

The mutually interfering character of the two processes cannot be eliminated, but it can be minimized by certain methods. One method for minimizing the dilemmas is to separate or differentiate the two types of decision processes as much as possible — by agenda, by people, by ground rules, by time, and by space. Another is to bargain over respective shares in advance of the problem solving to increase the joint gain. Still another technique is to develop norms governing the interaction system which discourage both parties from using certain bargaining tactics most disruptive to problem solving.

Problem solving and identity processes. First, an example illustrating identity competition that deteriorated interorganization decision making: The Neighborhood Center Pilot Program involved extensive interagency deliberations among HUD, BOB, OEO, DOL, and HEW. Those Bureau of the Budget officials who played important roles in the early development of the concept of the program endeavored to continue to play a central role in the substantive discussions of the procedures and guidelines to the field. The HUD chairmen were eager to establish *their* centrality in general and their leadership role in particular. The identity demands of the BOB and HUD officials were competitive. The consequences were interference with interagency problem solving and complications for interagency bargaining. The substantive decisions not only suffered in quality but were delayed in a way that greatly affected the program adversely.

A second example illustrates identity reinforcement that facilitated decision processes. In one city involved in the Neighborhood Center Pilot Program, the regional team representing four Federal agencies held its meetings with neighborhood leaders and officials of local agencies in the ghetto neighborhood. Problem solving and bargaining with local leaders were carried on under conditions more familiar to the neighborhood residents than to the Federal officials — meetings were held in the evenings in uncomfortable surroundings and were loosely structured. The ghetto meeting process was time consuming and inconvenient for Federal officials, but there is evidence that the investment in this effort to establish more mutually compatible identities paid off in the quality of the joint decision making. It is true that the unfamiliar format tended to deny the Federal executives their normal identity. However, a distinction must be made between current identity and desired identity. In this case, at least two key members of the Federal team preferred to establish a new image more identified with the local community. Thus, they preferred to establish and reinforce a *new* identity, rather than reinforce a prior identity.

It was stated earlier that participants in joint decision making are preoccupied with establishing their respective identities as long as the identities are not satisfactory. This does not necessarily mean that the *stated* agenda of the meetings is to negotiate status or identity of each participant. Most people are quite skillful in working on this social problem of establishing an identity in the context of the formal task, for example, an interunit decision task. However, the information introduced for this social purpose is often only superficially relevant to the decision task. Similarly, the initial disagreements about facts and meeting ground rules often reflect at least one of the participant's efforts to impress upon the other that he must be taken seriously as a person — indeed, as a particular type of person.

Mutually acceptable and acknowledged identities promote trust. Trust in turn enhances the accuracy of interpersonal communication and the willingness of one person to expose tentative ideas and judgments to another — both important ingredients of problem solving. Under identity-reinforcement conditions participants derive more gratification from and evidence more commitment to the interaction process, and as a result they assign less "cost" to the time they spend on the decision process. Why do we hypothesize that identity conflict interferes with problem solving? Our reasoning is as follows: While most people are quite skillful at working on their identity in the context of a task, interference occurs for several reasons. (*a*) The process of pursuing the temporarily denied but preferred identity often involves creating false issues and other behavior off-target to the issues at hand. (*b*) The denial of a satisfying identity increases the costs — subjective disutilities — that the participant associates with time he spends in the interorganization processes. (*c*) The denial of a preferred identity in the situation is experienced as more or less threatening, and this denial at higher levels of threat deteriorates cognitive functioning. (*d*) The competitive orientation induced by identity conflict is accompanied by perceptual distortions in the direction of underestimating areas of actual or potential agreement, and by judgmental distortions in the direction of overvaluing one's own contributions and downgrading the ideas of others.[3] Both of these distortions increase the likelihood of bargaining impasses. (*e*) The competitive orientation often leads to a substitution of objectives in the sense that the idea of defeating the other party begins to take on positive value.

Where the goals are compatible and both parties perceive the appropriate decision process to be problem solving and yet disagreements persist between the parties over assumptions, facts, decision making methods, and courses of action, it is highly likely that parties are pursuing mutually competitive identities.

Thus far we have explored the effects of identity processes on problem solving. To consider the reverse direction of influence, the effect of problem solving is to enlarge the area of identity affirmation and identity conflict. Why? Problem solving involves (*a*) focus on common goals that help enlarge the areas of common identification; (*b*) an open information-sharing process that promotes trust and mutual acceptance of each other; and (*c*) interdependently constructive activities that, if successful, tend to promote a sense of mutual accomplishment, self-worth, and respect for each other's competence. Thus, for example, if the participants enter into the interorganizational deliberations with negative stereotypes of members of the other organizations, and if the common interests are sufficiently compelling that problem solving occurs nevertheless, then stereotypes are likely to give way somewhat.

How can one minimize the extent to which conditions of identity conflict interfere with effective problem solving? (*a*) By selecting representatives who are least likely to trigger the identity conflict — in particular, persons who are relatively acceptable to the other participants and relatively accepting of them. (*b*) By clearly delineating the scope of decision making early in the process, thereby clarifying the degree of risk to identity that is at stake in the joint decision process. (*c*) By exploring problems in off-the-record sessions where organizational identities are deliberately deemphasized. (*d*) By confronting identity conflict as an agenda separate from the decision making problem. Separating identity conflict — both its expression and attempts to resolve it — from the decision process per se is often advisable. Not that one can completely separate it out. However, if the identity conflict is acknowledged and dealt with explicitly, there are two possible favorable results: (*a*) There is less need for the representative whose personal identity or whose group's identity is frustrated to work on the identity issues under the guise of decision making deliberations. (*b*) Frequently the process of direct confrontation of the identity issues enables the parties to work through

3. R. P. Blake and J. S. Mouton, "Reactions to Intergroup Competition Under Win–Lose Conditions," *Management Science* (1961) 7, 420–35.

to some partial resolution or to manage their behavior to make the identity conflict less salient. If this process is not well managed, there is a risk that the conflict will be escalated.

Bargaining and identity processes. On the one hand, identity conflict decreases (and identity reinforcement increases) the efficiency and effectiveness of bargaining in many of the same ways it affected problem solving.

On the other hand, an analysis of the tactics of bargaining and the behaviors associated with identity conflict and reinforcement reveals another and complementary picture. First, instrumental conflict or bargaining is entered into with additional motivation because the conflict tactics chosen primarily for bargaining purposes (listed earlier) have expressive value as well. Second, certain behaviors which are primarily expressive in their origin (namely, racial confrontations, spontaneous walkouts by workers, spontaneous student demonstrations) often also have value for instrumental conflict — improving bargaining power or directly winning certain substantive concessions. Third, certain actions instrumental to bargaining are more effective if they are accompanied by high identity conflict. For example, the uses of threats tactical to bargaining are more credible in the context of intense intergroup identity conflict. The above are ways the identity conflict can facilitate the bargaining efforts of one party vis-à-vis the other. It can be said to "promote" the interparty process, when the initially weaker of two parties wants to change the status quo and must utilize such tactics to force negotiations. There is nothing comparable to these consequences in the case of problem solving.

In view of all of the considerations above, if we assume two interdependent parties of comparable strength who are also predisposed to bargain with each other, then we can expect identity processes to have the following consequences for bargaining: Absolute identity affirmation would detract from the enthusiasm but enhance the technical proficiency with which bargaining is pursued by participants. A moderate level of identity conflict would promote bargaining behavior which is enthusiastic and imaginative with a slightly increased probability of impasse. A high level of identity competition would produce a process pursued both relentlessly and erratically and highly likely to create impasses; as face issues get confused with bargaining positions, default outcomes would become likely.

Turning to the other direction of influence, bargaining places a strain on an expressively positive relationship. Bluffs, information rationing, distortion, and the win-lose-compromise character of the process in its pure form — these all tend to create distance in a relationship, undermine trust and mutual respect and lead to attribution of unfavorable identities on the other.

The techniques for minimizing the effect of identity conflict on bargaining — when that is mutually desirable — include several of those discussed for ameliorating its effect on problem solving, namely, careful selection of representatives, clear delineation of scope of decision making, and off-the-record sessions.

The techniques for offsetting the tendency for bargaining to promote identity competition include depersonalizing the process as much as possible, giving it as little publicity as possible, and developing norms which constrain both parties from the more alienating forms of bargaining tactics.

Avoidance Versus Engagement Behavior in Joint Decision-Making Setting

In the preceding discussion we have assumed that even if participants to a joint decision-making situation are preoccupied with identity issues, they nevertheless are also engaged in either problem solving, bargaining, or both. Empirical observation, however, indicates they are often engaged in neither.

In the interagency decision-making meetings which I have observed I have been struck by the amount of behavior that is not directed toward either problem solving or bargaining over their respective preferences regarding the substantive issues that divide them, but rather is devoted to defeating the interagency process and making the outcome as ambiguous or innocuous as possible. Therefore, to fully understand interorganizational decision making, we must understand this avoidance phenomenon. Why (or when) is "avoidance" a viable alternative to problem solving and bargaining? Why (or when) is avoidance the preferred alternative?

Avoidance is frequently a viable alternative in the interagency systems referred to here because of the type of interdependence among the Federal agencies involved: First, in both the foreign affairs and urban fields, agencies' goals are interdependent only in the long run. For example, if education and health of a population must be improved before unemployment patterns can be altered in a stable way, then the goal achievement of the Labor Department depends in part upon the success of HEW. However, understanding this longer run interdependence does not provide a compelling reason for interacting today.

Second, while there is considerable intergrative potential among instrumental activities of agencies in the same field, there usually is no meaningful requirement to integrate or coordinate them. This means activities of several agencies are potentially interdependent in the sense that they could (*a*) eliminate duplicated administrative machinery and individually achieve their stated goals to a greater degree; (*b*) jointly gather and exchange information that would enable each to plan better; (*c*) simplify the Federal government liaison with other governmental units such as city governments, allowing for more integrative planning within these other units; (*d*) combine complementary types of expertise, e.g., in functional programs, in orientation toward citizen and institutional clientele, in contacts with different levels of government — making possible more comprehensive approaches to the solution of urban ills. However, despite the above integrative potential, there usually are little or no absolute costs associated with a failure to problem solve or bargain, (apart from the disapproval from bureaucratic superiors, a disapproval that is frequently more apparent than real). Failure to cooperate only involves opportunity costs, not regression from the status quo. Thus, ironically, joint decision making (including problem solving) is more likely where the agencies have been competing in a way that has incurred mutual costs of a tangible and accountable nature.

Why is avoidance the preferred alternative in the interagency relations studied? Consider four factors: First, compared with unilateral agency efforts, interagency efforts take more bureaucratic time and contain a higher risk that nothing will come of it. Bureaucratic time is enormous because of different geographical locations of agency offices and liaison positions which are not comparable from agency to agency. There are higher risks of failure to complete an interagency venture because: a second agency's red tape is layered on the first's; the areas of caution of two agencies preclude more alternatives than the areas of caution of one agency; actions have to be cleared through two agencies rather than one; moreover, more types of actions have to be cleared by the implementor in an interagency program than is the case of normal agency programs. The general point is that two sets of constraints are more cumbersome than one.

A second reason why avoidance often is a preferred alternative to engagement is that interdependent ventures very seldom have symmetrical gains for the two or more participating agencies.   .

Third, interdependent ventures increase the visibility of an agency's actions, and therefore increase the agency's vulnerabilities to attack and criticism. For example in a recent interagency program, the various participating agencies were variously criticized for incompetence, self-serving behavior, and being hopelessly bound by red tape. There are understandable fears that either additional controls will be imposed or that funds will be reallocated among agencies — as a result of the visibility.

Fourth, at the heart of much of the independence maneuvering is the desire to preserve a particular identity or status — even at the cost of foregoing integrative potential. For example, unfavorable stereotypes of the other agency lead to avoidance behavior as if contact would contaminate one's own identity. Similarly, there frequently is incongruity between the status of personnel representing the two agencies or between the agencies themselves; e.g., in an overseas mission Foreign Service officers have higher status but fewer resources under their control than their counterparts in AID and DOD. Another strain derives from engagement when one agency fears that its program's identity will be blurred. Also where two agencies have similar programs, contact increases the feelings of rivalry.

In the face of these many inhibiting factors, the stimulus for any engagement must be strong, sustained and coupled with some monitoring procedure if engagement is to result, giving support to the idea of treating "intervention" as an identifiable and strategic step.[4]

One should note that the alleged need for the Federal agencies to incur costs for not cooperating as well as potential gains from cooperating is acknowledging that the agencies are satisficing rather than maximizing goal achievement. Similarly, survival at the current level of performance is often at stake for one or both organizations in the case of organizational mergers — the most extreme movement toward interdependence, and/or the principals in one organization have become less cathected with the separate identity of his organization.

Returning to the question of problem solving, our analysis suggests this process would be enhanced by adding costs for not cooperating, reducing the identity competition, or bringing about a merger.

Change and Third Party Interventions

Let's assume that interunit decision making is not effective because of a superoptimal level of conflict in the interaction system.

If the immediate need is to break an impasse allowing a particular interunit decision to be made, then third party interventions can focus exclusively on interunit processes. To break a strictly bargaining impasse involves *mediation*; to break an impasse based on identity conflict involves *conciliation*.

If the need for change is longer run, the interventions must result in changes in the structure of the interunit system, its context, and the skills available in it; in particular in the degree of compatibility of instrumental objectives of the interaction the compatibility of identity needs pursued in the situation, and the strength of the avoidance forces. The first would involve either *changes in the payoff structure*, via superordinate goals, re-evaluation of goals or penalties for not cooperating; the second, *changes in the structure of interunit attitudes* via education or a working through process; the third, *changes in the many organizational factors that inhibit engagement*.

Summary and Conclusions

The importance of collective identity for interorganizational decision making should not be underestimated. Organizations, in contrast with subunits of an organization, usually have more latitude in just how interdependent they will become with particular other organizations. Secondly, the total organizations, more than organizational subunits, are explicitly concerned about the image they project to others with whom they deal. Thus, joint ventures between separate organizations are likely to raise identity concerns and the organization is often in a position to act on those concerns.

4. M. F. Tuite, "Toward a Theory of Joint Decision Making," this volume, chap. 1.

These identity concerns complicate interorganizational decision making. If the preferred identities of two organizations are compatible, the parties are more likely to be able to fully exploit the integrative potential which inheres in their respective goals and resource pools. If the preferred identities are in conflict the parties are not only less effective at problem solving but also their bargaining is more likely to result in miscalculations, impasses, and default outcomes.

The identity concerns can also contribute to a tendency for organizations in some settings to avoid interdependence with other organizations. Avoidance may be manifested by participant behaviors which deliberately defeat the very joint decision processes to which they are participants.

Collaborative interorganizational decision making can be increased by changes in the ratio of common to conflicting interests and by changes in the compatibility of the preferred identities of the participating organizations. The latter involves a strategy of attitude change, the accomplishment of which is often constrained by the interorganizational bargaining which must continue.

8

Decomposition Processes and Their Use in Joint Decision Making

JEROME E. HASS

Introduction

When an entity composed of a set of decision makers has a specific collective goal which is not the simple sum of the objectives of the individual decision makers and/or the decisions of one decision maker affect or are affected by the decisions of the other decision makers, the entity's goal will not be achieved unless the interdependencies of the decisions and their consequent impact on the collective goal are expressly taken into account. In many realistic settings, achieving the entity's goal through centralized decision making is a difficult, if not impossible, task. Centralization may be difficult because the entity may exert (or may wish to exert for motivational reasons) only limited control over the decision makers, information may be decentrally distributed and its redistribution may be limited by the capacity of information channels, and institutional or environmental restrictions may limit the transmission of proprietary information. In such situations decentralized decision making is a necessity.

Kenneth J. Arrow, in his Presidential Address to the International Meeting of The Institute of Management Sciences, defined the problem of achieving an entity's objective under decentralized decision making as one of choosing operating rules for these decision makers and enforcement rules for the operating rules so as to achieve the entity's objective.[1] Whereas operating rules under a centralized system take the form of "do this or that," under a decentralized system they take the form "do whatever is necessary to achieve a certain objective." Our objective is to develop operating rules (the objective functions used by decentralized decision makers) and a procedure in which they are to be embedded so that the decentralized entity may reach its goals through decentralized decision making. To this end we first describe two

---

1. Kenneth J. Arrow, "Control in Large Organizations," *Management Science*, X (April 1964).

algorithms (sets of rules and procedures) for decentralized decision making and then demonstrate the applicability of one of these algorithms by examining how it might be used for developing and implementing optimal water pollution treatment schemes.

The Problem

We limit our discussion to the case of two decision making units with decision variables X and Y, respectively. Generalizing to more than two units is straightforward. We consider the following entity problem:

$$
\begin{aligned}
\text{Maximize } \pi(X, Y) &= F(X) + G(Y) + H(X, Y) \\
\text{subject to} \quad & C_1 X + C_2 Y \leq R; \\
& f_i(X) \qquad \leq s_i, \ i \in \mathscr{L}_1; \\
& g_j(Y) \leq t_j, \ j \in \mathscr{L}_2; \\
& X, Y \geq 0,
\end{aligned}
\tag{8.1}
$$

where $X = [x_i]$, an $m \times 1$ column vector of real decision variables; $Y = [y_j]$, an $n \times 1$ column vector of real decision variables; $C_1 = [c_{1ij}]$, a $k \times m$ matrix of technical coefficients; $C_2 = [c_{2ij}]$, a $k \times n$ matrix of technical coefficients; $R = [r_i]$, a $k \times 1$ column vector of scarce resources; $\mathscr{L}_i = \{1, 2, \ldots, l_i\}$, a finite set of indices; F, G, and H are real functions concave in their arguments; f_i and g_j are real functions convex in their arguments; s_i and t_j are scarce resources; and $\pi(X, Y) \in C^2$, that is, is a continuous function with continuous first and second derivatives.

Table 8.1.

Conditions on equation (1)	Algorithm A	Algorithm B
$H(X, Y) = 0$; i.e., $\pi(X, Y)$ separable		Dantzig-Wolfe*
$\pi(X, Y)$ quadratic	Whinston†	Hass‡
$\pi(X, Y)$ linear	Dantzig-Wolfe§	Dantzig-Wolfe§

* Algorithm B differs slightly from the Dantzig-Wolfe formulation in this case. This difference, described later, is minimal except for the fact that finite convergence is more likely with our algorithm since they use linear approximations while we do not. George Dantzig, "General Convex Objective Forms," in *Mathematical Methods in the Social Sciences*, 1959, K. J. Arrow *et al.* (eds.) (Stanford: Stanford University Press, 1960), and George Dantzig and Philip Wolfe, "The Decomposition Principles for Linear Programs," *Econometrica*, XXIX (October 1961).

† Andrew Whinston, "Theoretical and Computational Problems in Organizational Decision-Making," in *Operational Research and the Social Sciences*, J. R. Lawrence (ed.) (London: Tavistock Publications, 1966).

‡Jerome E. Hass, "Transfer Pricing in a Decentralized Firm," *Management Science*, XIV (February 1968).

§Dantzig and Wolfe, *op. cit.*, and George Dantzig and Philip Wolfe, "Decomposition Principles for Linear Programming," *Operations Research*, VIII (February 1960).

Letting

$$S = \{X : f_i(X) \leq s_i, i \in \mathscr{L}_1, X \geq 0\} \text{ and}$$
$$T = \{Y : g_j(Y) \leq t_j, j \in \mathscr{L}_2, Y \geq 0\},$$

we further assume that S and T are bounded. Under the concavity and convexity specifications, if a local optimum to problem (8.1) can be found, it will be a global optimum.

Special cases of the two decomposition algorithms we present here have been developed by others. If we label our two algorithms A and B, respectively, Table 8.1 states these cases and their expositors. Our algorithm's are more general than these since the only requirements we impose upon $\pi(X, Y)$ are those stated in problem (8.1) and the conditions listed in Table 8.1 are more restrictive than these requirements.

Operating Rules and Procedures

STARTING ASSUMPTION

We assume the existence of the sequences $\{X^{(i)}\}$, $i = 1, \ldots, d$, and $\{Y^{(j)}\}$, $j = l, \ldots, e$, such that the master problem

$$\text{maximize } \pi_0(U, V) = F\left(\sum_i u_i X^{(i)}\right) + G\left(\sum_j v_j Y^{(j)}\right) + H\left(\sum_i u_i X^{(i)}, \sum_j v_j Y^{(j)}\right)$$

$$\text{subject to} \qquad \sum_i C_1 X^{(i)} u_i + \sum_j C_2 Y^{(j)} v_j \leq R \qquad (8.2)$$

$$\left(\sum_i u_i = 1, \sum_j v_j = 1, U, V \geq 0\right),$$

where $U = (u_1, \ldots, u_d)$ and $V = (v_1, \ldots, v_e)$, has an optimal solution, $(U^{(1)}, V^{(1)})$. It follows from the assumed properties of S and T that

$$\hat{X} = \sum_i X^{(i)} u_i \text{ and } \hat{Y} = \sum_j Y^{(j)} v_j \qquad (8.3)$$

is a feasible solution to problem (8.1) since $\hat{X}$ and $\hat{Y}$ are convex combinations of the feasible $X^{(i)}$'s and $Y^{(j)}$'s and the feasible region is assumed convex. Let the dual evaluators associated with the $k+2$ constraints of problem (8.2) be denoted by $\lambda = (\lambda_1, \ldots, \lambda_k)$, δ_1 and δ_2, respectively.

OPERATING RULES

Each decision maker is asked to solve a problem in his own decision variables. The X-decision problem is

$$\text{maximize } \pi_1(X^{(d+1)}) = X^{(d+1)} \partial \pi / \partial X \mid_{X = \hat{X}^{(t)}, Y = \hat{Y}^{(t)}} - \lambda^{(t)} C_1 X^{(d+1)} \qquad (8.4)$$

$$\text{subject to } X^{(d+1)} \in S$$

and the Y-decision problem is

$$\text{maximize } \pi_2(Y^{(e+1)}) = Y^{(e+1)} \partial \pi / \partial Y \big|_{X = \hat{X}^{(t)}, Y = \hat{Y}^{(t)}} - \lambda^{(t)} C_2 Y^{(e+1)} \quad (8.5)$$

subject to $Y^{e+1} \in T$,

where t is the iteration index.

THE PROCEDURE. ALGORITHM A:

i) Given the starting sequences, the central coordinator solves problem (8.2) for $(U^{(1)}, V^{(1)})$, $\lambda^{(1)}$, $\delta_1^{(1)}$, and $\delta_2^{(1)}$. Let t denote the iteration index: $t = 1$.

ii) Given $(U^{(t)}, V^{(t)})$, find $\hat{X}^{(t)}$ and $\hat{Y}^{(t)}$ using equation (8.3).

iii) Given $\hat{X}^{(t)}$, $\hat{Y}^{(t)}$, and $\lambda^{(t)}$, have decision makers X and Y solve problems (8.4) and (8.5), returning $\pi_1(X^{d+1})$, $X^{(d+1)}$, $\pi_2(Y^{(e+1)})$ and $Y^{(e+1)}$ to the central coordinator.

iv) If $\pi_1(X^{(d+1)}) > \delta_1^{(t)}$, set $d = d+1$ and extend the sequence $\{X^{(i)}\}$ by including $X^{(d+1)}$; if $\pi_2(Y^{(e+1)}) > \delta_2^{(t)}$, set $e = e+1$ and extend the sequence $\{Y^{(j)}\}$ by including $Y^{(e+1)}$. If $\pi_1(X^{(d+1)}) > \delta_1^{(t)}$ and/or $\pi_2(Y^{(e+1)}) > \delta_2^{(t)}$, resolve problem (8.2) by using the extended sequence(s) and go to (ii), setting $t = t+1$. If neither $\pi_1(X^{(d+1)}) > \delta_1^{(t)}$ nor $\pi_2(Y^{(e+1)}) > \delta_2^{(t)}$, terminate; the optimal solution is $(\hat{X}^{(t)}, \hat{Y}^{(t)})$.

If the functions f_i and g_j, for all i and j, are linear functions, the procedure is finite since problems (8.4) and (8.5) are linear programming problems and each iteration introduces at least one new extreme point into the master problem. If $\pi(X, Y)$ is linear, we have the Dantzig-Wolfe linear decomposition procedure; if $\pi(X, Y)$ is quadratic, we have Whinston's quadratic decomposition procedure.

Since it can be shown that

$$\lambda^{(t)} = \frac{\partial \pi}{\partial r_i} \bigg|_{X = \hat{X}^{(t)}, Y = \hat{Y}^{(t)}}$$

and

$$\delta_1^{(t)} = \hat{X}^{(t)} \frac{\partial \pi}{\partial X} \bigg|_{X = \hat{X}^{(t)}, Y = \hat{Y}^{(t)}} - \lambda^{(t)} C_1 \hat{X}^{(t)},$$

$\delta_1^{(t)}$ can be interpreted as the value, at the margin, of the decision $\hat{X}^{(t)}$. Thus, step (iv) is comparing the marginal value of $X^{(d+1)}$ with the marginal value of $\hat{X}^{(t)}$ and accepting $X^{(d+1)}$ if, at the margin, it is preferable to $\hat{X}^{(t)}$.

Numerical Example: the Quadratic Case

We wish to demonstrate the rules and procedures outlined above by solving the problem

maximize $6x - 2x^2 + 2xy - 2y^2$
subject to $x \qquad + y \qquad \leq 1.25 \qquad (0 \leq x \leq 1, 0 \leq y \leq 1).$ \qquad (8.6)

We assume the starting sequence $\{X^{(i)}\} = \{X^{(1)}\} = \{0\}$ and $\{Y^{(j)}\} = \{Y^{(1)}\} = \{0\}$. The master problem is

maximize $\pi_0(U, V) = 0u_1 + 0v_1$

subject to $\qquad\qquad 0u_1 + 0v_1 \leq 1.25$
$\qquad\qquad\qquad (u_1 = 1, v_1 = 1, u_1, v_1 \geq 0);$

and its solution is

$\qquad U^{(1)} = (1), V^{(1)} = (1), \pi_0 = 0, \lambda^{(1)} = 0, \delta_1{}^{(1)} = 0,$ and $\delta_2{}^{(1)} = 0.$

Correspondingly, $(\hat{X}^{(1)}, \hat{Y}^{(1)}) = (0, 0)$. Problem (8.4) becomes

$\qquad$ maximize $\pi_1(X^{(2)}) = x(6 - 4\hat{X}^{(1)} + 2\hat{Y}^{(1)}) - \lambda^{(1)}1x = 6x$

$\qquad$ subject to $0 \leq x \leq 1,$

with solution $X^{(2)} = 1$ and $\pi(X^{(2)}) = 6$; and problem (8.5) becomes

$\qquad$ maximize $\pi_2(Y^{(2)}) = y(2\hat{X}^{(1)} - 4\hat{Y}^{(1)}) - \lambda^{(1)}1y = 0y$

$\qquad$ subject to $0 \leq y \leq 1$

with solution $Y^{(2)} = \mu$, for all $0 \leq \mu \leq 1$, and $\pi_2(Y^{(2)}) = 0$. Since $\pi_1(X^{(2)}) > \delta_1{}^{(1)} = 0$, extend sequence: $\{X^{(i)}\} = \{0, 1\}$, and set $d = 2$. Since $\pi_2(T^{(2)}) = \delta_2{}^{(1)} = 0$, do not extend sequence: $\{Y^{(j)}\} = \{0\}$; $t = 2$. The master problem becomes

maximize $\pi_0(U, V) = 0u_1 + 6u_2 - 2u_2{}^2 + 0v_1$
subject to $\qquad\qquad 0u_1 + 1u_2 + 0v_1 \leq 1.25$ \qquad (8.7)
$\qquad\qquad\qquad (u_1 + u_2 = 1, v_1 = 1, U, V \geq 0),$

and its solution is $U^{(2)} = (0, 1), V^{(2)} = (0), \pi_0 = 4, \lambda^{(2)} = 0, \delta_1{}^{(2)} = 2,$ and $\delta_2{}^{(2)} = 0.$

Correspondingly, $(\hat{X}^{(2)}, \hat{Y}^{(2)} = (1, 0)$. Problem (8.4) becomes

$\qquad$ maximize $\pi_1(X^{(3)}) = (6 - 4)x$, subject to $0 \leq x \leq 1,$

with solution $X^{(3)} = 1$ and $\pi_1(X^{(3)}) = 2$; and problem (8.5) becomes

$\qquad$ maximize $\pi_2(Y^{(2)}) = 2y$, subject to $0 \leq y \leq 1,$

with solution $Y^{(2)} = 1$ and $\pi_2(Y^{(2)}) = 2$. Since $\pi_1(X^{(3)}) = \delta_1{}^{(2)} = 2$, do not extend sequence: $\{X^{(i)}\} = \{0, 1\}$. Since π_2 $Y^{(2)} > \delta_2{}^{(2)} = 0$, extend sequence: $\{Y^{(j)}\} = \{0, 1\}$, and set $e = 2$; $t = 3$.

The master problem at this iteration is

$$\text{maximize } \pi_0(U, V) = 0u_1 + 6u_2 - 2u_2{}^2 + 0v_1 - 2v_2{}^2 + 2u_2v_2$$
$$\text{subject to} \qquad 0u_1 + 1u_2 + 0v_1 + 1v_2 \leq 1.25,$$
$$u_1 + u_2 = 1,$$
$$v_1 + v_2 = 1;$$

and its solution is $U^{(3)} = (0, 1)$, $V^{(3)} = (\frac{3}{4}, \frac{1}{4})$, $\pi_0 = 4\frac{3}{8}$, $\lambda^{(3)} = 1$, $\delta_1{}^{(3)} = \frac{3}{2}$, $\delta_2{}^{(3)} = 0$. Correspondingly $(\hat{X}^{(3)}, \hat{Y}^{(3)}) = (1, \frac{1}{4})$. Problem (8.4) becomes

$$\text{maximize } \pi_1(X^{(3)}) = (6 - 4 + \tfrac{1}{2})x - x = 1.5x$$
$$\text{subject to } 0 \leq x \leq 1,$$

with solution $X^{(3)} = 1$ and $\pi_1(X^{(3)}) = 1.5$. Problem (8.5) becomes

$$\text{maximize } \pi_2(Y^{(3)}) = (2 - 1)y - y = 0y$$
$$\text{subject to } 0 \leq y \leq 1,$$

with solution $Y^{(3)} = \mu$, for all $0 \leq \mu \leq 1$, and $\pi_2(Y^{(3)}) = 0$. Since neither $\pi_1(X^{(3)}) > \delta_1{}^{(3)} = \frac{3}{2}$ nor $\pi_2(X^{(3)}) > \delta_2{}^{(3)} = 0$, terminate. Optimal solution is $(X, Y) = (\hat{X}^{(3)}, \hat{Y}^{(3)}) = (1, 0.25)$.

Algorithm B

While the numerical example above demonstrates the solution procedure, it also demonstrates the major drawback of the algorithm: the decision maker's "operating rules," i.e., the objective functions of (8.4) and (8.5), do not generally result in the optimal solution by these decision makers. Rather, the central coordinator must specify the X and Y decision once the optimal solution is attained by the process. We suggest here a slight modification in the process such that the operating rules will lead to the optimal solution if all our assumptions are met.

We posit solving (8.1) in a decentralized fashion by following the procedure outlined in the preceding section with two exceptions: (*a*) replace (8.4) and (8.5) in step (iii) by (8.4′) and (8.5′), where

$$\text{maximize } \pi_1(X^{(d+1)}) = \pi(X^{(d+1)}, \hat{Y}^{(t)}) - \pi(\hat{X}^{(t)}, \hat{Y}^{(t)}) - \lambda^{(t)} C_1(X^{(d+1)} - \hat{X}^{(t)})$$
$$\text{subject to } X^{(d+1)} \in S \tag{8.4′}$$

and

$$\text{maximize } \pi_{II}(Y^{(e+1)}) = \pi(\hat{X}^{(t)}, Y^{(e+1)}) - \pi(\hat{X}^{(t)}, \hat{Y}^{(t)}) - \lambda^{(t)} C_2(Y^{(e+1)} - \hat{Y}^{(t)})$$
$$\text{subject to } Y^{(e+1)} \in T; \tag{8.5′}$$

and (*b*) replace step (iv) by

iv′) If $\pi_1(X^{(d+1)}) > 0$, set $d = d + 1$ and extend the sequence $\{X^{(i)}\}$ by including $X^{(d+1)}$; if $\pi_{II}(Y^{(e+1)}) > 0$, set $e = e + 1$ and extend the sequence $\{Y^{(j)}\}$ by including $Y^{(e+1)}$. If $\pi_1(X^{(d+1)}) > 0$ and/or $\pi_{II}(Y^{(e+1)}) > 0$, resolve (8.2) using the extended sequence(s) and go to (ii), setting $t = t+1$. If neither $\pi_I(X^{(d+1)}) > 0$ nor $\pi_{II}(Y^{(e+1)}) > 0$, terminate; the optimal solution is $(\hat{X}^{(t)}, \hat{Y}^{(t)}) = (X^{(d+1)}, Y^{(e+1)})$.

By rewriting the objective function of (8.4) we can compare and contrast the two procedures. Since

$$\delta_1^{(t)} = \hat{X}^{(t)} \left. \frac{\partial \pi}{\partial X} \right|_{X = \hat{X}^{(t)}, Y = \hat{Y}^{(t)}} - \lambda^{(t)} C_1 \hat{X}^{(t)},$$

$\pi_I(X^{(d+1)}) > \delta_1^{(t)}$ is equivalent to $\Delta X \, \partial \pi / \partial X \big|_{X = \hat{X}^{(t)}, Y = \hat{Y}^{(t)}} - \lambda^{(t)} C_1 \Delta X > 0$, where $\Delta X = X^{(d+1)} - \hat{X}^{(t)}$. Hence the only difference between (8.4) and (8.5) when considered in conjunction with their respective criteria for acceptance occurs in their respective objective functions, where the approximate value of the increment in π in moving from $(\hat{X}^{(t)}, \hat{Y}^{(t)})$ to $(X^{(d+1)}, \hat{Y}^{(t)})$, ΔX $\partial \pi / \partial X \big|_{X = \hat{X}^{(t)}, Y = \hat{Y}^{(t)}}$ in (8.4), is replaced by the exact increment $\pi(X^{(d+1)}, \hat{Y}^{(t)}) - \pi(\hat{X}^{(t)}, \hat{Y}^{(t)})$ in (8.4').

Note that the essential operating difference between algorithms A and B lies in what has to be done once the optimum is attained. Under algorithm A, when the optimal solution has been attained, the optimal decisions must be given to the decentralized decision makers; another iteration with the current $\lambda^{(t)}$ and $\delta_1^{(t)}$ will not necessarily produce the optimal X decision when employed in problem (8.4) and used in step (iv). On the other hand, when the optimal solution has been attained under algorithm B, if the current $\lambda^{(t)}$ is used in problem (8.4'), the solution to (8.4') will be the optimal X decision, and the X decision maker will therefore not have to be told what to do; the operating rule employed leads him to make the optimal decision. Note, however, that (8.4') and (8.5') may be more difficult to solve than (8.4) and (8.5) since the latter have linear objective function while the objective functions of the former may be nonlinear; thus, algorithm B may be computationally more difficult to utilize than algorithm A.

Numerical Example: the Quadratic Case

We now wish to apply algorithm B to the example examined in the preceding section. The problem we wish to solve is labeled (8.6). Under identical starting sequences the master problem at $t = 1$ is the same as in the preceding section, with solution $U^{(1)} = (1)$, $V^{(1)} = (1)$, $\pi_0 = 0$, and $\lambda^{(1)} = 0$. Correspondingly, $(\hat{X}^{(1)}, \hat{Y}^{(1)}) = (0, 0)$. Problem (8.4') becomes

maximize $\pi_I(X^{(2)}) = (6x - 2x^2 + 2x\hat{Y}^{(1)} - 2\hat{Y}^{(1)2}) - \pi(\hat{X}^{(1)}, \hat{Y}^{(1)})$
$$- \lambda^{(1)} 1(x - \hat{X}^{(1)}) = 6x - 2x^2$$

subject to $0 \leq x \leq 1$,

with solution $X^{(2)} = 1$ and $\pi(X^{(2)}) = 4$. Problem (8.5') becomes

maximize $\pi_{II}(Y^{(2)}) = (6\hat{X}^{(1)} - 2\hat{X}^{(1)2} + 2\hat{X}^{(1)}y - 2y^2) - \pi(\hat{X}^{(1)}, \hat{Y}^{(1)}) - \lambda^{(1)} 1$
$$(y - \hat{Y}^{(1)}) = -2y^2$$

subject to $0 \leq x \leq 1$,

with solution $Y^{(2)} = 0$ and $\pi(Y^{(2)}) = 0$. Since $\pi_I(X^{(2)}) > 0$, extend sequence: $\{X^{(i)}\} = \{0, 1\}$ and set $d = 2$. Since $\pi_{II}(Y^{(2)}) = 0$, do not extend sequence: $\{Y^{(j)}\} = \{0\}$. $t = 2$.

The master problem is identical to (8.7) with solution $U^{(2)} = (0, 1)$, $V^{(2)} = (0)$, $\pi_0 = 4$ and $\lambda^{(2)} = 0$. Correspondingly, $(\hat{X}^{(2)}, \hat{Y}^{(2)}) = (1, 0)$. Problem (8.4') becomes

$$\text{maximize } \pi_I(X^{(3)}) = 6x - 2x^2 - 4$$
$$\text{subject to} \qquad 0 \le x \le 1,$$

with solution $X^{(3)} = 1$, $\pi_I(X^{(3)}) = 0$; problem (8.5') becomes

$$\text{maximize } \pi_I(Y^{(2)}) = 4 + 2y - 2y^2 - 4 = 2y - 2y^2$$
$$\text{subject to} \qquad 0 \le y \le 1,$$

with solution $Y^{(2)} = \frac{1}{2}$, $\pi_{II}(Y^{(2)}) = \frac{1}{2}$.
Since $\pi_I(X^{(3)}) = 0$, do not extend sequence: $\{X^{(i)}\} = \{0, 1\}$. Since $\pi_{II}(Y^{(2)}) > 0$, extend sequence: $\{Y^{(j)}\} = \{0, \frac{1}{2}\}$, $t = 3$.

The master problem becomes

$$\text{maximize } \pi_0(U, V) = 0u_1 + 6u_2 - 2u_2^2 + 0v_1 - \frac{1}{2}v_2^2 + u_2v_2$$
$$\text{subject to} \qquad 0u_1 + 1u_2 \qquad + 0v_1 + \frac{1}{2}v_2 \le 1.25,$$
$$u_1 + u_2 = 1, \ v_1 + v_2 = 1, \ U, V \ge 0,$$

with solution $U^{(3)} = (0, 1)$, $V^{(3)} = (\frac{1}{2}, \frac{1}{2})$, $\pi_0 = 4\frac{3}{8}$, and $\lambda^{(3)} = 1$. Correspondingly, $(\hat{X}^{(3)}, \hat{Y}^{(3)}) = (1, \frac{1}{4})$. Problem (8.4') becomes

$$\text{maximize } \pi_I(X^{(3)}) = 6x - 2x^2 + \frac{1}{2}x - \frac{1}{8} - 4\frac{3}{8} - x + 1 = 5.5x - 2x^2 - 3.5$$
$$\text{subject to} \qquad 0 \le x \le 1,$$

with solution $X^{(3)} = 1$ and $\pi_{II}(X^{(3)}) = 0$; problem (8.5') becomes

$$\text{maximize } \pi_{II}(Y^{(3)}) = 4 + 2y - 2y^2 - 4\frac{3}{8} - y + \frac{1}{4} = y - 2y^2 - \frac{1}{8}$$
$$\text{subject to} \qquad 0 \le y \le 1,$$

with solution $Y^{(3)} = \frac{1}{4}$ and $\pi_{II}(Y^{(3)}) = 0$. Since neither $\pi_I(X^{(3)}) > 0$ nor $\pi_{II}(Y^{(3)}) > 0$, terminate; the optimal solution is $(\hat{X}^{(3)}, \hat{Y}^{(3)}) = (X^{(3)}, Y^{(3)}) = (1, \frac{1}{4})$.

Thus, we see that algorithm B has the desirable property that if the operating rules are followed throughout the process, they lead to an "independent" optimal decision on the part of the dependent decision maker once the optimum is attained.

Some Comments in Implementation

The feasibility of implementing either of the above procedures depends heavily upon the speed of convergence of the process and the extent to which either the central coordinating mechanism can specify operating rules or the operating rules are consistent with the roles of the decision makers. While we have not been able to provide formal convergence proofs, numerous numerical experimental problems have converged satisfactorily; from this experimentation we wish to note that the process may be accelerated substantially by the use of solutions not obtained through iteration. If the central processor can make a "guesstimate" of the optimal solution and its associated λ, problems (8.4) and (8.5) or (8.4′) and (8.5′) can be solved to yield near-optimal solutions at an early iteration.

The extent to which the decomposition is consistent with the environment depends upon the problem and legitimizing the role of the central coordinator. For example, the use of the procedure to solve the transfer pricing problems of a divisionalized firm is highly feasible since "corporate headquarters" is clearly a legitimate coordinator and profit center planning and control schemes yield "natural" operating rules consistent with the objectives of the divisions and the objective function of (8.4) and (8.5) or (8.4′) and (8.5′). Another natural setting is centralized public decision making such as controlling river-basin pollution when a river-basin authority has the power to tax polluters in relation to their discharge. While the transfer pricing problem in the firm is, in essence, a problem of allocating scarce firm resources so as to maximize joint profits, the river-basin problem is a problem of allocating the assimilative capacities of a stream so as to minimize society's cost of maintaining clean water. A realistic simulation of the latter is informative, so we briefly present some results of such an application.

The posited problem is to minimize the total cost of achieving a given set of water quality standards (clean water) at various points along a river. The decentralized decision makers are the polluters, who must decide the extent to which they treat waste materials before discharge. To achieve the objective of least cost, a central water authority is assumed that can impose quality standards for the basin and enforce them via the levying of taxes upon the producers of waste discharging along the river. We consider only dissolved oxygen standards and oxygen-using waste for purposes of demonstration.

Let w_i denote the gross waste production per unit of time of the ith contributor (Biological Oxygen Demand Units, or BOD). The ith producer can treat this generated waste; let x_i denote the proportion of waste removed by treatment and the functional $\phi_i(x_i)$ denote cost of treating to remove the proportion x_i. The remaining portion discharged into the river, $w_i(1 - x_i)$, is taxed an amount λ_i, resulting in a tax bill amounting to $\lambda_i w_i(1 - x_i)$ for the ith producer. It is assumed that each producer wishes to minimize the total cost of waste disposal, that waste is treated in facilities independent of his production facilities, and that he does not alter the methods or level of production for the purpose of reducing w_i. After partitioning the length of the river into n reaches, it is further assumed that the technical relationships between the amount discharged and the effect of this discharge upon the quality of water at the jth reach are linear; letting a_{ji} denote the amount of dissolved oxygen demanded in reach j per unit of BOD discharged in reach i, $a_{ji} w_i(1 - x_i)$ is the total oxygen demand in reach j created by the discharge in reach i with x_i percent removal.

Given that total oxygen demand in each reach must be less than the oxygen available after the standards have been met, and if one lets S_j denote the excess supply in reach j, the mathematical form of the problem becomes

$$\text{minimize } \phi(x_1, x_2, \ldots, x_k) = \sum_{i=1}^{k} \phi_i(x_i),$$

subject to
$$
\begin{aligned}
a_{11}w_1(1-x_1) &\leq S_1, \\
a_{21}w_1(1-w_1)+a_{22}w_2(1-x_2) &\leq S_2, \qquad (8.8) \\
\vdots \qquad\qquad\qquad & \quad \vdots \\
a_{n1}w_1(1-x_1)+a_{n2}w_2(1-x_2)+\ldots+a_{nk}w_k(1-x_k) &\leq S_n
\end{aligned}
$$
$$(0 \leq x_k \leq 1, \text{ for all } k),$$

where there are n reaches and k treatable pollution sources.

Based on the logic developed above, a more complete model of the impact of BOD treatment was developed by Hass. The formulation of the a_{ji}'s and the s_j's for an arbitrary basin with arbitrary initial flow, hydrological characteristics, tributaries, and waste loads can be found in an earlier paper.[2] With this more complete formulation and data for the Lower Miami River Basin in Ohio during the months of low flow (July, August, and September), a constraint set was developed to represent the effect of treatment at the fifteen treatable sources of BOD pollution along the 58-mile stretch of the Lower Miami. A map of the Lower Miami appears in Figure 8.1. Partitioning the 58 miles from Dayton to the Ohio River into twenty-seven reaches, the constraints for the Lower Miami during the low flow period took the form displayed in Table 8.2 when a standard of 4 mg/l of dissolved oxygen (that sufficient to maintain aquatic life) was imposed at the end of each reach.[3] We also imposed a set of restrictions on each x_i, the percentage of BOD load w_i removed by treatment at source i, requiring each polluter to provide at least primary treatment (removal of solids), i.e., $x_i \geq .45$ for all i. Coupling these two sets of constraints with the treatment cost functions for each pollution source completes the formulation of the problem. But this coupling may be difficult to achieve because of informational location. While the constraint sets are logically developed by a central water authority with knowledge of the hydrological characteristics of the basin, treatment cost functions are best known by the polluters. Thus the problem is "naturally" decomposable since the information necessary to formulate the problem is held by the various participants in the basin. Furthermore, if taxes are to be imposed by the central authority, optimal taxes must be used so each polluter is led to the optimal treatment decision.

To simulate how the decomposition techniques described in the earlier sections of this paper could be used to solve this decentralized decision mak-

---

2. Jerome E. Hass, "Decomposition Algorithms and Decentralized Decision Making," unpublished Ph.D. dissertation, Carnegie-Mellon University, 1969.

3. Note that if $AW(\bar{1} - X) \leq S$, $-AWX \leq S - AW$ or $AWX \geq AW - S$. Thus, the constraints of (8.8) are compatible with those found in Table 8.2 since X is the vector of decision variables in Table 8.2.

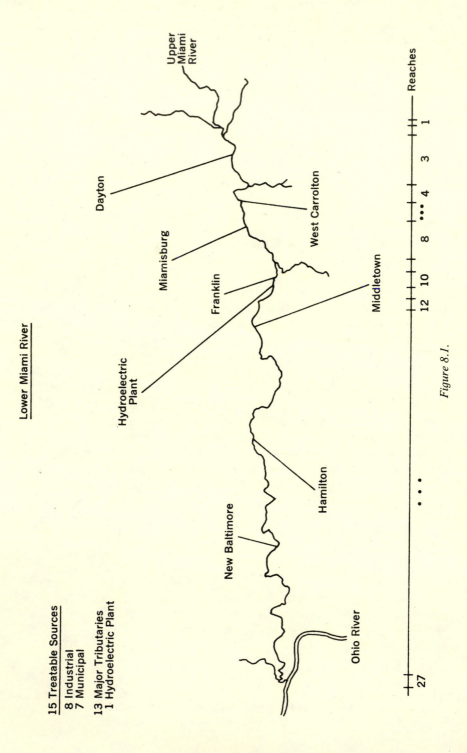

Lower Miami River

15 Treatable Sources
   8 Industrial
   7 Municipal

13 Major Tributaries
 1 Hydroelectric Plant

Ohio River

New Baltimore

Hamilton

Hydroelectric Plant

Franklin

Middletown

Miamisburg

West Carrolton

Dayton

Upper Miami River

27   12 10   8   4   3   1 — Reaches

Figure 8.1.

Table 8.2. Matrix representation of constraint set for Miami River Basin

															x_1	-3779
															x_2	-3333
																-3436
5989															x_3	2573
8840																5399
16553	989														x_4	14421
15985	1102	1576													x_5	14622
16394	1161	1947	242													15630
18029	1406	3524	1278	89												20220
19147	1590	4770	2108	161												23417
21004	1832	6181	3006	238	230											28187
22563	2059	7614	3943	318	483											32926
22959	2176	8610	4643	380	701											34969
22753	2172	8699	4723	387	735	108										34961
19846	1904	7691	4195	344	666	162	169									30222
19295	1871	7681	4227	348	697	290	495	164								30280
14288	1397	5820	3227	266	548	301	581	227								20653
14166	1394	5857	3263	269	564	355	718	295	909							21354
14028	1385	5856	3272	270	573	389	803	338	1495							21693
12447	1233	5234	2931	242	517	369	774	330	1720							18461
12249	1214	5156	2888	239	510	367	770	329	1747	65						18296
11967	1186	5045	2827	234	500	363	764	327	1786	158	40					18205
7551	758	3289	1862	154	341	299	656	292	2241	1435	585	188				15579
5534	561	2468	1406	117	264	256	574	260	2245	1774	732	239				7442
5509	559	2458	1401	116	263	256	573	260	2244	1777	733	239	57		x_{15}	7574
4103	420	1871	1072	89	206	216	492	226	2089	1823	755	249	2740	1698		12432
3332	343	1540	886	74	172	189	433	200	1914	1742	723	239	3634	2267		7233

(matrix $\cdot$ vector $\geq$ right-hand side)

ing problem, we employed the Dantzig-Wolfe variation of our algorithm B to solve the Miami River Basin problem.[4] In this case the dual evaluators, $\lambda^{(t)}$, can be used to develop a tax rate to be imposed upon each polluter by the central water authority at each iteration.[5] For treatment cost functions we

4. As noted earlier in this chapter, Dantzig and Wolfe have provided an algorithm very similar to our conjectured algorithm B for the case when $H(X, Y)$ in (8.1) is zero, i.e., the objective function of (8.1) is separable. The only difference from our conjectured algorithm B is that the master problem (8.2) objective function is a linear approximation, i.e., $\pi(U, V) = \Sigma_i u_i F(X^{(i)}) + \Sigma_j v_j G(Y^{(j)})$. This is extremely useful because the central coordinator does then not need to know the function form of $F(X)$ or $G(Y)$; at each iteration, if $X^{(d+1)}$ is accepted in the sequence $(X^{(i)})$, the X decision maker simply reports $F(X^{(i)})$ as well as $X^{(i)}$ to the central coordinator.

5. The auxiliary problem, following (8.4'), for polluter i then takes the logical form

$$\text{Min } \pi(X_i^{(d+1)}) = \phi_i(x_i) - \lambda^{(t)} A_i x_i,$$
$$\text{s.t.} \quad 0.45 \leq x_i \leq 0.99,$$

where $A_i' = (a_{1i}, a_{2i}, \ldots, a_{ni})$ is the ith column of the constraint matrix in Table 8.2, i.e., the ith polluter, given a tax rate of $T_i = \lambda^{(t)} A_i$ at the tth iteration by the central authority, minimizes the total cost of waste distribution (treatment plus taxes), $\phi_i(x_i) + (1 - x_i)T_i$. Since T_i is a constant,

$$\{\text{Min } [\phi_i(x_i) + (1 - x_i)T_i]\} = \{\text{min } [\phi_i(x_i) - x_i T_i]\},$$
$$0.45 \leq x_i \leq 0.99 \qquad\qquad 0.45 \leq x_i \leq 0.99$$

so that the solution to the problem faced by the polluter,

$$\text{Min } \pi(X_i^{(d+1)}) = \phi_i(x_i) + (1 - x_i)T_i$$
$$\text{s.t.} \quad 0.45 \leq x_i \leq 0.99$$

is identical to solving (8.4') if $T_i = \lambda^{(t)} A_i$.

used Frankel's treatment cost data to derive a quadratic function in plant size (capacity in million gallons processed per day) and percent BOD removed.[6]

To obtain the starting sequences we set $\lambda = \{0\}$ to get cost figures for 45 percent removal and then λ_{27}, the shadow price as the last reach, equal to 10. Table 8.3 reports the solution to the auxiliary problems under the starting

Table 8.3. Iteration numbers*

Pollution Source	1†	2†	3	4	5	6	7
1	45.0	99.0	72.0	85.5	92.3	88.9	87.2
	1368	4925	2257	3368	4091	3716	3539
2	45.0	99.0	61.8	69.7	73.9	71.8	70.8
	286	824	338	399	440	419	409
3	45.0	99.0	99.0	99.0	99.0	99.0	99.0
	.273	773	773	773	773	773	773
4	45.0	99.0	86.2	99.0	99.0	99.0	99.0
	257	712	521	712	712	712	712
5	45.0	93.0	51.8	54.5	56.2	55.3	54.9
	174	352	178	181	184	182	182
6	45.0	99.0	54.8	57.3	59.8	58.6	58.0
	193	469	202	207	214	210	209
7	45.0	99.0	49.8	47.4	48.6	48.0	47.7
	182	429	184	183	183	183	183
8	45.0	99.0	56.7	50.8	53.8	52.3	51.6
	177	408	188	180	183	181	180
9	45.0	99.0	50.5	47.8	49.2	48.4	48.1
	174	398	177	175	175	175	175
10	45.0	99.0	72.0	58.5	65.3	61.9	60.2
	246	672	353	273	306	288	280
11	45.0	99.0	57.3	51.2	54.2	52.7	51.9
	385	1198	427	396	409	402	398
12	45.0	99.0	55.7	50.4	53.0	51.7	51.0
	233	621	248	237	241	239	238
13	45.0	99.0	50.9	48.0	49.4	48.7	48.3
	177	408	180	178	178	178	178
14	45.0	99.0	58.8	51.9	55.4	53.6	52.8
	484	1573	555	502	524	512	506
15	45.0	99.0	56.5	50.7	53.6	52.2	51.5
	385	1198	422	394	406	399	397

Shadow prices of binding constraints‡ None $\lambda_{27} = 10.$

$\lambda_{12} = 0.22$ $\lambda_{12} = 0.40$ $\lambda_{12} = 0.46$ $\lambda_{12} = 0.43$ $\lambda_{12} = 0.42$

$\lambda_{26} = 0.38$ $\lambda_{26} = 0.19$ $\lambda_{26} = 0.28$ $\lambda_{26} = 0.24$ $\lambda_{26} = 0.21$

* The upper number in the table is the percentage of waste removed through treatment and the lower number is the daily cost associated with that treatment level.

† Starting iterations.

‡Subscripts on shadow prices refer to the constraint to which the shadow price applies.

6. Richard J. Frankel, "Water Quality Management: An Engineering-Economic Model for Domestic Waste Disposal," unpublished Ph.D. dissertation, UCLA, 1965.

condition and the iterative process, and Table 8.4 reports to solutions to the master problem for five iterations. We solved the problem directly using a quadratic programming code, and the optimal solution is found in the last column of Table 8.4.

Table 8.4.

Pollution Source	Central Authority Solution Number					Optimal Solution
	1	2	3	4	5	
1	89.5	87.7	86.9	86.8	86.8	86.8
2	45.0	61.8	69.7	69.7	69.7	70.5
3	99.0	99.0	99.0	99.0	99.0	99.0
4	99.0	99.0	99.0	99.0	99.0	99.0
5	45.0	51.8	54.5	54.5	54.5	54.8
6	45.0	54.8	57.3	59.8	58.6	57.8
7	45.0	45.0	47.4	47.4	47.4	47.7
8	45.0	56.7	50.8	50.8	52.3	51.6
9	45.0	45.0	47.8	49.2	48.5	48.1
10	87.8	56.4	61.1	61.6	61.9	60.2
11	45.0	57.3	51.2	51.2	51.2	51.9
12	45.0	55.7	55.7	53.0	51.7	51.0
13	45.0	45.0	48.0	49.4	48.7	48.3
14	45.0	55.3	51.9	51.9	52.0	52.8
15	45.0	45.0	50.7	50.7	50.7	51.4
Total cost per day	9218	8616	8340	8324	8317	8312
Shadow prices of	λ_{12} 0.223	0.404	0.459	0.432	0.418	0.4132
Binding constraints*	λ_{26} 0.377	0.189	0.283	0.236	0.212	0.2118

* Subscripts on shadow prices refer to the constraint to which the shadow price applies.

From Table 8.4 it is evident that the process converges toward the optimum quite rapidly under the Dantzig-Wolfe variation of algorithm B, with the individual polluters, by the end of iteration 5, responding to the tax rates imposed by the central water authority with near-optimal solutions.[7] Thus, the use of algorithm B to help solve the Miami's pollution problem not only provides us with a mechanism for solving the problem in a fashion consistent with the location of information and existence of "autonomous" polluters, but also provides us with automatic means of implementing the optimal decisions in a decentralized fashion as well.

Conclusions

This paper has described two nonlinear decomposition algorithms which are more general than algorithms available heretofore. We have argued that

7. We note that if the central water authority knew the function forms of the treatment cost functions faced by each polluter, algorithm B could have been used by the authority; if this were the case, the optimum would have been attained at the first iteration with optimal tax rates as a by-product.

the applicability of any decomposition algorithm in decentralized decision making relies heavily upon the legitimacy of the master-problem solver and the extent to which the operating rules prescribed by the algorithm are consistent with the operating rules used by the decentralized decision makers. We also believe that a highly desirable property is that once the optimum is attained, the procedures used to attain it are also appropriate for maintaining it. To these ends we posit algorithm B as a feasible vehicle for decentralized decision making in many situations. To demonstrate its applicability we simulated its use in determining the optimal treatment scheme to achieve a given set of standards for the Miami River of Ohio. The algorithm led to a set of tax rates to be imposed on each polluter such that when a polluter minimized the total cost of waste disposal (treatment plus discharge), the resultant level of treatment was consistent with the least-cost treatment scheme for the whole basin.

IV

Interorganizational Decision Making in a Business Context

The papers in the first three parts were predominantly theoretical in nature. The following three parts contain applied papers. However, the reader should not expect a precise distinction. Many of the papers in the following parts contain significant discussions of theoretical issues. Further, the applications, while pragmatic and realistic, are not simply descriptive, institutional, or "how to" oriented.

The applications papers are separated into three parts discussing, in turn, interorganizational decision problems arising in business, at the interface between government and business, and between various governmental units. Again, the boundaries are not precise, so the reader should not be surprised to find that Heskett's paper in the business section mentions governmental interactions and Whittaker's paper in the government section has a sizable part dealing with contractor-contractee relationships.

Further, the editors of this volume were not unaware of the existence of significant interorganizational decision problems in other areas of organizational endeavor. Obviously, many multi-organizational decisions must be made if delivery of health-care services is to be carried out in a way most beneficial to the recipients. Educational administration clearly requires the joint decisions of many groups. However, existing research seems to have concentrated on the organizations represented in this volume. It is the hope that the work reported here will stimulate work in other institutional sectors to the mutual benefit of all concerned.

As one reads the papers in the next three parts, one cannot but be impressed by the critical requirements for interorganizational decision making in any of the institutional contexts. Regardless of discipline, the authors, as they attempt to grapple with significant policy issues, find that the problems with which they must deal transcend the domain of any one organization. Many of our problems are now intersystem problems. This does not mean that all intrasystem issues have been solved, but it does represent a shift in

127

focus. As was stated in the Preface and is elaborated by Evan in Part V, there is increasing openness of organizations to their environment, and in many instances the most prevalent feature of the environment of one organization is other organizations. Thus, ways of interacting to solve mutual problems must be found.

Another theme, first stated in the Preface to this volume, is developed more fully by the authors of the papers in the next three parts. The idea is that inter-organizational decision problems arise at various systems levels. Thus, Tullock's paper deals with individuals within the corporation, and Baron examines the decision technology employable for decisions between divisions of the corporation. At the other extreme, De Strihou examines decisions at the level of NATO, an instance where a group of sovereign states must decide jointly. The models developed apply, therefore, regardless of the systems level at issue.

Decision models for business subsystems are readily available and plentiful in number. Yet, for interdepartmental and/or firm-wide decisions, the models fall far short of the needs. As Tuite pointed out in his paper in Part I, many of the decision models are suboptimizing at best and may transform what is essentially a cooperative effort into a game situation. A department employing a decision model may take the actions of other departments as a given or may even try to excel at the expense of another department, an action not necessarily optimum for the firm. Tuite's effort at merging marketing and production strategies is an example of the direction of development required.[1]

Much remains to be done in the business decision areas. Interorganizational decision making was defined above as an effort to reduce the conflict in a decision situation to allow interdependent units to achieve a higher optimum. Some of the shortcomings of models, such as Tuite proposes, lie in the behavioral area. Thomas, Walton, and Dutton and again Walton have illuminated the behavioral aspects of the conflicts which arise in the use of formal decision models. Yet, the incorporation of the insights of the behavioral scientist into the quantitative decision models remains incomplete at best.

Thus, the stage is set for further analysis of business decisions where multiple units of the same firm or several firms are involved in the decision process. Writing from the viewpoint of an economist, Gordon Tullock examines the structure of the business decision problem by taking as his subject the individual within the corporation. Thus he examines the behavior of a person; but the approach is structural, because it is the system which is really the central focus of Tullock's model. As a participant in the decision process, the individual is faced with a number of decision variables and an objective function which define the system. The individual will attempt to make those decisions which will optimize his contribution to his firm, gain the approval

1. M. F. Tuite, "Merging Marketing Strategy Selection and Production Scheduling: A Higher Order Optimum," *Journal of Industrial Engineering* (February 1968).

of his superior, and enhance his career. The individual is placed in the context of a nonzero-sum game relative to his co-workers and in a cooperative arrangement with his superior.

Tullock uses as his example a technological decision variable in an objective function which is clearly single valued. Yet, his model is similar to that of others in this volume, for his actor could just as easily have been a boundary person between decision units and the members of the unit taking the role of his superior in Tullock's model. Further, the recommendation made to the unit may have had consequences for conflict resolution between the actor's group and other groups. The nature of the conflict resolution might lead to maximizing the profit position of the firm while lessening the apparent contribution to that profit by the group in question. This would increase the disapproval by the group of the individual and might even threaten his career.

In the latter part of the paper, Tullock deals with the within-group problems such a boundary person might face. The example used is again related to a technical decision, but there is no reason why the same model would not hold for other decisions. The model would serve as a guide to optimizing behavior for the individual within his own unit when faced by the necessity of working out an interorganizational problem.

In Chapter 10, James Heskett examines the behavior of a number of firms involved in a real-world interorganization decision situation. The relationship of the firms was such that in a very large firm, the functions described might be performed by various units within the same firm. The same decisions would have to be made as the firm sought to optimize profits, so the model holds, a fortiori.

The functions or firms involved in this model are manufacturing, transporting, wholesaling, and retailing. There could be others, peripherally related. The nature of the decision remains the same, regardless of whether these are independent, profit-oriented firms or profit centers within the firm. The question is: How should they decide to act in order to optimize over the entire firm or group of firms? Thus, there is a system which is to be analyzed, and the linkages of this system are the foci of the interorganizational decision problems.

Interestingly, Heskett begins with a discussion of power relationships. Power is a behavioral concept, but power in this instance is tied to the structure determined by the system. Since the actors in this case were independent firms, each brought to the decision process certain economic power and power derived from other bases. Since any firm was always free to leave the decision process, the power of the others was circumscribed. Walton and Warren have discussed in detail the variables which influence the decision to participate. Thus, behavioral aspects are seen to substantially affect an otherwise purely economic relationship. Clearly, a nonzero-sum game is the result.

The firms studied were a coal-mining firm, a coal-using electrical-generating utility[2] and the intervening modes of transport including rail and water transportation. Within the existing power structure of the firms involved, the problem was to make decisions on an optimal distribution system. In the context of the decisions actually made, Heskett examines the power relationships, how the firms used their power in the decision process, and how they tried to maintain or improve their positions. Using concepts which have come to be called business logistics, Heskett develops a model for the identification of power bases and the means by which relationships might be maneuvered to obtain an optimal solution.

Finally, since the role of boundary personnel has been examined in several of the papers in this volume, it is interesting to consider the boundary personnel in Heskett's paper. Obviously, some of the details of any decision had to be worked out by staff personnel; but in this case it is clear that the top people in the various organizations were boundary personnel. Warren refers to this as a high-salience phenomenon. Obviously, the problem was an important one for the organizations involved. This point arises again in the context of government organizations as well. (See the introduction to Part VI.)

The technology of interorganizational decisions in a business context is examined by David Baron in "Joint Decision Technologies with a Production-Marketing Example." In this paper, he reflects the growing interest of decision technologists in decentralization by guidelines. The concept has been previously introduced in this volume by Tuite and Kortanek and will appear again below in the paper by Niskanen. The approach has much appeal as a pragmatic approach to decision problems. In fact, it may well be essentially the way many large organizations are indeed managed.

In this paper, he examines decision technologies which might be applied in a joint decision problem using the production and marketing departments of a single firm as the actors in his example. Other types of groups or organizations could be analyzed by this model with suitable modifications.

The three models examined are centralization, coherent decentralization, and decentralization by guidelines. Centralization implies a single decision maker or authority (which may be a committee). Coherent decentralization means independent decisions with an exchange of enough information for each unit to reach both its own optimum and a joint optimum for the system. Decentralization by guidelines is not a single model but a range of models interior to the extremes. As with most intermediate situations, it has some of the strengths and some of the weaknesses of the extreme alternatives.

Baron assumes a system where there is no possibility to opt out of the decision as is likely to be the case within a firm. Of course, there may be ques-

---

2. The fact that the utility was government run makes no significant difference here for it was behaving essentially as a business in this context, having no governmental authority in this instance.

tions of degree of cooperation of the various subsystems which Baron recognizes as implementation and control problems. There is no attempt to consider the behavioral variables which might influence the degree of cooperation or the likelihood that any subset would try to game the system.

Baron's organization is clearly Weberian in nature in that the central decision maker has authority which is imposed from the top down. In interorganizational decisions, there may be nothing corresponding to the central authority, and thus the guidelines must be developed by the subsystems as part of the decision process.

Baron recognizes that it may be necessary to acquire a great deal of information in order to set the guidelines. Presumably a guideline would take some form of instruction or rule issued by a central authority or agreed upon by the organizations. Using Reiter's notation where $\mathscr{A}$ was the entire action set, the instruction might be to take action a_1. This would presumably be a centralized decision. Complete decentralization might result in the instruction to take any action in A, where A is a subset of $\mathscr{A}$ and represents those actions which are perceived as optimal by the subunits. Guidelines might be stated as to anything between a_1 and a_n, where all $a_i \in A$. If a_1 and a_n are very close together, then a nearly centralized decision has been made. If they are very different, then they may nearly encompass all of A and approach decentralization. Baron does not deal with how close together or far apart the guidelines should be.

Baron considers a dynamic model in his paper. It is dynamic in the sense that there may be several periods over which the guidelines are specified. But there is no formal mechanism for review of the guidelines, nor a system to monitor changes as the organization itself changes over time. Thus, an organization theorist would view this model as incomplete.

The behavioral scientist might also want to suggest another form of guidelines. It may be possible to obtain some semblance of guidance simply by building an organization of people of similar skills and values who largely think and act alike, thus avoiding or keeping to a minimum the need for actually developing guidelines in a formal sense. This, however, as is the case for many of the theories in this volume, does not take into account the need for innovation and change – an issue requiring significant future research.

9

The View from Inside: An Individualistic Approach to the Corporation

GORDON TULLOCK

The apparatus presented below was originally developed as part of a general model of social interaction in which widely diverse situations could be represented simply by changing the parameters.[1] Basically, it is extremely individualistic. An individual is assumed to make decisions about action in the real world in an effort to maximize his own preference schedule. The anticipated reactions of other parts of the bureaucratic hierarchy in which he is operating are simply part of the environment in which he makes these decisions. Further, in many cases, he will face not a certain reaction from this environment, but a probability distribution of reactions. For ease of presentation, the expectation of the reactions will be used. This simplifies the model and, I think, causes no great difficulty.

The situation facing any man can be presented as a choice between different states of the world, the states being represented geometrically by points in a multidimensional space. There is one dimension for each variable the individual considers relevant. He has control over some of these dimensions; for example, he might be an automobile designer working for one of the large companies and in a position to recommend to his superiors the horsepower of one of the engine options for next year's car. Other variables are not within his control in a direct sense, but will be affected by his recommendation. For example, on the vertical axis of Figure 9.1, we have the degree of disapproval which he will receive from his immediate superior. My use of disapproval instead of approval does not indicate that I have fundamentally pessimistic or perverse views of the world. It seems to be my fate to use this negative or "cost" approach in many problems. It is, of course, possible to map this over into another graph in which positive approval instead of disapproval appeared on the left axis, but a general consideration of the problems seems to indicate that the "cost" approach will lead to fewer difficulties than the more conventional "benefit" approach.

1. See Tullock, "A Model of Social Interaction," *Mathematical Applications in Political Science V*, James F. Herndon and Joseph L. Bernd (eds.) (Charlottesville: University Press of Virginia), 1971.

133

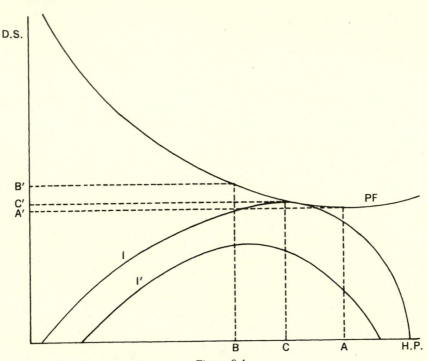

Figure 9.1.

Note that this figure does not assume that the superior has a definite view as to the horsepower of the engine and that the inferior is simply trying to reach that point. That might of course be so, but it might also be that the superior is solely interested in a salable engine and that a recommendation for a given horsepower together with reasons for believing that it is highly salable would be the recommendation that would lead to the least disapproval. If we wanted to discuss this problem extensively, we would have a number of dimensions for the recommendation, one of them being the horsepower and another perhaps the "packaging" in which the recommendation was wrapped. On the horizontal axis of our two-dimensional figure, however, we have only the horsepower recommendations.

The line labeled P.F. is the production function and shows the individual's estimate of the amount of disapproval he will obtain from his superior for any given recommendation with respect to horsepower. The individual could minimize the anticipated degree of disapproval from his superior by recommending horsepower *A* and obtaining *A'* amount of disapproval. The individual, however, has personal preferences with respect to the horse-power and, if he did not concern himself at all with the preferences of his superior, would choose horsepower *B*. If he made that recommendation, it would lead to an amount of disapproval *B'*. The fact that the individual has preferences both with respect to the horsepower of the engine and with respect to approval of his superior leads to a set of indifference curves of the general shape shown by the *I* lines. Note that the use of disapproval on the vertical axis rather than approval means that his optimum is down rather than up. The usual tangency solution leads him to recommend horsepower *C* and obtain *C'* amount of disapproval from his superior.

In the real world, of course, there are many more than two variables. For example, the horsepower of the engine is not its only technical characteristic, and there are, of course, innumerable other things which might turn up in an automobile design office. On the other hand, the disapproval of his immediate superior is not the only thing that the individual should be concerned with. Presumably, he is also interested in the disapproval of people of higher rank and, for that matter, people who are not directly in the formal hierarchy above him. He should also be concerned to some extent with the ultimate salability of the car, even if this is not likely at the moment to be reflected in the approval or disapproval of his superiors. It could be argued that his concern for the salability of his car is, however, indirectly an effort to obtain the favor of his superiors. He might even be interested in the opinion of people in a competing automobile company, if he had any idea of seeking a new employer. All of these variables, both those which he can directly control and those which he can't but which are affected by those which he can control, could be placed on an additional set of dimensions.

We can divide the dimensions of the many-dimensional space into two categories. The "control variables," our first set, are those variables which the individual himself can adjust as he wishes. The other variables, the "effect variables," are variables which the individual cannot directly control but which are, to some extent, affected by his choice of control variables. The individual, by choosing locations on the control variables, attempts to obtain the optimal adjustment to the entire manifold of variables. Thus, the effect variables influence his choice among the control variables. The model is extremely general; it can be used to discuss ordinary market situations, democratic voting, the problem of revolutions, despotic government, and crime. Its generality is largely a product of its simplicity. The situation the person finds himself in can always be described by a suitably designed production hypersurface in a suitably dimensional space. He will always have a set of indifferent hypersurfaces and can always seek the point where the highest indifference hypersurface is tangent to the production-function hypersurface.

It should be noted that we must be a little careful in the selection of our dimensions. If we are careless, it is possible that the individual will find himself in a position where the highest point of tangency of the highest indifference hypersurface in the particular space we have chosen is not actually available to him through manipulation of those variables which he can control. Under these circumstances, he would indeed be better off if he could get to this point, but he has no way of getting there. The individual will not have his action affected by the fact that he wants something that he knows he cannot get, and hence we must design our space in such a way that it contains only feasible positions. Note that it is not necessary that the number of control variables be as great as the number of variables which are affected. It is quite possible that an individual, by changing one of the things under his control, will affect a number of different dimensions such as, for example, his immediate superior's opinion, the opinion of the superior above his immediate superior, and total sales. With only one variable, of course, he cannot affect these various things independently.

Note also that the individual is not assumed to get his "payoff" entirely from the effect dimensions. He can have preferences with respect to the things which are under his control, too. He is, in our current very general mode, a utility maximizer and not a maximizer of any particular subset of variables. This extremely general structure fits widely different situations for the simple straighforward reason that the production function is different in a different situation. We keep the same model but we change the parameters. Our engineer making up a recommendation as to the horsepower of an engine might have a totally different subjective view of the production function that he faces than, let us say, the president of a corporation worried about an upcoming proxy fight.

The radically different nature of the worlds which they face turns up simply as a difference in the shape of the production function. Use of the model in any except the most abstract terms, therefore, will turn on specifying the nature of these preference functions and the production function which the individuals face. For the remainder of this paper, I propose to make such specifications to demonstrate that reasonably realistic statements about the actual situation can be thereby deduced. In all of the cases which I will present below I will radically simplify the situation for ease in presentation.

Let me begin by specifying a very, very simple preference system for executives in corporations—they just want to get ahead. In other words, they are unambiguous and single-minded promotion maximizers. I suppose no one would regard this as descriptive of the real world, but I also suppose that few would regard it as an extremely bad approximation of the real world. Let us further suppose that the manager feels that his own chance of getting ahead in the world is correlated with that of the profit position of any organization with which he happens to be connected. Increasing profit to the corporation, division, subdivision, etc., will lead to expansion and hence promotion and/or increased salaries to its executive personnel. It will, of course, also make managers from that organization more readily "salable" if they are interested in transferring to some other corporation, division, subdivision, etc.

In Figure 9.2, I have drawn in a production function, shown by the curved line, and a single indifference curve (I_A) for an official of Division A in a two-division corporation. Note that once again the figure is in what I call the cost form rather than the benefit form. Thus, the official's preference mountain rises as one moves down and to the left. The division official in Division A feels that an increase of $100,000 a year in profits to Division A will have an effect on his future promotion, and that an increase in the corporation's profits of $100,000 a year will also have a favorable net effect on his future career. He, however, feels quite rationally that the increase of profits of his division will have more effect – even though the total amount is the same – than the increase in the profits of the corporation as a whole. He would gain from increases in profits in Division B, but he feels that he would gain less than through the profits in his division. Note that I have not assumed that there is any particular positive feeling of rivalry between the two divisions or that the members of Division A are jealous of Division B, nor have I assumed any of what we may call sociological effects. These can be added in if desired, but at the moment I have not included them.

With these assumptions, we set the indifference line of I_A of the official in Division A more steeply inclined than 45°. The point of tangency to the assumed production function is at point A, and the individual, although genuinely interested in increasing profits (decreasing losses) both in Division B and in the corporation as a whole, would choose increasing profits to Division A

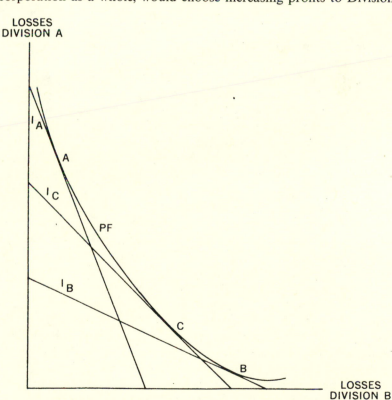

Figure 9.2.

even if this involves some reduction of profits to corporations as a whole. If our individual were to transfer to Division B, his preference function would immediately shift to line I_B, and his point of preference would become B. This would not be because there has been any change in his world or his perspective or his mental attitude; it would simply be that it is the indifference curve which is suitable to his new position, granted he faces the production function we have specified. If he is promoted to Chairman of the Board of the entire corporation, the 45° line (I_B) becomes his preference function and the highest preference point is at C. Needless to say, the indifference curve I_C is also an indifference curve of the stockholders.

The diagram we have just presented shows rather neatly the difference in attitude between different divisions in a corporation. We frequently find what appears to be "sociological" controversy between divisions, but they may well be the product of rational differences of the sort we have been describing. The difference in objective which we stated does pose distinct problems for the management. Traditionally there are two ways of dealing with this problem. The first, and I would say on the whole the older, of these methods is for the general manager to attempt to adjust the promotion possibilities of the officials in Division A and Division B in such a way that they will be impelled to act as if they were interested in the entire corporation rather than their respective divisions. Since the manager of the corporation knows less about what is going on in any given division than the division executives, this method is not entirely successful. It does, however, permit the integration of the different divisions into a whole, and for those who believed in centralized planning it is, of course, optimal. It should also be noted that even in the modern corporation with many "profit centers," it is still the basic reliance. The profit centers to which we will turn in a moment are, of course, subject to exactly the same process we have been describing internally. As a general rule, most corporations which have broken themselves down into a number of profit centers have only a few centers compared with the total number of managers. It is thus clear that centralized control is still the basic reliance.

The other method, however, the development of a number of profit centers, takes the form of changing the apparent production function by arranging the real world in a special way. To take the idea to its extreme, let us suppose we place Division A and B in sealed compartments so that the activity of Division A in no way affects Division B. Under these circumstances, if each of the division managers simply maximizes his own profit, he will also be making the maximum contribution to the corporation's profit. He retains exactly the same preferences, but the production function he faces is changed so that his action has no effect on anything except the profits of his own division and he is motivated to maximize them.

Corporations do not simply divide themselves up into the smallest possible units in order to give everyone this optimal incentive situation. The advantages of control and specialization of function are great enough so that direct supervision of individuals whose interests, to some extent, are conflicting is retained for a large part of the corporate chain of command. In these areas, the corporate manager substitutes his own judgment of individual behavior for a bookkeeping measure of the net output of each subarea. He may also attempt to establish an internal price system such that the individual's contribution to the total well-being in a corporation is assessed rather than his contribution to the well-being of whatever division he is in. Theoretically, we could, by setting off these different techniques, determine the optimum amount of disaggregation for a given corporation. This would, however, require a knowledge of parameters which we seldom have.

We can use the same general technique for dealing with any one of a large number of variables which might interest the individual. For example, the individual, in making recommendations to his superiors, might take into account the effect the recommendations will have on the ultimate sales of a given product. On the other hand, he might be interested solely in what his superior will think of him and feel that the superior's estimate of him will be more affected by the superior's personal biases as to the proper solution to the instant problem than by the ultimate effect on sales. A figure similar to Figure 9.2, or for that matter to Figure 9.1, could be drawn with a production function which combines on one axis the ultimate sales and on the other the actual degree of favor he anticipates obtaining from his superior, his recommendations being, of course, a control variable which is not on this particular two-dimensional diagram, and the individual's indifference surfaces would indicate what he would recommend. Both the ultimate sales and the immediate opinion of his superior would have some effect on the outcome, although the relative size of the effect would depend on the shape of both the production function and his particular payoff ratio between them. Note that here, as in the previous case, we have dealt with a possible conflict between two objectives, not by simply saying they are in conflict, but by saying that the individual should take both into account and should choose that point which optimizes his situation with respect to both.

In this last example, we again have a lesson for corporate management. In general, corporation managements should try to prevent their personal prejudices from affecting their promotion decisions with respect to their subordinates. The reason for this is simply that they will get better advice in terms of the objective functions which will eventually affect their own promotion in that way. One might say that, insofar as possible, a corporate executive in dealing with his subordinates should, to a very large extent, ignore anything except the results in terms of sales, costs, etc., that he gets from their performance. Some methods for achieving this result will be discussed below. In dealing with his superiors, he should, in general, also attempt to provide the best results, but he should at the same time try to maximize the degree to which his general appearance, demeanor, and advice meet the tastes of his superior.

In most cases, this advice already has been taken to heart by corporate executives, and the combination of efficiency and apple polishing that we would predict is what we observe. The Board Chairman, in choosing which among the vice presidents should be promoted to the executive committee, will find that all of them have done their best to conform closely to his prejudices — something which involves very little resources committment — and hence, can make his choice among them almost entirely in terms of their objective efficiency.

Let us now turn to another application of our basic model, which we may call "committeemanship". Returning to the situation in Figure 9.1 in which an engineer must recommend the horsepower for an upcoming car model, let us assume that there are several engineers all working in the same division, and that they are all going to appear at a meeting at which a decision will be made, naturally by their common chief, on the horsepower. In large organizations, committees are basically of two sorts. In some cases, they are genuinely collective bodies making collective decisions. More often, however, one member of the committee is "more equal than the others," and will make the ultimate decision both on the committee's current task and on eventual promotion of the members. In this case, the committee exists partly to give the actual policy maker advice, and partly to provide him with a sort of ceremonial backing in the event that he has difficulty later with his decision. It is this type of committee that we are discussing here. The other type of committee, in which genuine collective decisions are made, is rather more complicated. The engineers, no longer pure promotion maximizers, are interested to some extent in the horsepower itself, both for reasons of stability and for pure aesthetics, and to some extent in the recommendation which is most likely to meet with the approval of the superior. Each individual, then, could have his position represented by Figure 9.1. Each, however, knows that the other members of the committee will also make recommendations, and that the degree of approval or disapproval that each one gets from the manager will depend, to some extent, on this rivalry situation, i.e., on what other people also recommend.

We can sharpen the situation by assuming that, in the near future, one of the engineers making the recommendations is to be promoted, and that the man to whom the recommendations are made will make the decision as to which one. We can also sharpen the situation by assuming that the manager, the ultimate decision maker in this case, will probably select for promotion that engineer whose recommendation for engine size comes closest to the manager's own optimum. Under these circumstances, the initial production function closely approximates a subjective estimate of the relative probability of the manager's optimum being at any particular location.

For simplicity and in order to avoid drawing a new diagram, let us assume that the situation is as it was shown in Figure 9.1, and that all the engineers on the committee have indifference curves of the shape shown in Figure

9.1. Under these circumstances, the engineer has the problem of not only deciding what to recommend but also deciding when he shall make his recommendation or, more precisely, what target location in the series of recommendations he shall maneuver for. Under some circumstances, being the first person to make a recommendation gives a great advantage; and under other circumstances, making the recommendation later in the series is desirable. In order to discuss this problem, assume that we are again at the situation shown in Figure 9.1, and that an engineer has recommended point *C*. For a second engineer, who we will assume has exactly the same preferences as the engineer shown on Figure 9.1, the situation now becomes quite complex. The problem is complicated because if he simply repeats the first recommendation, he is unlikely to improve his own promotion possibilities. To the contrary, he is likely to improve the promotion possibilities of the first engineer and thus lower his own. If we assume temporarily that the basic production function has not shifted, his line now should look like the P.F. in Figure 9.3. In general, the closer he is to his predecessor's recommendation, the less likely it is that his boss will be impressed by him.[2] The farther away he is from his predecessor's recommendation, the less likely he is to, in essence, simply recommend his predecessor for promotion. On the other hand, it is likely that his predecessor's guess as to the optimum point to recommend is not too far wrong and therefore that simply taking a position far from his predecessor's estimate is also a mistake.

In Figure 9.3, I have drawn in another indifference curve, marked *I''*, which is essentially one of the same family as the two indifference curves shown on Figure 9.1. Note, however, that with the change in the production function that the individual faces because the other man has made a recommendation, he ends up at a different position even though his preferences are the same. Both of our engineers have the same indifference curves, and both have the same idea of the prejudices of the chief, but the fact that they are on a committee and one of them has to move first means that the other ends up in a position which is quite different from what he would originally have recommended. It will be noted also that this new position is somewhat closer to the optimum of the superior than was the original guess. This last, however, is not certain (although probable), and depends on the specific shape of our function.

So far, it would appear that the engineer who goes first has a distinct advantage over anyone who follows, and hence we would predict that there

---

2. It would, of course, be possible for the initial recommendation to be so convincing that the second engineer's estimate of his superior's opinion after the recommendation had been given would have a sharp downturn at the recommendation. Under these circumstances, he would have little choice other than to agree with his predecessor's recommendation. This would most assuredly mean that the first engineer was prompted. If this type of outcome was thought to be probable, one could predict that the members of the committee would maneuver to be the first to make recommendations.

would be a great deal of maneuvering for first place. Under some circumstances this may be so, but under other circumstances, making the recommendation late may be more desirable. The point here is simply that the
person to whom the recommendation is made will probably respond in some
way, even if only by a change in expression, to the first recommendation. This
response improves the information of the engineers as to the outcome that
he will reward, and hence, basically, moves the production function. It is the
possibility of acquiring information in this way which makes it perhaps
desirable to make one's recommendation late in the series instead of at the
beginning. If the engineer has a clear idea of his superior's desires, in other
words if the production function in Figure 9.3 is quite steep vertically, he
would be well advised to make his recommendation quickly and would, of
course, end up very close to the superior's optimum. If the production function shown on Figure 9.1 is subjectively very flat to him and he feels that it
will be so also for his rivals, he would be well advised to try to stall and to get
other engineers to make the first move; he can then plan his response in terms
of the information with respect to the production function which he derives
from observing the reaction to the first move.

So far, however, in discussing committee behavior, we have assumed that
the first person to make a recommendation makes it simply at his optimum

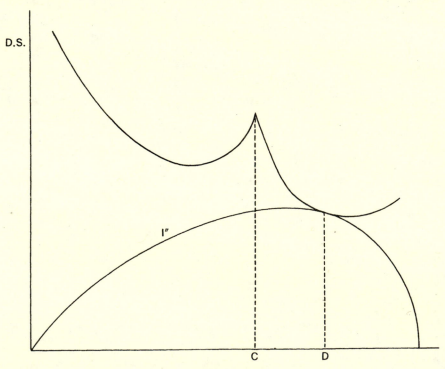

Figure 9.3.

without considering the fact that others will make recommendations later, and then that the second person makes his recommendation. We can inquire as to where our first engineer would choose as his recommendation point, granted that he knows that a second engineer will be replying. Note that the problem here is quite complex since the second engineer will always be able to choose the best counter-strategy to the person who goes first. The problem, in fact, is a close mapping of the reaction problem in duopoly, and, as is reasonably well known, this is one of the largest problems in the whole field of economics. Nevertheless, our engineer, like the practicing duopolist, must act, he cannot wait in the hope that the theorists, perhaps, will solve the problem. Practical men in many fields are called upon to act in areas where the theorists have not yet developed an elegant explanation.

So far we have been discussing this committee strategy from the standpoint of the individuals who are making the recommendation. It might be sensible to stop at this point, however, and point out that the outcome we have specified is quite desirable from the standpoint of the manager. Having two individuals making recommendations puts them under very considerable pressure to bring in recommendations that are close to the manager's optimum, or at least what they think are close to the manager's optimum. If the manager can give them a strong idea of the criteria he wants to be used in reaching the decision on the horsepower and can at the same time conceal from them any areas of ignorance he has about the application of these criteria, he puts them under great pressure to make recommendations that are very close to the optimum by those criteria. By this competition, he presses his subordinates into doing the necessary work to optimize according to those criteria without putting very much time into the problem himself. The apparatus is a great economizer of managerial time. In other words, the use of several competing engineers or engineering groups, although it appears superficially wasteful, nevertheless leads to a net outcome that is much closer to the objectives of the higher management than one would obtain with a single engineering group.

So much, however, for committeemanship. The model that I presented seems to me a very simple model and, as I said before, was originally designed for other purposes. It seems to me also, however, to give a rather realistic picture of the interior of a corporation, or for that matter of any large bureaucracy. Whether it is superior to other theories in realism and that criterion normally described as Occam's Razor, I must leave to you readers who are more familiar with the existing literature than I.

10

Interorganization Problem Solving in a Channel of Distribution

JAMES L. HESKETT

A number of hypotheses, a few of which are measurable, have been advanced regarding the nature of interorganization relations. These range from hypotheses about determinants of problem-solving efforts and outcomes in situations involving two or more organizations to personal problems of identification in interorganization "boundary" jobs. Several of them regarding the bases and uses of power were presented in a previous paper. It is the purpose of this presentation to set forth a detailed case example involving interorganization management activities and attempt to explain events in the framework of previously expressed theory regarding ways in which an organization can make effective use of existing power relationships to improve such relationships further in the future.

Power Bases and Uses[1]

POWER

Two concepts of power especially are helpful for this discussion. The first, advanced by Schopler,[2] measures power in terms of the net difference in probability that one actor will elect a behavior with or without intervention by a second actor. Thus, power is relative, measured in interpersonal or interorganizational terms.

Emerson's concept of power is one of dependence of one actor on another.[3] In it, the dependence of one actor upon another is said to be directly pro-

This paper is dedicated to the late Glenn A. Squibb, Vice President-Marketing, Bessemer and Lake Erie Railroad Company, without whose cooperation the study described would have been impossible.

1. Much of this section is drawn from James L. Heskett, Louis W. Stern, and Frederick J. Beier, "Bases and Uses of Power in Interorganization Relations," to be published.

2. John Schopler, "Social Power," in Leonard Berkowitz (ed.), *Advances in Experimental Social Psychology,* II (New York: Academic Press, 1965), 187.

3. Richard Emerson, "Power-Dependence Relations," *American Sociological Review,* XXVII (February 1962), 32–33.

portional to one's motivational investment in goals mediated by the other and inversely proportional to the availability of similar goals outside the relationship. Dependence, also termed commitment by Emerson, is a direct reflection of power. The power of one actor over another is reduced as the commitment of the second actor toward the first is reduced.

These two definitions of power are complementary, in that the second offers a possible explanation for behavior described in the first.

Some writers have attempted to distinguish between the concepts of power and influence. However, the distinctions raised do not appear to be sufficiently useful to discourage the use of these terms on an interchangeable basis throughout this paper.

BASES OF POWER

Although bases of power have been categorized in different ways, five such bases are especially relevant for this discussion: reward, coercion, expertness, legitimacy, and identification.

Reward power is based on the belief by one actor that another actor has the ability to mediate rewards for him. Naturally enough, it has been suggested that the degree of reward power varies directly with the magnitude of the reward which can be bestowed,[4] with successive demonstrations of the ability to bestow such rewards[5] within certain limits, and with points of diminishing returns for the successive use of similar rewards.[6] Rewards can have an uncertainty-reducing effect when they are employed to guarantee the success of an interorganizational venture, particularly in cases where there is little previous experience upon which to draw.

Coercion in many respects is the converse of reward power. It involves the ability of one actor either to mediate punishments for another or to withhold rewards from another.[7]

Expert power can be described in terms of the relative ability which one actor has to supply a special knowledge or expertness for another.[8] It is perishable in the sense that once supplied with the knowledge, the second actor may be able subsequently to provide it for himself, thus reducing the relative advantage of the first over the second.[9] Expertness may offer a second form of uncertainty absorption, particularly where the expertness of one actor results

4. John French and Bertram Raven, "The Bases of Social Power," in Dorwin Cartwright (ed.), *Studies in Social Power* (Ann Arbor: The University of Michigan Press, 1959), 156.

5. Dorwin Cartwright, "Influence, Leadership, Control," in James March (ed.), *Handbook of Organizations* (Chicago: Rand McNally, 1965), 11.

6. Paul Secord and Carl Backman, *Social Psychology* (New York: McGraw-Hill, 1964), 278.

7. Peter Blau, *Exchange and Power in Social Life* (New York: John Wiley & Sons, Inc., 1964), 116.

8. Cartwright, "Influence, Leadership, Control," *op. cit.* 30.

9. J. Thibaut and H. Kelley, *The Social Psychology of Groups* (New York: John Wiley & Sons, 1959).

from his ability to control and maintain the high quality of communications, perhaps through a central "message center" of some type. As March and Simon point out, by definition the recipient is unable to judge the correctness of such communications and must place his confidence in the communication, and perhaps editing, process.[10]

Legitimate power results from a legitimate right which one actor has to influence another and the obligation of the second to accept the influence of the first.[11] Legitimate power most often arises out of a contractual relationship which specifies the extent of the power. It may result from governmental action or protection. By its nature, legitimacy may result from a demonstration of expertness. Thus, quite often expert and legitimate power are interdependent.

Identification power results from the willingness or desire of one actor to be associated with another, or to maintain such an association.[12] The desire may result from the demonstration of desirable behavior on the part of the second actor, similar characteristics which the two actors possess, or perhaps just the fact that the two actors have been closely associated over time. In fact, Secord and Backman suggest that the repeated use of reward power by one actor toward another over time may create a situation in which the maintenance of the relationship is no longer as dependent on the specific applications of reward power as it is on the fact that a long-standing relationship has been maintained, a form of identification power.[13]

POWER RELATIONSHIPS IN A CHANNEL OF DISTRIBUTION

Several premises are important to an understanding of power relationships between and within channels of distribution involving manufacturers, transport carriers, wholesalers, retailers, and other types of business organizations. First, all measures of power are relative. One person or organization possesses more power than another, or more power than it did at a previous point in time. Absolute measures of power, even if they existed, would not be particularly useful.

Second, all parties to a channel relationship possess some degree of power; the relationship is not composed of a powerful and a powerless member. There must be some mutual perception of a need to complete a contractual agreement, for example. This perceived need on the part of both parties to a business relationship stems from the belief that each has something that the other needs; i.e., each possesses some type and amount of power relative to the other. As Alderson has observed, all members of an organized behavior

10. James March and Herbert Simon, *Organizations* (New York: John Wiley & Sons, Inc., 1958), 165.
11. John French and Bertram Raven, *op. cit.*, 159.
12. *Ibid.*, 161.
13. Paul Secord and Carl Backman, *op. cit.*, 376.

system occupy some position or status within its power structure.[14] Similarly, Cartwright has maintained that power is a relationship between two agents; it is not an absolute attribute of a single agent.[15]

Third, hypotheses and findings related to interpersonal relationships are valid equally for interorganizational relationships. Although there are several conflicting opinions about the validity of this statement, there is no evidence to the contrary.

Illustrations of the various power-base relationships in a channel of distribution are many and varied. For example, the producer of a product may bestow rewards or penalties on those with whom he potentially could deal by providing his product to, or withholding it from, various distributors. The importance of his act is related directly to the perceived need for the product on the part of potential distributors. The manufacturer can make his product more desirable by removing all potential alternatives to distributors through a campaign to differentiate the product from all competition, at least in the minds of consumers. On the other hand, in his decision to offer distribution services to the manufacturer, the distributor may bestow or withhold rewards also, particularly if he has distinguished his services from those of his competition, thereby removing acceptable alternatives by which the manufacturer can reach the market. The relative economic power of manufacturers and distributors has been the subject of extensive study by a variety of scholars.[16]

Expert power often is established by a member of a channel of distribution through a willingness to help those with whom it deals carry on their business more effectively. Thus, drug manufacturers long have assisted drug wholesalers by providing improved methods of managing inventory and by training wholesaler personnel in the use of these more effective methods. Automobile manufacturers provide nearly all ideas for promotional campaigns carried out by their dealers. Marketing research efforts in a channel of distribution typically are concentrated in one or two member organizations, with results disseminated either directly or indirectly to other channel members.

Legitimate power may be achieved through contractual provisions or by legal means. For example, a franchise agreement typically specifies the type of controls to be exercised by the franchiser over the franchisee. Fair-trade and unfair-pricing legislation has, in the past, afforded manufacturers some type of recourse against distributors failing to price their products as intended.

In a channel of distribution, identification power may result from the fact

14. Wroe Alderson, "The Analytical Framework of Marketing," in D. Duncan (ed.), *Proceedings: Conference of Marketing Teachers from Far Western States* (Berkeley: University of California, 1958), 22.

15. Cartwright, "Influence, Leadership, Control," *op. cit.,* 22.

16. See especially Joseph Palamountain, *The Politics of Distribution* (Cambridge: Harvard University Press, 1955); and John Galbraith, *American Capitalism* (Boston: Houghton-Mifflin Co., 1956).

that one party to an agreement carries a type or quality of product which another's product will complement. Product line decisions are based to a degree on identification power.

POWER-BASE INDICATORS AND THEIR MEASUREMENT

An individual or organization builds a power base resulting from a combination of various types of power discussed above. Thus, to measure the existence of power in a channel of distribution in terms of the ingredients of power held by one actor relative to another probably is a futile task. Instead, several references have been made to what might be termed power-base indicators, offering measurable evidence of the existence of power possessed by one individual or organization relative to another.

For example, Alderson has suggested that one measure of power in a transactional sense is the relative stake that parties to a transaction may have in the completion of the transaction or contractual arrangement.[17] Stake could be defined in terms of the proportion of the total business carried out by each party which the contractual arrangement might represent.

Evan has proposed that the innovative ability of one engineering organization might be measured by collecting data about the perceptions of personnel in a cross-section of other organizations or by the flow of people in innovative positions among competing organizations and the reasons for their mobility.[18]

Several power-base indicators and possible means of measuring them are indicated in Figure 10.1. They have been discussed in detail elsewhere.[19] The suggestion here is that through such indicators operational measures of power levels can be obtained. Even with operational measures, the problem of dimensional comparability among measures remains. These measurement problems are of sufficient magnitude that descriptive case study may remain the most feasible means of reporting observations for some time to come.

USES OF POWER AND THEIR MEASUREMENT

Given the existence of power relationships, how can an organization take steps to maintain (stabilize) or perhaps improve such relationships? Further, how can power relationships between organizations be manipulated to provide more effective problem solutions? Hypotheses, related to these questions in the form of suggested long-run constructive and long-run destructive uses of power, are presented in Figure 10.1. These are the major interests of this paper.

17. Wroe Alderson, *Dynamic Marketing Behavior* (Homewood, Ill.: Richard D. Irwin, Inc., 1965), 37–45.

18. For a hypothetical suggestion of how such a measure might be obtained, see William Evan, "Organization-Set: Toward a Theory of Interorganizational Relations," in James Thompson (ed.), *Approaches to Organization Design* (Pittsburgh: University of Pittsburgh Press, 1966), 175–91.

19. James L. Heskett, Louis W. Stern, and Frederick J. Beier, *op. cit.*

Figure 10.1. Selected Bases and Uses of Power in Interorganization Relationships:
Hypotheses and Possible Measures

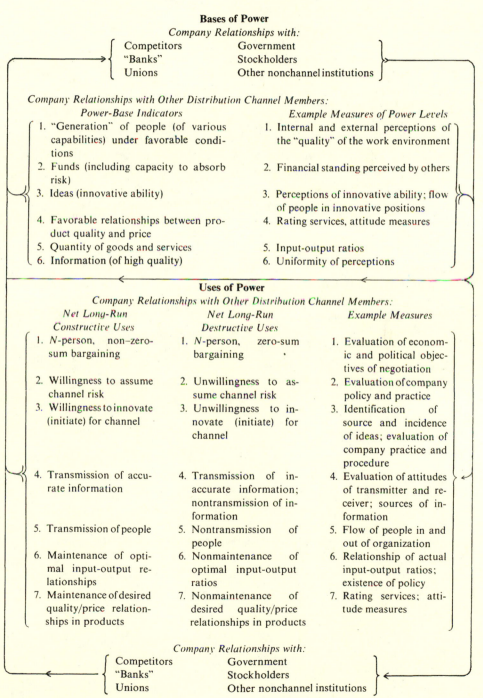

Bases of Power

Company Relationships with:

Competitors	Government
"Banks"	Stockholders
Unions	Other nonchannel institutions

Company Relationships with Other Distribution Channel Members:

Power-Base Indicators	*Example Measures of Power Levels*
1. "Generation" of people (of various capabilities) under favorable conditions	1. Internal and external perceptions of the "quality" of the work environment
2. Funds (including capacity to absorb risk)	2. Financial standing perceived by others
3. Ideas (innovative ability)	3. Perceptions of innovative ability; flow of people in innovative positions
4. Favorable relationships between product quality and price	4. Rating services, attitude measures
5. Quantity of goods and services	5. Input-output ratios
6. Information (of high quality)	6. Uniformity of perceptions

Uses of Power

Company Relationships with Other Distribution Channel Members:

Net Long-Run Constructive Uses	*Net Long-Run Destructive Uses*	*Example Measures*
1. N-person, non–zero-sum bargaining	1. N-person, zero-sum bargaining	1. Evaluation of economic and political objectives of negotiation
2. Willingness to assume channel risk	2. Unwillingness to assume channel risk	2. Evaluation of company policy and practice
3. Willingness to innovate (initiate) for channel	3. Unwillingness to innovate (initiate) for channel	3. Identification of source and incidence of ideas; evaluation of company practice and procedure
4. Transmission of accurate information	4. Transmission of inaccurate information; nontransmission of information	4. Evaluation of attitudes of transmitter and receiver; sources of information
5. Transmission of people	5. Nontransmission of people	5. Flow of people in and out of organization
6. Maintenance of optimal input-output relationships	6. Nonmaintenance of optimal input-output ratios	6. Relationship of actual input-output ratios; existence of policy
7. Maintenance of desired quality/price relationships in products	7. Nonmaintenance of desired quality/price relationships in products	7. Rating services; attitude measures

Company Relationships with:

Competitors	Government
"Banks"	Stockholders
Unions	Other nonchannel institutions

Long-run constructive uses of power in a channel of distribution are evidenced by an organization's willingness to enter into non–zero-sum bargaining activities, assume risk for other channel members, innovate or initiate new projects on behalf of the channel, transmit accurate information to other channel members, provide a talent pool for the channel as a whole, maintain effective input-output relationships with firms with which it deals, and maintain desired quality-price combinations in products and services which it attempts to market through the channel.

Non–zero-sum bargaining activities, because they lead to a basic alteration of cost structures, should produce benefits not only for the participants in a negotiation but also for the ultimate beneficiary of a channel of distribution, the consumer. In contrast, zero-sum activities, such as the renegotiation of a price, merely improve the cost or profit position of one member of a channel at the expense of another member, with little benefit accruing to the consumer, and consequently to the channel in its efforts to compete with other channel arrangements for the consumer's favor. A measurement of the economic objectives held out by an organization in its dealings with another should provide a basis for measuring the organization's willingness to enter into nonzero-sum bargaining situations.

Some parties to channel relationships are better able to assume risk than others. It is the organization that uses this ability to the advantage of its fellow members that is best able to maintain or improve its power base. This often occurs where the initiation of a new distribution concept requires the investment of money in equipment, advertising, or perhaps working capital. Company policies and past practices in such situations can provide means of determining the willingness to assume risk, perhaps in return for financial rewards, for other channel members.

An organization may use its resources to initiate new ideas which accrue benefits for the channel of distribution as a whole. For example, the proposal to use uniform pallet sizes among related organizations may require that one organization invest in material handling equipment which produces benefits for several companies with which it deals. If a continuing effort is made to monitor these types of efforts, it might be possible to identify the source and incidence of innovative ideas. Once again, organization practices and procedures related to innovative activities can be measured.

The degree to which an organization transmits useful information or knowledge and the relative reputation for expertness which it possesses may be measured by determining the extent to which such information actually is used in related organizations in a channel of distribution. An indirect measure of use might be the uniformity with which problems are approached. For example, drug manufacturers' past practices of providing an inventory control system for wholesalers with which they dealt produced a somewhat uniform concept of inventory control procedures for both manufacturers and wholesalers in the industry.

An effective strategy for maintaining or enhancing bases of power may be the "transmission" of people from one organization to another, especially under favorable circumstances. Thus, if one automobile manufacturer supplies engineering talent to another, under conditions in which the first organization is still held in high regard by its departing engineers, the transaction should lead to future enhancement of the power base of the "supplying" manufacturer. The measurement which suggests itself for this use of power would be the actual flows of people, in terms of numbers, types, and underlying causes, between competing organizations.

A firm wishing to maintain its power base typically would reduce its reliance on any one other firm at the same time that it might increase the reliance of other firms on itself. A means by which this might be done is suggested by the hypothetical example in Table 10.1. It is typical of the purchase-sales relationships maintained by some of the nation's larger retail organizations, in which the stake in the business relationship of the firms with which it deals is maintained at a higher level than for the retailing organization itself. In this case, the power base of the retailer would be stronger vis-à-vis manufacturer A than manufacturer B or C. Naturally, a basic means of creating a high proportion of favorable power relationships in matters of trade is by that of an increase in volume of sales and purchases of a firm.

Table 10.1. Improvement of input–output relationships in a channel of distribution

Sales Volume Relationships between Retailer and its Manufacturer-Suppliers

	Sales to Retailer X	Sales to Other Customers	Percentage of Total Sales Represented by Retailer X
Manufacturer A	$1 million	$2 million	33
Manufacturer B	$1 million	$3 million	25
Manufacturer C	$1 million	$4 million	20
	Purchases by Retailer X from Specific Manufacturers	Purchases of Similar Products by Retailer X from Other Sources	Percentage of Total Purchases of Product Represented by Specific Manufacturer
Manufacturer A	$1 million	$19 million	5
Manufacturer B	$1 million	$19 million	5
Manufacturer C	$1 million	$19 million	5

The existence of a definite policy regarding input-output relationships is evidence of the intent to control the use of power, leading to more effective future business relationships in the channel.

A significant factor in the economic success of a firm is the maintenance of desirable price-quantity relationships in the goods and services which it offers in relationship to those offered by its competition. This assumes, of course, that the maintenance of such relationships does not preclude a profit. Recent attempts to measure price-quality relationships are typified by the work of organizations such as Consumer's Union.

Interrelationships between bases and uses of power in a channel of distribution make experimental analysis and measurement difficult to apply. Problems of measurement are of sufficient magnitude to suggest that descriptive case studies may remain the most feasible means of reporting observations of power base and use relationships. The program of the Hydro-Electric Power Commission of Ontario (Ontario Hydro) to expand purchases of bituminous coal from the Fairmont district of West Virginia offers one such study.

A Case Study[20]

Late in 1962, Ontario Hydro issued a call for bids from bituminous coal producers capable of meeting the utility's requirements for quality. It represented the first time that long-term commitments were made to United States producers by the utility. Essentially, Ontario Hydro announced intentions to (a) purchase a base tonnage of 1,200,000 tons per year or 45 percent of Ontario Hydro's U.S. requirements, whichever were greater, from two sources, beginning in 1964 and continuing for five years; (b) establish relations with three other major sources to supply initially up to 1,500,000 tons on a year-to-year basis and convert, when feasible, to base tonnage or percentage of U.S. requirements, whichever might be feasible; and (c) leave at least 10 percent of the required purchases open for spot purchases or competitive bidding.

The offer came as the result of a need for the utility to increase its thermal power generating capabilities. Ontario Hydro had seen its hydroelectric sources of power decline with the water level of the eastern Great Lakes at the same time that the level of demand for electric power was increasing. Nuclear power sources were being brought on-stream only in limited quantities, primarily in areas which did not offer favorable economics for hydroelectric or thermal power sources.

Up to this time, Ontario Hydro had been a sporadic user of coal from sources other than Nova Scotia. However, the Canadian government limited to 750,000 tons per year the amount of coal on which it provided a subsidy to make high-cost Nova Scotian coal competitive with that from other sources. While these quantities had been adequate to meet nearly all of the utility's past needs for coal, they would fall far short of future needs.

The utility's use of United States sources as fill-in suppliers in the past had somewhat damaged its credibility as a customer with these sources.

Although several destinations were involved in the utility's program, a

20. All estimates presented in this section of the paper are those of the author and have not been confirmed by the parties to the transactions.

description of the potential channels of distribution for supplying the Toronto plant provides a typical profile for consideration. Routes by which small amounts of coal had been shipped from the Fairmont coal fields in West Virginia to Ontario Hydro's Toronto plant in 1962 and previous years are sketched in Figure 10.2. Five routes shown in Figure 10.2 were the most important among those that had been employed: (1) Pennsylvania Railroad to Ashtabula, Ohio, and by boat to Toronto; (2) Pennsylvania Railroad to Sodus Point, New York, and by boat to Toronto; (3) B&O Railroad to Fairport, Ohio, and by boat to Toronto; (4) B&O Railroad to Port Charlotte, New York, and by boat to Toronto; and (5) Consolidation Coal Company barge to Bessemer, Pennsylvania; Bessemer & Lake Erie Railroad to Conneaut, Ohio; and by boat to Toronto.

Figure 10.2. Map of Geographical Relationships in the Distribution of Bituminous Coal from West Virginia to Toronto, Canada

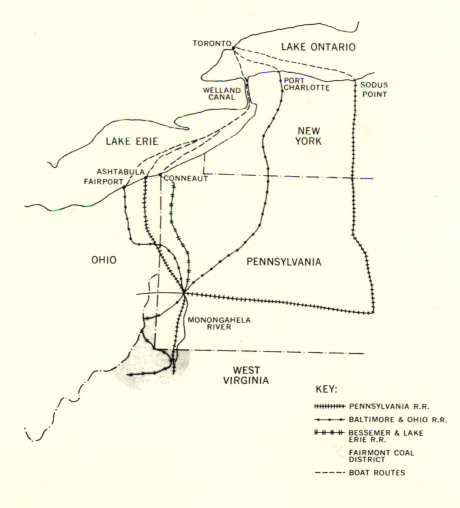

Terms under which coal was purchased by Ontario Hydro from West Virginia coal producers typically were f.o.b. the lake boat employed for the movement. The utility contracted for water transportation service on the Great Lakes, and took title to the coal as it was tendered for delivery to the vessel at the United States port.

ELEMENTS OF THE DISTRIBUTION PROBLEM

Executives responsible for the procurement of coal for Ontario Hydro were most anxious to encourage new practices which might lead to lower landed costs for the coal which they would have to obtain in the foreseeable future. In order to meet the internal competition from nuclear power development, it was felt that a 15 percent reduction in the landed cost of coal would be necessary.

A number of problems had characterized past practice in the procurement and shipment of coal to Toronto. Because of its lower price, for example, coal had been purchased from a number of strip mines in Pennsylvania and Ohio. However, the quantities supplied by any one mine were often quite small, making consolidation for rail and water shipment difficult.

Methods for shipping coal to Ontario Hydro's Toronto plant were somewhat limited. Unit train shipments direct from the United States mine to the plant were precluded by the Toronto plant's lake-front location which made rail delivery difficult and time-consuming. Further problems of coordination had arisen between railroads which would have to cooperate to make all-rail shipment possible. The investment required for a slurry pipeline for all or any part of the distance was very great.

However, rail-lake methods of distribution had serious shortcomings as well. The coordination of rail and water shipments, particularly at the United States lake ports, was difficult. Even when trainload quantities could be assembled, trains of 100 70-ton cars (7,000 tons of coal) would have to be loaded onto lake vessels with 10,000 to 12,000 tons of capacity. Either loaded rail equipment had to be assembled in advance of the arrival of the boat or the boat had to wait until a second trainload arrived at the port in order to complete its load. As a result, rail equipment was delayed at the port for six days, on the average. Rail tariffs accommodated this situation by allowing five days of "free time" at the port before the assessment of equipment demurrage charges for delays. Delays also resulted for lake vessels.

The ports of Fairport, Ashtabula, and Conneaut were capable of being expanded to accommodate boats of any size. The New York ports, however, were situated in such a way that expansion would be difficult and expensive. Rail-to-lake transfer equipment at the ports was not of the most advanced in design, offering transfer rates of from 1,500 to 2,000 tons per hour.

A combination of uncertainties at the port, relatively slow loading times, and uncertainties in the time required to transit the Welland Canal between

Lake Erie and Lake Ontario had discouraged boat operators on Lakes Erie and Ontario from committing themselves to the construction of vessels larger than 12,000 tons even though the Welland Canal was equipped to handle vessels of up to 25,000 tons in size.

Transportation between the mines and Toronto had to be accomplished on a seasonal basis. Lakes Erie and Ontario became impassable with ice during a portion of each year, and the lakes officially were closed to traffic from about November 30 through April 15 each season. This reduced the incentive for railroads and boat operators to commit specially designed equipment to the service.

Although coal producers served a variety of markets, utility customers had grown in importance in recent years. The utility market, in combination with others, produced a relatively constant demand for coal throughout the year. Thus, although the Ontario Hydro contract would involve a considerable amount of incremental business for West Virginia producers, it represented seasonal business added to a relatively constant current demand.

Storage capabilities for coal in the channel were severely limited except at the utility's plant in Toronto. At the mines, the rough terrain prevented ground storage, although at the larger underground mines in the Fairmont district there were sufficient railroad sidings to accommodate cars needed to make up a 7,000-ton unit train. Port facilities provided only for car storage sufficient to supply boats of 12,000 or more tons. Ground storage facilities at Ontario Hydro's Toronto Plant were capable of holding about 2 million tons of coal, an amount sufficient to supply the plant during the period that the lake was frozen each year.

Custom dominated many of the practices in the production and distribution of bituminous coal. In the so-called lake trade, for example, there was little precedent for coordinated effort among the railroads serving the area. Typically, railroads had not quoted joint rates for services which would allow loaded cars to be interchanged and consolidated in such a way that more efficient handling could be designed for a given commodity. Thus, each railroad maintained its own coal transfer facility on the south shore of the Great Lakes.

POWER BASES

Power-base indicators in the channel in question largely were limited to those involving economics. It was not possible to measure others, except in a highly qualitative way.

Quite naturally, Ontario Hydro executives were able to influence the behavior of a number of organizations by the manner in which they went about the purchase of the coal. However, the fact that they had no viable short-term alternatives to the purchase of large amounts of coal tempered their aggressiveness in approaching the problem.

Several years earlier, the terms of sale for the purchase of coal by Ontario Hydro had been altered from f.o.b. the Toronto plant to f.o.b. the boat at the United States lake port. This allowed the utility to negotiate its own vessel contracts, of some importance because of the desire on the part of the utility to have its coal hauled in fewer ships of larger capacity in order to obtain better utilization of its unloading facilities in Toronto. Also, the change in terms of sale allowed the utility to specify the lake port at which it desired to take possession of the coal, indirectly influencing the choice of railroad which the producers would have to make, either directly or through the brokers which handled their marketing efforts. Thus, Ontario Hydro executives had gained the authority to specify participants at all levels in the channel of distribution used to supply coal.

Among the railroads which had participated in the small amount of coal trade between West Virginia and Canada, the Baltimore and Ohio Railroad Company, New York Central System, and the Pennsylvania Railroad Company were situated in such a way that they could originate coal directly on their lines or those of subsidiary companies. By far the largest proportion of coal was located on the Baltimore and Ohio, which made that line an important factor in any volume movement of coal from West Virginia to Canada. Thus, the B&O held perhaps the greatest amount of reward power of all the producers and carriers in the channel because of its strategic location.

There were perhaps no more than eight or nine coal producers with facilities of a size sufficient to generate the quantities of coal required under the impending contract, particularly if unit train quantities had to be moved. Of these, the Consolidation Coal Company had perhaps the greatest volume and the largest amount of potential capacity which could be developed if the projected quantities of coal were to be supplied.

Other organizations that could participate in the channel possessed relatively little economic leverage. The lake-boat operators could obtain only temporary leverage through the amount and type of carrying capacity which they might happen to have in their fleets at a given point in time. At the time of the impending contract, there was a shortage of capacity of the larger, self-unloading type of boat which the utility desired for the supply of its coal. However, potentially it could turn to any one of several operators in contracting for the service which would be required in 1964. An eighteen-month lead time was required for the construction of necessary vessels.

Geographically, the Bessemer and Lake Erie Railroad Company was in a vulnerable position, because it did not serve underground mines directly with its line. All of the coal moving over the B&LE had been placed in Consolidation Coal Company barges, moved up the Monongahela River, transferred to B&LE equipment at Bessemer, Pennsylvania, and hauled to Conneaut, Ohio. In addition, the railroad's ore traffic, which had provided a major source of business, had declined with the depletion of the Mesabi pits in Minnesota. Replacement for the Mesabi ore, originating in Labrador and Venezuela, was shipped in from the east and interchanged onto the B&LE's line only 50 miles from Pittsburgh. As a result, the railroad's profit performance had declined dramatically.

As a subsidiary of the United States Steel Corporation, the B&LE did have a source of capital which presumably could be made available if it were needed.

At the time of the Ontario Hydro request for bids, executives of at least two of the Canadian boat operating companies, Canadian Steamship Lines and upper Lakes Shipping, the Bessemer and Lake Erie Railroad Company, and several of the coal producers, including Consolidation Coal Company, evidenced the greatest interest in the potential business which the proposed transactions represented. It was necessary, however, to develop a strategy which would lead to the coordinated problem-solving effort necessary to provide lower-cost distribution for coal landed at Toronto. This strategy, and the results which it produced, can be explained in terms of the frame of reference of power-base use discussed earlier.

SEQUENCE OF EVENTS

In announcing their request for bids, Ontario Hydro executives also distributed the most accurate estimates of the company's long-term bituminous coal needs that they could prepare. These estimates indicated a high probability that a dramatic increase in coal would be needed to meet the demands on the Toronto and other facilities operated by the company. Further, this information was distributed to all organizations that conceivably might be interested in participating in the business. In the power-base-use framework discussed earlier, Ontario Hydro thus positioned itself (1) as an uncertainty-reducing force through its willingness to engage in a five-year contract and (2) as a reliable information center, assuming that its long-run estimates proved roughly correct.

The call for bids and the informal indication of the utility's desire to reduce the landed cost of its coal by about 15 percent, or about $1.30 per ton (U.S. currency) from its current weighted average cost at Toronto of an estimated $8.81 per ton, produced action on the part of the railroads. Within sixty days, all competing railroads had announced a 60-cent reduction per ton in their rates for coal moving from West Virginia to the utility's facility in Toronto. This type of action could be interpreted as non–zero-sum bargaining, characterized by a cut in price with no attendant change in the method of doing business. The net result of this action was merely to reapportion profits among parties to the channel with no change in the overall economics of the channel of distribution.

Fortunately, the next round of railroad rate negotiations did produce benefits for the channel of distribution. In this round, following the first by about ninety days, the B&LE Railroad announced a reduction of 59 cents per ton on coal moving in trainload minimum quantities of 7,000 tons. Further, this tariff change provided that the free time for the holding of cars at the port would be reduced from the previous five days to two days. It was estimated that each day of improved utilization for the typical railroad equipment used in this service saved approximately 5 cents per ton in cost. By reducing the free-time provision in the tariff, the railroad provided an incentive for improved coordination between the coal producers responsible for moving the coal to the port and the utility responsible for arranging the water leg of the move. Although other railroads opposed the move, they followed the B&LE's lead quickly in adjusting their rates once the latter organization declared its independent action. What amounted to non–zero-sum bargaining had taken place. Further, the B&LE railroad had begun to build a base of expert and referent power with the utility and coal producers that was to produce dividends later.

In the fall of 1963, several matters negotiated simultaneously provided the setting in which significant change in the organization of channel activities could take place. Given the assurance of Ontario Hydro support through the specification of routing by way of Conneaut, Ohio, B&LE executives announced that the railroad would invest from 4 to 5 million dollars in the development of a coal storage and rapid handling facility at Conneaut. It would feature expandable ground storage initially for 1 million tons and a mechanical reclaim device and loading machine which could pick up coal from the ground for subsequent loading onto lake boats at the rate of 4,500 tons per hour. At the same time, the railroad announced a set of rates for the winter storage of coal, 15 cents per ton, and a reduced rate for transferring the coal into lake boats.

At about the same time, Ontario Hydro negotiated a new lake-boat rate agreement under which it agreed to compensate boat operators for undue delays encountered at the Welland Canal which were beyond their control.

Both of these actions served further to absorb uncertainty in the channel. The lake-port storage facility created an opportunity to accumulate coal in quantities sufficient to guarantee the availability of boatload quantities on demand and to load it at rates more than twice as fast as those possible previously. Further, it made it much more feasible for railroad equipment to be turned around rapidly at the port, eliminating demurrage charges which could have resulted under the new rapid-turnaround tariffs. The lake-boat tariff eliminated a major source of operating risk for the boat operators.

The immediate result of efforts to absorb risk was a decision by Canadian Steamship Lines to place an order for a 25,000-ton self-unloading boat, to be delivered by the start of the shipping season in April 1965. Because of the fact that few extra crew members were required to operate a boat of twice the size used previously, the per-ton economics of water transportation were affected greatly by the decision to construct and operate the larger boat in the coal trades.

At this point, B&O and Pennsylvania Railroad executives were weighing the possibility of constructing improved port facilities for their roads. Possibly to discourage such moves, the B&LE next announced that it would offer a joint rate to both the B&O and the Pennsylvania for coal tendered to its interchange points by either railroad. Thus, the new port at Conneaut was made available potentially for use by all three railroads. More important, the operating economies at Conneaut possible through the consolidation of all of the Toronto tonnage which would be moving in the early years of the contract possibly could be preserved by such a move.

In April of 1964, Upper Lakes Shipping announced that it too had ordered a 25,000-ton self-unloader for use in the Ontario Hydro coal trade. This would accommodate the remainder of the traffic expected to develop during the first five years of the trade.

At the time that the Conneaut port facility did become operative at the outset of the winter storage season in December, 1964, the B&O Railroad did in fact begin making use of the B&LE's joint rate rather than construct its own port facility. Pennsylvania Railroad officials continued to consider the possibility of a new facility on their line. Thus, an organization with a small base of power at the outset of the interorganization negotiation, the Bessemer and Lake Erie Railroad Company, had captured for its line a large proportion of the volume moving on the Ontario Hydro coal trade.

It is interesting to consider the sequence of events summarized briefly above in another manner, that of lapsed time between significant action points.

About six months elapsed between the time of the first uncertainty-absorbing announcement of Ontario Hydro and any demonstration of non–zero-sum bargaining activity on the part of the railroad organizations. Once the process of creative problem solving started, however, significant decisions were made quickly. For example, the structure of the entire channel of distribution was altered within a period of about two weeks in the fall of 1963 when the utility committed itself to a risk-reducing boat tariff and the railroad announced its intent to construct the coal storage and handling facility.

For significant change to take place in the channel under consideration, a critical mass of announced actions or intent was necessary on the part of those possessing sufficient power to have legitimacy in the eyes of other channel members. Further, credibility had to be established by actions which reflected announced intent.

This behavior appears to be especially important in situations where favorable end results, expressed in terms of improved economics of a channel of distribution, result only from the interrelated decisions of executives in a number of independently managed organizations.

RESULTS

Any estimates of the results of the interorganization process described above must be extremely rough. However, it is possible to provide some idea of the significant changes which took place in cost-profit relationships as a result of the development of a new structure for the distribution of bituminous coal from West Virginia through Conneaut to the Toronto, Canada, facility in question.

As indicated in Table 10.2, the small quantity of coal moved through the Conneaut port facility in 1962, about 183,000 tons, probably produced a loss for the channel participants, if it is assumed that full costs are assessed to the channel. Information in Table 10.3 indicates that the railroad and boat operators were absorbing this loss for the channel. As a result of the restructuring of the channel, the railroads especially benefited by obtaining a year-round flow of traffic on a regular basis. Boat operators too were encouraged to construct boats of a size which greatly improved the operating economies of the service. To a lesser extent, coal producers obtained a new source of year-round business which allowed them to make better use of existing facilities.

Table 10.2. Net result of the initiation of a new method of coal distribution, in terms of interorganization costs, revenues, and profits or losses per ton

	1962	1966
Revenues	$8.81	$7.47
Costs		
Coal mining	$2.80	$2.77
Barge	.48	.48
River-to-rail transfer, Bessemer	.15	.15
Rail	3.22	1.18
Rail-to-lake transfer, Conneaut	.22	.238
Canadian import duty	.46	.46
Boat	1.75	.96
Total	$9.08	$6.238
Profits or (Losses)	($0.27)	$1.23

In terms of volume, an estimated 4,300,000 tons of coal was moved through Conneaut in 1966 compared with the 183,000 tons in 1962. The increased volume produced an estimated profit of $1.23 per ton to channel members as well as an average price reduction to Ontario Hydro of $1.34 per ton.

Summary

Basic structural changes in ways of doing business in a channel of distribution often result from a complex set of negotiations between participating channel organizations. The success of such negotiations, measured in terms

Table 10.3. Net result of the initiation of a new method of coal distribution, in terms of interorganization dollar revenues and profits

	Per Ton		Total Dollars*	
	1962	1966	1962	1966
Revenues			$1,613,000	$33,282,000
Profits (by activity center)				
Coal mining	$0.68	$0.575	$124,000	2,472,000
Barge	0.00	0.00	—	—
River-to-rail transfer (Bessemer)	0.01	0.01	2,000	43,000
Rail	(0.51)	0.25	(93,000)	1,074,000
Rail-to-lake transfer (Conneaut)	(0.02)	0.037	(4,000)	159,000
Boat operation	(0.43)	0.36	(89,000)	1,548,000
Utility	NA	1.34†	NA†	5,760,000†
Totals	($0.27)	$2.57	$(50,000)	$11,056,000

* Based on the movement to Ontario Hydro through Conneaut only of about 183,000 tons in 1962 and an estimated 4,300,000 tons in 1966.

† In this case, only the reduction in price per ton of coal bought, $1.34, is known. It is possible that some portion of this saving was passed on to consumers of electric power subsequent to this time.

of the favorable impact on the operating economics of the channel, depends to a great extent on the way in which power is used by those organizations that possess it. Ways in which power can be used to provide the setting for creative problem solving were presented in the form of a set of hypotheses.

An example of creative problem solving in a channel of distribution was described and analyzed briefly as a means of suggesting a type of research which will be useful if relationships between sources and creative uses of power in interorganization relationships are to be investigated further.

11

Joint Decision Technologies with a Production–Marketing Example

DAVID P. BARON

Introduction

The increased complexity of modern organizations and their environments has created an important class of problems involving interdependencies that span subsystem boundaries. The subsystems may be functional departments within a firm, subsidiaries of a corporation, or autonomous organizations. Because of the interdependence of the subsystems, separate or individual decision making will not result in optimal returns. A joint decision problem is said to exist if cooperative action by the subsystems will result in a total reward greater than that which would result from individual action by the subsystems. The concern in this paper is the alternative decision technologies that may be employed in situations necessitating joint action. A technology is a formal structure for arriving at a decision given some objective. The three technologies to be considered are centralization, decentralization, and decentralization by guidelines. This paper is intended to suggest certain aspects of joint decision technologies that may be important to organizational design. The analysis focuses on aspects of information, computation, and implementation of the three technologies. The technologies will be discussed both at an abstract level and in the context of a model of marketing-production decision making within a firm. A deterministic, single-period model is used, and a dynamic extension is suggested.

Joint Decision Technologies

Before joint decision making can take place, the decision makers must recognize the interdependencies that give rise to the joint decision problem and must agree to cooperate in an attempt to achieve the increased rewards that will result from cooperative action. Both the formation of the agreement or coalition and the stability of the coalition are important. Formation and

162

stability require an acceptable sharing of the increase in joint rewards resulting from cooperative action. Intraorganizational and interorganizational joint decision problems differ in this respect because a formal central authority with power over the subsystems exists in the former but not in the latter. Problems of formation, stability, and hence implementation are more difficult in interorganizational situations because of the absence of a formal authority. Since the concern here is with the technologies for joint decision making, coalition formation and stability will be presumed.

A formal statement of a joint decision problem involving two decision makers with respective decisions x_1 and x_2 is

$$\text{Maximize } \pi(x_1, x_2)$$
$$\underset{x_1, x_2}{}$$

$$\text{subject to } h_i(x_1, x_2) \le b_i; i = 1, ..., m. \tag{11.1}$$

If there are no interdependencies between x_1 and x_2 in equation (11.1), the optimization is equivalent to

$$\text{Maximize } \pi^1(x_1) \qquad\qquad \text{Maximize } \pi^2(x_2)$$
$$\underset{x_1}{} \qquad\qquad\qquad\qquad \underset{x_2}{}$$

$$\text{subject to } h_i^1(x_1) \le b_i^1 \qquad \text{subject to } h_i^2(x_2) \le b_i^2$$
$$(i = 1, ..., k), \qquad\qquad (i = k+1, ..., m), \tag{11.2}$$

where π^1, h_i^1 and π^2, h_i^2 are the respective objective functions and constraints for the individual decision makers. Since individual action results in optimal returns, joint decision making is not required. A joint decision problem is said to exist only when the optimal value of the objective function in (11.1) is greater than the sum of the optimal values in (11.2).

Centralization is represented formally by (11.1) and involves locating the decision making responsibility with some central authority.[1] The subsystems are then responsible for the implementation of the decisions. Some of the difficulties involved in centralization are: (1) A central authority may not exist and may be prohibited because of legal restrictions, for example; (2) the central authority may not have or the subsystems may not want to supply the information required for determination of the joint objective function or the constraints; (3) the centralized program in (1) may be too large or complex to solve with existing equipment;[2] (4) centralization may result in problems of implementation and control because of the exclusion of the subsystems from the decision making process.

An alternative to centralization is coherent decentralization of authority.

1 .The "central authority" may or may not be some existent entity and may or may not be "central." For example, decision makers 1 and 2 could be autonomous organizations that form a "committee" to act as a central authority. Alternatively, one decision maker may give the other authorization to make the decisions for both.

2. This difficulty originally motivated the study of decomposition of linear programs, reported in George B. Dantzig and P. Wolfe, "Decomposition Principle for Linear Programs," *Operations Research*, VIII (February 1960).

Coherent decentralization is defined by Charnes, Clower and Kortanek as the structuring of the program for each subsystem in such a manner that optimization of each subprogram will result in optimization of the entire program.[3] Letting π^a and π^b be the structured objective functions for the subprograms and $h_i^a(x_1) \leq b_i^a$, $h_i^b(x_2) \leq b_i^b$ the structured constraints, coherent decentralization requires that the optimal decisions for

Maximize $\pi^a(x_1)$ Maximize $\pi^b(x_2)$
$\quad x_1$ $\quad x_2$

subject to $h_i^a(x_1) \leq b_i^a$ subject to $h_i^b(x_2) \leq b_i^b$
$(i = 1, \ldots, I_1)$, $(i = 1, \ldots, I_2)$,   (11.3)

result in optimization of the centralized objective function in (11.1). Coherent decentralization is possible in most programs as demonstrated by Charnes, Fiacco and Littlechild.[4]

Coherent decentralization has been suggested as a means of alleviating certain behavioral limitations of centralization, such as program implementation, by letting each subsystem make its own decisions for the subprograms in (11.3). Decentralization may also have computational advantages in that solving a set of subprograms may require less effort than the solution of one large program. Also, decentralization often yields meaningful transfer prices that can be used for control purposes.

Decision making in a decentralized process may proceed in an iterative manner. The coordinator or central authority sends information required for the subprograms to the decision makers who optimize conditionally on that information. The decision makers then report certain information to the coordinator, who determines new information for the subprograms. This process continues until the optimum is achieved. One difficulty in such an iterative process is that the decision makers may attempt to "game" the system by reporting false information in the hope of obtaining a greater value of the objective function of their subprograms.

An important dimension for measuring the desirability of a decentralization process is the nature and amount of information transmitted in an iterative process. An extension of Hurwicz's[5] concept of informational decentralization can be used to consider the degree of decentralization[6] in terms of the

3. A. Charnes, R. W. Clower, and Kenneth O. Kortanek, "Effective Control through Coherent Decentralization with Preemptive Goals," *Econometrica*, XXXV (April 1967).

4. A. Charnes, A. W. Fiacco, and S. C. Littlechild, "Convex Approximants and Decentralization: A SUMT Approach," System Research Memorandum No. 165; Evanston, Ill.: Northwestern University.

5. Leonid Hurwicz, "On the Concept and Possibility of Informational Decentralization," *American Economic Review*, LIX (May, 1969), 513–24.

6. Charnes, Clower, and Kortanek, *op. cit.*, discuss a more limited concept which they use to classify the structure of coherency.

information requirements.[7] Informational decentralization requires that each subsystem be unaware of the structure of the programs of the other subsystems and that the dimension of the information equal the dimension of the commodity space for the program. Commodities in a joint decision problem refer to transfers within the system involving flows of materials and funds. In the model considered below, the production department transfers finished goods to the marketing department. A stronger requirement imposed here is that the central authority or coordinator does not know the structure of the subsystem programs but knows only what information it must transmit, what information it must receive, how to determine new information for the next iteration, and some stopping rule that indicates when optimality has been achieved. If in addition the information received by the coordinator is not the subsystem decisions but some aggregate information (e.g., output rather than factor employment), decentralization of authority is said to be informationally decentralized and efficient.

Decentralization by guidelines is a technology intended to give many of the benefits of coherent decentralization while avoiding the cost and time involved in an iterative process. Decentralization by guidelines involves a set of guidelines or policies imposed upon the individual decision makers by the central authority and can be thought of as an approximation to centralization and coherent decentralization. The guidelines may involve alterations in subsystem reward functions, restrictions on the feasible decision space, or both.[8] The individual decision makers make optimal decisions, subject to the guidelines, without iteration. Guidelines reduce the possibility of gaming the system and reduce the cost and time involved with information transmittal. The greatest weakness of the guideline approach is that it does not necessarily result in optimal decisions.[9] Another limitation is that the coordinator or central authority must have more information than that required for iterative decentralization in order to set "proper" guidelines. Informational decentralization and informational efficiency are thus not generally present in decentralization by guidelines.

Decentralization by guidelines may be the most prevalent form of decision

7. Informational aspects of decentralization have also been considered in W. J. Baumol and T. Fabian, "Decomposition, Pricing for Decentralization and External Economies," *Management Science,* XI (September 1964); A. Charnes and W. W. Cooper, *Management Models and Industrial Applications of Linear Programming* (Vols. I and II, New York: John Wiley and Sons, Inc., 1961); Charnes, Clower, and Kortanek, *op. cit.*; Charnes, Fiacco, and Littlechild, *op. cit.*; Jerome Hass, "Transfer Pricing in a Decentralized Firm," *Management Science,* XIV (February 1968); Jerome Hass, "Decomposition Processes and Their Use in Joint Decision Making," this volume, chap. 8; and Andrew Whinston, "Price Guides in Decentralized Organizations," *New Perspectives in Organization Research,* W. W. Cooper, H. J. Leavitt, and M. W. Shelling II (eds.), New York: John Wiley & Sons, Inc., 1964.

8. For linear models, guidelines are analogous to goals in goal programming. See Charnes and Cooper, *op. cit.*, and Charnes, Clower, and Kortanek, *op. cit.*

9. The model of production-marketing decision making will demonstrate that decentralization by guidelines may result in optimal decisions.

making in complex organizations. Guidelines take the form of budgetary restrictions, long- and short-range plans, performance criteria, policies relating to customers and employees, and standard operating procedures. While guidelines do not in general lead to optimal decisions, they may be the only practical alternative in many situations.

A Marketing–Production Model

The model represents joint decision making involving marketing and production departments within a single product firm. The marketing department is assumed to have two decision variables: price p and advertising expenditures A. The demand function for the firm is a function of both price and advertising or $x = g(p, A)$. Initially, the marketing department is constrained only by the nonnegativity of price and advertising. The production department has two decisions variables: standard hours employed w and overtime hours w_o. The production department is constrained by available standard hours w^*, by the requirement that overtime must not exceed some fraction k of the standard hours employed, and by nonnegativity of w and w_o. Since the analysis is short-run, capital will be assumed fixed. The firm's production function is thus $x = f(w, w_0)$. The firm is assumed to not produce more than the quantity demanded or $g(p, A) \geq f(w, w_o)$. This requirement is appropriate in a single-period, deterministic model because inventory considerations are not present. The firm does not stipulate the equality of demand and output because it may be desirable to leave some demand unsatisfied if output is restricted by the constraints on labor inputs. The next three subsections consider joint decision making which uses the technologies of centralization, coherent decentralization, and decentralization by guideline. An extension to a multiperiod model is then considered.

CENTRALIZATION

The centralization technology for joint decision making will be considered first in order to analyze the nature of the interdependencies between marketing and production. The firm is assumed to maximize profit

$$\pi = pf(w, w_o) - A - cw - c_o w_o \tag{11.4}$$

subject to $w^* - w \geq 0$, $g(p, A) - f(w, w_o) \geq 0$, $kw - w_o \geq 0$, $p, A, w, w_o \geq 0$,

where c and $c_o(c_o > c)$ are the wages for standard and overtime hours, respectively; $0 < k < 1$ represents the maximum proportion of overtime hours to standard hours; $\partial g/\partial p < 0$ and g is strictly concave in p and A; $f(w = 0, w_o = 0) = 0$, $f \geq 0$; f is strictly concave in w and w_o; and f and g have continuous first derivatives.

In (11.4) total revenue is pf rather than pg because the firm may choose not to satisfy demand when output is constrained by available labor hours.

The Lagrangian for the constrained maximization program is

$$L = pf(w, w_o) - A - cw - c_o w_o + \lambda_1(w^* - w) + \lambda_2(kw - w_o)$$
$$+ \lambda_3[g(p, A) - f(w, w_o)], \qquad (11.5)$$

where λ_i $(i = 1, 2, 3)$ are nonnegative multipliers. Necessary conditions for a maximum are[10]

$$\partial L/\partial p = f + \lambda_3 \, \partial g/\partial p \le 0 \quad \text{and} \quad p \, \partial L/\partial p = 0; \qquad (11.6)$$

$$\partial L/\partial A = -1 + \lambda_3 \, \partial g/\partial A \le 0 \quad \text{and} \quad A \, \partial L/\partial A = 0; \qquad (11.7)$$

$$\partial L/\partial w = p \, \partial f/\partial w - c - \lambda_1 + k\lambda_2 - \lambda_3 \, \partial f/\partial w \le 0 \quad \text{and} \quad w \, \partial L/\partial w = 0; \qquad (11.8)$$

$$\partial L/\partial w_o = p \, \partial f/\partial w_o - c_o - \lambda_2 - \lambda_3 \, \partial f/\partial w_o \le 0 \quad \text{and} \quad w_o \, \partial L/\partial w_o = 0; \qquad (11.9)$$

$$\partial L/\partial \lambda_1 = w^* - w \ge 0 \quad \text{and} \quad \lambda_1 \, \partial L/\partial \lambda_1 = 0; \qquad (11.10)$$

$$\partial L/\partial \lambda_2 = kw - w_o \ge 0 \quad \text{and} \quad \lambda_2 \partial L/\partial \lambda_2 = 0; \qquad (11.11)$$

$$\partial L/\partial \lambda_3 = g - f \ge 0 \quad \text{and} \quad \lambda_3 \partial L/\partial \lambda_3 = 0; \qquad (11.12)$$

$$p \ge 0, \; w \ge 0, \; w_o \ge 0, \; A \ge 0. \qquad (11.13)$$

For the firm to stay in business it is evident that $p > 0$ and $w > 0$ or else total revenue is zero. For $p > 0$ the equality holds in (11.6) or

$$f + \lambda_3 \, \partial g/\partial p = 0, \qquad (11.14)$$

which implies that since $f > 0$ and $\partial g/\partial p < 0$, $\lambda_3 > 0$. If $\lambda_3 > 0$, then from (11.12) $g - f = 0$, indicating that if the firm is in business it will always equate output and demand even in the presence of constraints on the decision variables.

The multiplier $\lambda_3 = \partial L/\partial g$ is the change in the Lagrangian, or the marginal contribution to profit, due to a change in demand. The necessary condition in (11.7) for the firm not to advertise is $\lambda_3 \, \partial g(p, A = 0)/\partial A < 1$. If the marginal contribution times the change in demand due to a dollar of advertising is less than the marginal cost of advertising, the firm does not advertise. The firm finds it desirable to advertise only when $\lambda_3 \, \partial g(p, A = 0)/\partial A > 1$, and it will increase A until equality holds. Since $\lambda_3 > 0$, $\partial g/\partial A > 0$ which implies that at the optimum an additional dollar of advertising will increase demand but the contribution of that dollar will not be greater than the cost of a dollar of advertising.

In order to analyze the necessary condition for employment of standard hours w, assume initially that $\lambda_2 = 0$ and $0 < w < w^*$. The condition in (11.8) can be rewritten as

$$\partial f/\partial w \, (p - \lambda_3) = c. \qquad (11.15)$$

---

10. See H. W. Kuhn and A. W. Tucker, "Non-linear Programming," *Proceedings of the 2nd Berkeley Symposium on Mathematics and Probability,* J. Neyman (ed.) (Berkeley: University of California Press, 1950).

Because $c>0$ and $p>\lambda_3$, marginal physical product $\partial f/\partial w$ is positive at the optimal employment of standard hours. Since λ_3 is marginal contribution, $(p-\lambda_3)$ is marginal cost which equals $c(\partial f/\partial w)^{-1}$ or the wage rate divided by marginal physical product. Alternatively, $\lambda_3 = p-c(\partial f/\partial w)^{-1}$, or marginal contribution equals price less marginal cost.

The firm will use overtime if from (11.9)

$$\frac{\partial f(\bar{w}, w_o = 0)}{\partial w_o}(p-\lambda_3)>c_o, \tag{11.16}$$

where $\bar{w}$ is the optimal employment of standard hours, or if the marginal physical product times marginal contribution is greater than marginal cost. Since $c_o>c$, it is not optimal to use overtime when standard hours are available.[11] If (11.16) is satisfied, then $\lambda_1>0$ and (11.15) is $(p-\lambda_3)\partial f/\partial w = c+\lambda_1$, indicating an increase in marginal cost. If $\partial f/\partial w = \partial f/\partial w_o$, $\lambda_1 = c_o-c$ which represents a jump in marginal cost when $\bar{w} = w^*$ and $\lambda_2 = 0$.

To further analyze the marketing decisions, solve (11.14), (11.15), and (11.7) for λ_3 and equate to obtain

$$\lambda_3 = -f\left(\frac{\partial g}{\partial p}\right)^{-1} = \left(\frac{\partial g}{\partial A}\right)^{-1} = p-c\left(\frac{\partial f}{\partial w}\right)^{-1} \tag{11.17}$$

Substituting g for f in the second expression and rearranging the second and fourth expressions gives

$$p\frac{\partial g}{\partial p}+g = c\left(\frac{\partial f}{\partial w}\right)^{-1}\frac{\partial g}{\partial p}. \tag{11.18}$$

The left-hand side of (11.18) is marginal revenue with respect to price which must be negative, since $\partial g/\partial p<0$ and marginal cost is positive. The firm thus prices such that an increase in price will decrease total revenue. Using the second and third expressions and rewriting gives

$$f = g = -\frac{(\partial g/\partial p)}{(\partial g/\partial A)}, \tag{11.19}$$

which indicates that demand equals the negative of the marginal rate of substitution between price and advertising. The firm thus determines the optimal marketing point on the optimal isoquant.

Joint decision making is required for the firm since both the objective function and the constraint $g-f \geq 0$ are not separable (in the sense of (11.2)) in the marketing and production variables. Because of the nonseparability the constraints on available standard and overtime hours affect the optimal levels of the marketing variables. For example, a tightening of the constraint $w^* - w \geq 0$ may reduce output, but because an increase in λ_1 affects λ_3 the

---

11. It is assumed that the marginal physical product of standard hours is greater than or equal to that of overtime hours.

firm will adjust price and advertising in order to reduce demand until it equals output.

Constraints on marketing variables also affect the optimal levels of the production variables. Two possible constraints on advertising are

$$A^* - A \geq 0, A^* \geq 0; \tag{11.20}$$

$$\alpha p f(w, w_o) - A \geq 0; 0 < \alpha < 1. \tag{11.21}$$

The first is a budget constraint, and the second requires advertising not to exceed a fraction α of revenue. When the advertising constraint tightens, the firm adjusts the optimal levels of price and employment.

The centralization technology requires that the marketing and production departments inform the central authority of the nature of the demand function, the production function, and the wage rates. The central authority optimizes the program in (11.4) and directs the departments to implement the optimal decisions. One difficulty in centralization is that the departments may report false information to the central authority in an attempt to obtain decisions that more nearly meet their individual goals. Also, it may be difficult to enforce the implementation of the decisions determined by the central authority because centralization does not necessarily motivate the departments to carry out the decisions. This is particularly true if the best interests of the departments do not coincide with the goals of the firm.

COHERENT DECENTRALIZATION

The coherent decentralization technology determines objective functions π^a and π^b and constraints $h_i^a \leq b_i^a$, $h_i^b \leq b_i^b$ such that the optimization of the individual subprograms in (11.3) yields the maximal profit for the firm. This can be accomplished by using the subprograms:

Marketing Department:

$$\text{Max } \pi^a = (p - \beta)g - A$$
$$\underset{p, A}{}$$

$$\text{s.t. } p, A \geq 0. \tag{11.22}$$

Production Department:

$$\text{Max } \pi^b = \beta f - cw - c_o w_o$$
$$\underset{w, w_o}{}$$

$$\text{s.t. } w^* - w \geq 0, kw - w_o \geq 0, w, w_o \geq 0. \tag{11.23}$$

If $\beta' = p' - \lambda'_3$, where the prime denotes optimal, the optimization of (11.22) and (11.23) yields the maximum profit for the firm. The transfer price β' is marginal cost given in (11.15). The marketing department is thus charged the marginal cost for each unit g it sells, and the production department is given revenue β for each unit produced.

The optimal value of β can be determined in either of two ways. If the central coordinator knows the demand and production functions and has the relevant cost information, the centralized program in (11.5) can be optimized to determine $\beta' = p' - \lambda'_3$. The transmission of information β' to the departments is then sufficient to ensure optimality of the subprograms without iteration. Such a procedure is not informationally decentralized nor informationally efficient, but it does eliminate the time and cost involved in iterating.

Alternatively, any value of β may be chosen by the central authority and given to the departments. The departments determine optimal decisions for that β, marketing reports demand g, and production reports output f to the coordinator. If $g > f$, the coordinator increases β in order to reduce demand and increase output; if $g < f$, he decreases β to increase demand and decrease output. Iterations continue until $g = f$ which indicates that optimal decisions have been reached. It is important to note that the coordinator need not have any specific knowledge of the subprograms in (11.22) and (11.23) but only need know the stopping condition $g = f$ and a rule for changing β.

One weakness of the iterative procedure is that the departments must be told when they have reached the optimal decision.[12] To somewhat temper this weakness, the departments can be told to terminate the iterations if their decisions are the same on two consecutive iterations. Since the optimal β is the same for both departments, each will determine new decisions for every change in β, and both will terminate on the same iteration. Also, during the computations there will be no idleness of one division while the other iterates.

The objective function for the firm in (11.5) is nonseparable with respect to the marketing and production variables because of the total revenue term pf. Price information alone in the form of β is sufficient for coherent decentralization, however, because demand and output are equated at the optimum. This coherent decentralization process is both informationally decentralized and efficient. In addition, each department is unaware of the structure of the other department's program, as is the coordinator. It is informationally decentralized because one transfer price is required and only one transfer, finished goods, is made. Even with the addition of the nonseparable advertising constraint in (11.21), the decentralization in (11.22) and (11.23) is informationally decentralized and efficient. The constraint $\alpha p f - A \geq 0$ is added to (11.22) and $\beta' = p' + \alpha p' \lambda'_4 - \lambda'_3$, where λ'_4 is the optimal value of the multiplier for the advertising constraint.

The term $\beta' f = \beta' g$ represents a transfer payment from the marketing department to the production department and can be the basis for profit-center control in the firm. Consequently, coherent decentralization in this case not only permits the decision makers to participate in the decision process but also provides a means for control and monitoring of their decisions.

12. Baumol and Fabian, op. cit., and Hass, op. cit.

DECENTRALIZATION BY GUIDELINES

Joint decision making by guidelines is an attempt to approximate coherent decentralization with the hope of avoiding certain of the limitations of that technology and arriving at a value of the objective function not "too far" from the optimal level. Two of the main objections to decentralization that may be alleviated by using guidelines are avoidance of gaming the system and a reduction in the time (iterations) and cost required to reach a decision. The primary advantage of decentralization by guidelines over centralization is that it avoids certain of the implementation problems associated with centralization in that the individual decision makers are able to make their own decisions (subject of course, to the guidelines).

Guidelines may affect the feasible decision regions, the objective functions, or both. For the production-marketing model, constraint guidelines might limit the feasible price to some range $p_L \leq p \leq p_U$ where p_L and p_U are lower and upper bounds. Guidelines for advertising might involve constraints such as the budgetary or percent sales constraints in (11.20) and (11.21). Guidelines for the production department might require output at a particular level or employment within some range. For example, the subprogram for the marketing department might be

$$\text{Max } \pi^a = pg - A$$
$$\substack{p,\, A}$$

$$\text{s.t. } 0 \leq p_L \leq p \leq p_U,\ A^* - A \geq 0,\ A \geq 0. \tag{11.24}$$

For the production department the subprogram might be

$$\text{Min } \pi^b = cw + c_o w_o$$
$$\substack{w,\, w_o}$$
$$\text{s.t. } f = g^*,\ w^* - w \geq 0,\ kw - w_o \geq 0,\ w,\, w_o \geq 0, \tag{11.25}$$

where g^* is the demand determined by the marketing department. One difficulty with the use of constraint guidelines is that the guidelines may be inconsistent and yield no feasible solution. The objective then might be to come as "close" (in terms of some metric) as possible to the guidelines in a manner analogous to goal programming.[13]

Such a guideline approach requires that the central authority have more information than that required for coherent decentralization using the iterative process but less than that required for centralization. What is required for decentralization by constraint guidelines is that the coordinator have some knowledge of the range of the optimal levels of the decision variables. While decentralization by constraint guidelines generally results in a lower value of the objective function, optimal decisions can be achieved. For example, if p_{opt} and A_{opt} are the optimal price and advertising expenditure, then a feasible range of $p_L \leq p \leq p_{\text{opt}}$ and a constraint $A_{\text{opt}} - A \geq 0$ will ensure that price

13. Charnes and Cooper *op. cit.* and Charnes, Clower, and Kortanek, *op. cit.*

and advertising are optimal and consequently that the production decisions are optimal. Informational efficiency is decreased, however, and the decentralization of authority is not informationally decentralized.

Guidelines which affect the objective function of the departments but do not affect the feasible decision region cannot lead to inconsistency of constraints. The natural reward function for marketing is

$$\pi^a = pg - A. \tag{11.26}$$

If the central authority charges a variable cost charge γ per unit of demand, the marketing department would

$$\text{Max } \pi^a = (p - \gamma)g - A$$
$$\underset{p, A}{\text{subject to }} p, A \geq 0. \tag{11.27}$$

Similarly, the production department could be given a "revenue" per unit η, and the decision problem would be

$$\text{Max } \pi^b = \eta f - cw - c_o w_o$$
$$\underset{w, w_o}{\text{subject to }} w^* - w \geq 0, \; kw - w_o \geq 0, \; w, w_o \geq 0. \tag{11.28}$$

Such decentralization is informationally decentralized and efficient. Clearly, if $\gamma = \eta = \beta'$, the objective function guidelines yield coherent decentralization, but if the coordinator does not have complete information or cannot use the iterative process, the optimal values of γ and η cannot be readily determined. The difficulty with such an approach is that demand and output will not be equated for $\gamma \neq \beta' \neq \eta$. In a more realistic model, inventory would alleviate this difficulty. Alternatively, constraint guidelines requiring output to equal the demand determined by marketing could be added. In (11.27) and (11.28) profit-center control is also possible as in coherent decentralization. Decentralization by guidelines in (11.27) and (11.28) is thus an approximation to coherent decentralization.

Guidelines may be determined in an adaptive manner. The guidelines can be based upon past performance and revised when new performance information is obtained. Such a method of determining guidelines would be more successful if the firm's environment is stable rather than rapidly changing.

A DYNAMIC EXTENSION OF COHERENT DECENTRALIZATION[14]

Research on decentralization has been concerned with static models, but in reality decision makers may plan over some time horizon. This section takes a first step toward generalizing the production-marketing model to dynamic

14. For a different approach see David P. Baron, "Dynamic Decentralization of Marketing, Finance and Production Decision," paper presented at the TIMS 10th American Meetings, Atlanta, October, 1969.

situations. Let I_0 be the inventory of the firm at the beginning and I_1 the inventory at the end of the current period. Let $k(I_1)$ be the strictly concave, optimal return for the remaining periods in the planning horizon. The optimal return is assumed to depend only on the ending inventory of the current period.[15] The function $k(I_1)$ may have been determined by dynamic programming. The firm seeks to maximize the return over the planning horizon or (omitting overtime possibilities without loss of generality)

$$\pi = px - cw - A - hI_1 + k(I_1)$$
$$\text{subject to } w^* - w \geq 0, g \geq x \geq 0, p, A, w, I_1 \geq 0, \qquad (11.29)$$

where x is the amount sold and h is the holding cost per unit of inventory carried into the next period. The material balance equation is

$$I_0 + f = x + I_1. \qquad (11.30)$$

Substituting for x from (11.30), the Lagrangian is

$$L = p(I_0 + f - I_1) - cw - A - hI_1 + k(I_1) + \lambda_1(w^* - w)$$
$$+ \lambda_3[g - (I_0 + f - I_1)] + \lambda_5(I_0 + f - I_1). \qquad (11.31)$$

The necessary conditions for optimality are

$$\partial L/\partial p = I_0 + f - I_1 + \lambda_3 \, \partial g/\partial p \leq 0, \quad \text{and} \quad p \, \partial L/\partial p = 0; \qquad (11.32)$$

$$\partial L/\partial A = -1 + \lambda_3 \, \partial g/\partial A \leq 0, \quad \text{and} \quad A \, \partial L/\partial A = 0; \qquad (11.33)$$

$$\partial L/\partial w = p \, \partial f/\partial w - c - \lambda_1 - \lambda_3 \, \partial f/\partial w + \lambda_5 \partial f/\partial w \leq 0, \quad \text{and}$$
$$w \, \partial L/\partial w = 0; \qquad (11.34)$$

$$\partial L/\partial I_1 = -p - h + \partial k(I_1)/\partial I_1 + \lambda_3 - \lambda_5 \leq 0, \quad \text{and} \quad I_1 \, \partial L/\partial I_1 = 0; \qquad (11.35)$$

$$w^* - w \geq 0; \lambda_1(w^* - w) = 0; g - (I_0 + f - I_1) \geq 0; \lambda_3[g - (I_0 + f - I_1)] = 0;$$
$$I_0 + f - I_1 \geq 0, \lambda_5(I_0 + f - I_1) = 0. \qquad (11.36)$$

As in the static model, $\lambda_3 > 0$ for the firm to remain in business so $x = g$ and $\lambda_5 = 0$. From (11.35) it is evident that inventory is carried into the next period if

$$\frac{\partial k(I_1 = 0)}{\partial I_1} > [(p - \lambda_3) + h]$$

or if the marginal return for future periods is greater than the marginal contribution in the current period plus the cost of holding that inventory during the current period.

---

15. More general assumptions regarding $k(\cdot)$ can also result in coherent decentralization that is informationally decentralized and efficient. For example, this will be true if $k(\cdot)$ is a function of any of the production variables, or if $k(\cdot) = k_1(\cdot) + k_2(\cdot)$, where k_1 is a function of the marketing variables and $k_2(\cdot)$ a function of the production variables. If $k(\cdot)$ is nonseparable and a function of both marketing and production variables, coherent decentralization is still possible, but it is not generally informationally decentralized nor efficient.

Coherent decentralization is possible with the following subprograms:
Marketing Department:

$$\text{Max } \pi^a = (p - \beta)g - A$$
$$\underset{p,\,A}{}$$
$$\text{subject to } p, A \geq 0. \tag{11.37}$$

Production Department:

$$\text{Max } \pi^b = \beta(I_0 + f - I_1) - cw - hI_1 + k(I_1)$$
$$w, I_1$$
$$\text{subject to } w^* - w \geq 0;\ w, I_1 \geq 0;\ I_0 + f - I_1 \geq 0. \tag{11.38}$$

Revenue for the marketing department is based upon demand g, while for production revenue is based upon sales ($I_0 + f - I_1 = x$). When $\beta' = p' - \lambda'_3$, the optimality conditions for (11.37) and (11.38) are identical to those for (11.31). If the iterative process for determining the optimal value of β is used, the stopping rule is $g = I_0 + f - I_1$. Such a decentralization procedure requires the central coordinator to have considerably more information than in a single-period model because the coordinator must determine the optimal return function $k(I_1)$ for the remaining periods in the planning horizon. The coordinator does not need to know the costs and relationships for the current period, however. Also, for the current period decentralization is informationally decentralized and efficient, since the production department reports ($I_0 + f - I_1$) and the marketing department reports g to the central coordinator.

Conclusions

Three general technologies for joint decision making — centralization, coherent decentralization, and decentralization by guidelines — have been considered at an abstract level and in the context of a marketing-production model. Centralization and coherent decentralization can be thought of as the ends of a spectrum with decentralization by guidelines covering the range between the two. As indicated by the production-marketing example, the limiting cases of decentralization by guidelines can be thought of as centralization and coherent decentralization. The principal factors involved in choosing between the technologies are (1) the behavioral implications for implementation and control of the decisions; (2) the informational requirements of the decision process; (3) the complexity, time, and cost of the iterations required to arrive at a decision; and (4) the value of the objective function obtained.

Coherent decentralization has advantages in implementation and control and in the informational requirements (except for the gaming possibilities). In models more general than the one presented here, informational decentralization and efficiency may be reduced, however. Coherent decentralization may not be practical in many cases because of the cost and time involved in iterations. Decentralization by guidelines avoids the problems involved with iterations but generally at a sacrifice in the value of the objective function. The advantage of centralization lies in arriving at the optimal solution without possibilities of gaming the system during iterations, although gaming may be present in the information acquisition process. Centralization has disadvantages with respect to implementation and control and possibly in the difficulty of solving the centralized program.

V

Decision Making at the Government–Business Interface

The cooperative–competitive nature of interorganizational decision making is perhaps most clearly seen when one organization is a private firm and the other is public, such as an arm of some level of government. Many interactions of this sort are business deals, the same as are made every day between two firms. But the strictly business view is too simplistic. There is too much involved to imply that the usual market-transaction models are applicable.

Traditional bargaining models may be of some help, especially in overcoming the lack of market prices. However, an employee may change employers while an organization is usually not free to change governments; i.e., nonparticipation is not an option. An employer may go out of business, but a government is not likely to take this course. Further, the literature of political science contains models of lobbying and other behavior which lead one to doubt that the simple bargaining models apply very well.

From the point of view of organizational theory, there may be reasons why special problems may arise. When a government and a business come together, the two organizations interact with varying degrees of ability to act on the matter at hand. More important, they may approach the interaction with widely different goal sets and time horizons. Thus, there are inherent organizational differences which must be overcome if effective decision making is to take place.

The literature of economics contains additional questions about the decision process when government makes a decision jointly with a private organization. Even with bargaining, the transaction may be made in a nonmarket situation which raises the question of allocation of resources without market guidance. The possibilities of externalities when one party to a decision is the government seem to be enhanced. Finally, instead of a question of moving to a Pareto-optimal solution, the decision may well involve a redistribution of income. For this, there are fewer economic guidelines than theological models.

Obviously, the variables influencing the decision to participate in joint decision making as discussed by Walton and Warren must be modified here. What is at issue is not the decision to interact, but the degree of cooperation. Warren's use of the concept of salience is also applicable here. For some firms, a government contract is all that keeps them in business, so they must interact. Whittaker places this fact in clear relief in his paper in Part VI. For other firms, their environment is dominated by a regulatory agency, as Evan illustrates in his paper. And as Perlmutter points out, the multinational firm has made a conscious decision to enter a country other than its home nation, so it must have some degree of awareness of the need to interact with the host government.

William Evan focuses on the behavioral aspects of the government-business problem. In his paper he uses a systems approach in developing his sociological perspective. The formal organization is viewed as an open social system. From this perspective, Evan derives the postulate that the system is embedded in an environment composed of other organizations and is surrounded by a complex of norms, values, and roles constituting the structure of the encompassing society. Thus, he justifies the use of sociological techniques to examine interorganizational relations.

Building upon role-theory concepts, especially the role-set and the focal position, several analogous concepts at the level of analysis of the organization are developed, such as the organization-set and the focal organization. The organization-set, in turn, is partitioned into an input and an output set. Structural dimensions of organization-sets are identified, namely, size, diversity, and network configuration. In addition, the concept of the role-set is joined with that of the boundary role in order to provide empirically observable linkages in interorganizational relations. Several dimensions of boundary personnel are singled out. With the aid of the various concepts introduced, hypotheses are formulated concerning organizational processes. In lieu of any available body of systematic data to test the organization-set model of interorganizational relations, several cases of relations between industrial organizations and government agencies are considered. The actions of the ICC, FDA, FTC, and SEC are examined as they interact with their constituent industries. Finally, some as yet unsolved problems of a methodological and pragmatic nature are discussed in the concluding section of the paper.

In moving from consideration of Evan's paper to Perlmutter's paper, it is interesting to compare the approach of the two authors. Evan sees the problem in sociological terms. As a result, while he is talking about behavior, his approach is structural in that he focuses on the system in which the problem will be solved. Perlmutter comes to the problem with the perspective of a social psychologist. Thus, his approach, while also behavioral, focuses on attitudes which are individual centered. The system, or structure, is simply the arena in which people behave in certain ways because of the attitudes they hold.

His paper focuses on business–government joint decision problems which are even more complex in that he deals with international firms which interact with more than one government. His work is based on a careful analysis of around 200 actual government–business bargaining or decision situations.

The outcome of the decision process was found to be influenced by the attitudes which governed the behavior of the boundary personnel in the decision process. Four general categories of people could become boundary personnel: (1) decision makers in the headquarters of the firm whereever located, (2) decision makers in the subsidiary of the firm engaged in a joint decision with some government, (3) government officials of the country where the firm's headquarters are located, and (4) government officials of the host country where the decision process is underway.

Perlmutter describes the attitudes found and shows how varying combinations of attitudes held by boundary personnel lead to different structures and outcomes of decision processes. The prospect for conflict reduction, in both the short and the long run, is discussed in light of the attitude configurations. Indeed, cooperation fostered by economic incentives may lead to changes in attitudes which lead in turn to reduced conflict. The special cases of underdeveloped countries and Communist countries are analyzed. The payoff matrix, in terms of the outcomes or states of conflict to be expected, is analyzed in some detail.

Edna Loehman and Andrew Whinston have contributed a paper which deals with the decision technology which may be employed to yield optimal decisions at the government-business interface. The situation they model deals with firms located along a stream, with the upstream firm discharging a pollutant and the downstream firm suffering the damage. Thus, the structure of the problem is determined by geography, and the organization-set well defined. Whether there is conflict to be reduced or whether it is a non–zero-sum game depends on the particular situation. The only assumption about behavior is the usual assumption of economic models of profit maximization, though the government agency may have other goals.

For the problem at hand, the attitudes of the participants, though not the same as those which Perlmutter discusses, color the situation considerably. Further, once a governmental agency enters, it is not possible to avoid the decision situation, regardless of the threat which the agency seems to pose. However, it is important to note that this may not be a government–business decision problem, but rather one to be solved by the businesses alone. It can be shown that some optimum level of water quality exists for both firms so the two firms could be merged, thereby forming a single decision unit to solve the problem. But outright purchase may be out of the question, and merger or other joint action could bring antitrust action. Thus, in practice, the situation is usually solved by a third party, and something like Evan's structural model of regulated industries emerges.

As Loehman and Whinston demonstrate, one way to achieve an optimum joint decision is for the government to impose by fiat a standard for water quality. The authors show that an optimum water quality standard exists. The government might determine the standard by anything from a careful cost–benefit analysis to a purely arbitrary statement. Of course, the likelihood of choosing the optimum standard is reduced if the choice is arbitrary. The polluting firm would be fined if the standard was not met, and the fine would be sufficiently high to assure compliance. A problem arises in that income may be redistributed by the levy and thus the Pareto-optimal position may change. While the authors do point out the need to resolve the problem when some of the variables change, there is once again a lack of means within the system to monitor or produce change in a systematic way rather than simply reacting to it.

The alternative to a fine would be to impose one of two types of taxes on the polluting firm. The authors show by their model that it is possible to devise a tax on each unit of output which will assure that the polluting firm will just meet the water standard established. This tax will be sensitive to the rate of water flow and will have to be recomputed frequently. Thus, there will be a substantial cost to the joint decision process.

The tax could be computed another way. It could be zero on all units of production up to the point where the clean water standards were no longer met. Then, the tax on each additional unit of production would be very large, perhaps confiscatory, assuring that the firms would jointly decide to meet the water quality standard.

The authors point out that while an optimal decision will result from the optimal tax, the problem of redistributing the tax revenues remains. The government could contribute the money to the injured party, use it to build a treatment plant, or use it to achieve some other social goal. The latter portion of the decision model is not covered by the optimization model employed in determining the optimal tax.

It is important to note at this point that such a precise optimal point may in practice be difficult to find. In some instances, the source of the imprecision will be the inability of the managers of the firm to perceive clearly the nature of the loss functions implied. Or, there may exist broad areas of indifference when, even if the losses occurring are accurately perceived, the management simply fails to react to them. Whatever the reason, strict convexity does not apply and the resulting weak-convexity model results in a range of outcomes.

The authors go on to consider a variety of complications and extensions of the model proposed. These extensions include the case of multiple firms, the treatment of discharge and stochastic stream flow.

12

An Organization-Set Model of
Interorganizational Relations

WILLIAM M. EVAN

The pattern of research in the field of organizational behavior over the past two decades has been the reverse of that in behavioristic psychology. Instead of looking at the stimulus and response, social scientists, with the exception of some economists,[1,2] have studied what behaviorists refer to as the "black box," that is, the internal structures and processes of an organization. This strategy is justified in view of the complexity and variability of formal organizations, but it is a highly restricted approach to the analysis of organizational phenomena which consist of many external as well as internal interactions. It has nevertheless provided an indispensable prologue to the analysis of the problems of interorganizational relations that some social scientists and practitioners are now attempting to study.[3]

1. Oliver E. Williamson, "A Dynamic Theory of Interfirm Behavior," *Quarterly Journal of Economics,* LXXIX (November 1965), 579–607.

2. Almarin Phillips, "A Theory of Interfirm Organization," *Quarterly Journal of Economics,* LXXIV (November 1960). 602–13.

3. Eugene Litwak with the collaboration of Jack Rothman, "Toward the Theory and Practice of Coordination between Formal Organizations," *Organizations and Clients,* William R. Rosengren and Mark Lefton (eds.) (Columbus, Ohio: Charles E. Merrill Publishing Co., 1970); William M. Evan, "A Systems Model of Organizational Climate," *Organizational Climate,* Rennato Tagiuri and George H. Litwin (eds.) (Boston: Division of Research, Harvard Business School, 1968); Roland L. Warren, "The Interorganizational Field as a Focus for Investigation," *Administrative Science Quarterly,* XII (December 1967), 396–419; Burton R. Clark, "Interorganizational Patterns in Education," *Administrative Science Quarterly,* X (November 1966), 224–37; Warren B. Brown, "Systems, Boundaries and Information Flow," *Journal of Academy of Management,* IX (December 1966), 318–27; William M. Evan, "The Organization Set: Toward a Theory of Interorganizational Relations," *Approaches to Organizational Design,* James D. Thompson (ed.) (Pittsburgh: University of Pittsburgh Press, 1966); F. E. Emery and E. L. Trist, "The Causal Texture of Organizational Environments," *Human Relations,* XVIII (1965), 21–31; and Eugene Litwak and Lydia F. Hylton, "Interorganizational Analysis: An Hypothesis on Coordination between Formal Organizations," *Administrative Science Quarterly,* VI (March 1962), 397–420.

The purpose of this paper is twofold: (*a*) to outline a model of interorganizational relations; and (*b*) to apply the model to some case materials on the interrelation of business and government organizations.

A Systems Model

For several decades social scientists engaged in research on organizations have conceived of formal organizations as social systems. However, they have rarely pursued the implication of this conceptualization, which is to acknowledge that a systems analysis is required to guide the conduct of research. A systems approach to organizational phenomena begins with the postulate that organizations are "open" systems which, of necessity, engage in various modes of exchange with their environment.[4]

In further postulating the interrelationships of components of a given system, a systems approach identifies input elements, process elements, output elements, and feedback effects. Moreover, it focuses attention on the interrelation of at least three levels of analysis: the subsystems of an organization, the organizational system in its entirety, and the suprasystem. Analyzing the subsystems of an organization entails a study of the interaction patterns of various subunits. Analyzing the organizational system includes an examination of (*a*) the cultural components, viz., its values and goals, (*b*) the structural components, which consist of the various relationships among the subunits, and (*c*) the technological components. The suprasystem level of analysis of an organization necessitates, at the very least, an inquiry into the network of interactions or linkages of a given organization with various organizations in its environment.[5]

The particular systems model of interorganizational relations explored here is one elsewhere referred to as an "organization-set" model.[6] The points of departure of this model are several concepts in role theory developed by Merton[7] and Gross *et al.*[8] Instead of selecting a status as the unit of analysis and charting the complex of role relationships in which the status occupant is involved, as Merton does in his analysis of role-sets, let us take as the unit of analysis an organization or a class of organizations and trace its interactions with the various organizations in its environment, viz., its "organization-set." Following Gross, Mason and McEachern's use of the term "focal position" in their analysis of roles,[9] the organization or class or organi-

4. Daniel Katz and Robert L. Kahn, *The Social Psychology of Organizations* (New York: John Wiley & Sons, Inc., 1966).

5. Evan, "A Systems Model of Organizational Climate," *op. cit.*

6. Evan, "The Organization-Set," *op. cit.*

7. R. K. Merton, *Social Theory and Social Structure* (rev. ed.; Glencoe, Ill.: The Free Press, 1957), 368–80.

8. N. Gross, W. S. Mason, and A. W. McEachern, *Explorations in Role Analysis: Studies of the School Superintendency Role* (New York: John Wiley & Sons, Inc., 1958), 48–74.

9. *Ibid.*, 50–56.

zations that is the point of reference is referred to as the "focal organization."[10] As in the case of role-set analysis, the focal organization interacts with a complement of organizations in its environment, i.e., its "organization-set." A systems analysis perspective, however, suggests that we partition the organization-set into an "input-organization-set" and an "output-organization-set." By an input-organization-set, as the term suggests, a complement of organizations is meant that provides resources to the focal organization. Similarly, by an output-organization-set is meant all organizations which receive the goods and/or services, including organizational decisions, generated by the focal organization. Furthermore, a systems analysis requires that we trace feedback effects from the output-organization-set to the focal organization and thence to the input-organization-set, or directly from the output- to the input-organization-set. These feedback effects can, of course, be positive or negative, as well as anticipated or unanticipated, but it is easier to postulate these effects than to operationalize them to facilitate empirical inquiry.

The four components of the model — focal organization, input-organization-set, output-organization-set, and feedback effects — may jointly be conceived as comprising an "interorganizational system." Figure 12.1 summarizes the structural elements of the model of interorganizational relations.

For purposes of illustration, if we take as a focal organization the Ford Motor Company, the input-organization-set may include a variety of suppliers of raw materials, trade unions, government agencies, courts, universities, research and development organizations, etc. The input resources are very heterogeneous, including human, material, financial, legal, etc. These inputs are transformed by the focal organization's social structure and technology into products and services that are exported to the members of the output-organization-set, which include principally automobile dealers. The output-organization-set may also include advertising agencies concerned with increasing the sale of its products, trade associations to which information is provided and which may undertake to influence the course of future legislation, community chest organizations to which financial contributions are made, etc. The success with which the focal organization, in this case the Ford Motor Company, manages its multifaceted relations with the members of its output-organization-set, in turn, has feedback effects on itself as well as on the input-organization-set which again triggers the cycle of interorganizational systemic relations.

If instead of the Ford Motor Company we take as a focal organization all four automobile manufacturers for the purpose of studying how they "negotiate their environment,"[11] the analysis would focus on the "interfirm

10. Evan, "The Organization-Set," *op. cit.*, 178.
11. Richard M. Cyert and James G. March, *A Behavioral Theory of the Firm* (Englewood Cliffs, N.J.: Prentice-Hall, Inc., 1963), 119–20.

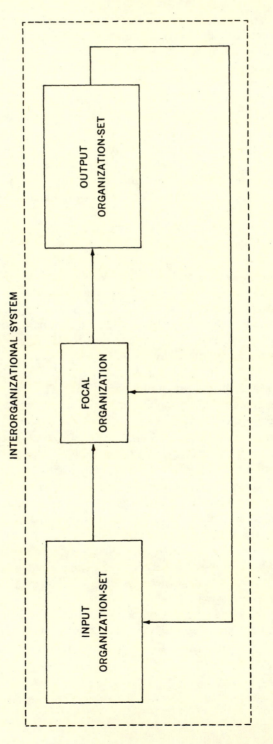

Figure 12.1. Some Elements of an Organization-Set Model of Interorganizational Relations

organization"[12] in a simple oligopolistic market and the members of the output-organization-set. Such questions as the following might be asked: How does the focal organization decide on output, prices, policies with respect to automobile dealers, strategy with respect to trade associations, legislatures, etc.? In other words, given the problem formulation, it may not be especially relevant to inquire about the interactions of the focal organization with members of its input-organization-set. If the analysis of this particular focal organization were extended to the members of the input-organization-set, two potential members would be the Department of Justice and the Federal Trade Commission, one or both of which might inquire into possible violations of antitrust law.

Dimensions of Organization-Sets

It should be clear from the context of this analysis that the phrase "member of an organization-set" refers to an organizational entity with which a focal organization interacts, not an individual member of one of the environing organizations. Apart from distinguishing between input- and output-organization-sets, various other dimensions of organization-sets need to be explored if we are to generate some propositions about interorganizational interactions. For present purposes three dimensions may be singled out that, prima facie, have significant consequences for the focal organization, viz., the size and diversity of the input- and output-organization-sets and the network configuration.[13] Size of set, of course, refers to the sheer number of input and output organizations with which the focal organization interacts; by diversity of the input- and output-organization-set is meant the number of organizations in the input- and output-sets differing in gross, manifest functions such as industrial organizations, courts, legislatures, community organizations, prisons, professional associations, hospitals, etc. The network configuration refers to the formal properties of interaction among the members of the input- and output-organization-sets. At least four types of interaction configurations, shown in Figure 12.2, that have loomed large in the experimental literature on group communication network experiments will be mentioned: (a) a dyad, in which focal organization A interacts with B, an individual organization or a class of organizations, in either the input- or output-set; (b) a wheel network, in which the focal organization interacts with more than one organization of a particular type but where there are no mutual interactions among the members of the set; (c) an all-channel network, in which all members of the set interact with each other and each interacts with the focal organization; and (d) a chain network, in which the members of a set are linked in series

12. Phillips, *op. cit.*
13. For other dimensions of organization-sets, see Evan, "The Organization-Set," *op. cit.*, 178–80.

with the focal organization which has only direct interaction with the first link, so to speak, in the chain.

Examples of network configurations from the real world might make these four types appear more plausible. An illustration of a dyadic relationship

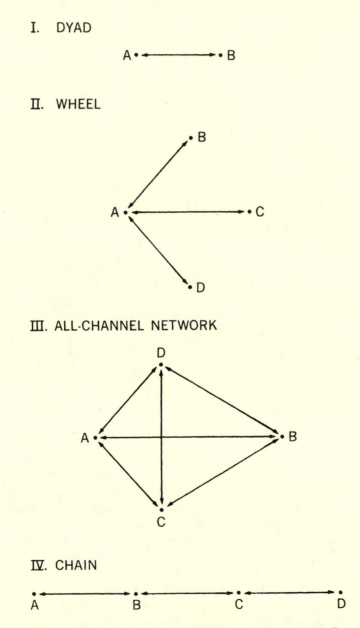

I.   DYAD

A ●◄————————► ● B

II. WHEEL

III. ALL-CHANNEL NETWORK

IV. CHAIN

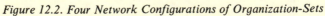

Figure 12.2. Four Network Configurations of Organization-Sets

is the interaction of a trade union with a business organization. A wheel-type configuration would describe the interaction of automobile manufacturers with 30,000–40,000 individual automobile dealers prior to the formation of the National Automobile Dealers Association.[14, 15] With the establishment of this association, the interaction configuration was transformed to a modified channel network, thus increasing the relative bargaining power of the automobile dealers. The chain configuration commonly occurs in manufacturing and in distribution processes, e.g., the sequential pattern of interaction of automobile suppliers, automobile manufacturers, and automobile dealers. Obviously these four network configurations are meant to be only illustrative of the formal properties of input- and output-organization-sets. Other types may be postulated, such as a limited-channel network with only one link to the focal organization. An exploration of the empirically observable formal properties of sets is but one of the many unsolved analytical problems of interorganizational relations.

An analysis of the formal properties of organization-sets points to an intriguing question concerning the relationship between these formal properties and modes of interaction between the focal organization and members of the input- and output-sets. Thus, for example, under what conditions in a dyadic linkage between the focal organization and a member of its input-set will we observe evidence of cooptation, bargaining, and amalgamation? In a wheel-type configuration, do we find the focal organization dominating the members of the set? If so, under what conditions will pressures emerge to transform the dominance-submission relationship into a bargaining relationship? In an all-channel network or a limited-channel network, would we find a tendency for a coalition to emerge, vis-à-vis the focal organization? And, finally, under what conditions would we find in a chain network both cooperation and conflict because of the pressures arising from the constrained pattern of interdependence? Inasmuch as the focal organization will often be involved in diverse network configurations with members of its input- and output-sets, the question arises as to the relative frequency of different modes of interaction, given the frequency of different network configurations.

Apart from having consequences for modes of interaction between the focal organization and members of its input- and output-sets, each of the formal properties probably has some reverberations in the internal structure and internal processes of the focal organization, such as in the formation of new subunits, the formation of new organizational norms, and the articulation of new goals. One hypothetical example will suffice: A state university

14. S. Macaulay, "Changing a Continuing Relationship between a Large Corporation and Those Who Deal with it: Automobile Manufacturers, Their Dealers and the Legal Systems" *Wisconsin Law Review* (Summer 1965) 483–575, and (Fall 1965) 740–858.

15. Henry Assael, "Constructive Role of Interorganizational Conflict," *Administrative Science Quarterly*, XIV (December 1969), 573–82.

whose principal source of financial support is derived from the state legislature is an illustration of a dyadic linkage between the focal organization and a member of the input-organization-set. In this familiar situation it is difficult to justify substantial budget increases over time for various departments and schools of a university unless new functional units are established. As a consequence, financial constraints encourage subunit differentiation in the focal organization; for example, sociology and anthropology are divided into separate departments; similarly, operations research and statistics, finance and economics, etc. By establishing new organizational subunits, which may increase student enrollment, it becomes easier to justify substantial increases in the budget of the total university as well as of its components.

Role-Sets of Boundary Personnel

An analysis of modes of interaction between the focal organization and members of its organization-sets, with the aid of the three dimensions discussed above, has one serious limitation. On this level of aggregation there is not only a danger of hypostatizing organizations, i.e., treating them as disembodied entities, but also of losing sight of the intervening mechanisms that contribute to the various modes of interaction. It is, therefore, essential to descend to a lower level of aggregation of social structure and examine the system linkages observable in the role-set relations of boundary personnel. It is through the behavior of incumbents of various statuses at the boundary of the focal organization, such as top executives, lawyers, purchasing agents, marketing specialists, personnel officers, etc., that various environmental interactions are mediated. Corresponding to the distinction between an input- and output-organization-set, let us distinguish between input and output boundary roles. As a result of the network of role-set relations of boundary personnel of the focal organization, with their role partners in organizations comprising the input- and output-organization-sets, various transactions occur involving the flows of people, information, capital, influence, goods and services, etc.

Apart from distinguishing between input and output boundary roles, other dimensions need to be identified if we are to generate new propositions about interorganizational relations. The most obvious way of distinguishing between the input and output boundary personnel of one organization compared with another is in sheer number, absolute or relative. One could devise various ratios of boundary to nonboundary personnel of the focal organization's input- and output-sets. A second dimension is the quality of formal education or the degree of expertise of boundary personnel. It makes a substantial difference whether the house counsel, for example, is a graduate of an Ivy League law school or a night law school.

A third dimension is position in the organizational hierarchy. Whether the boundary person is a shipping clerk, a director of research and development, or a top executive will obviously influence his relationship to his role partners in other organizations. Is the boundary person authorized to engage in organizational decision making, in pre–decision making activities, such as information gathering, or in non–decision making activities, viz., in the internal technical activities of the organization? Parsons's conceptualization of the three levels in the hierarchical structure of organizations is especially suggestive when applied to boundary roles.[16] At the "technical" level in an organization there may be a relatively large number of boundary roles as well as boundary personnel engaged in the primary operations of the organization, such as foreman, supervisors, purchasing agents, salesmen, clerks, etc. Individually they may have little impact on interorganizational relations, but collectively their effect may be of considerable significance. At the "managerial" level in an organization, the number of boundary roles is smaller but the salience of the manager's behavior, individually and collectively, for interorganizational relations is probably greater than the behavior of boundary personnel at the "technical" level. Managers also differ from the personnel at the "technical" level in that they are preoccupied with the tactics of organizational goal formation and decision making. At the "institutional" level in an organization's hierarchy, where the focus is on strategies of goal formation and decision making,[17] there are substantially fewer boundary roles and boundary personnel than at the managerial level, and the decision making power of such personnel — top executives, members of board of directors, or boards of trustees — in their role-set relations at the interface of the focal organization, is appreciably greater.

A fourth dimension of boundary roles is the normative-reference-group orientation of boundary personnel. Do they orient themselves to the norms and values of their own organization, i.e., of the focal organization, or to those of some other organization? Boundary personnel whose normative reference group is their own organization, i.e., the focal organization, will exhibit greater loyalty in their external role-set relations than those whose normative reference group is an outside organization. Organizations employing large numbers of professionals, such as universities, hospitals, research and development organizations, bear the brunt of a "cosmopolitan" normative-reference-group orientation which may result in behavior impeding organizational goal attainment, including the costs entailed in a high turnover rate.[18]

An analysis of the personnel occupying the boundary roles of a focal organization would be guided by the dimensions identified above as well as

16. Talcott Parsons, *Structure and Process in Modern Societies* (Glencoe, Ill.: The Free Press, 1960), 60–69.

17. Alfred D. Chandler, Jr., *Strategy and Structure* (Cambridge: M.I.T. Press, 1962), 13–21.

18. A. W. Gouldner, "Cosmopolitans and Locals: Toward an Analysis of Latent Social Roles, I, "*Administrative Science Quarterly*, II (December 1957), 281–306; and "Cosmopolitans and Locals: Toward an Analysis of Latent Social Roles, II, "*Administrative Science Quarterly*, II (March 1958), 444–80.

by the dimensions of its input- and output-organization-set. By way of illustrating the heuristic value of our model, we suggest the following hypotheses:

1. As the size of the input-organization-set increases, the number of input boundary personnel of the focal organization increases.

2. As the diversity or heterogeneity of the input-organization-set increases, the input boundary roles within the focal organization become increasingly differentiated.

3. A similar positive relationship is anticipated between the size and diversity of the output-organization-set and the number and role differentiation of output boundary personnel of the focal organization.

4. As the input- and output-organization-sets become more "turbulent"[19] and uncertain, the input and output boundary roles of the focal organization become more functionally differentiated.

5. If the boundary personnel of the focal organization are not commensurate in number, quality of education or expertise, position in the organizational hierarchy, and normative-reference-group orientation with the boundary personnel of organizations comprising the input- and output-organization-sets, the effectiveness of the focal organization will be impaired.

Implications of the Model for a Theory of Organizational Change

The organization-set model outlined above is incomplete in two respects: it needs to be further developed theoretically and also operationalized before it can be put to an empirical test. In its present state it is principally a systems approach to organizational structure and ecology. At first blush, the model may suggest a static approach to organizational phenomena. Upon closer examination, however, it should be evident that it has implications for a "positive" as well as a "normative" theory of organizational change. Insofar as it generates explanations for organizational stability as well as predictions concerning organizational change, it qualifies as a positive or a descriptive theory; and insofar as it suggests guidelines for effecting organizational change, it meets the test of a normative theory. In either case, the level of analysis of this model and its implications for a theory of organizational change are principally sociological in nature.

In attending to the internal structure of the focal organization, we are focusing on the structure of roles at the three levels in the hierarchy (technical, managerial, and institutional) and inquiring into (*a*) the characteristics of the boundary roles and boundary personnel in terms of the four dimensions identified above and (*b*) the functions performed by boundary personnel in

19. Emery and Trist, *op. cit.*

relation to their role partners located in organizations comprising the input- and output-organization-sets. In examining the input- and output-set of the focal organization, such structural dimensions as size, diversity, and network configuration are considered in order to ascertain the sources of support for, opposition to, and constraints on, the focal organization.

From the concepts and assumptions of our model it follows that the effectiveness of the focal organization, regardless of its objectives, is a function of (a) internal structure, particularly its role structure, and (b) the characteristics of its input- and output-sets. We may also infer the following proposition, of a positive nature, with respect to organizational change: as the input- or output-organization-set undergoes change as regards size, diversity, network configuration, etc., the internal structure and level of effectiveness of the focal organization will also change. The direction of causality is in principle reversible; i.e., if the focal organization's internal structure (role structure and/or technology) undergoes change, the input- and output-organization-sets will likewise change. Neither of these propositions, of course, precludes the occurrence of time lags before adaptive responses are triggered.[20] Organizational change, in the sense of growth, occurs when the feedback effects are positive but of a controlled nature. It goes without saying that uncontrolled positive feedback effects can destroy the focal organization; that excessive time lags before adaptive responses occur, especially on the part of boundary personnel at all three hierarchical levels of the focal organization, can undermine organizational effectiveness; and that if no "appreciable" structural change occurs, within a given time interval, in the focal organization as well as in its input- and output-sets, the focal organization can be characterized as "stable."

Our model also has implications for a normative theory of organizational change in that it in effect directs change agents — whether internal or external — to intervene at several crucial junctures in organizational functioning. First and foremost, in recruiting personnel for boundary roles at the three hierarchical levels, special attention is warranted in assessing their potential efficacy in interactions with role partners in organizations comprising the input- and output-sets. Second, to the extent that the socialization of new and old members involves formal and planned activities, particular attention should be devoted to the handling of role-set problems of boundary personnel. In all likelihood, the incidence of role conflicts and role ambiguities is higher among the occupants of boundary roles than nonboundary roles. Hence, if boundary personnel were helped, via specially designed training programs, to increase their level of competence in managing role-set conflicts and ambiguities, it could noticeably improve their role performance. Third, special efforts are necessary at each of the three levels in the hierarchy of the focal organization for redesigning the interaction network in the input- and

20. William M. Evan, "Organizational Lag," *Human Organization*, XXV (1966), 51–53.

output-organization-sets, with a view to increasing organizational effectiveness. Innovative ideas designed to alter the organizational ecology of the focal organization may include proposals for cooperation, cooptation, bargaining, coalition formation, consortia formation, amalgamation, etc.[21] with members of the input- and output-organization-sets.

Clearly, normative guidelines, such as these, that are derived from our model differ from, but are not incompatible with, the psychological and social-psychological propositions of theories of change emerging under the rubric of organization development.[22] Since few organizational field experiments have thus far been performed,[23] we are not yet in a position to assess the relative merits of different normative theories of organizational change. Much systematic field experimentation will be needed to test the validity of propositions derivable from our model as compared with those derivable from "organization development" models.

Analysis of Some Cases of Interorganizational Relations

In the absence of systematic empirical research designed to test some of the propositions derived from the organization-set model and to further develop it, an analysis of four cases of "organizational failure"[24] may be made with the aid of the model, which might prove instructive. The cases selected are four administrative agencies — SEC, ICC, FDA, and FTC — charged with regulating industry in order to protect the "public interest." Our purpose is confined to using our model in order to throw light on some of the well-known defects of these regulatory bodies. We shall not seek to develop remedies for the "organizational failures" which would, of course, far exceed the scope of this paper.

SECURITIES AND EXCHANGE COMMISSION

Charged with the mission of regulating the securities industry, the SEC's organizational defects, compared with those of the other three regulatory agencies, are least conspicuous.[25] If we consider the SEC as the focal organization for our analysis, as is shown in Figure 12.3, the members of its input-set, at a given point in time, may include: Congress which votes on its annual

21. Evan, "The Organization-Set," *op. cit.*, 183–84.

22. Richard Beckhard, *Organization Development: Strategies and Models* (Reading, Mass.: Addison-Wesley Publishing Co., 1969); Warren G. Bennis, *Organization Development: Its Nature, Origins, and Prospects* (Reading, Mass.: Addison-Wesley Publishing Co., 1969), and R. R. Blake and J. S. Mouton, *Building a Dynamic Corporation Through Grid Organization Development* (Reading, Mass.: Addison-Wesley Publishing Co., 1969).

23. William M. Evan, ed., *Organizational Experiments* (New York: Harper & Row, 1971).

24. Oliver E. Williamson, *The Vertical Integration of Production: Market Failure Considerations* (University of Pennsylvania, Fels Discussion Paper in Economics and Bureaucracy, #1 [mimeo], 1970).

25. For a report of an extensive inquiry into the SEC, see Report of the Special Study of Securities Markets of the Securities and Exchange Commission H.R. Doc. No. 95, 88th Cong., 1st sess., pts. 1–5 (Washington, D.C.: U.S. Government Printing Office, 1963).

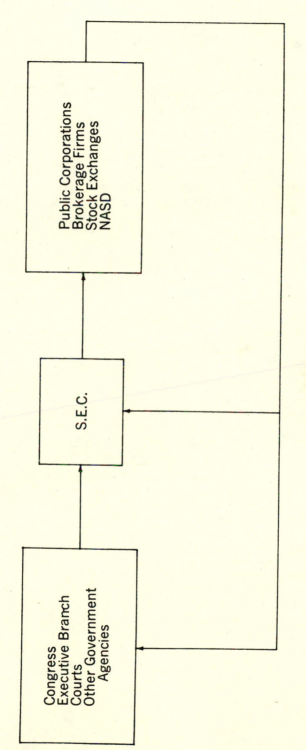

Figure 12.3. An Organization-Set Analysis of SEC

appropriations; the President who appoints the Commissioners with the confirmation of the Senate; the U.S. Court of Appeals and the Supreme Court which may accept some of the decisions of SEC for judicial review; and other government agencies with which it may interchange information, people, etc. The SEC's output-set is huge: it considers of many thousands of public corporations, whose securities come under the scrutiny of the SEC in accordance with the rules of disclosure promulgated in the Securities Exchange Act of 1934. In addition, the output-set includes many thousands of brokerage firms selling securities to the investing public. In view of the enormous size and diversity of the SEC's output-set, the Securities Exchange Act provides for self-regulatory bodies, namely, the fourteen stock exchanges which exercise control over its member firms and the National Association of Securities Dealers which regulates the conduct of corporations whose securities are sold in the over-the-counter market and not on the stock exchanges. Any corporation or brokerage firm that is found in violation of the Securities Exchange Act may be investigated by the SEC. Some of its decisions may in turn be appealed in the courts, whose decisions in turn affect the SEC's actions. And to the extent that the securities industry engages in direct lobbying with the SEC or in indirect lobbying via Congress to protect itself against the enforcement efforts of the SEC, it becomes a member of the SEC's input-set, thus illustrating a positive feedback effect.

Given the SEC's mandate to regulate the securities industry, the complexity of its output-set poses many problems. The SEC's efforts at regulating the stock exchanges apparently have been more effective than either the NASD's efforts in relation to its members or the efforts of the several stock exchanges in relation to their member brokerage firms. This difference in enforcement effectiveness of the law may be largely a function of the size of the output-sets of the different focal organizations. The SEC's regulatory problems in relation to the fourteen stock exchanges are considerably fewer than are those of the fourteen exchanges vis-à-vis their thousands of brokerage firms, or of the NASD's problems in relation to its thousands of member firms.

Another facet of the pattern of interorganizational relations that may significantly affect the enforcement efficiency of the SEC is the flow of personnel from the regulatory to the self-regulatory agencies and to the regulated organizations. Although the interchange of SEC boundary personnel with members of its output-set has not been documented in the 1963 study,[26] it is a plausible conjecture that the normative-reference-group orientation of many of its boundary personnel is the securities industry rather than the SEC. "If the reference group of a substantial proportion of the personnel of the SEC is the brokerage community rather than the regulatory bodies, then the SEC's enforcement efficiency of legal norms is likely to be impaired."[27]

26. *Ibid.*

INTERSTATE COMMERCE COMMISSION

The formal composition of the input-set of the ICC is similar to that of the SEC. As for the output-set, it is probably smaller in size, consisting of approximately 17,000 railway, trucking, shipping, and pipeline companies engaged in interstate commerce; it is probably more diverse; and, unlike the securities industry, there is no provision for self-regulatory agencies. The members of the output-set are organized into several influential trade and professional associations: American Association of Railroads, American Trucking Association, Water Carriers Association, Motor Carrier Lawyers Associations, and ICC Practitioners.[28] Conspicuously absent from the output-set is any organization representing consumer interests. Compared with the large number of company lawyers and lobbyists representing industry interests, the staff of the ICC numbering 1,906 in 1969 appears minuscule.

Further hampering effective regulation of the transportation industry is the ICC's extensive informal and formal contacts with industry. Notwithstanding the ICC Canons of Conduct prohibiting employees from engaging in any behavior which could affect their impartiality or adversely affect the confidence of the public in the integrity of the Commission, "industry regularly pays for luncheons, hotel rooms . . ., Commissioners and upper staff are commonly transported around at their convenience by corporate jets, private rail cars, and pleasure yachts."[29] There are recurrent conferences between the ICC and seventeen organized groups representing the interests of the transportation industry, none of which represents consumers or the "public interest."[30] Through these informal and formal contacts, members of the output-set become, in the course of time, members of the input-set, influencing information gathering as well as policy formulation.

Promoting this type of feedback effect is a frequent flow of ICC employees to industry. Of the last eleven Commissioners to leave the ICC, six became top executives of companies in the transportation industry, three became ICC practitioners, and two retired.[31]

> The manner in which agency officials lay down the regulatory cudgel and pick up the industrial cudgel by changing jobs indicates that they feel an identity between the two roles. . . . Aware that the door to industry employment is open, a Commissioner may keep it ajar by passive regulation that does not step on industry's toes.[32]

27. William M. Evan and Ezra G. Levin, "Status-Set and Role-Set Conflicts of the Stockbroker," *Social Forces*, VL (September 1966), 73–83.
28. Robert C. Fellmeth, *The Interstate Commerce Commission* (New York: Grossman Publishers, 1970).
29. *Ibid.,* 16, 19.
30. *Ibid.,* 346–49.
31. *Ibid.,* 20–21.
32. *Ibid.*

Under the circumstances, the boundary personnel of the focal organization and the members of the output-set tend to develop a common normative-reference-group orientation. This factor, together with the absence of an effective countervailing organization representing consumer interests in the input- and output-sets, encourages "passive regulation" of ICC statutes.

FOOD AND DRUG ADMINISTRATION

A regulatory agency which is a division of the Department of Health, Education, and Welfare, the FDA, as the name implies, is charged with regulating two mammoth industries. From its annual budget of over $70 million, $23 million is allocated to programs designed to protect the food supply and the balance to protect the supply of drugs and cosmetics.[33] To enforce the various FDA statutes, this agency employs approximately 5,000 people, including inspectors, scientists, other specialists, and technicians.

The members of FDA's input-set, apart from the administration of HEW, is similar to that of the SEC and the ICC. Its output-set, however, is larger and more diverse than that of the ICC. It consists of about 50,000 food manufacturing firms, over 1,000 pharmaceutical firms, several trade associations such as the Pharmaceutical Manufacturers Association and the Grocery Manufacturers of America, and professional associations, notably the American Medical Association. Once again we note the absence from the output-set of any organized consumer group to exercise countervailing power against other organized interest groups. The coalition between AMA and PMA has been especially effective in that it has succeeded in exercising direct influence on FDA decision making as well as indirect influence, through Congress, by means of political campaign contributions. Since the agency engages in very little original research on food and drugs, it has become increasingly dependent on the research of industry: "seventy percent of all food standards are initially proposed by the food industry. Nearly all research on food additive safety is conducted by industry, not FDA."[34] Thus, as in the case of the ICC, the "regulatees" have succeeded in the course of time in obtaining access to the input-set of the "regulators."

Further resembling the ICC, the boundary between the FDA and members of its output-set is indeed permeable. Between 1959 and 1963, of the 813 scientific, medical, and technical employees who left the FDA, 83 transferred to companies FDA regulates, 632 were not employed in regulated industries, and information on the remaining 98 was unavailable.[35] Dr. Louis Lasagne, a pharmacologist, commenting on the interchange of personnel noted that the

subtle and potentially most dangerous aspect of the FDA setup [is] the well traveled, two-way street between industry and Washington. Men from the drug

33. James S. Turner, *The Chemical Feast* (New York: Grossman Publishers, 1970), 2–3.
34. *Ibid.*, 103.
35. Morton Mintz, *The Therapeutic Nightmare* (Boston: Houghton Mifflin Co., 1965), 177.

industry have gone on to FDA jobs and — more important — FDA specialists have gone on to lucrative executive jobs in industry. . . . It does not seem desirable to have in decision-making positions, scientists who are consciously or unconsciously always contemplating the possibility that their futures may be determined by their rapport with industry.[36]

Mintz, who has conducted an extensive study of FDA's regulation of the drug industry, points to yet another pattern of interchange of boundary personnel between the FDA and members of its output-set:

There has also been a rather more complicated series of movements among the three power centers, the Food and Drug Administration, the Pharmaceutical Manufacturers Association and its member firms, and the American Medical Association — the three components of the FDA-PMA-AMA molecule.

The following are cases in point. Before becoming head of Winthrop Laboratories, Dr. Theodore G. Klumpp had in the late 1930's been chief medical officer of the Drug Division at FDA, subsequently leaving to take a post in the AMA. C. Joseph Stetler, who had been counsel of the AMA and head of its Socioeconomic Division, found it possible to improve his socioeconomic position by becoming executive vice president of the PMA. Dr. Jean K. Weston was with Parke, Davis from 1951 to 1962, when he left his position as head of the firm's Department of Clinical Investigation to join Burroughs Wellcome & Co. In June 1964, Dr. Weston became director of the AMA's Department of Drugs and secretary of its Council on Drugs.[37]

In view of these flows of personnel, it is not surprising that the FDA has opted for a program of "voluntary compliance" rather than a program of strict enforcement of the law:

Under the FDA's voluntary compliance program, thirty-four thousand representatives of five thousand regulated firms have attended 325 workshops and forty national conferences between 1965 and 1970. The purpose of this massive effort was to help give industry a better understanding of the law and FDA regulations, to make available to industry benefits of FDA research and methodology to help solve contamination and other problems, and to encourage maximum self-regulation.[38]

FEDERAL TRADE COMMISSION

As an independent regulatory agency, the FTC has a dual mission: to counteract monopoly practices (restraints of trade, unfair methods of competition, etc.) and consumer fraud ("deceptive acts and practices"). In 1969, its staff numbered 1,154, of whom 400 were lawyers and 200 were economists and other professionals; its budget was $16,900,000.[39] In investigating com-

36. *Ibid.*, 175–76.
37. *Ibid.*, 178.
38. Turner, *op. cit.*, 105.
39. Miles W. Kirkpatrick, *Report of the ABA Commission to Study the Federal Trade Commission* (1969), 8.

pliance with various statutes, FTC lawyers perform a crucial function as boundary personnel. Hence, the questions raised about the quality of the education and the expertise of FTC lawyers touch on an important facet of the enforcement effectiveness of this agency.

In recruiting attorneys, the FTC evidently attaches more significance to regional background, old school ties, and political endorsement of applicants than to their ability as reflected in grades or in the quality of the law schools they attended.[40] "As a result, graduates of prestigious law schools such as Harvard and Pennsylvania, which have very capable antitrust departments, have a poor chance of joining the FTC, compared with graduates of law schools like Kentucky and Tennessee."[41] The author's analysis of data[42] on graduates of classes 1967 and 1968 from five Northern law schools (N.Y.U., Georgetown, George Washington, St. John's, and Brooklyn) and three Southern law schools (Texas, Kentucky, and Tennessee) yielded the following result: 21 percent of applicants from Northern schools were offered appointments compared with 52 percent from Southern schools, a difference statistically significant at the .05 level. Moreover, according to a bureau chief of the FTC,

> He preferred to hire older men — who had been out in the world for ten years or so and had come to appreciate that they were not going to make much of a mark — because they tended to be loyal and remain with the FTC. He also reported that he gave less weight to law school grades than to other factors.[43]

To compound the problem of the expertise of its boundary personnel, the FTC lacks medical, scientific, and engineering specialists in its various bureaus that require them:

> The FTC's large staff of lawyers also poses a problem of quite a different order — legal competence alone is often not enough for the job. The Division of Food and Drug Advertising in the Bureau of Deceptive Practices is a good case in point. It is responsible, among other things, for detecting and preventing deception in drug-product advertising. Yet it is staffed entirely by lawyers and has no doctors or scientists to advise it. . . . It is then not surprising that the Division of Food and Drug Advertising operates at a low level of energy. . . . It also does nothing at all to enforce the agency's laws on therapeutic devices.[44]

The formal composition of the input-set of the FTC is the same as that of any other independent regulatory agency such as the SEC or the ICC. Its output-set, however, is both larger and more diverse, consisting of "hundreds of thousands of businesses".[45] Of this enormous population of firms engaged

40. E. F. Cox, R. C. Fellmeth, and J. E. Schulz, *Report on the Federal Trade Commission* (New York: Grove Press, 1969), 150.
41. *Ibid.*, 151.
42. *Ibid.*, 228.
43. Kirkpatrick, *op. cit.*, 33.
44. Cox, Fellmeth, and Schultz, *op. cit.*, 158.
45. *Ibid.*, 57.

in manufacturing and merchandising activities, the FTC tends to shy away from investigating the compliance of large companies and disproportionately devotes its resources to relatively small firms, especially in textiles and furs.[46] "The FTC's reluctance to go after big companies often lies in its fear of their vast and brilliant legal staffs — particularly if formal action is called for."[47]

Like the FDA, the FTC has deemphasized formal complaint procedures and concentrated on a program of voluntary compliance. Among the informal devices it employs, each of which lacks the force of law, are (1) industry guides, (2) advisory opinions, (3) trade regulation rules, and (4) assurances of voluntary compliance and informal corrective actions.[48]

An analysis of various measures of FTC enforcement activities over a ten-year period has prompted the recent ABA Commission to conclude:

> Through lack of effective direction, the FTC has failed to establish goals and priorities, to provide necessary guidance to its staff and to manage the flow of its work in an efficient and expeditious manner. All available statistical measures of FTC activity show a downward trend in virtually all categories of its activities in the face of a rising budget and increased staff. Moreover, present enforcement activity rests heavily on a voluntary compliance program devoid of effective surveillance or sanctions. It thus appears that both the volume and the force of FTC law enforcement have declined during this decade.[49]

This impressive record of "organizational failure" on the part of FTC and various other regulatory agencies has stimulated some observers to call for major organizational reforms and others to wonder whether these agencies ought not to be abolished in favor of "greater reliance on market processes and on the system of judicial rights and remedies."[50]

Conclusion

Analysis of case materials, however instructive or suggestive it may be, is no substitute for systematic empirical inquiry designed to test and further develop a model. Let us consider, by way of conclusion, some implications of the model for organizational research. This may be regarded as yet another test of the heuristic value of the model. Given a particular substantive problem, the research procedure might be as follows: (1) ascertain the boundary roles and the boundary personnel of the focal organization; (2) ascertain the role-set relations and the transactions mediated by the role-set interactions; (3) map the members of the input- and output-sets; (4) establish the formal properties and modes of interaction with the input- and output-sets,

46. Kirkpatrick, *op. cit.,* 27.
47. Cox, Fellmeth, and Schultz, *op. cit.,* 57.
48. Kirkpatrick, *op. cit.,* 8–9.
49. *Ibid.,* 1.
50. Richard A. Posner, "Separate Statement," in Miles W. Kirkpatrick, *Report of the ABA Commission to Study the Federal Trade Commission* (1969), 92–119.

especially as they have changed over at least two time intervals; (5) trace feedback effects from the output-organization-set to the focal organization and to the input-organization-set.

This is indeed a tall order; the methodological imponderables underlying each of these five research procedures should not be minimized. Nevertheless, if a full-scale empirical study of organization-sets were successfully carried out, it might do for interorganizational theory what Gross, Mason, and McEachern[51] and Kahn and his colleagues[52] have done for role theory. In addition, it would in all likelihood yield various "spin-offs" for a normative theory of organization-set change, namely, how to modify input- and output-set interactions in order to increase the effectiveness of the focal organization.

51. Gross, Mason, and McEachern, *op. cit.*
52. R. L. Kahn, *et. al., Organizational Stress: Studies in Role Conflict and Ambiguity* (New York: John Wiley & Sons, Inc., 1964).

13

Attitudinal Patterns in Joint Decision Making in Multinational Firm–Nation State Relationships

Introduction

Our concern here is to develop a model and testable hypotheses concerning the interorganizational decision making process involving the multinational firm and the nation state. This objective evolves from our work in a neonate field of the applied behavioral sciences we call social architecture, defined as the art, discipline, and science of building and/or renewing society's indispensable institutions which are both viable and legitimate from the view of the institution's various claimants.[1] The multinational corporation is a fascinating new setting for the testing of a theory of the social architecture of worldwide institutions.[2]

A number of observers have suggested that as multinational firms grow in size and influence, they will be perceived by the host nation states as threatening and intrusive.[3] Even though the managerial and technological capabilities of multinational firms might be attractive for host countries, the domain in which this kind of firm is growing could be construed as belonging to the "sovereign nation state." Since the decisions of a multinational corporation involve the host country's physical and human resources, political decision makers are aware of their dependence on a foreign firm's decision makers. The social architectural issue thus becomes: How do multinational firms legitimize the use of a nation state's resources? The joint decision making process between multinational firm and nation state is of central importance.

We feel that new concepts and data are needed if we are to improve our understanding of the conditions under which the activities of a multinational firm would be legitimized, by the leaders of countries interdependent with the

1. H. V. Perlmutter, *Towards a Theory and Practice of Social Architecture: The Building of Indispensable Institutions* (London: Tavistock No. 12, 1965).
2. *Ibid.*
3. R. Vernon, "Economic Sovereignty at Bay," *Foreign Affairs,* October 1968.

multinational firm. This would constitute an important opportunity to understand the process by which the multinational firm, as a new institution, is seen as necessary and benevolent versus dispensable and malevolent by the nation state with which it shares, uses, and transfers resources.

Thus we see the study of joint decision making between these two units or "systems" as one route to building a more solid basis for a theory and practice of social architecture. As a first step, we need a theory which accounts for the vicissitudes of relations between the multinational firm and the nation state in a precise way by focusing directly on the interactive processes between the two systems.

The Character and Significance of the Multinational Firm

Multinational firms are defined in various ways in the current literature.[4] For our purposes, however, we need a definition that allows the establishment of measurable attributes as a basis of theory building and hypothesis testing. We consider those firms who sell, provide services, and/or manufacture outside their home nation to be multinational to a degree. Export-oriented companies who have foreign sales agents are less multinational since their foreign direct investment is minimal.[5] The more multinational firm will own sales and distribution or productive facilities in different nation states simultaneously. This means that as multinational firms grow they gain access to resources which are considered parts of host sovereign nation states. In system terms, the multinational firm is a system whose subsystems exist in more than one nation-state system.

Three generalizations about multinational-firm–nation-state decision making, about which most observers agree, are:

First, the multinational firm is usually a complex, geographically decentralized organization whose activities require it to use and contribute resources to nation states. Coordination and joint decision making are indispensable for both firm and state.

Second, the multinational firm is not a transient phenomenon. Such firms have access to more capital, men, markets, and ideas than national firms; they are diversified as to risk in many economies, and they have an image of trust in many countries. No single nation state can destroy the firm, and, although there are certainly nationalizations on record, most political leaders in advanced countries try to avoid this extreme approach since the foreign assets of their own multinational firms would be vulnerable to the same tactics.

4. See, for example A. Robinson, *International Business Policy* (New York: Holt, Rinehart & Winston, Inc., 1964), and C. P. Kindleberger, *American Business Abroad* (New Haven: Yale University Press, 1969).

5. The multinational corporations operate in the following businesses: plantations or agribusiness, oil and extractive, manufacturing, and commercial or service industries including trade or banking. The overseas expansion of banks and advertising agencies are illustrative of the last two categories.

Third, the boundary relations between multinational firm and the nation state are complex. The worldwide firm, as a total system, has literally hundreds of environmental interfaces. Thus, the boundary relationships and boundary personnel between multinational firm and nation state are complex and must be defined in any given joint decision making situation.

Toward a Model of Multinational-Firm–Nation-State Relations

In developing a model for the joint decision making process between the multinational firm (MNF) and the nation state (NS) we need to identify the *outcomes or consequences* of joint decision making as a function of a variety of parameters, conditions, and alternatives.

A survey of some 200 episodes involving negotiations between multinational firms and nation states led us to consider these variables:

1. *The global industrial and political system* as a context in which the joint decision making process between multinational firm and nation state takes place.
2. *The interpolitical context* involving the two nations in which the firm acts in a given episode – for example, headquarters and subsidiary.
3. *The interests, values, and objectives* of each multinational firm and nation state.
4. *The relevant actors* especially those at the interfaces. These actors are called boundary personnel. Examples would be Head of State, Vice President Manufacturing.
5. *The personal attributes* of these actors, especially their *attitudinal orientations* – for example, their fear versus receptivity toward foreigners.
6. *The key decision areas or issues* on which joint decision making is focused—for example, whether a plant will be built in a given country.
7. *The central interactive* processes – for example, bargaining, rewarding, communicating.
8. *The joint decision making structure* and its *technology* – for example, face to face versus intermediaries.
9. *The alternatives* in the decision making process – for example, invest or not invest.
10. The various dimensions of *outcomes or consequences* – for example, a mutually satisfactory decision versus failure to agree.

Since a complete consideration of all parameters is beyond the scope of this chapter, we shall focus on a selected few in the hope that testable hypotheses related to the institution-building process will be forthcoming.

MNF-NS JOINT DECISION MAKING IN THE CONTEXT OF THE
GLOBAL INDUSTRIAL-POLITICAL SYSTEM

The global industrial system is a construct referring to the network of all industrial, technological, scientific, financial, and commercial activities on the planet Earth. This global system cuts across nation states with the help of intertwined multinational firms who, along with the economic industrial-commercial activities of the nation state, are conceived of as subsystems. It follows that the global industrial system is irreversibly linked with the global political system,[6] i.e., the network of alliances, blocs, and political communities of the planet Earth.

We hold that identifiable worldwide trends and emergent processes make a difference to MNF-NS joint decision making. Forces of internationalization, integration, and harmonization complement a given MNF-NS relation, whereas forces which reinforce national differences, fragment national interest, differentiate national objectives, and encourage countries to compete with other countries through nationalistic policies inhibit MNF-NS joint decision making. Joint decision making structures appear to be on the increase to the extent that:

1. There is under way a global concentration process wherein firms in Europe and Japan are combining to prevent takeover by the U.S. firms, and to build a base for worldwide expansion.

2. There is an increased cross-national tendency for firms to develop joint decision making structures in functional areas, limited mergers, or mergers of subsidiaries. Such agreements represent recognition of the need for greater interdependence within the global industrial system.

3. There has been a degree of intergovernmental cooperation in regional economic communities. The EEC in West Europe is the best-known example. These arrangements may facilitate joint decision making structures between nation states by helping both parties recognize limitations of any given nation's human and material resources.

4. There is evidence that more transideological enterprises will be established wherein market-oriented enterprises in the West develop joint decision making structures with state-owned enterprises in the command economies of the socialist states. Fiat, for example, is helping the USSR build an automobile factory.

5. Cooperative arrangements with governments of developing countries for the manufacture of components for worldwide export — as, for example, IBM's manufacture of card sorters for world markets from India — are on the increase. There are instances, especially in Latin America, where a multinational firm, in order to achieve economies of scale, will oblige two countries to cooperate by specializing production of components in each country.

6. H. Spiro, *World Politics: The Global System* (Homewood, Ill.: The Dorsey Press, 1966).

These trends illustrate the greater responsiveness of firms and countries to the increasing interdependence of the world's national economies, and contribute to the turbulent conditions of the existing global system.[7] Such turbulent conditions create a system-wide need to share parts, to develop overlapping functions, and to increase the need for joint decision making structures involving multinational firms and nation states.[8]

GLOBAL SYSTEM TRENDS INHIBITING MULTINATIONAL-FIRM–NATION-STATE JOINT DECISION MAKING

There is also evidence that there are global system trends and processes which may be acting to subvert or negate the effectiveness of the joint decision making structures in the global industrial political system.

1. There are rising new nationalisms wherein joint decision making structures with foreign groups are suspect and disloyal.[9]

2. There is evidence of continuing distrust for joint ventures between multinational firms and local interests. Conflicts result because the multinational firm often takes a worldwide view of resource allocation whereas local interests take a chauvinistic national view.

3. Multinational firms tend to be based in the rich countries, and often inhirit the ill feelings harbored by the poor countries for their rich and powerful neighbors. The "have-not" nations resent the affluence of the "have" nations, and political leaders in the poorer countries are apt to feel exploited in that the payoffs received by their nation are inequitable in contrast to the payoffs to the rich nations.[10]

4. East-West ventures are presently considered precarious at best to the degree that ideological factors continue to be important.[11]

5. In general, governments have resisted supernational structures for political and other reasons. An institution which has the power to allocate the resources of a nation, without the nation's being consulted or allowed to veto, is considered very threatening.

6. There is some feeling that many multinational firms constitute a threat to the autonomy of the nation state. European countries, for example, object to the possibility that decisions concerning local employment may be made in Detroit.[12]

7. There is increasing resentment concerning attempts by governments

7. F. E. Emery, "The Next Thirty Years: Concepts, Methods and Anticipations," *Human Relations,* XX (1967).

8. F. E. Emery and E. L. Trist, "The Causal Texture of Organizational Environments," *Human Relations,* XVIII (August 1965), 21–32.

9. K. Deutch, *The Analysis of International Relations* (Englewood Cliffs, N.J.: Prentice-Hall, Inc., 1968); L. I. Snyder, *The New Nationalism* (Ithaca, N.Y.: Cornell University Press, 1968).

10. J. E. Hartshorn, *Oil Companies and Governments* (London: Farber, 1962).

11. Howard V. Perlmutter, "Emerging East-West Ventures: The Transideological Enterprise," *Columbia Journal of World Business* (September–October 1969).

12. J. J. Servan-Schreiber, *The American Challenge* (New York: Avon Books, 1969).

to apply their laws in other countries. For example, the attempt by the U.S. Department of Justice to apply antitrust laws to French subsidiaries of U.S. companies who the French claim are subject only to French law.[13]

SOCIAL, CULTURAL, AND POLITICAL CONTEXT BETWEEN TWO NATIONS

In any interaction between members of a multinational firm and a nation state, we would expect social, political, and cultural factors to play some part. Consider the political leaders of a lesser developed country (LDC) in Latin America trying to decide whether a U.S. based multinational firm would be allowed to buy a local firm to be managed by U.S. expatriates. If sensitivity to U.S. influence is great, if differences in concepts of bargaining and agreement exist, if dependence on foreign aid is found necessary or distasteful, we could expect that joint decision making between Latin political leaders and U.S. executives would not be based primarily on "rational" considerations.

These factors, coupled with problems of cross-cultural communication, make the barriers to joint decision making seem formidable.

ORGANIZATIONAL OBJECTIVES, INTERESTS, VALUES, AND DISTINCTIVE COMPETENCE

The firm's executives are usually concerned with profitability, earnings per share, market penetration, and volume of sales. The nation state's leaders are more apt to be concerned with their sovereignty, welfare of citizens, and military capability, as well as the economic viability of the state.[14]

THE RELEVANT ACTORS AND THEIR ATTRIBUTES

The actors include primary actors and key decision makers from the firm and the state, as well as the secondary actors who try to influence the primary actors. A political leader, for example, might respond to a local business interest, the secondary actor, by favoring restriction of investment by foreign-owned firms, despite the possibility that foreign firms may increase the quality of goods and services at a lower price.

Personal attributes thus include the orientations of the actors as determined by their attitudes, values, motivations, expectations toward foreign and domestic firms and political leaders, and respective polity stands and actions. Other relevant attributes include amount of experience overseas, knowledge of foreign languages, and communications skills.

---

13. J. J. A. Ellis, "The Legal Aspects of European Direct Investment in the United States," in *The Multinational Corporation in the World Economy,* S. E. Rolfe and W. Damm (eds.) (New York: Frederick A. Praeger, Inc., 1970).

14. B. Gross, *The State of the Nation: Social Systems Accounting* (London: Tavistock, 1966).

THE KEY DECISION AREAS AND ISSUES, AND ALTERNATIVES

Key decision areas and issues in joint decision making would be very likely to center on the following issues: distribution of equity and dividends, investment of profits, capital investments, product mix, quality standards, percentage of host country suppliers, local borrowing, and location of R&D.[15]

THE CENTRAL INTERACTIVE PROCESSES AND STRUCTURES

The central interactive processes in joint decision making would include correlation of objectives, allocation of tasks and resources, distribution of authority and responsibility, application of values and standards, determination of payoffs, communication and information sharing, and selection of decision makers.[16]

ALTERNATIVES, OUTCOMES, AND CONSEQUENCES

Conceptually it is important to consider which alternative outcomes are open to the joint decision makers. These are choices, such as nationalization, raising tariffs, and increasing the rate of host-country nationals in key positions. Outcomes are the choices or alternatives taken, and result from a bargaining process around a finite set of issues. Outcomes have consequences associated with them which may result in quasi-balanced and quasi-unbalanced states for the system.

A quasi-balanced state is a social perceptual, cognitive, affective condition where two sets of actors hold constant, and the tendency to change is low at a given time. A quasi-unbalanced state is a condition where dissonance, incongruence, and disharmony exist between the orientations of two sets of actors, and where the tendency to change attributes is high.[17] In our view, a quasi-balanced state occurs when two parties *reinforce* each other's attitude or belief systems, and quasi-unbalanced states occur wherein the joint decision makers act and express opinions which *do not support the other's* attitudes and belief systems.

We also distinguish viability versus legitimacy outcomes for the multinational firm. Viability outcomes are those outcomes which relate directly to each organization's effectiveness measured by return on invested capital, market share for the firm, and balance of payments for the country. Legitimacy outcomes are those outcomes wherein the key actors have the pre-

15. F. Sagasti, "A Proposed Framework for the Study of Conflict Between the Multinational Firm and the Nation State" (Philadelphia: Division for Research and Development of Worldwide Institutions, Wharton School, University of Pennsylvania, 1970).

16. Emery and Trist, *op. cit.*

17. F. Heider, *The Psychology of Interpersonal Relations* (New York: John Wiley & Sons, Inc., 1958); M. Horowitz, J. Lyons, and H. V. Perlmutter, "Induction of Forces in Discussion Groups," *Human Relations,* IV (1951), 57–76; M. Jahoda, and N. Warren, *Attitudes* (New York: Penguin Books, 1966).

vailing sentiment that the other party has a right to autonomous existence and is necessary as an organization (something like it would be needed if it did not exist), and wherein each party is interdependent with the other.

As a new institution, the multinational firm can be seen as involved in a legitimizing process, with principal claimants being the home government and the host government. Studies concerning the conditions under which host political leaders feel that the multinational firm has a right to autonomous existence and is indispensable, shed light on the legitimizing process. Joint decision making may or may not contribute to legitimacy and/or viability outcomes.

Finally, we could consider value payoff-outcomes, the qualitative and quantitive consequences of joint decision making which imply both immediate and potential delivery of values, or a better sharing of values between the two parties. In this respect both multinational firm and nation state are conceived of as multiutility or multivalue delivery systems.

In choosing among the many parameters of this model we sought first, to develop hypotheses which were particularly promising for testing, and second, to apply existing theory and related observations on the joint decision making process involving nation states and multinational firms.

Thus, we shall now limit our study to the relations between the attitudinal orientations of the key decision makers of the multinational firm in home country (HQ) and the subsidiaries (SUB), and of the key decision makers of the home nation state (HM) and the host nation state (HS). We will focus on attitudes directed toward selected issues to determine which attitudinal orientations lead to quasi-balanced states (QBS) or quasi-unbalanced states (QUBS). These patterns would be the basis for formulating hypotheses to test how patterns of attitudinal orientations, and of quasi-balanced and quasi–unbalanced states, may be related to perceived legitimacy.

Attitudinal Orientation of Decision Makers as a Critical Concept

In our discussions with political and business leaders of their joint decision making process, we have come to regard the attitudinal *orientation* of the key decision makers as critical determinants of the "atmosphere" surrounding the process and its outcomes.

We observed negotiations and analyzed written and verbal reports of negotiations between executives of a multinational firm and representatives of given nation "states." These observations indicated that one of the parties to the joint decision making process frequently developed dispositions to interpret the other's behavior in rather consistent ways. These predispositions seem consistent with the concept of "attitudes," defined as "more or less enduring sets, orientations towards objects or situations."[18] Thus while

18. *Ibid.*

situational constraints might alter the overt expression of hostile behavior in the joint decision making process, some light could be shed upon the patterns of collaboration between firm and state by systematically examining the attitudes of the key actors on both sides.

The Function and Functioning of Activities

Social psychological research on interpersonal behavior indicates that the attitudes of one person are experienced as crucial by the other person. A decision maker can easily recall the facial expression, the warmth, the posture, the premises on which his protagonist's arguments were based, how the other talked, why he did not or did listen, etc. Both parties built up an impression of the attitude of the other.

From the view of the holder, Katz feels that attitudes serve multiple functions.[19]

First, attitudes have instrumental, adjustive, utilitarian functions. To feel that foreigners are untrustworthy may make it easier to "adapt" to a foreign way of life, usually by living in an enclave abroad.

Second, attitudes have an ego-defensive function; they protect the individual's self-esteem by defending him from acknowledging deficiencies in his own compatriots.

Third, attitudes have a social function; they permit persons to fit into a social group, to experience belonging by talking about the inferior aspects of foreigners.

Fourth, attitudes have a value-expressive function; they allow the person to express the values he cherishes: nationalism, loyalty to in group.

Fifth, attitudes have a knowledge function; they help the individual build a world which is consistent, stable, and predictable.

Finally, attitudes have a function in action. They support moving toward or against other persons or groups, and enable *policy stands* defining a particular kind of collective action.[20]

Attitudes toward Foreigners as a Central Focus

In the context of joint decision making between delegates of multinational firms and nation states, the more relevant categories of attitudes are those which involve foreigners and compatriots. The members of the parent firm are usually of the same nationality as key decision makers of the home country of the firm, and of a different nationality from key decision makers

19. D. Katz, "The Functional Approach to the Study of Attitudes." *Public Opinion Quarterly,* XXIV (1960), 163–204.

20. J. S. Bruner, M. B. Smith, and R. W. White, *Opinions and Personality* (New York: John Wiley & Sons, Inc., 1956).

of the host nation state. Usually, but not always, the key decision makers of a subsidiary include some of local nationality.

The choice of the dimension attitudes toward foreigners as a strategic concept has ample empirical support. We have evidence that the process of viewing foreigners versus compatriots necessarily involves a greater tendency to stereotype foreigners.[21] This relates to the syndrome of ethnocentrism, first cited by William Graham Sumner in his *Folkways of 1906,* as a condition for group formation and intergroup competition. Campbell and Levine summarized some of the facets of ethnocentrism as shown in Table 13.1.[22]

Attitudes and Behaviors toward In Group	*Attitudes and Behaviors toward Out Group*
1. See selves as virtuous and superior.	1. See out group as contemptible, morally inferior.
2. See own standards of value as universal, intrinsically true.	2. See out group as having inferior standards.
3. See own customs as original—centrally human.	3. See out group as less than human.
4. See selves as strong.	4. See out group as weak.
5. Cooperative relations between in-group members.	5. Absence of cooperative relations with out-group members.
6. Obedience to in-group authorities.	6. Absence of obedience to out group's authorities.
7. Willingness to fight and die for in group.	7. Blaming of out group for in-group trouble.
	8. Disgust and fear of out groups.

In addition to ethnocentrism, four other syndromes will be discussed. First, we distinguish xenophobia, which is usually linked with ethnocentrism, but which focuses on the fears of foreign influence and anxieties about foreign intrusiveness. The second syndrome we call "xenophilic," wherein there is an admiration for the foreign way, a rejection of the domestic. Xenophilic attitudes are the reverse of ethnocentric attitudes: the domestic is seen as weak, and the foreign as strong. The complexity of xenophilic attitude comes from the inner conflict it produces. The self-identity with regard to the home nation is negative; thus the ambivalence is characteristic of this attitude. The third attitude, polycentrism, involves reaction to the emotional undercurrents of xenophobic ethnocentrism; for here persons and groups avoid foreigners, seeing them as different and difficult. Polycentrism no doubt has elements of a ethnocentrism as well, but it is a passive, withdrawing approach

21. J. Bruner and H. V. Perlmutter, "Compatriot and Foreigner: A Study of Impression Formation in Three Countries," *Journal of Abnormalities and Social Psychology,* LV (September 1957); and H. C. Kelman, ed., *International Behavior: A Social Psychological Analysis* (SPSSI; New York: Holt, Rinehart & Winston, Inc., 1965).
22. D. T. Campbell and R. A. Levine, "Propositions about Ethnocentrism from Social Science Theories" (Evanston, Ill.: Northwestern University, March 1965) (Mimeographed).

to the foreigners. Fourth, there are geometric attitudes wherein foreigners and compatriots are treated with minimal stereotypy.[23]

Attitudinal Orientation of Key Decision Makers

We distinguish three attitudinal orientations of a HQ decision maker in the multinational firm as ethnocentric, polycentric, and geocentric, and three attitudinal orientations of subsidiary decision makers as xenophilic, xenophobic, and geocentric. We further distinguish respectively similar kinds of attitudinal orientations for political leaders of the home and host countries. (Other variations are omitted from this discussion, although in reality they are mixed.)

Attitudinal Patterns in Joint Decision Making

Consider now a joint decision making situation wherein the key decision makers of a multinational firm and a nation state meet to discuss one or more central issues (e.g., whether a plant will be built in a given host country , or what products will be manufactured, to what standards, etc.). We seek to answer the questions given:

1. The variety of attitudes (which will be expressed symbolically): (*a*) ethnocentric (ETH), (*b*) polycentric (POLY), (*c*) xenophilic (XPL), (*d*) xenophobic (XPB), and (*e*) geocentric (GEO).
2. The following classes of decision makers: (*a*) home country (HM) and parent company headquarters (HQ) of the multinational firm (MNF), (*b*) host country (HS) and subsidiary (SUB), (*c*) between the multinational firm (MNF) and the home (HM) and host countries (HS).
3. Under what conditions should we expect (*a*) quasi-balanced states (QBS), or (*b*) quasi-unbalanced states (QUBS)?
4. As a further application of this analysis, we can ask: What kinds of joint decision making situation and attitudinal patterns ought we find between the developing countries and the Communist countries?

On the basis of our analysis of anecdotal accounts of multinational-firm–nation-state relations, we hypothesize that some attitudinal configurations of HS, HM, and SUB are more likely to lead to a measurable condition defined as QUBS. While obviously the next step is to devise rigorous tests of these hypotheses, the pragmatic consideration in getting decision makers in firms and nations to submit to this kind of systematic and controlled observation has yet to be worked out.

Thus we now focus on these questions by presenting in a concise way our analyses of multinational-firms–nation-state "episodes."

23. Bruner and Perlmutter, *op. cit.*

Within-Firm Attitudinal Patterns that Lead to Quasi-balanced
States (QBS)

THE ETHNOCENTRIC-XENOPHILIC PATTERN

The ethnocentric-xenophilic pattern is expressed as:

$$HQ_{ETH} + SUB_{XPL} \rightarrow UBS.$$

The ethnocentric approach of HQ executives is likely to be accommodated to by SUB executives who comply with HQ directives.

The attitudes, values, and sentiments of the senior executives of the multinational firm in the ethnocentric pattern are, crudely put, that "We (people of X company of one nationality) are superior, have superior resources, facilities and competences than you (people) of Y country. We will be willing to build facilities in your country if you accept our inherent superiority and our methods and conditions for doing the job." Despite the attempts at presenting a friendly facade, the message described above is conveyed to the subsidiary executives. A not untypical reaction of local executives is to accept that the need for the capital and skills and know-how is great. Local leaders adopt what could be called the xenophilic attitude: "We accept your superiority and our inferiority. We shall do as you say and shall comply with the methods and standards you apply to us."[24] Conflict may be contained in the joint decision making process — usually by the presence of a few loyal executives who are strongly and positively oriented toward the nationals of the headquarters of the multinational firm.

THE POLYCENTRIC XENOPHOBIC PATTERNS

The polycentric xenophobic pattern is expressed as

$$HQ_{POLY} + SUB_{XPB} \rightarrow QBS.$$

The headquarters gives in to the SUB's demands usually on the basis that the local conditions are unique, and local executives resist their advice.

There are firms which, by experience or by inclination of a top executive in power, begin with the assumption that the locals are so culturally different that they are too difficult to understand. The belief here is that local people know what is best for them, and that the part of the firm which is located in the host country should be as "local in identity" as possible. In the joint decision process, local executives try to demonstrate how their needs are really different, that local culture and standards make their country quite unique.

24. Howard V. Perlmutter, "Correlates of Two Types of Xenophilic Orientation," *Journal of Abnormal Social Psychology*, LII (1956), 130–35.

THE GEOCENTRIC-GEOCENTRIC PATTERN

The Geocentric-Geocentric pattern is expressed as

$$HQ_{GEO} + SUB_{GEO} \rightarrow QBS.$$

Both HQ and SUB collaborate to work out each other's roles in the world-wide enterprise.

This pattern is just beginning to emerge. It is one where senior executives do not assume the inherent superiority of either home-office or foreign executives, but seek to find the best men, regardless of nationality, to solve the company's problems everywhere in the world. The senior executives attempt to create a subsidiary which is not only a good citizen of the host state but also a leading exporter from this nation state in the international community, with optimal benefits for the nation state as regards balance of payments, taxes, new skills and knowledge, improvement of the country's capabilities. The response of subsidiary executives is to recognize that this kind of enterprise is necessary and a positive step toward improving the host country's position in the world economy. Such a firm provides needed men and information for the nation state. The internationalistic tendencies of subexecutives are thus aroused and supported.

In the joint decision making process the HQ and SUB executives experience membership in a worldwide team concerned with solving the problems of relating the subsidiary as part-system to the total worldwide system.

INTRAFIRM PATTERN INSTABILITY OVER TIME

Over longer periods we regard the first two patterns as relatively unstable. A balanced state is not necessarily durable over longer periods of time; rather, it is one in which, at a given time, the strains toward change are not great. We could further distinguish quasi-balanced states which are relatively unstable as QBS (I) from quasi-balanced states which are relatively stable, OBS (D). The destructive conflict latent in the ethnocentric-xenophilic relation is perhaps most obvious. Subsidiary executives eventually come to resent the "arbitrary and egocentric" practices of the multinational firm. The implication that local executives will never be trusted sufficiently to be capable of assuming senior posts in the company, even in the local country, becomes harder to bear, over time. The distrust becomes greater among nationals of the host country as regards the impact on the economic contribution of the firm to the country. An important result is perhaps the negative effect on the self-confidence of SUB executives, employees of the host country. The need to shed off these "superiors" becomes greater and greater, often leading to the polycentric-xenophobic pattern.

But the polycentric-xenophobic pattern is also unstable in the long run since it becomes clear to senior executives and subsidiary executives that the xenophobic attitudes of subexecutives cuts them off from ideas, innovations, and trends in other countries. While their locally manufactured goods may be protected by tariffs, they soon find that they are unable to export into the world economy. Besides, a costly duplication of facilities and errors is more than likely due to the lack of communication between subsidiaries of the same company in different countries. Host-country political leaders may come to doubt whether such an enterprise is really efficient in the long run and may conclude that it might just as well be locally owned.

The geocentric-geocentric pattern we hypothesize is the one least likely to generate distrust and destructive conflict between the HQ executives of the multinational firm and subsidiary executives. But once in evidence, it may in a given firm not endure over time — if the HQ feels that only HQ nationals are needed again in key posts of it, HS may become more xenophobic.

WITHIN-FIRM ATTITUDINAL PATTERNS THAT LEAD TO QUASI-UNBALANCED STATES (QUBS)

Other attitudinal combinations seem to imply a more conflictive and perhaps less constructive problem solving, in joint decision making.

The ethnocentric-xenophobic pattern is expressed as

$$HQ_{ETH} + SUB_{XPB} \rightarrow QUBS.$$

HQ and the SUB are in strong conflict as to whose standards will prevail. HQ finds its recommendations are not carried out, and SUB object to the useless character of advice from headquarters. Subsidiary executives in joint decision making may find it necessary to maintain a facade of compliance if HQ puts pressure on them, but SUB feels strongly that they need the responsibility and authority to decide what should be done, especially since SUB executives are "the company" in the country. SUB executives say they must maintain a local identity and thus see attempts to influence by HQ executives as identity denial processes.[25]

Since $HQ_{ETH} + SUB_{XPB}$ is an unbalanced state, we hypothesize that there should be immediate pressures in the joint decision making structures to seek a QBS, as, for example,

Alternative A: $HQ_{ETH} + SUB_{XPL} \rightarrow QBS.$

Headquarters may, for example, decide to remove the uncooperative host-country manager and replace him with a home-country national who sees things their way and appears more trustworthy.

Alternative B: $HQ_{POLY} + SUB_{XPB}.$

HQ may decide that it is too risky to force compliance from or to remove the host-country manager. HQ may "withdraw psychologically," saying, "We will let SUB do it their way. But if they fail, we can move in. However, they will not get much help from HQ now."

25. Walton, this volume.

Our own observations indicate that for alternative A to result ($HQ_{ETH} + SUB_{XPL}$), SUB tends to be located in a small market, where political considerations are not important, and where present profitability is low. For alternative B to result, SUB manager must be "a strong personality" with considerable political influence in a politically risky country, and preferably operating in a large market which is currently quite profitable.

Attitudinal Patterns in MNF-NS Relationships: Quasi-balanced States

WITHIN THE HOME NATION

1. One possibility is quasi-balanced states involving the home-country decision makers holding ethnocentric attitudes along with the key decision makers of the MNF: $HM_{ETH} + HQ_{ETH} \rightarrow QBS$.

There are many U.S. multinational firms who would still consider that they should further U.S. foreign interests – and if these interests are ethnocentric, we assume that joint decision making between HM + HQ should be relatively easy as regards, for example, rapid repatriation of profits.

2. Another possibility would be $HM_{POLY} + HQ_{POLY} \rightarrow QBS$.

This is illustrated by Swiss multinational companies who are frequently anxious to fit with their country's neutralist orientation. Agreement would be relatively easily established to maintain a "low Swiss profile" in given countries, and not to embarrass foreign posture.

3. A third possibility is $HM_{GEO} + HQ_{GEO} \rightarrow QBS$.

This occurs, for example, when in a regional community's political leaders and executives agree to selective industrialization, recognizing that areas of competence exist in other countries and thus increasing opportunities for reciprocal trade.

WITHIN THE HOST COUNTRY

1. Between the key decision makers and the subsidiary decision makers in the host country we find $HS_{XPL} + SUB_{XPL} \rightarrow QBS$.

Both political leaders of the host country and subsidiary managers would find that they see the foreigner's methods, procedures, men and/or technology as superior and usually try to agree on how to bring more of these resources into the host country. The political leaders might generally seek help in getting foreign capital and managers through the subexecutive's contact in HQ.

2. Similarly, in $HS_{XPB} + SUB_{XPB} \rightarrow QBS$, the subsidiary decision maker identifies with the host country political leaders' fears of foreign intrusion.

Such joint decision making outcomes as agreement to sell stock locally, to engage in joint ventures with the government, and to use only local executives might result. Subsidiary managers would work with political leaders of the host country by insisting that infant industries be protected and tariffs be increased to protect the host country from "foreign competition" and propensities to dump products at low prices, thus providing evidence that the subsidiary wants to affirm the identity of the host nation state.

3. Finally, $HS_{GEO} + SUB_{GEO} \rightarrow QBS$, where, for example, host political leaders can agree to avoid import substitution by building costly, small, inefficient plants, and instead seek to develop a worldwide capability in one product line.

Attitudinal Patterns in MNFS-NS Relationships:
Quasi-unbalanced states within the Home Nation

The quasi-unbalanced states in joint decision making which arise in the home country include $HM_{ETH} + HQ_{POLY} \rightarrow QUBS$.

The home country attempts to get a polycentric headquarters to carry out its foreign policy, as, for example, when the U.S. Congress or an official of the U.S. State Department urges a U.S. owned multinational firm to threaten the host country with punitive acts from the United States if the host country nationalizes a U.S. subsidiary of this company. The headquarters executive may prefer not to stir up resentment toward the firm's subsidiaries in host countries around the world. Thus, some U.S. firms in Latin America urged the U.S. Congress not to apply the Hickenlooper amendment to countries who nationalize U.S. subsidiaries.

How is this QUBS resolved? One alternative is $HM_{POLY} + HQ_{POLY}$, wherein the home country is convinced that it should not attempt to dominate overseas.

Another recourse is for the home government to get the HQ to comply; thus, $HM_{ETH} + HQ_{ETH}$ is an alternative wherein the headquarters agrees to behave like a loyal home country institution and "teach a lesson" to foreign countries.

Attitudinal Patterns between MNF and Host and Home
Nation States

QUASI-UNBALANCED STATES

In joint decision making involving the $MNF + HS + HM + SUB$, a QBS in the home country is usually not a guarantee for a QBS in the host country. For example, $(HM_{ETH} + HQ_{ETH}) + (HS_{XPB} + SUB_{XPB})$ is likely to produce a QUBS during the joint decision making process. The coalition of home-country factions will be pitted against the host-country factions. This is a dangerous polarization, not especially conducive to problem solving.

Nor does a QBS between headquarters and subsidiary guarantee collaborative problem solving during the joint decision making process. We observe $HM_{ETH} + (HQ_{GEO} + SUB_{GEO}) + HS_{XPB} \rightarrow QUBS$. That is to say, if there is ethnocentrism to a high degree in the home country, and xenophobia to a high degree in the host country, then the attempt by the MNF to work out intraorganizational decision making in a geocentric way may be seen as threatening by both host and home political decision makers. The reward/payoffs for the worldwide firm may be more obvious to the political leaders than the payoffs to each nation state. Besides, the geocentric $(HQ + SUB)$ may seem to deny the identity needs of home or host countries when the ethnocentrism and xenophobia, respectively, are strongly held attitudes.

How could collaborative, identity-reinforcing problem solving take place? Suppose HQ_{GEO} changed to HQ_{ETH}. Then $HM_{ETH} + HQ_{ETH} \rightarrow QBS$. But then $(HM_{ETH} + HQ_{ETH}) + (SUB_{GEO}) + HS_{XPB} \rightarrow QUBS$.

Or suppose SUB_{GEO} changed its orientation to SUB_{XPB}. Then $HS_{XPB} + SUB_{XPB} \rightarrow QBS$. But then $(HM_{ETH} + HQ_{GEO}) + (HS_{XPB} + SUB_{XPB}) \rightarrow QUBS$.

Thus these two routes both tend toward quasi-unbalanced states.

QUASI-BALANCED STATES

Under what conditions, then, would we hypothesize a QBS to occur? There are three possible cases for QBS to occur in a quadripartite situation.

Case 1 — In this situation, problem solving proceeds under geocentric conditions. If HM_{ETH} changed to HM_{GEO} and HS_{XPB} changed to HS_{GEO}, the result would be $HM_{GEO} + HQ_{GEO} + HS_{GEO} + SUB_{GEO} \rightarrow QBS$.

While this hypothesis needs testing, the possibility that $HM_{GEO} + HS_{GEO}$ will occur is not great at the present time, except in such regional communities as EEC.

Case 2 — $(HM_{ETH} + HQ_{ETH}) + (HS_{XPL} + SUB_{XPL}) \rightarrow QBS(I)$.

In this situation, headquarters, reinforced by the political leaders of the home country, are able to get the host country to accept its status of dependence on the home country of the multinational firm. The SUB then finds few difficulties in carrying out parent-company policy. But long-term instability should be expected as HS political leaders begin to resent dependency.

Case 3 — $(HM_{POLY} + HQ_{POLY}) + (HS_{XPB} + SUB_{XPB}) \rightarrow QBS(I)$.

Here political leaders of the home country are aware of the sensitivities of the host country shortly after independence of the host country from HM. HM colludes with HQ to help the local political leaders express their nationalist sentiments, however irrational they may appear — e.g., by giving aid to build costly, small-scale steel plants, automobile factories, etc. In the longer term, the host country will find itself with noncompetitive, obsolescent plants; hence, we would hypothesize that this solution is unstable over the long term.

Some Further Applications

It is also possible to study the variety of attitudinal patterns that might occur between home and host nations in developing countries and in command (Communist) economies.

ATTITUDINAL DETERMINANTS OF JOINT DECISION MAKING IN
THE DEVELOPING COUNTRIES

From the point of view of the multinational firm, lesser developed countries (locations) are frequently riskier, smaller, less profitable markets, handicapped by a shortage of management talent. On the other hand, lesser developed countries (LDC's) like India and Zambia are very sensitive to foreign control and "neocolonial influences." The developing countries of Latin America are especially sensitive to the power of the Yankee dollar to influence their country's fate.

In general, it is difficult for the people of poorer countries to feel that a level of cooperativeness and parity in power is possible in joint decision making structures with representatives of such foreign countries. The demand for about $600 million of reparations for past injustices by the Peruvian government from a Canadian subsidiary of the Standard Oil Company in Peru has caused a crisis. As we indicated above, decision makers in Peru felt that the stronger firms either exploit them or manipulate them. Even apparent acts of "helping" are distrusted. A powerful international firm may say it wants to do good for an LDC by assembling automobiles in Brazil or building a chemical plant in Argentina, but the belief will reign among the host leadership that very high profits are the main motive. Host political leaders doubt that joint payoffs between MNF's and host nation states are desired by HQ executives. Political and economic actors from the host country believe that the rich international firm, who has more to begin with, will gain an unfair part of the rewards of joint ventures. In short, what may be "fair" for one may be perceived as exploitation by the other; the perceptions are thus not mutual enough. In the states where the post-colonial nationalist sentiments are strongest, there is great difficulty in allowing mutual perceptions of a state of mutual satisfaction and interdependence by political leaders and their constituents. This is probably the situation today in Peru and in those countries where, in the view of the host country, which feels that its growth is primary, the multinational corporation is getting too high a return on its invested capital. So $MNF_{ETH} + HS_{XPB} \rightarrow QUBS$.

The perceived power imbalance of MNF over LDC is a serious problem, especially where the home nation, as for American owned companies, supports its firms with punitive legislation for foreign countries who expropriate possessions of MNF without repayment: $(HM_{ETH} + MNF_{ETH}) + HS_{XPB} \rightarrow QUBS$.

Swiss and Swedish companies have apparently not had such difficulties in developing countries since they have fewer temptations to invoke home-country punitive actions. Thus, $HM_{POLY} + MNF_{GEO}$ appears easier in Sweden and in Switzerland.

In the case of Union Carbide, which built a meat-casing plant in Puerto Rico as a worldwide export base, Puerto Rico gains a worldwide technical competence and worldwide markets through Union Carbide's distribution system. On the assumption that Puerto Rico seeks its geocentric niche, there is likely a state of mutual satisfaction and interdependence.

In my recent research with multinational firms operating in LDC's, political and economic leaders demand equity in foreign-owned firms under threat of nationalization. In Mexico, encouraged by some economists, there is a demand for "fade-out" by the multinational firms after a specified number of years. The economists and political leaders hold that in the long term the multinational firm is not indispensable. It should provide management and know-how, on a contractual basis, and should be preparing to leave as soon as it enters an economy. This fits into the pattern $HS_{POLY} + MNF_{POLY} \rightarrow QBS$ (I).

But if the subsidiary is treated polycentrically by the HQ of the multinational firm, it receives little of the distinctive competence of a geocentric firm, it receives little of the distinctive competence of a geocentric firm which includes continually updating products technologically, improving know-how and training, human and material resources, as well as access to a worldwide marketing system. In this connection, some serious errors have been already recognized by political leaders by not distinguishing MNF_{POLY} from MNF_{GEO}, that is, a polycentric versus a geocentric multinational firm.

Thus in the long run, the MNF_{POLY} is more likely to lead to a state of value deprivation in HS and to a conflict about the worthwhileness of MNF. However, the MNF_{POLY} approach seems appealing because it permits HS to feel autonomous and not dependent on the foreign firm, but the trade-off in values lost becomes more costly over time.

ATTITUDINAL DETERMINANTS OF JOINT DECISION MAKING:
THE EAST–WEST DIMENSION

Elsewhere we have tried to show why for ideological reasons joint structures are difficult in East–West relations.[26] It is obvious that the ideological conflict makes durable and reciprocal relationships between the U.S. and the USSR rather tenuous. The explanation is in terms of two sets of concepts of building on East–West economic systems. What we call submergence theory in East and West relations is another form of ethnocentrism in the nation state. This involves ethnocentric-submergist assumptions such that (1) there must be a winner between East and West, (2) a world market can only be achieved by world conquest, and (3) trade is economic warfare.

26. Perlmutter, "Emerging East-West Ventures," *op. cit.*

By contrast, the polycentric and xenophobic divergence theorists, who wish to keep East and West separated, hold that nobody can win a world war. They favor military containment theory, and feel that trade should be restricted to nations with similar ideologies and that there should be only minimal trade between East and West.

We call joint production systems between East and West, like the Togliatti automobile plant in Moscow established with the advisory services of the capitalist firm Fiat of Italy, transideological. It is obviously more difficult for American MNF's to enter into such transideological structures than, for example, politically neutral Sweden. An explanation of how such joint decisions are made is contained in a widely circulated quote from one auto industry executive: "We don't talk politics when we are designing automobiles. If there is an ideologist present, he is permitted to give a short speech. Then he will leave so we can continue the business of designing the automobile, which really has nothing to do with Marx."

Boiled down to attitudes, we should find $MNF_{GEO} + HS_{GEO} \rightarrow QBS$; but HS_{GEO} in an Eastern European country is at best precarious, given the watchfulness of the Eastern ideologists and marshals! Nevertheless, there is a growing belief among some Western capitalists and some Eastern Communists that we need more such "joint decision making structures" of a transideological character.

Discussion

In this exploratory essay we have attempted to develop a set of hypotheses suitable for testing, and related to the building of viable and legitimate worldwide enterprises. We have been concerned with a class of decision problems characterized by the existence of various degrees of interdependence between the multinational firm and the nation state as decision units. We have tried to show, implicitly, that the degree of perceived interdependence between these decision units in part depends on the attitudes held by the interacting parties. The fact that coordination between two sets of decision makers might not take place—that joint rewards may not be considered high enough to maintain contact—could be related to such attitudinal orientations in key decision makers described as ethnocentric, polycentric, xenophilic, xenophobic, and geocentric. We have tried to determine the attitudinal patterns involving host and home multinational-firm decision makers which were quasi-balanced and quasi-unbalanced. We have further attempted to distinguish which processes were set in motion by these two types of relationships. And finally we have attempted to develop hypotheses concerning the conditions under which the perception of legitimacy by the decision maker in nation states would be relatively high or low.

We recognize the inherent circularity of the argument that attitudes determine joint decision making outcomes and perceived legitimacy. This methodological problem, while not new or unique, can in part be dealt with by developing operationally distinct measures. Thus much work lies ahead in creating feasible hypothesis-testing situations.

There are, to be sure, oversimplifications in any theory-building activity to label attitudes of key decision makers as ethnocentric or geocentric or xenophobic. The role sets of key decision makers like politicians are sufficiently complex that attitudinal inputs of local business leaders, union officials, home-based multinational firms, suppliers, distributors, shareholders, and even consumers exert influence on the key decision makers' resultant attitudinal orientation. The key decision makers' attitudinal orientation is multidetermined. His own inclinations are influenced vectorially by his role set, and it is rare that he does not respond to these influences.

A diadic view of the multinational-firm–nation-state relation is incomplete. Explanatory power is increased by virtue of a perspective, whereas a given international system (of MNF and nation state) is related to a more inclusive system which we called global industrial and political systems. The risk here in the global system, as Singer has put it, is to emphasize unduly the abstract while glossing over the relatively autonomous decision making power that resides at the level of the nation state.[27] Singer's fears are no doubt warranted when one considers how few worldwide institutions operate without direct control by the nation states. But it is our view that the multinational firm is rapidly becoming competent as an effective worldwide institution. In terms of a global system, in a given domain the multinational firm is as influential as the nation state. Thus previous theorizing about the primacy of the nation state which did not take account of this emerging phenomenon is necessarily limited.

Finally, it is clear to us that the behavioral sciences — especially those which provide insights, concepts, theory, and data about joint decision making between interdependent decision making units — are fundamental to the development of a theory and practice of building viable and legitimate worldwide institutions. But the task ahead is full of blind alleys, overly abstract propositions, and unsupported hypotheses.

It is hoped the yet neonate character of multinational firms will invite those who are interested in the more rigorous testing of hypotheses about building worldwide institutions, as well as those who see scholarly opportunities, to study joint decision making in an institution which may be destined to reshape the industrial and political system of the planet Earth.

27. J. D. Singer, "The Level of Analysis Problem in International Relations," in *The International System*, K. Knorr and S. Verba (eds.) (Princeton, N.J.: Princeton University Press, 1961).

14

Some Welfare Problems of Intertemporal Decision Making

EDNA LOEHMAN AND ANDREW WHINSTON

Introduction

The theory of decentralized decision making for a static one-period model has been extensively developed. For the case of a convex technology and no externalities Debreu has surveyed and summarized the field.[1] Pigou is historically credited with raising the difficulties associated with the case of externalities, and various solutions and analyses have appeared subsequently. Nonconvexity of the technology raises seemingly insurmountable problems and, unfortunately, for an economic allocative problem nonconvexity is realistic to expect.

Consideration of dynamic resource allocation models has drawn renewed interest in economics, especially with the adoption of techniques from optimal-control theory. The structure of such models is to maximize an integral over time subject to differential equation restraints, and perhaps some inequality constraints also. Some models which have been formulated in this way have included allocating capital and labor between the capital goods and consumption sectors to achieve "economic maturity" in minimum time[2] and allocating labor between technological and nontechnological sectors in order to maximize output.[3]

The static theory of resource allocation was concerned with the coincidence of action by conscious decision makers in a market environment and

This paper is sponsored by the Office of Naval Research and the Army Research Office.

1. G. Debreu, *Theory of Value, An Axiomatic Analysis of Economic Equilibrium* (New York: John Wiley & Sons, Inc., 1959).
2. M. Kurz, "Optimal Paths of Capital Accumulation Under Minimum Time Objective," *Econometrica*, XXXIII (1965), 42.
3. L. E. Ruff, *Optimal Growth and Technological Progress in a Cournot Economy* (Technical Report 11, Institute for Mathematical Studies in the Social Science, Stanford University, Stanford, California, 1968).

the optimality properties of a resource allocation model. This study carries over naturally to the dynamic models: does profit maximization behavior of producers and utility maximization of consumers in a dynamic market environment lead to the satisfaction of the optimality conditions? In the dynamic case these conditions are referred to as the Euler-Lagrange or the adjoint equations, and market prices appear as adjoint variables. As in the static case, if there are no imperfections in the market system, profit and utility maximization can result in the maximization of a social welfare function at every point in time.

It is interesting to explore the problems that arise in the dynamic case in the presence of imperfections in the market system. This paper will consider the case of technological externalities in a dynamic setting. Two producers, one upstream from the other, are considered. The externality is assumed to be effluent discharge by the upstream producer, which causes damage to the downstream producer in the form of increased production costs. The usual static argument is extended to the dynamic case: first, the two producers act independently and the upstream producer ignores the social cost over time of his effluent discharge; second, the case of joint production is considered to see what the solution would be if social costs are accounted for; third, paralleling the Pigouvian theory, an optimal tax is derived. The fourth case indicates a new direction which arises in the dynamic case. While the second and third cases deal with a social welfare or Pareto solution, the solution is optimal in a limited sense only. Mutually beneficial investment in treatment facilities can be made that will lead to an improved solution for both producers. Thus, in this paper we propose the concept of social investment to mitigate the effects of externalities. Given the restrictions on behavior such as limitation of effluent discharge and economies of scale in waste treatment, there are social gains that can be achieved through mutual investment.

Some Background Information about Water Pollution and Introduction to the Mathematical Model

Water pollution is an example of a technological externality; that is, the costs of a pollution-producing activity are borne not by the polluter but by some independent economic unit somewhere downstream. Public good externalities are also associated with water pollution, but this aspect will not be dealt with here. Because of the failure of the market to allocate water resources efficiently, it has become necessary in many areas for some authority to impose pollution standards. The standards may be based on cost-benefit analysis or may be quite arbitrary. Often, "equal treatment" criteria have been imposed. That is, every plant on a stream must treat its wastes to the same extent as the others. Recently, it has been argued that the recuperative powers of a stream and the varying stream quality in different sections imply that a better solution would be for different dumping levels to be allowed in different sections. Thus, a typical problem studied is the one of minimizing piping and/or treatment costs subject to achieving various quality goals in different sections of the stream. Questions of building regional treatment plants are also often considered. The models used are usually linear, and in these it is implicitly assumed that steady-state conditions hold. That is, externalities and joint treatment decisions are considered at a fixed point in time. In physical terms, this means time variations in the distributions of dissolved oxygen (DO) and oxygen demand by organic wastes (BOD) are neglected. DO is a measure of stream quality, and BOD measures how much oxygen per unit volume is required to decompose the organic wastes in a given unit volume. For further discussion of these terms see Kneese and Bower.[4]

In this steady state, stream flow and velocity are assumed to be constant. However, many steams have a varying flow pattern consisting of a rise in the spring and a prolonged drop to a low steady flow during the late summer and early fall. During this low period, minimal dilution, which raises the BOD concentration, and high temperature, which lowers the amount of oxygen dissolved in the water, combine to produce poor water quality. Treatment plants are planned to meet these low conditions. Linear programming models are also formulated corresponding to these conditions. If a linear programming problem to determine the optimum waste-dumping levels for industries along a stream were solved, the optimum levels would be constants corresponding to what could be tolerated under the worst stream conditions. However, since rapidly flowing water is conducive to better water quality, optimum dumping levels would in fact vary throughout the year, corresponding to various conditions of flow and temperature.

The relationship between volumetric flow rate and water quality is given by the following:

$$\frac{\partial c}{\partial t} + \frac{F}{A}\frac{\partial c}{\partial x} = \pm \Sigma S(c, x, t), \tag{14.1}$$

where c stands for BOD or DO, A is the cross-sectional area of the stream (assumed to be constant), F is the volumetric flow rate (assumed to be a function of time only), x is the distance downstream, and $S(c, x, t)$ stands for sources and sinks of DO or BOD.

We assume one source at $x = 0$ which is discharging at a constant rate of W lbs./day and $S(L, x, t) = k_r L$, where L is the BOD concentration and k_r is the BOD reaction rate constant (per day).

Then the BOD distribution is given by

$$L(x, t) = \frac{W}{F(\tau)} \exp\left[-k_r(t-\tau)\right], \tag{14.2}$$

---

4. A. V. Kneese and B. T. Bower, *Managing Water Quality: Economics Technology, Institutions* (Resources for the Future; John Hopkins Press, Baltimore, Maryland, 1968).

where $\tau = \tau(x, t)$ is the time that the BOD observed at point (x, t) was released.

Also, if O is the dissolved oxygen concentration, and k_a the reaeration coefficient,

$$O(x, t) = \frac{W}{F(\tau)} \frac{k_r}{k_a - k_r} \{\exp\left[-xk_r(t-\tau)\right] - \exp\left[-xk_a(t-\tau)\right]\}. \quad (14.3)$$

The coefficient k_a also depends on the flow:

$$k_a = (cF^n)/H^m, \quad (14.4)$$

where H is the average depth and c is a constant. If there is more than one polluter, the BOD and DO distributions are determined by summing at each point the distributions due to each pollution source. These equations for DO and BOD are given by DiToro and O'Connor[5] and O'Connor[6].

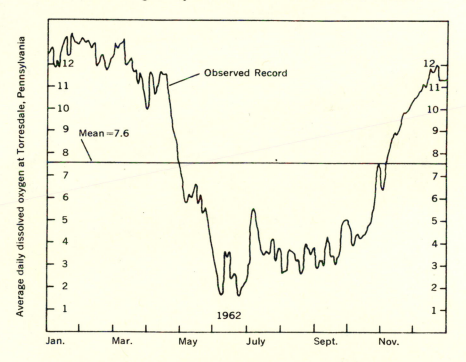

Figure 14.1. Average Daily Dissolved Oxygen at Torresdale, Pennsylvania.

Source: R. V. Thomann, D. J. O'Connor, and B. M. Di Toro, "The Management of Time Variable Stream and Estuarine Systems," *Chemical Engineering Progress Symposium Series,* LXIV (1968), 21.

5. D. M. Di Toro and D. J. O'Connor, "The Distribution of Dissolved Oxygen in a Stream with Time Varying Velocity," *Water Resources Research,* IV (1968), 639.

6. D. J. O'Connor, "The Temporal and Spatial Distributions of Dissolved Oxygen in Streams," *Water Resources Research,* III. (1967), 65.

From these relationships we see clearly the inverse relationship between water quality and flow. Also, since in reality the flow $F(t)$ will vary throughout the year, $L(x, t)$ and $O(x, t)$ will vary through the year. Figure 14.1 shows this time variation for DO. Because of this, dynamic models are more suitable than static ones in water pollution models.

Consider the case of a polluter at $x = 0$ causing damage to a downstream plant or municipality at $x = x_0$ which uses stream water for some purpose. Suppose dumping limits are imposed so that

$$O(x_0 t) = \bar{O} = \text{constant}$$

is the standard that is to be achieved at x_0. Then since $F(t)$ varies, $\bar{O}$ can be achieved for different values of W during the year. That is, to achieve a given standard the upstream polluter can be allowed to dump more during some times of the year than others. If problems of maximizing revenue are considered, clearly the optimal solution will be better if W is allowed to vary than if W is fixed at the lowest value throughout the year.

Under the imposed standard $O(x_0, t) = \bar{O}$, then if the upstream firm desires to produce more than the amounts corresponding to the standard, it must build a treatment plant. Likewise, if the downstream firm desires better water quality than $\bar{O}$, it too must employ additional treatment to the water it uses. Suppose that $\bar{O}$ is imposed by some authority (either by law or by an optimal tax) and both the upstream and the downstream firms are not satisfied with the corresponding production levels. Then, because of the significant economies of scale involved (and the advantage to the downstream firm of treating the wastes before they enter the stream), the two firms will be better off to build a joint treatment facility. The savings due to economies of scale may be quite significant as illustrated in Figure 14.2.

Thus, in the case of an imposed water quality standard, if the damaged firm would like to have lower damage costs than those corresponding to the standard, and if the polluting firms would like to produce more than is allowed under the standard, there will be incentives to build joint treatment facilities and costs can be further reduced due to economies of scale.

To satisfy the upstream and downstream firms, the amount that is to be treated will vary with stream flow (at higher flows, not as much will have to be treated to satisfy both). Thus, different flow determines different demand periods. There is a question of what capacity the treatment plant should have. If it is built to satisfy the peak demand, then the same fixed costs will have to be covered during lower demand periods. The optimal capacity is determined by balancing the cost of a certain capacity against the amounts the plants are willing to contribute in the different periods. The equilibrium production level for each producer corresponds to when the per unit contribution to the treatment plant just equals the net revenue of the last unit produced. Thus, the optimal treatment plant capacity, amounts treated, and the production levels are jointly determined.

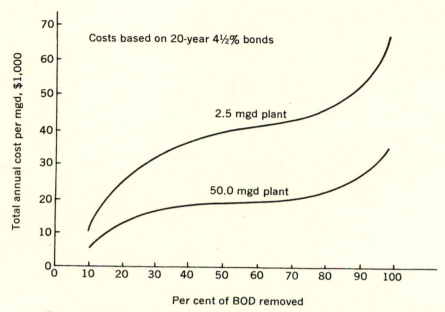

Figure 14.2. Relationship between Degree of BOD Removal and Costs.

Source: R. J. Frankel, "Cost-Quality Relationships in an Engineering-Economic Model for Municipal Waste Disposal," ASCE Water Resources Engineering Conference, Mobile, Alabama, 1965, in A. V. Kneese and B. T. Bower, *Managing Water Quality: Economics, Technology, Institutions* (Resources for the Future) (Baltimore: Johns Hopkins Press, 1968).

These issues will be formulated in a time-varying context. Thus, instead of the usual linear or nonlinear programming methods, the Pontryagin maximum principle[7] and a theorem due to Hestenes[8] will be used. Both of these theorems give necessary conditions for solution of an optimization problem. The ideas of this section are formalized in two models presented in the next sections. For simplicity a zero discount rate is assumed, although this is not necessary for any of the conclusions.

Model I

The purposes of this model are to determine what a rational pollution standard would be based on a Pareto-efficient distribution of the water resource and to describe the properties of Pareto-efficient production levels.

Suppose that there is a downstream firm B who has a net return function $V_B(q_B)$. V_B reflects the demand conditions for B's product, the production

7. L. S. Pontryagin, V. G. Boltyanskii, R. V. Gamkrelidze, and E. F. Mishchenko, *The Mathematical Theory of Optimal Processes* (Interscience Publishers, New York, 1962).

8. M. R. Hestenes, "On Variational Theory and Optimal Control Theory," *J. SIAM Control,* III (1965).

function, and input costs. That is, if q_B units are produced, B receives a net profit $V_B(q_B)$. The properties of $V_B(q_B)$ are assumed to be (see Figure 14.3)

$$V'_B \geq 0, \ V''_B < 0, \ V'''_B \leq 0. \tag{14.5}$$

The best production level for B would be where $V'_B = 0$, i.e., at $q_B{}^0$. We assume B needs to have water of a certain quality as an input in his production.

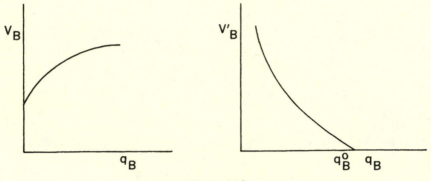

Figure 14.3

Now suppose firm A builds a plant upstream from B, and let A have a net return function $V_A(q_A)$ with the same properties

$$V'_A \geq 0, \ V''_A < 0, \tag{14.6}$$

and A's best level of production would be where $V'_A = 0$, or at $q_A{}^0$. Assume A's production produces water pollutants which cause B to have additional production costs. Let $D[w_A, F(t)]$ denote B's per unit damage costs, where $F(t)$ is the streamflow, and w_A is the pounds of waste which A dumps in the river per day. Let A's production be proportional to his waste production, i.e.,

$$q_A = k_1 w_A, \ k_1 > 0. \tag{14.7}$$

Then if A is producing q_A units a day and $F = F(t)$, B's total extra costs due to pollution at time t will be $D(w_A, F)q_B$ if B produces q_B units.

By this characterization, the damage is nonseparable in nature; that is, every unit of waste does not result in the same amount of damage. There is some evidence that this is realistic. The properties of the damage function are assumed to be

$$\frac{\partial D}{\partial w_A} = D_1 > 0, \frac{\partial D}{\partial F} = D_2 < 0, \frac{\partial^2 D}{\partial F^2} = D_{22} > 0,$$

$$\tag{14.8}$$

$$\frac{\partial^2 D}{\partial w_A{}^2} = D_{11} > 0, D_{12} = D_{21} < 0.$$

An example of such a function would be

$$D = c_1 \frac{e^{c_2 w_A}}{F(t)} \quad (c_1, c_2 > 0).$$

After pollution costs are added, to maximize net returns, B will produce at a level corresponding to $V'_B = D$ (see Figure 14.4). Clearly, this will be less than the amount B would have produced if A had not been polluting. Damage costs per unit may even be so high that B's production level would be near zero. This situation may be unacceptable, for B could be a municipal water plant or B might produce something which was socially desirable (such as recreation).

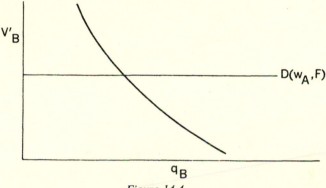

Figure 14.4.

Mathematically the situation where there is no interaction between the firms could be described as follows:

Firm A:

$$\underset{0 \le q_A \le q_A{}^0}{\text{Max}} \int_0^T V_A(q_A)dt;$$

Firm B:

$$\underset{0 \le q_B \le q_B{}^0}{\text{Max}} \int_0^T [V_B(q_B) - D(w_A, F)q_B]dt. \tag{14.9}$$

By the first-order conditions Firm B will maximize his profits for $V'_B(q_B) = D(w_A, F)q_B$ at each time t.

If A decides to produce $q_A{}^0$ units (which maximizes A's revenues), then B's revenues will be maximized where q_B satisfies $V'_B(q_B) = D(w_A{}^0, F)$. The following curve is derived from the functions $V'_B(q_B)$, $D(w_A{}^0, F)$ and the relationship $V'_B(q_B) = D(w_A{}^0, F)$ (see Figure 14.5). This curve defines B's optimal production as a function of flow. For the given level of A's production $q_A{}^0$, B's production decreases with decreasing streamflow [and increasing $D(w_A{}^0, F)$]. If instead A decided to produce $q'_A < q_A{}^0$, *the* production possibilities would be given by a curve shifted to the right of the one above. Note that B has only to know the value of the damage function, and not A's production level or the flow, in order to determine his production.

If the resulting production q_B is socially unacceptable, then A's dumping will have to be restricted, perhaps by some regional authority. How could fair standards be set?

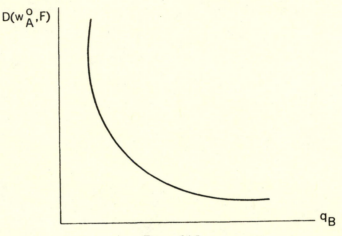

Figure 14.5.

One criterion that economists use is "Pareto efficiency." Here we want to find the Pareto-efficient allocation of the water resource between water quality uses and water used for waste assimilation so that joint returns are maximized. If both firms were jointly owned, then the Pareto-efficient production levels would be actually attained.

If one plant were very efficient and the other inefficient, then the revenue-maximizing result might be that the inefficient one shut down entirely. However, this situation is not very interesting and might be socially unacceptable, so we will assume this situation does not hold. Thus we assume that both $w_A > 0$ and $q_B > 0$. Let us also assume for the joint solution $w_A^0 > w_A$ and $q_B^0 > q_B$; that is, A's production actually affects B's production so that in the joint solution neither will produce the maximum possible. By these two assumptions, the solution for w_A and q_B will be an interior one.

The mathematical model is

$$\text{Maximize} \int_0^T [V_A(q_A) + V_B(q_B) - D(w_A, F)q_B]dt$$

$$\text{subject to } \dot{q}_B = k_2[V'_B(q_B) - D(w_A, F)], k_2 > 0$$

and $\qquad\qquad 0 < w_A < w_A^0, 0 < q_B < q_B^0, \qquad\qquad (14.10)$

where $q_A = k_1 w_A$, $k_1 > 0$, and k_2 is a constant which gives B's speed of adjustment. The control is w_A; the trajectory is q_B. We do not consider the flow F as a control variable, although it could be somewhat controlled by flow augmentation. For a discussion of this point see the section on extensions of the model. The differential equation is a behavioral equation which says that B will increase his production if his marginal revenue is above the per unit damage costs, decrease production if per unit damage costs are greater than marginal revenue, and remain at the level of production where marginal revenue just equals per unit damage cost. In other words, this constraint describes B's behavior as a profit maximizer.

Let the unit of time be in days. At time $t = 0$, A's and B's production levels are some fixed values in $[0, w_A{}^0]$ and $[0, q_B{}^0]$, respectively. Also assume T is a fixed time, but $w_A(T)$, $q_B(T)$ are not required to have any fixed value. Under these assumptions, the Pontryagin theorem may be applied.

We form the Hamiltonian function

$$H[q_B, w_A, t, \lambda_1(t)] = \{V_A(k_1 w_A) + V_B(q_B) - D[w_A, F(t)]q_B\}$$

$$+ \lambda_1 k_2 \{V'_B(q_B) - D[w_A, F(t)]\}. \tag{14.11}$$

We use the notation

$$\hat{H} = H[q_B{}^*, w_A{}^*, t, \lambda_1(t)],$$

where $q_B{}^*$, $w_A{}^*$ indicate the optimal trajectory and control. As in nonlinear programming, $\hat{H}$ can be interpreted to be the total value of the system at each time t, and $\lambda_1(t)$ has the interpretation of the value at time t of a change in $\dot{q}_B{}^*$. The necessary conditions are

$$\frac{\partial \hat{H}}{\partial w_A{}^*} = 0 \text{ (since } 0 < w^*{}_A < w^0{}_A \text{ and hence is an interior point of the control}$$

$$\text{region)}, \tag{14.12}$$

$$\dot{\lambda}_1 = -\frac{\partial \hat{H}}{\partial q_B{}^*} = -[V'_B{}^* - D^* + \lambda_1 k_2 V''_B{}^*], \lambda_1(T) = 0 \tag{14.13}$$

the asterisks denoting the functions evaluated at $q_B{}^*$ and $w_A{}^*$, and $\lambda_1(T) = 0$ by the transversality condition. From (14.12) we obtain

$$\lambda_1(t) = \frac{k_1 V'_A{}^* - D_1{}^* q_B{}^*}{k_2 D_1{}^*}. \tag{14.14}$$

The interpretation of $\lambda_1(t)$ is the social value of a change in $\dot{q}_B{}^*$ at the time t. From (14.14) we see that $\lambda_1(t) = 0$ if and only if $k_1 V'_A{}^* = D_1{}^* q_B{}^*$, or the marginal unit of q_A is bringing in revenue just equal to the resulting damage costs. If w_A were increased at this point, the damage costs would exceed the additional revenue, so in maximizing revenue jointly, it would not be advantageous to increase w_A. Since k_2 and D_1 are both positive, then $\lambda_1(t) > 0$ if and only if

$$k_1 V'_A{}^* > D_1{}^* q_B.$$

That is, the revenue due to the marginal unit of q_A exceeds the damage it causes. Here the value of the objective function can be increased by increasing w_A until $\lambda_1 = 0$ occurs. We may solve for $\dot{\lambda}_1$ from (14.14) and set this equal to $-\partial \hat{H}/\partial q_B{}^*$ given in (14.13). After solving and simplifying, we obtain an expression for $\dot{w}_A{}^*$, the differential equation which the optimal control must satisfy.

$$\left[-D_{11}\frac{k_1 V'_A}{D_1{}^2} + \frac{k_1{}^2 V''_A}{D_1} \right] \dot{w}_A$$

$$= -k_2 V''_B \frac{(k_1 V'_A - q_B D_1)}{D_1} + \frac{k_1 V'_A}{D_1{}^2} D_{12}\dot{F}. \qquad (14.15)$$

(The asterisk notation has been omitted for simplicity, but all functions are in terms of the optimal trajectory and control.) The expression

$$C \equiv -D_{11}\frac{k_1 V'_A}{D_1{}^2} + \frac{k_1{}^2 V''_A}{D_1} < 0$$

since $D_{11} > 0$, $D_1 > 0$, $V'_A > 0$, $V''_A < 0$. Thus, $\dot{w}_A$ is positive if and only if the right-hand side of (14.15) is negative. That is, the optimal waste discharge (and hence A's production) is allowed to increase if and only if that expression is negative. The derivative $\dot{w}_A$ is negative if and only if the right-hand side is positive, and $\dot{w}_A$ is constant if and only if the right-hand side is zero. The expression for $\dot{w}_A$ is the condition for optimality of the problem. The expression for $\dot{q}_B$,

$$\dot{q}_B = k_2[V'_B - D], \qquad (14.16)$$

is the condition for feasibility.

Consider the right-hand side of (14.15).

$$-k_2{}^2 V''_B \lambda_1 + \frac{k_1 V'_A}{D_1{}^2} D_{12}\dot{F} \qquad (14.17)$$

From this, we can describe properties of the optimal feasible solution depending on the stream flow:

CASE I. $\dot{F} = 0$. The flow is constant.

Since $V''_B < 0$, $\dot{w}_A < 0$ only if $\lambda_1 > 0$ or the value of a decrease in w_A is positive; $\dot{w}_A = 0$ only if $\lambda_1 = 0$ or the damage cost of the last unit of q_A equals its marginal revenue; and $\dot{w}_A > 0$ only if $\lambda_1 < 0$ or the value of a decrease in w_A is negative.

CASE II. $\dot{F} < 0$. The flow is diminishing over time.

Since D_{12} is negative, the expression in (14.17) is greater than zero ($\dot{w}_A < 0$) if $\lambda_1 > 0$ and can be less than zero ($\dot{w}_A > 0$) only if λ_1 is sufficiently negative.

CASE III. $\dot{F} > 0$. The flow is increasing.

$k_1 V'_A D_{12}\dot{F} < 0$. The expression in (14.17) is negative ($\dot{w}_A > 0$) if $\lambda_1 < 0$. If

$\dot{F}$ is positive but not sufficiently large to make (14.17) negative, then

$$0 > k_1 V_A' D_{12}\dot{F} > k_2 V_B'' D_1{}^2 \lambda_1$$

For the above in equality to hold, $\lambda_1 > 0$. Thus, it is of social value to increase production of q_B even though w_A should not be increased.

Summarizing these three cases, for an optimal, feasible solution for Model I, the optimal dumping level for A is allowed to increase only when $\dot{F}$ is sufficiently large. If flow is constant, then A's production level is constant only if the damage due to the last unit of q_A produced equals its marginal revenue: otherwise A's production should decrease until this is accomplished. If flow decreases, then A's production level must decrease. This describes A's optimal production as a function of flow, and these results correspond very well to the intuitive presentation in the first section of this chapter. Phase-diagram techniques can be used to show the shape of the time paths of w_A and q_B for initial points in various regions. Stability of the system may also be considered by using phase diagrams. However, there are difficulties in obtaining phase diagrams for our system

$$\dot{w}_A = \frac{1}{C} \left[-k_2{}^2 V_B'' \lambda_1 + \frac{k_1 V_A'}{D_1{}^2} D_{12}\dot{F} \right]$$

$$\dot{q}_B = k_2[V_B' - D]$$

$$\lambda_1 = \frac{k_1 V_A' - D_1 q_B}{k_2 D_1} \tag{14.18}$$

since F and $\dot{F}$ are nonautonomous terms. Because of this we first proceed under the assumption that $\dot{F} = 0$, i.e. F is a given constant for some time period.*

Time paths for which both $\dot{q}_B = 0$ and $\dot{w}_A = 0$ are called stationary points. If there is one and only one such point such that $\dot{q}_B = 0$ and $\dot{w}_A = 0$, it is called the equilibrium path. The phase diagram consists of dividing the (q_B, w_A) – plane into regions by the locus of (q_B, w_A) which satisfy $\dot{w}_A = 0$ and the locus of (q_B, w_A) which satisfy $\dot{q}_B = 0$.

Consider the locus $\dot{w}_A = 0$. $\dot{w}_A = 0$ if and only if $\lambda_1 = 0$. Taking the differentials of both sides of the equation $\lambda_1 = 0$

$$\frac{dw_A}{dq_B} = \frac{D_1}{k_1{}^2 V_A'' - D_{11}q_B}$$

By our assumptions, $\dfrac{dw_A}{dq_B} < 0$ and $\dfrac{d^2 w_A}{dq_B{}^2} > 0$ for the curve $\lambda_1 = 0$.

Now on one side of this curve $\lambda_1 > 0$ (i.e., w_A is decreasing), and on the other $\lambda_1 < 0$ (w_A is increasing). To determine which is which, we find

$$\frac{\partial \lambda_1}{\partial q_B} = -\frac{1}{k_2} < 0$$

*Thanks are due to Bruce A. Forster and John Logan, Australian National University, for corrections in the manuscript at this point.

Therefore, we get the (q_B, D) – plane divided into regions as shown in Figure 14.6.

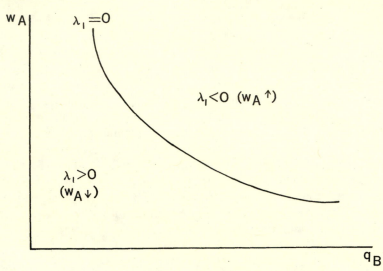

Figure 14.6

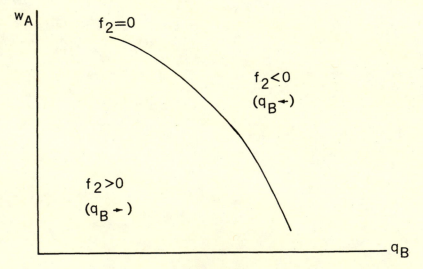

Figure 14.7

Similarly, consider $\dot{q}_B = 0$. The derivative $\dot{q}_B = 0$ if and only if $f_2 = [V'_B - D] = 0$. The locus $f_2 = 0$ yields

$$\frac{dw_A}{dq_B} = \frac{V''_B}{D_1} < 0, \frac{d^2w_A}{dq_B^2} = \frac{V_B'''}{D_1} \leq 0$$

so that the locus (q_B, w_A) satisfying $\dot{q}_B = 0$ has negative slope. Also

$$\frac{\partial f_2}{\partial q_B} = V_B'' < 0.$$

Thus, the locus $f_2 = 0$ divides the plane as shown in Figure 14.7. In the region where $f_2 < 0$, q_B is decreasing over time; and where $f_2 > 0$, q_B is increasing over time.

Since both $\lambda_1 = 0$ and $f_2 = 0$ have negative slope, the curves can intersect once, twice, or not at all in the positive quadrant. If there is an intersection of the two curves, it satisfies the conditions

$$k_1 V_A' - D_1 q_B = 0$$
$$V_B' \quad - D \quad = 0$$

which are the static welfare maximization conditions. A necessary condition for a solution to exist is that the Jacobian of the system

$$\begin{vmatrix} k_1{}^2 V_A'' - D_{11} q_B & -D_1 \\ -D_1 & V_B'' \end{vmatrix}$$

be nonvanishing.

Assuming a unique solution of the static welfare maximization conditions exists, the following phase diagram in the (q_B, w_A)−plane is obtained:

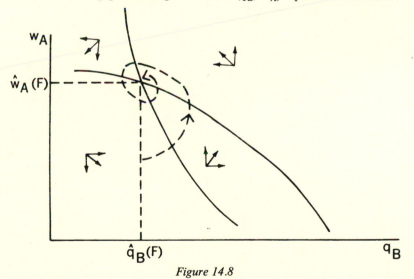

Figure 14.8

From this phase diagram we see that the optimal solution eventually converges to the static equilibrium point $(\hat{q}_B(F), \hat{w}_A(F))$. This equilibrium is stable since the Hessian is negative definite by our assumptions.

We have assumed a constant flow level to obtain this phase diagram. If the flow changes from one constant level to another, both curves $\lambda_1 = 0$

and $f_2 = 0$ shift. The direction of the shift is obtained from differentiating $\lambda_1 = 0$ and $f_2 = 0$ with respect to F. The new equilibrium $(\hat{q}_B, \hat{w}_A)$ for a decrease in flow is pictured below in Fig. 14.9.

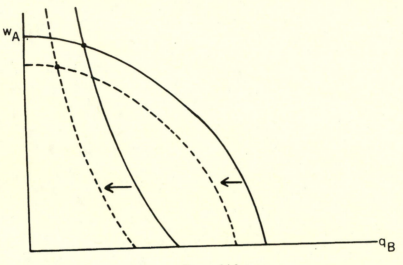

Figure 14.9

For continuous changes in flow, we may extrapolate these results to obtain the path of equilibrium points as shown in Fig. 14.10.

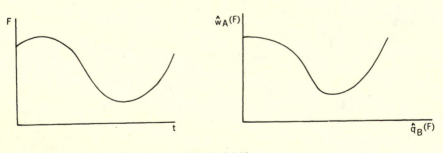

Figure 14.10

The time path of solutions to (14.18) would approach this path of equilibrium points.

Note that for $\dot{F} = 0$, it is possible that there is no equilibrium solution. In this case possible phase diagrams are given in Fig. 14.11. In these cases, the solution may eventually converge to no production of w_A or no production of q_B.

Where an equilibrium exists for $\dot{F} = 0$, the equilibrium may not be reached if the time period under consideration is not long enough. However, once reached, the system will remain at this point until the flow is changed. That is, if A and B were jointly owned, once A and B attain this production path, they will be content to remain there. For this reason, if an authority were to set a limit on A's dumping, it would make sense to base the standard on the equilibrium $\hat{w}_A(F)$. In other words, A would be allowed to dump various amounts during different flow periods.

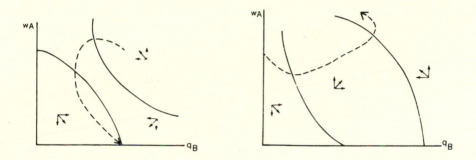

Figure 14.11

Waste disposal for A is then allowed to increase only when $\dot{F}$ is sufficiently large. Waste disposal must decrease when F is decreasing, and when F is constant, A's production depends on the level of damage to B.

So far the results obtained have dealt with the necessary conditions for optimality under the assumption of an interior solution. By Mangasarians's results,[9] these conditions are also sufficient if the integrand in (14.10) and $V''_B(q_B) - D(w_A, F)$ are concave and differentiable in (q_B, w_A). We can check the concavity of these by the Hessian necessary and sufficient condition for concavity. By the Hessian condition the integrand is concave if and only if

1. $k_1^2 V''_A - D_{11} q_B \leq 0;$
2. $V''_B \leq 0;$
3. $\begin{vmatrix} k_1^2 V''_A - D_{11} q_B & -D_1 \\ -D_1 & V''_B \end{vmatrix} = V''_B(k_1^2 V''_A - D_{11} q_B) - D_1^2 \geq 0.$

Since we assumed $V''_A < 0$, $D_{11} > 0$, $q_B > 0$, the first condition holds for our problem and by assumption the second does also. If D_1 (the change in per unit damage to B due to the marginal unit of A's wastes) is sufficiently small or k_1 is sufficiently large (firm A is inefficient), then condition 3 can be made to hold.

9. O. L. Mangasarian. "Sufficient Conditions for the Optimal Control of Nonlinear Systems," J. Slam Control, IV (1966), 139.

$V'_B(q_B) - D(w_A, F)$ is concave in (q_B, w_A) if and only if

1. $\qquad\qquad\qquad V'''_B \leq 0;$
2. $\qquad\qquad\qquad -D_{11} \leq 0;$
3. $\qquad\qquad\qquad \begin{vmatrix} V'''_B & 0 \\ 0 & -D_{11} \end{vmatrix} = -D_{11} V'''_B \geq 0.$

Since we assumed $V'''_B \leq 0$ and $D_{11} > 0$, conditions 1 and 2 are fulfilled, and 1 and 2 imply that 3 holds.

Given our initial assumptions (14.5), (14.6), (14.7), and (14.8), and assumption of an interior solution, if D_1 is sufficiently small or k_1 sufficiently large, we have obtained both the necessary and sufficient conditions for a Pareto-efficient allocation of the water resource between firms A and B. For this reason the waste disposal level $\hat{w}_A(F)$ would be a logical one for a regional authority to impose.

Taxation Schemes

The optimal tax in the Pigouvian sense is a charge per unit of production such that A's revenue maximization results in his producing corresponding to the waste level $\hat{w}_A(F)$.

Mathematically, the problem is to find a per unit tax τ so that

$$\underset{q_A}{\text{Max}} \int_0^T [V_A(q_A) - \tau q_A] dt$$

has the solution $\hat{q}_A = k_1 \hat{w}_A(F)$.

Taking the derivative with respect to w_A, we see that

$$\tau = V'_A[k_1 \hat{w}_A(F)] = \frac{D_1 \hat{q}_B(F)}{k_1}$$

satisfies the first-order necessary conditions; and since $V''_A < 0$, this condition is also sufficient that the tax be optimal. Notice that τ varies with flow so that the optimal tax would have to be recalculated for each flow change.

Suppose such a tax structure is used. Then the regional authority will collect an amount τ from A for every unit he produces. Although the optimal waste level is achieved (assuming that A acts according to the economic theory of setting marginal costs equal to marginal revenues), there is the problem of the tax monies collected. The distribution of income is affected by the tax collection. Also, what should be done with the money collected? Should treatment facilities be built with it (in which case there are problems of what size and type the plant should be and the authority's decisions about treatment may not lead to the social optimum)? Or should it be given to the damaged party in payment for damages? As Turvey says,

> Whether A or B are persons or firms, to levy a tax on A which is not received as damages or compensation by B may prevent optimal resource allocation from being achieved. . . . The reason is that the resource allocation which maximizes A's gain less B's loss may differ from that which maximize A's gain less A's tax less B's loss.[10]

Another taxation scheme would be that the regional authority tax none of A's production until A exceeds the limit $\hat{w}_A(F)$. When $\hat{w}_A(F)$ is exceeded, the authority would fine or tax A equal to the entire amount of revenues in excess of that corresponding to $\hat{w}_A(F)$. If A was aware that he would be taxed in this way, there would be no incentive for him to discharge more than $\hat{w}_A(F)$. So this would be an optimal tax scheme. However, again we would have problems with what to do with the money collected.

Alternatively, $\hat{w}_A(F)$ could just be established by law to be the most A could discharge. Of course, sufficiently strong penalities would have to be established so that A would have no desire to cheat.

For any of these tax schemes, because of the nonseparability of the damage function, the authority would have to know the production function of both firms as well as the damage function. So from an informational standpoint, any tax scheme requires as much as any other. However, using legal restrictions does save the authority some computational work as well as not presenting the income-distribution problems mentioned above. It may be argued that this is undemocratic, but such legal restrictions are in the same spirit as zoning laws and speed limits. In the following model we will assume that such legal restrictions on dumping are imposed.

Model II

Suppose now that A's waste disposal via the stream has been fixed at $\hat{w}_A(F)$ by legal restrictions as discussed in an earlier section, so that without treatment facilities, A can produce at most

$$\hat{q}_A = k_1 \hat{w}_A(F)$$

(note that $\hat{q}_A$ varies with the stream flow) and receive revenue $\hat{V}_A = V_A(\hat{q}_A)$. By assumption, A's production capacity is $q_A{}^0 > \hat{q}_A$ so if $\hat{q}_A$ is sufficiently below $q_A{}^0$, then it would pay for A to build a treatment facility. (If $\hat{q}_A$ is "close" to capacity production $q_A{}^0$, then the trouble involved might mean that no plant would be built.) We will suppose that A is willing to pay some amount c_A for each unit of production to produce at a level higher than

10. R. Turvey, "On Divergences Between Social Cost and Private Cost," *Economica*, XXX (1963), 309.

$\hat{q}_A$. In effect, A is taxing himself on his own production; the resulting equilibrium production level is where $V'_A = c_A$. The "tax" c_A will vary as the flow varies because when flow is higher, A is allowed to produce more and hence additional production is not worth as much as at lower flows. Likewise, when the stream flow is lower, A must diminish his production and so additional production is worth more than at higher flows. Thus the equilibrium production level will also vary with flow. Firm A will use the amount $c_A q_A$ to build treatment facilities to treat all wastes above $\hat{w}_A(F)$.

Since A has a legal right to dispose of wastes up to the amount $\hat{w}_A(F)$, the upstream firm A has no reason to treat more than an amount $s_A = w_A - \hat{w}_A(F)$ so that the per unit damage to downstream production is still at the constant level $\hat{D}$. If B's corresponding production level $\hat{q}_B$ is sufficiently below capacity $q_B{}^0$, then B has an incentive to "bride" A to dump less wastes than $\hat{w}_A(F)$ via the stream. In other words, B would like A to treat an amount s_B so that only $\hat{w}_A(F) - s_B$ is disposed of in the stream. We suppose that B is willing to pay A $c_B q_B$ for this so that B's equilibrium production will be where $V'_B - D = c_B$. Here again, in effect B is taxing himself on each unit produced. The amount B is willing to pay to A depends on the damage that A is causing, and hence c_B varies with flow, resulting in an equilibrium production which varies with flow also.

Now, the total funds available for the treatment plant are $c_A q_A + c_B q_B$. If A desires that an amount s_A be treated and B desires that an additional amount s_B be treated, then because of the economies of scale and sharing of the fixed costs, it costs less per unit to treat $s = s_A + s_B$ in a jointly financial treatment plant than it would if only s_A or only s_B were treated. Thus, to achieve their goals through a joint treatment plant, both A's "taxes" and B's "bribes" can be lower than the amount they were originally willing to contribute. Payments c_A and c_B will adjust, and the equilibrium production levels will be higher.

Suppose the treatment plant was built to have capacity corresponding to the highest treatment demand. Then in lower demand periods, this high fixed cost would still have to be met at the same time that A and B would want to contribute less. This affects the amount which could be treated. Thus, A and B must choose the optimum capacity for the treatment plant, as well as their financing of it. At each time t (days), the cost of a treatment plant of capacity K is

$$B(K)s + C(K)$$

to treat an amount $sB(K)$ is the variable cost per unit treatment, and $C(K)$ is the daily fixed costs. We suppose that $B'(K) < 0$ and $C'(K) > 0$ due to the economics of scale. We assume that the cost of operating the plant must be covered at each time t. The financing constraint is then

$$c_A q_A + c_B q_B \geq B(K)s + C(K),$$

where $K \geq s$. Once chosen, the capacity is fixed so that K is a control parameter.

By acting jointly to build the treatment plant, the firms A and B are in effect internalizing the externality. Supposing that A and B can reach an agreement and the coalition does not break down during the time period, we have the following model for the situation (as before $q_A = k_1 w_A$):

$$\text{Maximize}_{K, s, c_A, c_B} \int_0^T [V_A(k_1 w_A) + V_B(q_B) - D(w_A - s, F)q_B - c_A k_1 w_A - c_B q_B] dt \quad (14.19)$$

$$\text{subject to } \dot{q}_B = k_2[V'_B(q_B) - D(w_A - s, F) - c_B], k_2 > 0; \quad (14.20)$$

$$\dot{w}_A = \frac{k_3}{k_1}[V'_A(k_1 w_A) - c_A], k_3 > 0, k_1 > 0, \quad (14.21)$$

$$0 \leq s \leq K, \quad (14.22)$$

$$c_A k_1 w_A + c_B q_B \geq B(K)s + C(K), \quad (14.23)$$

$$\int_0^T [V_A(k_1 w_A) - \hat{V}_A - c_A k_1 w_A] dt \geq 0, \quad (14.24)$$

$$\int_0^T [(V_B(q_B) - Dq_B) - (\hat{V}_B - \hat{D}\hat{q}_B) - c_B q_B] dt \geq 0, \quad (14.25)$$

$$\hat{w}_A(F) \geq w_A - s, \quad (14.26)$$

$$0 \leq c_A \leq \hat{V}'_A, \quad (14.27)$$

$$0 \leq c_B \leq \hat{D}, \quad (14.28)$$

$$\hat{w}_A(F) \leq w_A \leq w^0_A, \quad (14.29)$$

$$\hat{q}_B \leq q_B \leq q^0_B. \quad (14.30)$$

At time $t = 0$, A produces $\hat{q}_A$ and B produces $\hat{q}_B$. A and B's objectives are to maximize joint revenues, since they are cooperating in the treatment plant, and this is given by (14.19). Constraints (14.20) and (14.21) give A's and B's individual profit-maximizing behavior. Constraint (14.21) corresponds to the condition $\dot{q}_A = k_3[V'_A - c_A]$, $k_3 > 0$ since w_A is proportional to q_A. Expression (14.23) is the financing constraint, and (14.22) is the capacity constraint. Expressions (14.24) and (14.25) say that by cooperating in this way, neither A nor B should suffer a loss compared to their profit position in Model I. Expression (14.26) is the quality constraint, i.e., that no more than $\hat{w}_A(F)$ can be dumped in the stream. Expressions (14.27), (14.28), (14.29), and (14.30) give ranges on the other variables. The notation is as before in Model I. For instance, (14.27) says that A will not contribute more than $V'_A(\hat{q}_A)$, for he could produce at the level $\hat{q}_A$ without paying any treatment costs. The constants k_2, k_3/k_1 are B's and A's speeds of adjustment. From the

Hestenes theorem, the multipliers associated with constraints (14.24) and (14.25) are constants, whereas those associated with the rest are continuous or piecewise continuous functions of time.

For simplicity, we will assume that

$$\int_0^T [V_A - \hat{V}_A - c_A k_1 w_A]\, dt > 0$$

and

$$\int_0^T [(V_B - Dq_B) - (\hat{V}_B - \hat{D}\hat{q}_B) - c_B q_B]\, dt > 0;$$

i.e., that both find cooperation profitable over the time period. Then the corresponding multipliers are zero by the Hestenes theorem. Also, assume that

$$\hat{w}_A(F) > w_A - s;$$

that is, that B is better off at each time in the period. If not, then at some point he might not wish to cooperate further. Under this assumption the multiplier associated with this constraint is identically zero. Likewise, we will assume that the inequalities in (14.27)–(14.30) hold strictly.

Now, only the two inequalities (14.22) and (14.23) are assumed to be able to hold with equality. The rank condition is then satisfied since

$$\begin{vmatrix} c_A k_1 & k_1 w_A & q_B & -B(K) \\ 0 & 0 & 0 & -1 \end{vmatrix}$$

has rank two. So the Hestenes theorem can be applied to give the necessary conditions for an optimum solution to the problem under the above assumptions.

The Hamiltonian expression is given by

$$H = \lambda_0 (V_A + V_B - Dq_B - c_A k_1 w_A - c_B q_B)$$

$$+ \lambda_1 k_2 (V'_B - D - c_B) + \lambda_2 \frac{k_3}{k_1}(V'_A - c_A)$$

$$+ \mu_1(K - s) + \mu_2 [c_A k_1 w_A + c_B q_B - B(K)s - C(K)]. \tag{14.31}$$

Denote by H^* the Hamiltonian evaluated at the optimal trajectories and controls w_A^*, q_B^*, K^*, s^*, c_A^*, c_B^*. The following necessary conditions are obtained from the Hestenes theorem:

$$\lambda_0 \geq 0 \text{ is a constant}, \tag{14.32}$$

$$\dot{\lambda}_1 = -\partial H^*/\partial q_B^* = -\lambda_0(V_B^* - D^* - c_B^*) - \lambda_1 k_2 V''_B - \mu_2 c_B^*, \tag{14.33}$$

$$\dot{\lambda}_2 = -\partial H^*/\partial w_A^* = -\lambda_0(k_1 V'_A^* - D_1^* q_B^* - c_A^* k_1) \\ + \lambda_1 k_2 D_1^* - \lambda_2 k_3 V_A^* - \mu_2 c_A^* k_1 \tag{14.34}$$

(where D_1 denotes the partial of D with respect to $w_A - s$),

$$\partial H^*/\partial s^* = \lambda_0 D_1{}^* q_B{}^* - \mu_1 - B(K^*)\mu_2 + \lambda_1 D_1{}^* k_2 = 0, \qquad (14.35)$$

$$\partial H^*/\partial c_A{}^* = -\lambda_0 k_1 w_A{}^* - \lambda_2 k_3/k_1 + \mu_2 k_1 w_A{}^* = 0, \qquad (14.36)$$

$$\partial H^*/\partial c_B{}^* = -\lambda_0 q_B{}^* - \lambda_1 k_2 + \mu_2 q_B{}^* = 0, \qquad (14.37)$$

the transversality condition $\displaystyle \int_0^T \frac{\partial H^*}{\partial K^*}\, dt = 0,$ (14.38)

$\mu_1(t)$, $\mu_2(t)$ are nonnegative, and

$$\mu_1[K^* - s^*] = 0, \ \mu_2[c_A{}^* q_A{}^* + c_B{}^* q_B{}^* - B(K^*)s^* - C(K^*)] = 0$$
$$\text{for all } t. \qquad (14.39)$$

Let us drop the asterisk notation with the understanding that all equations refer to conditions about the optimal trajectories and controls. Substituting for $\lambda_0 q_B$ from (14.37) into (14.35), we obtain

$$\mu_1(t) = \mu_2(t)[D_1 q_B - B(K)], \qquad (14.40)$$

from (14.36)

$$\lambda_2(t)\, k_3/k_1 = k_1 w_A[\mu_2(t) - \lambda_0], \qquad (14.41)$$

and from (14.37)

$$\lambda_1(t)k_2 = q_B[\mu_2(t) - \lambda_0]. \qquad (14.42)$$

Note that all the multipliers are related to $\mu_2(t)$ which is the social value of increasing treatment-plant financing. This says that the value of increasing financing depends on the social value of increasing production for A and B and also depends on the value of increasing treatment.

Suppose λ_0 is zero. Then if any of μ_2, λ_1, or λ_2 is also zero at any time t, we see from (14.40), (14.41), and (14.42) that all the multipliers will be zero at that time. This contradicts the condition that $[\lambda_0, \lambda_1(t), \lambda_2(t)]$ be nonvanishing. Thus we either have to suppose that λ_0 is positive or assume that none of μ_2, λ_1, or λ_2 is ever zero. Under the latter assumption, it will always be of social value to increase production of q_A, q_B and increase treatment. This is clearly an unsatisfactory assumption. Thus we may suppose that λ_0 is nonzero and hence normalize it to be unity. Since $\lambda_1(t)$ and $\lambda_2(t)$ are nonnegative and q_A and q_B are positive, then we see that $\mu_2(t) \geq 1$. Since $\mu_2(t)$ is nonzero, then by condition (14.39).

$$c_A k_1 w_A + c_B q_B - B(K)s - C(K) = 0 \quad \text{at every time } t. \qquad (14.43)$$

This means that at every time t, A and B will contribute just enough to cover the treatment plant costs and no more. (This condition presupposes that the production possibilities are completely divisible.) Now let us consider the question of the optimal treatment-plant capacity. From (14.39)

$$0 = \mu_1(K-s) = \mu_2[D_1q_B - B(K)](K-s) \quad \text{at each time } t, \quad (14.44)$$

or

$$0 = [D_1q_B - B(K)](K-s) \quad \text{since } \mu_2 \geq 1.$$

If we can show that $\mu_1(t) > 0$ for some t, then the above expression gives a functional relationship between K, s, w_A, and q_B. (If μ_1 were positive for all t, then $K \equiv s$.) If $\mu_1 = 0$ for all t, then the above gives no information about K and s.

From (14.38) we obtain

$$\int_0^T \mu_1(t)dt = \int_0^T \mu_2(t)[B'(K)s + C'(K)]dt \quad (14.45)$$

$$\geq \int_0^T B'(K)s + C'(K)dt$$

since $\mu_2(t) \geq 1$. Now

$$\int_0^T B'(K)s + C'(K)dt \geq \int_0^T [B'(K)K + C'(K)]dt = T[B'(K)K + C'(K)] \quad (14.46)$$

since K is constant, $K \geq s$, and $B'(K) < 0$. We assume

$$B'(K)K + C'(K) \equiv \partial/\partial K[B(K)s + C(K)]\big|_{s=K} > 0. \quad (14.47)$$

This expression is the marginal cost of an extra unit of capacity, and it is reasonable to assume that the cost of expanding capacity is positive.

Combining (14.45), (14.46), and (14.47), we find

$$\int_0^T \mu_1(t)dt > 0. \quad (14.48)$$

That is, $\mu_1(t)$ is positive for some t and, from (14.40), $\mu_1(t)$ will be zero only if $D_1q_B = B(K)$. The function $\mu_1(t)$ is interpreted to be the "shadow price" of increasing treatment. When $K > s$, the plant is operating below capacity and $\mu_1(t) = 0$. When $\mu_1(t) > 0$—that is, when the "shadow price" of increasing treatment is positive—then $K = s$, or the plant is operating at capacity level and to increase treatment would mean that the plant would have to be expanded. Below plant capacity, $D_1q_B = B(K)$ means that the short run marginal cost of treating a unit of A's wastes is equal to the marginal damage cost to B which is averted due to one less unit of A's wastes. So, below treatment-plant capacity we have that the optimal production and treatment levels satisfy the usual profit-maximizing condition of marginal cost equaling marginal revenue. However, because of the dynamic nature of the problem, this condition does not hold when $\mu_1(t) > 0$.

From (14.44), either $s(t) = K$ or $s(t)$ satisfies

$$D(w_A - s, F)q_B = B(K). \tag{14.49}$$

This gives $s(t)$ as an implicit function of K, w_A, q_B, and F:

$$s(t) = f(K, w_A, q_B, F). \tag{14.50}$$

When $K = s(t)$, we have

$$s = f(s, w_A, q_B, F). \tag{14.51}$$

Denote the solution of this equation by $\bar{s}(t)$. Then the optimal capacity is

$$K = \underset{0 \le t \le T}{\text{Max}}\, \bar{s}(t). \tag{14.52}$$

Thus, once we know the optimal trajectories w_A, q_B and control s, K can be determined.

Let us summarize the results obtained so far. There will be a treatment plant built whose size can be determined as above, and it will be financed in such a way that A and B contribute exactly enough at each time t to run the plant. In addition, below plant capacity the condition that marginal treatment cost equals marginal damage averted holds.

Using (14.20), (14.21), (14.33), (14.34), (14.41), and (14.42) with $\lambda_0 = 1$, we can obtain two simultaneous equations in $\dot{\mu}_2$ and μ_2 which can be solved for $\mu_2(t)$ and $\dot{\mu}_2(t)$:

$$\dot{\mu}_2(t) = \frac{k_2}{q_B}\mu_2(-V''_B q_B - V'_B + D) + k_2 V''_B, \tag{14.53}$$

$$\mu_2(t) = \frac{V''_B k_2 - k_3 V''_A}{V''_B k_2 - V''_A k_3 - (k_3/k_1)(D_1 q_B - k_1 V'_A)/k_1 w_A + k_2(V'_B - D)/q_B} \tag{14.54}$$

$$= \left\{ 1 - \frac{1}{V''_B k_2 - k_3 V''_A}\left[\frac{k_3 (D_1 q_B - k_1 V'_A)}{k_1}\frac{}{k_1 w_A} - \frac{k_2(V'_B - D)}{q_B} \right] \right\}^{-1}.$$

(Since $\mu_2(t) \ge 1$, we see that the denominator above must be less than or equal to 1 and positive.) Now, since $\mu_2(t)$ is known, expressions for $\mu_1(t)$, $\lambda_1(t)$, and $\lambda_2(t)$ are obtained only in terms of functions of w_A, q_B, and s. So, in theory, once the multipliers are obtained, the time paths of the variables of the system may be obtained.

Expression (14.42) for λ_1 may be differentiated with respect to time, and by using (14.33), $\mu_2(t)$, $\dot{\mu}_2(t)$ we can solve for $c_B(t)$ in terms of functions of w_A, q_B, and s. Likewise by using (14.41) for λ_2, (14.34), $\mu_2(t)$, and $\dot{\mu}_2(t)$, we may obtain $c_A(t)$ in terms of functions of w_A, q_B, and s. Using (14.52) and (14.43), we have another expression in terms of c_A, c_B and s, w_A, q_B. Since we now have three equations in c_A, c_B, and s in terms of w_A, q_B, these may be solved to give time paths of c_A, c_B, and s in terms of q_B and w_A. Then the time paths of all the controls and state variables are known.

No explicit expressions for these time paths will be given in this paper because of the complicatedness of the expressions. The important point is that we see how these paths can be obtained. Numerical approximation methods and use of a computer would enable us to obtain these time paths more explicitly, given knowledge of the functions involved.

Since we have not explicitly obtained all of the time paths, it is not possible, as was done in Model I, to discuss stability of the system. However, the optimality conditions which were obtained yielded some plausible results. Thus, the purpose of constructing these dynamic models, which was to show that such models can be useful in understanding externalities over time, has been fulfilled.

Extensions of the Model

It is clear that the model given in the previous section is almost too complicated to deal with by just using the Maximum Principle. Fortunately numerical approximation methods are available. One approach is to write all differential equations as difference equations and all integrals as sums. From there, different solution methods are possible. One method would be to use nonlinear programming; another is presented in a paper by Kendricks.[11]

Gradient or steepest-ascent techniques, generalized Newton-Raphson techniques applied to the Euler-Lagrange equations, and dynamic programming can also be used. These methods and a comparison of their efficiency are discussed in a book edited by Balakrishnan and Neustadt.[12]

The use of numerical techniques makes it feasible to consider models involving more than two firms. As in Model I, we can form a model to determine the Pareto-efficient waste disposal levels for n firms on a stream. These levels can then be imposed on the firms by an authority. The problem is complicated by the fact that each pollutor can also be a damaged party.

After the waste levels are imposed by the authority, firms have the incentives to form cooperative groups to build treatment plants for the same motives as those given in the previous section. The size of the coalition will depend on the relative location of the firms. A firm will not want to join with firms which are so far away that waste-piping costs become important.

Another extension of the model is to introduce stochastic processes. Stream flow cannot be predicted completely accurately because of random

11. D. A. Kendricks, and L. J. Taylor, *Numerical Solution of Nonlinear Planning Models* (Economic Development Report #98, Harvard University, May 1968).

12. A. V. Balakrishnan and L. W. Neustadt (eds.), *Computing Methods in Optimization Proceedings* (Conference on Computing Methods in Optimization Problems [New York: Academic Press, 1964]).

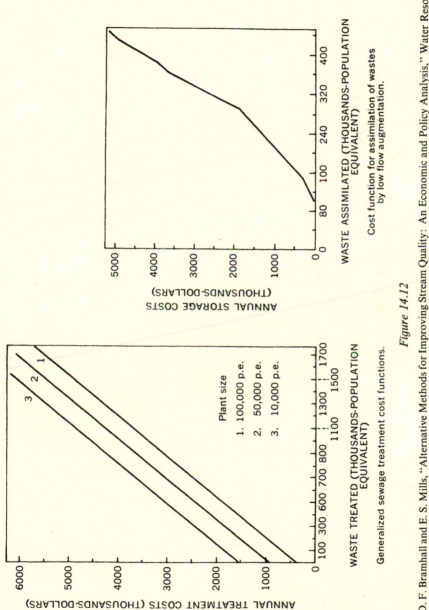

Figure 14.12

Source: D. F. Bramhall and E. S. Mills, "Alternative Methods for Improving Stream Quality: An Economic and Policy Analysis," Water Resources Research II, 358–59.

fluctuations. Stochastic control processes are discussed by Bellman,[13] and it is possible to include this in the models.

Finally, flow could also be introduced as a control variable in the models. By low flow augmentation through dam building, stream flow could be somewhat controlled. In low-flow periods, water would be released from the dam. The main effect of the released water would be to dilute wastes. However, reservoir storage may actually result in water which is quite low in dissolved oxygen, so that water releases to achieve a given effect are large and relatively costly. Thus, it seems that low-flow augmentation alone is not an efficient method of water treatment. Bramhall and Mills believe that

> Given present knowledge of stream assimilation processes and the economics of waste treatment and storage, it is very likely that the optimum waste reduction process combination includes a high level of waste treatment and relatively little low-flow augmentation.[14]

They conclude this from cost functions constructed from data from the Maryland portion of the Potomac River Basin. Their cost functions for standard treatment facilities and low-flow augmentation are given in Figure 14.12. It is clear from their model that it costs relatively more to achieve a given standard by flow augmentation than by standard treatment facilities. Thus while flow augmentation could be used for water treatment in our models, it cannot take the place of building joint treatment plants, and so flow was not considered as a control variable.

Summary and Conclusions

After observing that water-pollution externalities may result in socially undesirable resource allocation, a model was discussed in an earlier section to exhibit the necessary optimality conditions for a Pareto-efficient water resource allocation. It was shown that under certain conditions the optimality and feasibility conditions were both necessary and sufficient for a globally stable (D, q_B) system so that if the upstream and downstream firms were jointly operated, the equilibrium production levels could eventually be attained. For these reasons, it was argued that these production levels should be the ones imposed by the central authority. The technological externalities still exist after the standard is imposed, but the allocation of water resources is socially efficient. Because of the information requirements and computations necessary, it was argued that the Pareto-efficient production levels should be imposed by legal restrictions and property rights rather than by taxes.

13. R. Bellman, *Adaptive Control Processes: A Guided Tour* (Princeton, New Jersey: Princeton University Press, 1961.).

14. D. F. Bramhall and E. S. Mills, "Alternative Methods for Improving Stream Quality: An Economic and Policy Analysis," Water Resources Research, II, 355–365.

Next it was observed that such restrictions would encourage the firms to enter into negotiations and cooperate in building a treatment plant. Through this social investment, a higher level of social welfare is attainable than the Pareto-efficient level in Model I. Thus certain conditions imposed by a central authority can result in even greater social welfare through decentralized joint decision making by the firms. Davis and Whinston suggested that in the case of nonseparable technological externalities, the "natural unit" for decision making would be formed by mergers until the externalities were internalized.[15] In our model, externalities are internalized by joint treatment decisions; while this is not quite the same as a merger, it is closely related to this idea of the natural decision making unit. Note that the questions of the optimum size treatment plant and optimum joint social investment as formulated here could be formulated only in a dynamic model because of the time-varying demand for water resources. The dynamic model which was constructed contained individual profit-maximizing conditions as behavioral constraint conditions so that the model considered both individual and joint welfare maximization. The necessary conditions for optimality which were obtained showed that optimal financing should only just cover treating costs in all periods, and showed how optimum treatment-plant capacity could be determined. The time paths for all the variables of interest could best be obtained by numerical methods.

One final issue should be discussed. The joint treatment-plant financing model hinged on the authority's imposition of the Pareto-efficient equilibrium waste disposal level on the polluting firm. The authority's knowledge of this level depends on his knowing the demand conditions for the firm's products, their production functions, and the damage function, and then solving the problem formulated in Model I. The information requirements are thus formidable, especially if more than two firms are involved. Suppose the authority cannot obtain the exact Pareto-efficient equilibrium waste disposal. (For instance, the authority does not know all necessary functions exactly, or the computational requirements force it to simply make educated estimates as to what the correct waste level should be.) Then, what is the effect on the decentralized joint decision making? If the authority sets the standards too high, then the polluter will have to contribute more than the optimal amount to the treatment plant and the downstream firm will be overly benefited; the resulting production levels will of course not be optimum. The opposite situation holds if the authority sets the standard too low. However, the pressures toward joint social investment by the firms will still exist. Thus by defining property rights, the central authority designates the status quo point which determines the final distribution of income. Any status quo point selected will encourage decentralized decision making which

15. O. A. Davis and A. Whinston, "Externalities, Welfare, and the Theory of Games," *Journal of Political Economy*, LXX (1962), 215.

will lead to a higher level of social welfare than would have occurred without such encouragement. However, the final social welfare may not be the highest possible if the stutus quo point is not the Pareto-efficient one.

This idea of defining property rights to encourage negotiation is not new in literature dealing with externalities and is directly related to the discussion by Davis and Whinston on the proper role of the legal system:

> It may be the proper role of the legal and/or the judicial system to choose a status quo point ... so that the parties are free to determine a final settlement by bargaining methods.[16]

However, optimal social investment over time to mitigate the effects of externalities is a new concept which follows naturally when dynamic models are considered. We have applied this idea to a water-pollution model which is an example of a time-varying, nonreciprocal, nonseparable externality. It is clear that such dynamic bargaining models need not be limited to water pollution. Decentralized decision making and social investment can be encouraged by proper legal restrictions in other areas such as air pollution and municipal zoning.

16. O. A. Davis and A. Whinston, "Some Notes on Equating Private and Social Cost," *Southern Economic Journal*, XXXII, (1965), 113.

VI

Interorganizational Decision Making in Government

The papers in this section are directed to the problems arising when decisions must be made across the boundaries of multiple governmental organizations. One need only consider the layer upon layer of governmental units to begin to see the difficulties which may arise.

Government agencies are generally tied into the same overall hierarchical structure, which implies a power relationship and a chain of command. But in many instances decisions must be made involving units of roughly equal stature. It is the latter problem which is examined here.

Organization for Decision Making

In one sense, a discussion of organization for decision making should be deferred until the problem area and goal sets have been examined. Hurwicz, in his paper, discussed the problem of designing an optimal organization for joint decision making. The problem in the government context is often that there is an existing structure which was not designed to consider the decision at hand. The situation is more in the spirit of seeing the decision process as it is, not as it might be.

Some of the existing Federal governmental organization goes back to the 1920's. The Hoover Commission succeeded in altering the existing structure somewhat in the 1940's. Since then, there have been some additions, but few real alterations (despite the new cabinet posts) and almost no deletions. Any

Some of the ideas in this introduction and the case materials were developed in a panel discussion on the Management of Environment held at the Conference. The moderator was Lynton K. Caldwell, Political Science Department, Indiana University. Panelists were Sam Lawrence, Director Commission on Marine Science, Engineering and Natural Resources; Walter A. Hahn, ESSA, Department of Commerce (now a member of the National Goals Commission); and Ellison Burton, partner Ernst & Ernst. Other participants in the discussion were James T. Godfrey, Northwestern University; Jerome E. Hass, Cornell University; Hollis B. Vail, Department of the Interior and Matthew F. Tuite, Northwestern University.

organizational structure devised tends to become respected and solidified. This process extends beyond the government. In academic circles, one excels within his discipline, and jurisdiction is an important word to the governmental agency and to the labor union. But the problems are becoming too complex to deal with in the context of a discipline or jurisdiction. Interdisciplinary research into interorganizational decision making or management of environment is initiated; and interagency commissions are set up to deal with such problems as the development of marine resources.

In many respects, it would be easier if there were no preexisting organizational structure. The interested parties could then organize optimally for the decision to be taken. But a complex decision problem may require an equally complex structure, necessitating adapting to the existing structure. Thus, the theory of teams is less helpful than it might be because the theory must be applied within a fairly rigid preexisting organizational structure.

Merely throwing together organizations which can find a slot in the new structure or subsume several agencies may not be enough. The resulting organization must be strong enough to withstand any conflicts which develop. For example, in ocean exploitation, Department of Interior, Commercial Fisheries, the Geological Survey, ESSA, and the Navy all employ ships which do undersea charting. The questions of who has jurisdiction, what scale charts are to be produced, duplication of effort, and who may eventually have to give up their ships arise and must be resolved. In a non–zero-sum game, the need for strong as well as complex organizations is obvious, if the players are to return to play another round.

Example of Decision Organizations

Examples of complex decision organizations of the type discussed above may illuminate some of the additional decision problems which develop when multiple governmental bodies, each with independent decision making powers, are introduced into the system. One example involves Federal, state, and local governments in the solution of urban problems.[1] A second example, drawn from the conference panel discussion, is of an organization of organizations for decision purposes. It is the Council on Marine Research and Engineering. Its decision problems were to analyze existing marine programs in light of user requirements and benefits; to formulate national objectives and implement plans; to extend technology; and to consider the interfaces between the Federal government and lower levels of government, the private sector, and foreign governments.

The Vice President chairs the Marine Council which is part of the executive branch, almost a mini-cabinet. The council has a secretariat, which oversees

---

1. This example is not drawn from the panel discussion. Instead, it derives from research by the editors of this volume as a part of the larger NASA-supported project as acknowledged previously in this volume. See the Postscript for a fuller description of this decision situation.

the actions of the council and the professional staff which are part of the council. Under the secretariat are four committees which deal with various aspects of marine development plus a fifth parallel committee which is in the Department of State and which deals with the international aspects of marine development and use.

The committees are the arenas where the various agencies interested in marine development come together. The representatives to these committees are at the assistant-secretary or bureau-chief level (GS 17 or GS 18) for the civilian agencies and captains or admirals from the Navy. The Committee on Ocean Exploration has seventeen agency members. When it meets, about forty people are in the room by the time all the participants and observers gather. And there exist four other committees.

There are even elements of government-private sector decision interfaces because there exist, roughly parallel to the government committees, a series of subpanels of civilian consultants, in total about sixty-five to seventy-five people, who advise the Marine Council. Add several individuals who directly advise the Marine Council plus a few other little groups which do not fit neatly into the organization chart, and it becomes apparent that this decision making organization is complex. The structure follows not only from the complexity of the problem but also from behavioral attributes of bureaucracies.

The Objective Function and Goal Sets

Interorganizational decisions by government units are not distinguished by complexity of organization alone. The concept of an objective function was introduced by Kortanek, Hass, Baron, Loehman, and Whinston in preceding chapters in this volume. The objective function plays a key role in decision technology. As was shown, what is maximized by the decision process may differ somewhat depending on the situation, but in many instances at least one knows what is to be maximized. In the government case, the decision process may well involve the very definition of the goal set. The payoff matrix becomes part of the decision process rather than something to be discovered. Further, in most of the other decision processes described by the authors mentioned, there were market prices which served as relevant guides for resource allocation, although the Hurwicz and Reiter models did not necessarily require this information. In the government case, the decision frequently involves a non–price situation and, all too often, a situation in which the market system has failed to allocate well according to some criterion.

In decision technology, there is an objective function which is a statement of that which is to be maximized by the use of the decision technique. The economist talks of maximizing profits. In more general terms, it is usual to speak of goals and priorities. The question of the goal set has some interesting implications for the decision process.

Broadly stated, goals may obtain wide support but little action results when there is low operational content. Even the articulated goal of putting a man on the moon had to be refined in order to become a guideline for action, i.e., an objective function which would serve as a guide for decision making.

Some of the most interesting interorganizational decisions among government units come down to decisions of what will be the goal set, i.e., what is the objective function to be maximized. Present formal decision technologies are not well suited to resolving such issues. The goal of putting a man on the moon could not be stated in such a way that the NASA computers could go to work. After some initial decisions were made, the goals could be reformulated in terms which were amenable to the use of maximization techniques.

The Marine Sciences Commission has been able to take a broadly stated goal, such as wise development of the resources of the sea, and convert it to goal statements such as preserving specific recreational areas or developing commercial mining operations of a particular type in a certain location. The National Air Pollution Control Administration states goals in terms of achieving fewer than a fixed number of parts per million of any given pollutant. At this point, decision technology becomes applicable whether one or many organizations are involved.

There are a number of interesting problems associated with goal sets. One problem in formulating goal sets arises because perception of the problem area differs. The public at large is the ultimate arbiter of the actions taken. If the public perceives smog and sees black smoke pouring from the smokestacks in factories or from exhaust pipes of diesel engines, pressure is placed on the governmental agencies to adopt a goal of preventing black smoke. Dirt from black smoke and the problems it causes should not be minimized, but such a goal is not very helpful. The damage to health is likely to be caused by sulfur dioxide and other totally invisible pollutants. Similarly, oil floating on a body of water is visible, but a temperature rise caused by an atomic-fueled generating plant is not as easily noticed. In each case, the invisible pollutant may be the more damaging but the goal becomes to prevent the visible pollutant.

Another problem is that there may be a multiplicity of goals both within and outside the system which may or may not be conflicting. The Commission on Marine Science found that, in addition to private groups and business, all levels of government from the lowest up to the Federal had goals related to use of the resources of the sea. The goal of preserving commercial fishing may not conflict with the goal of providing sport fishing or other recreation; but both may conflict with undersea oil drilling, the use of sea water to cool atomic-fueled power plants, or the goal of using the sea for disposal of atomic wastes. Of course, the decision technologist will say that the problem is one of goal programming. But achievement of one goal may be a constraint to achieving others—a situation not suited to goal programming. Further, the goals may not yet be stated in quantitative terms consistent with goal-programming techniques. Moving from a zero-sum to a nonzero-sum game through conflict resolution is the decision problem. Finally we have both the problems of discrepancies between formal and stated goals and those actually sought by members of the predominant coalitions in organizations, and the fact that there may be significant but low-visibility goal shifts over time.

Goal sets may change rapidly over time. Wise use or improvement of the environment as a general goal has risen rapidly up the ladder of priorities. In recent times, any firm or government agency interested in pursuing a goal related to the sea was free to do so. There was no national goal for development of this resource. In the past few years, the priority of sea use has risen and the formation of the Marine Science Commission is in part the result of the higher priority and in part a cause of it. Yet, top priority in the goal structure cannot yet be assigned to development of ocean resources.

Change in ranking is not the only dynamic aspect of goals. The statement of the goal itself may change. Such change is not necessarily unrelated to a change in ranking. The goal may have the aspects of a moving target. The Marine Science Commission began work early in 1967, and the goal it perceived then became altered with the passage of time. This does not mean that decision technology is of no help, but it is often rendered less useful because the objective function once stated is already out of date.

Another aspect of dynamics in goal sets is the possibility of trade-offs between goals. In some instances, pairs of goals exist which, in order to maximize utility, should both be met. In a one-industry town, the goal of clean air may be attainable, failing some subsidy, only at the expense of losing the major employer. The decision may be all or none, unless it is possible to specify some mix. The objective function must be either the socialutility function or else the application of formal decision technology only to the problem of obtaining the desired mix once a decision on what the mix should be is obtained.

There is a means-ends chain or interchange within any goal set. It is often difficult to state a set of independent goals because one goal is simply a near-term goal—a means to a higher-level, longer-term goal. There may be both horizontal and vertical strata of goals which make difficult a precise statement of an objective function.

An operational goal (which is a means to the goal of lessening pollution) is the implementation of the Air Quality Act. It is a goal of the National Air Pollution Control Administration (NAPCA) whose responsibility it is to implement the provisions of the law. The problem is that there is no ready translation of the stated goal into an objective function. The difficulty here is not so much that there exists an hierarchy of goals. Instead, the problem is that decision technology might fail to serve the NAPCA very well if the result is vigorous enforcement of the Air Quality Act. It is entirely possible that the achievement of the goal of implementing the law would be at odds with other goals which are parallel but perhaps more salient. There is the necessity to preserve and perhaps expand the agency. Increased appropriations for the agency is a goal. But rigid enforcement of the law may provoke enemies in the Congress. Further, each individual within the agency has his career to consider. Self-preservation takes precedence over budgets, and the agency is more important than clean air. Thus, there is a subtle weighing of goals which is not easily included in the usual form of the objective function.

There may be goals which are horizontally stratified or parallel. Some of these may be conflicting, others not. Several examples related to the management of marine resources were given above and need not be repeated here. In the air-pollution case, conflict also arises. States and municipalities face the trade-off situation mentioned above. Rigid enforcement of stringent requirements may scare off industry. Setting standards at the Federal level reduces the chance of losing an industry for there is nowhere to go unless the firm goes out of business. At the other extreme, many municipalities find themselves besieged by groups of local citizens demanding cleaner air, and some local enforcement groups are influenced by such pressures so that maximum reduction of air pollutants becomes the goal. Thus, goals related to the use of the atmosphere for waste disposal, on the one hand, conflict with goals of breathing on the other. But, it still need not be a zero-sum game, and a joint decision may achieve a higher-order optimal solution.

The dual questions of goal setting and design of organizations may be summarized as follows. If there exists a public good, then there are, in all probability, several subsets of the public at large which have interests in the public good. The problem of organizations is to bring together representatives of the various interests and to explore fully the interrelated nature of the situation. There are then two criteria to be met. First, the organization must be efficient in performing its purpose, in both its decision making and implementation aspects. Second, it must produce an efficient solution in that it maximizes welfare over the various interests connected with the solution.

Impediments to Decisions

One paper in each of the preceding parts of this volume has concentrated on technical models of joint decision processes, and Tuite, Kortanek, and Baron discussed decentralized decision models explicitly. In each paper, benefits to coordinated decisions were demonstrated. If such coordination can be shown to be beneficial, why are organizations not more ready to coordinate their decision processes? Perhaps the reward system does not assure each party that he is receiving an equitable share of the joint benefit resulting from coordinated action.

In government organizations, the reward system has an unusual interpretation. Remembering that it is a public good which is being enhanced by the joint decision process, one must look to how the individuals involved in the decision process are motivated and rewarded. Even if the agency is credited for the improved resource allocation, will the boundary personnel involved in the decision be similarly rewarded?

On the contrary, in most instances the reward system penalizes the boundary personnel for doing anything which will achieve conflict resolution or an improved resource allocation through a joint decision. The evaluation or reward system is usually designed to promote and reward the employee who most advances the interests of the agency of which he is a member. Thus, if he bargains away any of the agency's prerogatives, he is penalized even though a conflict has been resolved.[2] Interorganizational decision making requires a reward system which motivates the individuals and their agencies to work together to achieve the collective goals.

Another impediment to the interorganizational decision process is the cost of communication and coordination. The decentralized decision models discussed in several papers above usually implicitly assumed a costless, noise-free channel of communication. In fact, a substantial resource cost is involved.

Several additional comments on the coordination and decision process are warranted here. First, for communication purposes, the selection of boundary personnel is a decision of great import. It is an unwise administrator who sends his most expendable clerk to represent his agency in the decision making process. At the interface, only persons of comparable rank and stature can comfortably be expected to reason together. In any such interorganizational decision group, holding the right position with the right people can have substantial impact on the decision reached. Communication requires a situation in which all may talk and expect to be listened to, not one in which some persons are capable of giving orders.

Second, the role each boundary person plays may differ from time to time. Sometimes a message may be sent to or through a particular person because of who he is, who he knows, who he can influence, or other reasons of personal power of the individual involved. At other times, a message will be directed to or through a person because of the position, job, or role he has. It may be convenient for all interested parties to "play it both ways." Yet neither the decision theorists nor the behavioralists have models which can fully deal with the subtleties of such a situation.

Third, the question of what is to be communicated, and through what channels, must be examined. In many instances, communication consists entirely of items related to the budget for the agency involved. Ultimate centralized control is often maintained through this process. It is often suggested that other messages are required for optimal coordinated decisions, but there are costs associated with the assembly, processing, and trans-

2. Heskett speaks of the power base of an organization, and Warren refers to the domain of the organization. Both assume that in decision making, organization will attempt to preserve or enhance their domain or power.

mission of these additional messages. Thus, if additional data are to be recommended for transmition, the benefit over the cost must be demonstrated.

The above impediments aside, decisions among government organizations are being made, and hopefully with some good results. The following three chapters relate to specific instances of such interorganizational decision making by such government agencies.

Articles on Joint Decisions by Governmental Organizations

Each of the three chapters in Part VI takes a slightly different view, but some of the considerations mentioned above are seen to apply in each case.

The first paper, by J. Van Ypersele de Strihou, examines a joint decision problem where the organizations are sovereign states. The decision process examined is the level of military power to commit to NATO. As such this discussion represents the largest level of interacting systems presented in this volume.

The paper examines the nature of the objective function, the payoff matrix of a nonzero-sum game. Presumably, there could be some optimal allocation of military-force commitments to produce maximum defense. Defense activities produce externalities which accrue unevenly, and the perception of being part of a larger system varies from country to country. While the perceived need for defense of the homeland is quite different, the salience concept used by Warren seems to play a big role here. Walton's discussion of when an organization will decide to not participate in a decision is also important here. De Strihou notes that an analysis on strictly economic terms such as ability to pay or cost benefit fails to explain actual NATO contributions. He goes on to propose a decision model which seems to better explain the observed NATO commitment.

Philip Whittaker was associated with NASA at the time his paper was written, and the examples are drawn from the NASA context. The striking aspect of this paper, prepared from the practitioners' viewpoint, is that he perceives the multidisciplinary aspects of the joint decision problem even though he does not employ the jargon of the academic disciplines. In fact, his perception of the problem is, if anything, clearer because he is free of a discipline-bound set when he approaches the problem. He describes the structure of NASA, which seems on the surface to fit the decentralization model fairly well. The headquarters group plays the role of coordinator in the decentralization model. It is interesting to note that in the NASA case, the various units tend to make independent decisions and the messages to headquarters take the form of demands.

The role of boundary personnel in the NASA decision process is described. It is noted that they are often top people in each of the decision units and each has considerable personal power when confronting the headquarters group.

Whittaker points out that the decentralization model may not fit well many of the interunit decisions in the government situation. He notes that one person ultimately makes most decisions. This person may be a member of one of the groups rather than an external coordinator. As such, he is well aware of the objective function of his own group. He may, and usually does, receive enough messages so that he is informed of the objective function of the other group(s). On this basis, he makes the decision.

As with many papers in this volume, the discussion often ranges beyond the primary focus to deal significantly with other issues. Whittaker goes on to examine decisions at the government-business interface as they occur in the context of NASA. The decision or negotiation of a contract is examined in some detail, with a discussion of the nature of the decisions made independently. It is in this discussion that Whittaker points out some of the second-order linkages of a decision system, something known to the practitioner but which none of the other authors in this volume have treated explicitly.

The point is made that parts of the system have considerable power. Obviously NASA has the power to cancel a contract for nonperformance, but exercise of this power may destroy the system or at least a key part of it. This is the nature of the second-order linkage. Cancellation of a contract destroys that contractor. But he may be the only supplier, and thus other NASA programs now and in the future are jeopardized. Even more complex is the effect that such actions would have on NASA's reputation and hence on its general long-term relations with its contractees and subcontractees. The need of NASA to control the second-order relations between "primes" and "subs" (contractors) is of special interest.

In the third paper, William Niskanen describes an attempt to use a decentralized decision model in a real-world context. The example is drawn from the Department of Defense, and the successes and difficulties are examined.

The paper focuses on the problem of establishing appropriate objective functions for each of the relevant decision units. Following the point raised by both Kortanek and Baron, Niskanen tries to deal with the tendency of the various units to game the system by establishing a series of incentives which will cause the units actually to maximize their objectives. He does not deal with the behavior which creates the gaming activities nor with changes in the entire system which arise as the subsystems develop new goal sets. Niskanen recognizes that it is possible to achieve coordination through close supervision by headquarters, but he notes, as did Baron, that the information costs are high and that this effectively recentralizes decision making, losing the benefits of decentralization.

Two further questions related to decentralization models are also examined. The first question deals with how much additional information the central decision makers must acquire concerning the production functions of the various decision units in order to function well. The second question discusses the difficulties arising because of noise in the decision channels.

15

Defense Organizations and Alliances

JACQUES VAN YPERSELE DE STRIHOU

Economists and political scientists in the United States have frequently argued over the last ten years that the decision making process by which the NATO allies decided on the level of forces they would contribute to the alliance has been deficient. The United States, they argue, has been contributing too large a share of the common-defense burden. The relative defense burden of each country is best expressed by the ratio of defense expenditures to GNP which indicates the share of its output that a country sacrifices in order to obtain security. The critics of NATO burden sharing point out that in 1963, for instance, while the U.S. allocated 10 percent of its GNP to defense, France, the United Kingdom, and Germany were contributing 8, 7, and 6 percent, respectively, and most of the smaller members of NATO contributed only between 3 and 5 percent of their GNP.[1] The critics also indicate that even in Europe itself the American forces represent a large percentage of total allied forces and are in a better state of combat readiness than those of many of their allies. This situation has led to frequent exhortations by U.S. Secretaries of Defense to their European colleagues to increase the amount and quality of their countries' contribution.

The purpose of this paper is not to define criteria for equitable burden sharing, but rather to try to understand the decision making process and to explain in economic terms why the allies have devoted very different shares of their total resources to the common-defense effort.

Any views expressed in this paper are those of the author and should not be interpreted as reflecting those of the organization to which the author belongs. This paper draws on some elements of the author's Ph.D. dissertation on: *Sharing the Defense Burden Among Western Allies.* Yale University, 1966.

1. Total defense expenditures of each country are measured according to the common and standard definition adopted by NATO. We have adjusted the data as published by NATO to take into account the differences between the opportunity and actual costs of conscripts. See the author's "Sharing the Defense Burden Among Western Allies," *Review of Economics and Statistics*, November 1967, 527–34.

The ability-to-pay principle does not provide an explanation to the differences in the relative burdens of each country. There is no positive relationship between the percentage of GNP allocated to defense and the per capita income of NATO countries. Nor do countries contribute according to the benefit they receive from the alliance. Indeed, as I have tried to argue elsewhere,[2] the benefit approach would lead to a higher proportion of GNP devoted to defense by smaller countries than by the larger ones. As I will indicate, it is just the reverse relationship that is found.

Before going into the details of the explanation, let me describe its main lines. The first and major factor of this explanation is that defense expenditures of the allies produce a service: common security, which is to some extent an international public good. This means that once an ally provides security for itself, to some extent it automatically also provides security to the other allies whether they contribute or not. The second factor is that in addition to common security, defense expenditures also provide joint products, which are not or are only partly shared with the other allies. Such benefits are, for instance, the internal security that can be provided by the armed forces, or nonalliance political benefits which can be obtained through the possession of a strong military force or the actual use of it. The existence of these joint products may induce countries to provide more security than they would provide if there were only the common-security benefits. A third factor is that countries have assessed differently the defense effort required to achieve a given level of security. A clear example of this are U.S. defense expenditure in Viet Nam which some allies do not view as contributing to the overall security of the West.

To develop the first argument, we have to analyze the concept of external security, then see to what extent it can be considered a public good, and finally analyze the consequences of this fact for burden sharing.

If one assumed a given threat common to all Western countries, then the security of the citizens of any NATO country, A, involves at least the following four aspects at a given moment.

1. The deterrence controlled by country A and that provided by its allies to deter the enemy from attacking country A or any other NATO country whose security is directly related to A's security. As is well known, deterrence is based on a force capable of inflicting upon an aggressor, even after a massive surprise attack, enough losses to deter him from launching such an attack and on the willingness to use these forces to make the threat of retaliation credible. Deterrence can be expressed in terms of probability of nonattack by the enemy.

2. If deterrence fails, security then depends on the country's ability with its allies to defend itself and escape destruction. This is what Secretary of Defense McNamara called the "damage limitation capability." It can be

2. See the author's "Sharing the Defense Burden Among Western Allies," *Yale Economic Essays* (Spring 1968), 261–320.

expressed in terms of number of men saved in cases of enemy attack.

3. A third element of security is the ability possessed by the given NATO country and its allies to prevent, by deterrence or the actual use of force or any other means, limited enemy gains in other parts of the world when such gains are considered to influence indirectly the security of the given country.

4. A fourth aspect of security is the ability each country has to prevent being drawn into another country's war against its own will.

Let us now recall the two characteristics of a public good.

a. The nonrivalness characteristic, or as Samuelson has expressed it, the condition that each individual's consumption of such good leads to no subtraction from any other individual's consumption.

b. The nonexclusion characteristic, which means that it is either not possible or not economical to exclude people who do not pay for the services from the benefits that result.

Let us now analyze how the two first aspects of security can be considered as a public good for the citizens of a given country, A. We will then transpose the problem to the international scene.

First, deterrence on the national level is the closest example of a pure public good. The first characteristic of a public good is fully met indeed. The enjoyment of deterrence, for instance, by a New Yorker does not decrease the security of a Californian. The cost of applying this deterrence to one more individual coming into this country is zero. The second characteristic of nonexclusion is also fully met. No one can be excluded from the benefit of national deterrence once it is provided.

The second aspect of security—defense if deterrence fails—does not fully meet in all cases the characteristics of a pure national public good, and in some cases it is even a private good.

Once deterrence fails, one meets a capacity problem, even in the use of the equipment initially designed for deterrence. The means of defense will not necessarily provide security to all the citizens of the country. While many instruments of defense will provide the same degree of protection to the whole country, others will extend their protection only to limited areas and will be public goods only for the citizens of this area, and not for those outside it. Indeed, in this case, if citizens of one area receive more protection, then fewer resources will be left for the protection of citizens in other areas.

Examples of defense instruments with strictly local impact are community shelters or local antimissile defenses. In some cases, even the protection provided will be a private good because consumption of security by one individual will rival that of another. Examples of this are private nuclear shelters which provide a certain external security but which do not meet the first nor the second characteristic of the public good, once deterrence fails.

Let me now transpose the problem onto the international level and see to what extent security can be considered an international public good in the NATO alliance.

(*a*) Deterrence meets to a large extent the first characteristic of a public good. Indeed, assuming for a moment that the alliance is composed of two members, the United States and Europe, one may consider that a certain amount of deterrence against enemy attack on Europe is a part of U.S. security. Since this deterrence for Europe is already part of the security the United States provides for itself, the cost of extending this deterrence to Europe is zero.

However, the deterrence against attack on Europe which is part of the security of the United States is not necessarily the same as the amount of deterrence provided to U.S. citizens. Pledging the same deterrence to Europe in all circumstances as to the United States may indeed include positive marginal costs and may even decrease the level of U.S. security, if we recall the fourth aspect of security: the ability to stay out of other countries' conflicts.

The second characteristic of a public good, nonexclusion, is largely but not perfectly met. Even in an alliance, the United States, for instance, could decide to decrease its deterrence for a European power by decreasing the credibility of its defense of this ally. It is partly the awareness of this possibility which has led France to start building its own deterrence.

France believes that the deterrence provided by the United States to its allies is not perfectly automatic and not of the same value as the one provided to American citizens, due to different costs and risks. France emphasizes that while the deterrence of attack on the United States rests unambiguously upon nuclear retaliation, this is not the case in Europe.

(*b*) The second element of security, defense if deterrence fails, is not a pure public good. The first characteristic of public good indeed is not necessarily met. If the deterrence fails, a capacity problem is met in the ability to defend citizens. So, in some cases for the United States, providing more defense for European countries may mean less protection for the United States, although the defense of different countries will not necessarily be rival in all cases. For instance, the use of U.S. missiles to destroy attack centers of the enemy will also protect any allies who face the same threat. Secretary of Defense McNamara has emphasized this aspect by saying, "We do not view damage limitation as a question of concern only to the U.S. Our offensive forces cover strategic enemy capabilities to inflict damage on our allies in Europe just as they cover enemy threats to the continent".[3]

The second characteristic of a public good — non exclusion — is not met perfectly, either. If deterrence fails, the United States, for instance, is not bound to give the same protection to Europe as to itself.

Now let us see what the consequences are for burden sharing of security being partly, at least, an international public good and of defense expenditures providing joint products private to each country. For presentation purposes,

---

3. Secretary of Defense McNamara: Statement to the House Armed Services Committee, cited by the *New York Times* (February 19, 1965).

let us first analyze the consequences of defense expenditures providing a pure public good, common security, and no private joint products. We will then see the implications of softening this principle by recognizing that security is only partly an international public good and that defense expenditures provide private joint products.

The consequences of defense being a pure international public good, for the sharing of the burden between a large country, A, and a small country, B, are relatively easy to forecast. For simplicity's sake, let us assume that all citizens in both countries have each the same income and the same indifference curve between security and other goods. The only difference is that there are twice as many citizens in country A than in country B. Small country B knows that the large country A will provide a higher amount of security than country B itself would be ready to provide in the absence of an alliance and that the amount of security will be automatically extended to B. As a result, B will not be induced to contribute at all. It knows that A will provide the good anyway, whether B contributes or not, and it knows that A will not be able to bargain with B since at the margin A places a higher value on security than B. This conclusion will not be altered even if when one takes into account the income effect caused in country B by the fact that it receives free security, provided the difference in size between the two countries is large. These points have been well developed by Mancur Olson and Richard Zeckhauser in their RAND paper entitled "An Economic Theory of Alliances".[4]

Thus, if security were a pure public good and defense expenditures provided no joint products, the big country would be contributing everything and the smaller countries nothing. As already indicated, we will have to relax both assumptions. However, as an explanation of the divergence between the defense burden of the United States and that of its allies, this factor — namely, that part of the security provided by the United States is an international public good — is a main element. Numerous acknowledgements of this can be found in studies of the contributions of smaller allies.

A student of European contributions to NATO, analyzing the fact that NATO goals were not met, summarized this point well:

> Implicit in the European unwillingness to meet the established goals was a reluctance to divert more public goods, funds, and services to building a weapons-use system when, in effect, the United States with its nuclear capability provided a 'defense' for Europe. In this connection, the existence of United States forces in Europe provided the Europeans with the assurance that, if Europe were attacked, the United States would be automatically committed to a response. Thus, the cost of building to the NATO desired strengths were assessed as too high in relation to the utilization of materials for domestic policies.[5]

4. M. Olson, Jr., and R. Zeckhauser, "An Economic Theory of Alliances" (RAND Paper RM-4297-ISA, October 1966).
5. Murray La Tourette Warden, "A Systems Approach to European Integration" (mimeographed, San Francisco, 1964).

As already noted, this first argument, although of prime importance, is not enough to explain the divergence between the relative burdens borne by the allies. Indeed, taken alone, this argument would lead to a situation where the United States would contribute all the defense expenditures of the alliance and the other countries nothing. Thus, while this first factor is a partial explanation of the importance of the burden borne by the United States relative to that borne by its allies, it does not explain why middle-sized European countries also devote a substantial share of their GNP to defense. Nor does it explain why the smaller countries of the alliance devote a much smaller percentage of their GNP to defense than the medium-sized countries. To explain this, we have to recognize that security is not a pure international public good and that defense expenditures provide private joint products.

We have already pointed out that the deterrence and the damage limitation capabilities were not pure public goods. In other words, only a part of the security the United States provides for itself is automatically extended to the allies. Those who emphasize this point with regard to deterrence look especially at the changes in strategy adopted in the alliance. Hedley Bull expresses this point of view well:

> The whole retreat of the United States from the doctrine of massive retaliation as a general formula for military containment of communism has been based upon the premise that the costs which are acceptable in repelling attacks and the risks shouldered in deterring them differ according to which country it is that is being attacked. They are not the same in the case of other countries as they are in the case of attacks on North America itself, and among other countries they are not the same in the case of attacks on NATO Europe. Deterrence of attack on North America rests unambiguously upon nuclear retaliation; deterrence of ground invasion of Western Europe rests upon 'the threat that leaves something to chance'; deterrence of attacks on other areas except where the opponent is without nuclear weapons, contains a very slight element of commitment to nuclear force.[6]

In summary, the expenditures on deterrence by the United States, while providing a public consumption good for U.S. citizens, are not considered by its allies as automatically providing the same degree of security. As indicated before, this is still more the case for the damage limiting capability aspects of security.

The total security provided automatically as a pure public good by the United States to citizens of its allies may be lower than what they would choose according to their own preference schedules and costs (taking into account the income effect caused by the security which is automatically provided).

So these countries may be induced to supplement the amount of security which is provided automatically by the big country.

They can supplement this security by providing themselves with their own

6. Hedley Bull, *Strategy and the Atlantic Alliance* (Policy Memorandum No. 29, Center for International Studies, Princeton University, September, 1964).

means of security, and by trying to render the U.S. response more automatic than the United States considers strictly necessary for its own security. A way to render the U.S. response more automatic is to keep an important contingent of American forces in Europe, and to accept the U.S. conditions for this, i.e., the provision by the Europeans of sizable conventional forces.

This last point was expressed well by Kissinger when analyzing the significance of the European contribution:

> Despite our commitment to retaliatory strategy, we constantly pressed for a European contribution of ground forces. The Europeans, though they agreed to a succession of NATO force goals, never really believed in the doctrines used to rationalize them. Rather, they saw in their military contributions a form of fee paid for United States nuclear protection. The Europeans agreed to our requests but they tried to see to it that their actual contribution would be large enough to induce us to keep a substantial military establishment in Europe, yet not so high as to provide a real alternative to nuclear retaliation.[7]

This analysis is not complete, however, because we have not yet included the reactions between the medium-sized and the small allies themselves. What I have in mind here is that the additional forces that the allies provide to supplement the security provided automatically by the bigger ally are themselves partly an international public good. For instance, the German forces, and the additional U.S. guarantee that they bring, are themselves partly a public good for the other allies. So we may apply here again, for the relationship between the medium-sized and the small countries, the arguments developed for the relationship between the big country and its smaller allies. This aspect of our analysis thus helps to explain the divergence between the relative size of the contribution of medium-sized countries as the United Kingdom, France, and Germany, and the smaller relative burden borne by the smaller allies.

The fact that defense expenditures provide joint products private to each country also helps to explain the level of contributions made by the allies. For instance, the armed forces can be used for internal security objectives. It may be noted that the NATO definition includes as defense expenditures some payments for internal security forces which are available for external security. Moreover, in emergencies, the armed forces themselves can be used to maintain order. These costs and benefits can be assumed to be a fixed proportion of the GNP. One could try to infer a very rough estimate of this benefit expressed as a percentage of GNP by looking at the situation in Ireland and Austria where defense expenditures are incurred almost solely for internal security. Between 1956 and 1963, these two countries devoted each about 1.3 percent of their GNP, on the average, to defense. Small NATO countries, even in the absence of external security problems, could be

---

7. Henry Kissinger, "Coalition and Nuclear Diplomacy," *Foreign Affairs,* XXXXII (July 1964), 525–45.

expected to devote about the same percentage of GNP for internal security. This helps us to explain the contribution of small NATO countries.

Other private joint products are the nonalliance political benefits that can be derived from the possession of a strong military force or the actual use of it. For instance, France in the Algerian war was deriving strictly national benefits from the use of its armed forces.

The main factor of this explanation is that security is partly an international public good, whether provided initially by the big ally or as a supplementary contribution by the medium-sized countries.

This implies, as shown in the analysis of security as an international public good, that the main determinant of a country's contribution will be its total GNP, not its per capita GNP. This is due to the fact that there is no supranational authority in the alliance which could determine the contribution of each member according to its ability to pay. On the contrary, each country will decide on its contribution according to its self-interest, and if it knows that a bigger country will value the good more highly at the margin than itself, it will not be induced to contribute.

Since the explanations suggest a positive relationship between the percentage of GNP devoted to defense and the absolute magnitude of GNP, we have tested this relationship for two years: 1955 and 1963.

Before discussing the test, however, we should note that the costs are only an imperfect measure of the burden borne by each country. For instance, from the defense expenditures of Greece and Turkey one should deduct part of the economic aid provided for these countries by their allies just to offset the burden of their military effort. One should also deduct from each country's defense expenditures the strictly national benefits in order to obtain a measure of the burden borne by each country for the provision of the international public good.

In addition to the fifteen NATO countries included in the test, we also added four neutral countries in 1955 (Sweden, Switzerland, Ireland, and Finland); and Austria was added in 1963. This was done in order to test the argument that the explanations given in this paper are also partly valid for the European neutral countries since they benefit implicitly from the alliance.

We found significant positive relationships between the percentage of GNP at factor cost allocated to defense, and the logarithms of real GNP at U.S. prices for various groups of Western countries, both in 1955 and 1963. These are indicated in Table 15.1.

Expressed differently, the relationship we are testing is:

$$\frac{D}{GNP} = a + b(GNP^*),$$

where D = defense expenditures according to the NATO definition in national prices, GNP = gross national product at factor cost in national prices, and GNP^* = logarithm of gross national product measured in U.S. prices.

Table 15.1. Coefficient of variation and t-test

Countries Included	r^2	$b/(\sigma b)$	Level of Significance against a Hypothesis of No Relationship
1963			
NATO countries minus			
Portugal, Greece and	0.89	0.942	0.001
Turkey = 12 countries		(0.106)	
NATO countries minus	0.81	0.902	0.001
Portugal = 14 countries		(0.125)	
NATO countries minus			
Portugal, Greece, and Turkey, plus	0.83	0.910	0.001
5 neutral countries* = 17 countries		(0.107)	
NATO countries minus			
Portugal, plus 5 neutral countries =			
19 countries	0.75	0.866	0.001
		(0.121)	
1955			
NATO countries minus			
Greece and Turkey = 13 countries	0.71	0.844	0.001
		(0.162)	
NATO countries minus Portugal,			
Greece, and Turkey = 12 countries	0.72	0.849	0.001
		(0.167)	
NATO countries = 15 countries	0.66	0.816	0.001
		(0.149)	
NATO countries plus 4 neutral			
countries† = 19 countries	0.63	0.793	0.001
		(0.148)	

* Sweden, Switzerland, Finland, Austria, Ireland.
† The same as in 1963, with the exception of Austria.

16

Joint Decisions in Aerospace

PHILIP N. WHITTAKER

This paper is concerned with the aerospace area and, in particular, the business area of the National Aeronautics and Space Administration (NASA). With over 90 percent of NASA's budget being paid out in contracts and grants as it is today, there certainly is a joint involvement of government, industry, and universities in the space program. Within the government itself, there is also an enormous amount of interorganizational interplay.

As one sits in NASA and looks about, one sees a large number of other executive agencies of government that have related and sometimes seemingly overlapping roles, missions, and responsibilities. There is the General Services Administration, which has a large centralized responsibility for procuring all of the standard items that are used within government and for managing the government's office buildings and this type of thing. There is also the Department of Defense with its own massive space and aeronautics programs. The Department of Transportation includes the Federal Aviation Administration, again clearly involved in the area of aeronautics. The Bureau of the Budget has broad control over financial matters. So clearly, within the government there is an enormous amount of joint involvement.

NASA Organization Structure

NASA, itself, consists of some eleven centers that are geographically scattered around the United States, each of which enjoys a considerable measure of autonomy and whose individual charters contain some elements of overlap and competition. Included are such centers as the Marshall Space Center in Huntsville headed by Dr. Von Braun, a pretty strong man in his own right with his own constituency, the Lewis Research Center headed by Dr. Silverstein at Cleveland, and the Manned Space Center at Houston headed by Dr. Gilruth. Each one of these and other entities has a tendency to strike out on its own in many areas, to be master within limits of its own destiny,

270

and, for completely human and understandable reasons, to turn to NASA headquarters and simply demand the money needed to get on with whatever projects are thought by them to be particularly important at the time. In addition, there are four program offices at NASA headquarters to which the centers report. For example, the three centers involved in manned space flight, that is, the Marshall, Houston, and Kennedy space centers, report into a single program office of Manned Space Flight. The centers whose main thrust is in the research area report into a program office called the Office of Advanced Research and Technology: and the remaining centers, those that are involved in the unmanned programs, the planetary probes, the weather and scientific satellites, and so forth, report to the Office of Space Science and Application. The fourth program office is for tracking and data acquisition. No specific centers report into it, but it is responsible for the worldwide networks that the agency uses. A small group called NASA Headquarters coordinates all of this.

NASA today has approximately 31,000 government employees, with an additional 200,000 people in industry, universities, and nonprofit organizations involved in performing NASA's programs. These are largely administrators, scientists, engineers, and the like. NASA's present budget is about $4 billion, which is down from the almost $6 billion of several years ago, at which time there were some 400,000 people involved in performing NASA's programs. I have presented this very brief organizational outline so as to be able to discuss some of the principal interfaces that one sees sitting from the particular vantage point of an administrator in NASA.

NASA has many characteristics in common with other organizations both in government and industry, where one could observe patterns which are quite similar to the one I have described. Such complex organizations have their own line, their own staff, their own semi–self-sufficient, self-sustaining, self-governing, self-operating entities, be they NASA centers, university departments, or corporate divisions. Within the organization the age-old line-staff complexities exist, as well as other issues which may not neatly be contained within one center, one staff structure, or one department. One evidence of this condition lies in the so-called acting or decision documents that come replete with concurrences from a vast number of people and that, by virtue of what is known in government as the coordination process, sometimes seem to get issued very slowly. Beyond that, in NASA's case, is the extremely complex spread of agencies and instrumentalities comprising the Federal government, many of which relate to NASA on a day-to-day basis. There is also the large family of contractors who have a special kind of relationship in the performance of space-related tasks.

Patterns of Decision Making

I have been careful so far not to labor the term "joint decision." While talking about the interfaces and the interrelationships which do exist, let me try to express my uncertainty on the use of the term "joint decision making." My observation is that there probably is no such thing as joint decisions. Somebody has to make a decision. It may be, and almost undoubtedly is, influenced by a great number of external pieces of information in the factors, but nonetheless the decision making process in the final analysis involves a single person, without crossing organizational lines. Having said this, I am forced back to the actualities of this fairly complex world in which we all live. While a decision in the final analysis is made by one party, many decisions are so shaped by the environment and the interplay of the organizations as to constitute what might be called a de facto joint decision. The final decision maker is put in the position, by virtue of all the inputs he receives, of something approaching inevitability as to the decision making in which he finally indulges.

Let us look at a pattern of decision making. The government in general and NASA in particular have largely rejected the "arsenal" concept, the idea of setting up government-owned and -operated research and development laboratories and manufacturing plants, aircraft and spacecraft construction facilities, and the like. There is a policy directive put out by the Executive Office of the President which enunciates the policies of the government to generally rely on the private enterprise system to supply its needs. As indicated, over 90 percent of NASA's budget dollars are spent in industry, the universities, and nonprofit organizations. The real question is that imposed by the importance of there being an optimum working relation between the agencies such as NASA, who on behalf of the government and the taxpayer want to obtain needed goods and services, and the private sector which supplies them. It certainly should be apparent that by optimizing this relation everyone will benefit. NASA will get more boost for its money; technology will be better advanced; and industry will improve its technological confidence, its prestige, and its economic and financial success.

We are talking here, particularly in the space agency of enormously complex systems and kinds of acquisitions, which are most difficult to describe in advance: what is wanted, how it should be designed and built, what its exact specifications should be, how much it should cost, how long it should take to get it, and so forth. Of NASA's appropriations since it started, 82 percent have been in the category of research and development effort. It is necessary to examine some of the interfaces which exist between NASA and the industries, universities, and nonprofit organizations with which it deals, areas that must be optimized in order for the relation to be rewarding to both parties. Long before an agency is ready to go out for a procurement it must have as good an understanding as possible of the technological capabilities that exist in industry. NASA should know, for example, what the possibilities are in space power, how much weight one has to put in a satellite in order to generate how many kilowatts of power, for how long a period, and with what reliability. Another example: What are tomorrow's possibilities in communicating from space? How many data, in other words, can you send back to earth from a spacecraft in orbit in a given period of time? NASA must know what industry's capabilities are today and what they are likely to be tomorrow. Only by knowing this kind of thing could the agency make the right decisions as to its future programs. In turn, the contractors who are interested in working in the space program must know what NASA's future plans and requirements are.

All major aerospace contractors have their independent research and development (IR&D) programs. These are conducted by the contractor at his own election in areas of his own choosing, but are considered an allowable cost in overhead spread over the contractor's stable of government contracts. It would be unfortunate and a waste of taxpayers' money, not to mention scarce technical talent, if the contractor were to use his IR&D effort to go off in some direction which clearly has no applicability to the nation's needs as visualized by the government contracting agencies. The closest kind of communication is required in order that the contractor's decisions as to his research and development activities, his future market planning, and his thrusting technological effort result in their being linked with government needs. The government must do its planning in recognition of what technology is and will be available to it as it implements its programs. A two-way flow is necessary in order for the right decisions to be made separately by the parties. This activity is not being as well done as it should be, and there are a number of cases of discontinuity between the two parties.

Establishment of a Contract

Here is a clear case of a situation in which the decisions are made separately by each of the parties, but only after, hopefully at least, a heavy input from the other party. From the time period prior to initiation of a particular procurement or even the identification of a specifically defined and approved program we move into the time frame during which the contractor's selection process takes place. Here again there is a tremendous amount of interface activity and interaction taking place between the government agency and the contractor. As the establishment of a contract becomes more imminent, the adversarial relationship between the parties is considerably accentuated. The contractor is trying to sell the government on his selection, his price, his time requirements, and a set of specifications as undemanding as possible. The government is trying to do exactly the opposite. Even in this adversarial relationship it is important to note that there is a mutuality of interests, a striking of a balance, and an establishment of a relation which will optimally motivate both parties and be desirable for both of them. It is not of real long-term benefit to the government to induce contractors to undertake contracts on which industry will incur substantial losses or fail from the standpoint of technical performance.

It is important at this time that the government use every means at its command to describe completely, accurately, and coherently to prospective contractors what it is that the government wants to buy. It is essential that the contractor in turn submit a proposal which is clear, concise, and factual and which describes the best possible and most responsive product that the contractor can provide to satisfy the government's request. Just as in the independent research and development area, the contractor's bid and proposal costs are included in his overhead and charged across all of his contracts, and for that reason alone it is to the best interest of both parties to be sure that the contractor is not going to spend money on putting together proposals that are way off target. The proposal cycle is full of decision making, and the decision making had better be independent, as between the contractor and the government, for a number of legal reasons. One party's decisions will be better and sounder if based heavily on inputs from the other.

Once the proposal cycle has been completed and the winning contractor has been selected, the parties will negotiate the contractual relationship. The closest thing to joint decision making takes place here. First of all, in a negotiation one has to be sure that both parties understand, and reduce to writing, exactly what the technical scope of the work will be. There has to be agreement on the reporting requirements, the management system requirements, and the like. The contractor must prepare cost estimates which are subject to analysis and audit, and only then can the price be negotiated. An understanding has to be reached as to the types and amounts of control that will be imposed on the contractor during the performance. The resulting contract reflects in a very real sense the separate judgments and decisions of the parties as to the relative sharing of the risks between them. After the contract is entered into, there is a continuing and usually protracted period during which the contractor is working and the government is watching what is going on. Frequently changes in direction are being established as the contract progresses. Each one of these changes in direction or scope in itself goes through the same sort of negotiation cycle as the initial contract. In each of these cases an interorganizational decision process is involved. Also during contract performance, and immediately thereafter, a number of other government agencies may become involved. These may include the General Accounting Office—the Congressional watchdog which, as some agencies view it, second guesses the agency and the contractor—the renegotiation board, which examines the contractor's overall profits on an annual basis and determines whether they have been excessive, and also a number of nongovernment parties, including, of course, the subcontractor, the teammates associated with the prime contractor, the competitors of the winning contractor, and probably other divisions and organizations within each one of these entities.

This brings up the special question of the amount of control that NASA exercises over its subcontractor. The agency looks upon itself as being budget-constrained rather than project-constrained; the agency must stay within the budget. There is, in theory, no direct contract between the government and the subcontractor; however, the agency often selects the subcontractor or looks in on the one that the prime contractor has selected. The government then withdraws, and the prime contractor is responsible for the management of the subcontractor. You might ask whether, in this case, the contractor would have an incentive always to pick the best subcontractors and to establish sound financial relations with them. In fact, some prime contractors have exacted a terrible price from some subcontracting companies to get into that program. They have forced subcontractors to come in on a fixed-price basis although their prime contract is not a fixed-price contract. They have forced fixed-price contracts on their subcontractors, with some of these losing millions of dollars. There is only one thing worse than doing business with the government, and that's doing business with a prime. One of the problems is that if you don't like it, you can be told to go somewhere else. The facts of life are that you can't always go somewhere else. If you have a plant that is specialized to turn out portions of a wing of aircraft, you can't convert that overnight to making metal furniture. You're trying to keep your labor force together. Perhaps there is no commercial aircraft work available at the moment, and so the only option open to you is the space or defense subcontract. What you do is exercise all the optimism that you can and take a high risk and perhaps later find yourself in a tough spot. This may not be healthy for the industry. We should not be in a position in which we see government play God.

Conclusions

What I have attempted to catalog briefly are some of the organizational units and forces that come into play in the government procurement process. Most decisions are made by one party or the other—by the government, by the prime contractor, by the subcontractor, and by the independent government agency. However, almost all of these decisions are influenced by agencies outside the one making the particular decision. A challenging problem facing the government and the aerospace industry today is how to create an environment in which decisions can be made which will be most beneficial to both parties.

There is an old saying in government negotiations and industry negotiating circles that a good negotiation is one from which both parties will walk away slightly dissatisfied. There are all different degrees of satisfaction as to the results of a negotiation. I, therefore, see no such things as a joint decision. Even though two parties are sitting across the table with a contractual document lying between them, there is an affirmative separate act taken by each party as to how he will agree to that contract. In spite of the fact that it is done in proximity and done at a very close time cycle, the two actions are separate actions. I have been a party to several negotiations in which, when the discussions reach their end, one party or the other walks out. It's not fruitful to become involved in a semantics debate as to whether there are or are not joint decisions; what is important is to recognize that there are separate determinations being made by the two parties.

We should not move in the direction of joint decision, but we should move in the direction of decisions that take into account the interest of both sides of the equation, that is, both government and industry. The key element is to have as full and complete information shared between the parties as is possible throughout this entire cycle. For, with such complete information, better decisions will result, thereby resulting in better procurements, greater technological advances, enhanced economies in government spending, and improved economic health for the industries involved.

17

Coherent Decentralization of U.S. Defense Force Planning

WILLIAM A. NISKANEN

Introduction

The Department of Defense is the third largest planned economy in the world. Annual U.S. defense expenditures are now around $80 billion plus $10–15 billion of additional resources which are expropriated or provided by other government agencies. The Department of Defense directly employs around 5 million people and indirectly employs, through the defense contractors, around 3 million additional people. Among the planned economies, total expenditures by the Department of Defense rank behind only the total economies of the Soviet Union and, possibly, Communist China — the two nations, ironically, which are our major potential adversaries.

For all the literature on the organization and decision processes of planned economies and multidivisional private firms, the Department of Defense has been virtually ignored as an appropriate subject for study. As you might suspect, I think this is unfortunate. Several years in the Pentagon greatly increased my personal understanding of the problems of the socialist economies; I expect, correspondingly, that the lessons so painfully learned by the socialist economies would be of considerable value to the Department of Defense. I am less hopeful that the theoretical developments of the last decade concerning the conditions for coherent decentralization of private economies and firms will provide very valuable insights for the organization and management of defense. These developments have been characterized as proving that everything is for the best in this best of all possible, freely competitive, profit-maximizing linear worlds. This may or may not be reassuring, depending on whether one views this as mathematical support for Adam Smith or for Voltaire. I am not in a position to judge the value of these insights to the private economy or the difficulty of implementing them in a specific firm. These models are not (yet) very valuable for either descriptive or prescriptive purposes to the management of defense, for the following primary reasons:

The Department of Defense and its subordinate agencies are not profit maximizers.

There are no objective market prices for the defense outputs.

There are only a few rudimentary internal markets for the transfer of resources among subordinate agencies.

Competition among the subordinate agencies is often limited by high fixed costs and economies of scale and also, more importantly, by a doctrinal division of "roles and missions."

For these and several other reasons, everything is not for the best in the Department of Defense.

At the present time, the Department of Defense is among the most centralized of large modern institutions on the basis of both the type and level of issues resolved by the top management level and the approved latitude of subordinate managers. The basic force planning system operates by a flow of production function and cost information from subordinate agencies to the Office of the Secretary of Defense, calculations and decisions by OSD, and a flow of orders from OSD to the subordinate agencies. At various times since 1961, no type or level of decision has been immune from OSD attention, and the approval latitude of the subordinate managers is often very small. Secretary McNamara personally intervened in the selection of belt buckles and butcher smocks. A change of one unit in the level of a program element formally requires OSD approval.

Some change in the present management procedures of the Department of Defense is important because the cost-output performance, with few exceptions, has been poor. This is not the place to document this assertion, but I am prepared to do so at some length. There is no reason to be doctrinaire on the issue of whether a different centralized or a more decentralized management system would be better. The evidence of the last several years is that the present centralized management system does not work very well. The potential success of a strongly centralized system is dependent on all of the following conditions:

The objectives of the subordinate managers must be consistent (not necessarily identical) with the objectives of the central manager.

Information available to subordinate managers must be effectively transmitted to the central manager.

The central manager must know how to use the available information and be prepared to make decisions on this basis.

The subordinate managers must understand and be prepared to carry out orders from the central manager.

In a bureaucratic environment, such conditions exist only under very special circumstances. Objectives are most nearly consistent throughout the organization only when the total organization is faced by strong output pressure (such as that caused by an organization-threatening crisis or war) or as a consequence of the tolerance and uncertainty by subordinate managers during the rather short "honeymoons" at the start of a new administration. Under normal conditions, the behavior of subordinate managers can best be described by a budget-maximizing model. Even when objectives are consistent, information is lost in transmission, partly depending on the number of echelons which process the information before it reaches the central manager. When objectives are not consistent, the central manager should expect the information provided to be self-serving to the subordinate managers. The rare central manager may know how to use the detailed production function and cost data provided by the subordinate managers. Under most circumstances, however, he and his staff will have less professional experience in the relevant areas than the subordinate managers and will be particularly handicapped in handling problems where the information is subject to some uncertainty and cannot be directly evaluated. Again, even when objectives are consistent, information about the intent of orders is degraded by transmission through several echelons to the relevant subordinate manager. When objectives are not consistent, of course, implementation of orders can be seriously undermined by the lack of complete information by the central manager on the actions of subordinate managers.

One other condition that limits the effectiveness of centralized organizations is not sufficiently appreciated. Some amount of management responsibility is positively valued in our society. Most people will prefer to work in response to impersonal forces or general direction, however deterministic their behavior appears to be in retrospect. As a consequence, subordinate managers must usually be compensated in some form (such as larger budgets) in exchange for a reduction in their management authority. One should expect the increasing centralization of a bureaucracy, therefore, to be associated with larger budgets, and decreasing centralization, conversely, with smaller budgets. A decentralization of defense management to give the military more management responsibility may be a necessary condition for reducing the defense budget as the war in Viet Nam is (hopefully) resolved.

For these reasons a strongly centralized formal management system, except during a sustained crisis, tends to lose control to an increasingly decentralized actual management system over time. The primary power of the subordinate managers is their control over information flow—about what they can do and what they are doing. The more complex the production processes, the more difficult it is for the central manager to acquire information in which he has confidence about the lower level organizations. One would expect that it would be relatively easy for a central manager to understand and monitor the production processes of a subordinate group for which the inputs are dominated by a few major items of capital equipment and the output has only a few dominant characteristics. For example, OSD has been relatively successful in managing the strategic offensive forces but most unsuccessful in managing the ground forces, support programs, and research and development. Decentralization on the basis of information control is a most probable consequence of the end of tightening budgets or an output crisis, but the dimensions of this decentralization have only a nominal correspondence to those of a coherent decentralization.

The organization and management of the Department of Defense, thus, is influenced by two counteracting forces: Some degree of central management is requisite to effective political control over defense outputs and budgets and may be dictated, to some degree, by the nature of the production and cost functions. Some degree of de facto decentralized management is a consequence of subordinate managers' control of information. An exploration of the necessary conditions for the coherent decentralization of the Department of Defense may lead to a conclusion that either a more or a less centralized system is desirable; in any case, it should provide some insights about the appropriate roles of the central and subordinate managers, the necessary types of information flow, and other general characteristics of an efficient defense management system.

A Representative Force Planning Problem

The primary problems of decentralizing defense force planning are illustrated by the representation of a U.S. tactical (or "general purpose") forces planning model given in Table 17.1.

The master force planning problem is to select the set of U.S. tactical forces which minimize

$$C(X_P, X_C, X_E, \triangle X) \tag{17.1}$$

subject to

$$O(X_P) + S_{PI} = R_{PI}O(Y_{PI}), \tag{17.2}$$

$$O(X_P, X_C S_{PI}) \geq R_{PS}O(Y_{PS}), \tag{17.3}$$

$$O(X_C, X_E S_{EI}) \geq R_{ES}O(Y_{ES}), \tag{17.4}$$

$$O(X_E) + S_{EI} = R_{EI}O(Y_{EI}), \tag{17.5}$$

$$X_P + X_C + X_E - \triangle X \leq X^0, \tag{17.6}$$

$$X_P, X_C, X_E, \triangle X, S_{PI}, S_{EI} \geq 0. \tag{17.7}$$

In this representation of the master force planning problem, the total budget for the tactical forces is minimized subject to achieving certain tactical objectives. The elements in the cost function (17.1) are the present value of the cost of maintaining and operating the X_P, X_C, and X_E forces during the planning period plus the procurement cost for any new forces.

Table 17.1.

Variable	Description
X_P	U.S. tactical forces in Pacific theater or specifically committed to this theater
X_C	U.S. tactical forces in continental U.S. for potential employment in either theater
X_E	U.S. tactical forces in Europe or specifically committed to this theater
ΔX	Total increment to U.S. tactical forces during planning period
X^0	Total U.S. tactical forces at beginning of planning period
Y_{PI}	Enemy forces in Pacific theater during initial phase of conflict
Y_{PS}	Enemy forces in Pacific theater during sustained phase of conflict
Y_{EI}	Enemy forces in European theater during initial phase of conflict
Y_{ES}	Enemy forces in European theater during sustained phase of conflict
R_{PI}	U.S. objectives in Pacific theater during initial phase of conflict
R_{PS}	U.S. objectives in Pacific theater during sustained phase of conflict
R_{EI}	U.S. objectives in European theater during initial phase of conflict
R_{ES}	U.S. objectives in European theater during sustained phase of conflict
S_{PI}	"Slack" U.S. objectives in Pacific theater during initial phase of conflict
S_{EI}	"Slack" U.S. objectives in European theater during initial phase of conflict

Cost Function

$C(X_P, X_C, X_E, \Delta X)$. Present value of total cost of U.S. tactical forces during planning period

Production Function

$O(X_P, Y_{PI})$, "Output" of interaction of U.S. and enemy forces in Pacific during initial phase of conflict

$O(X_P, X_C, Y_{PS}, S_{PI})$. "Output" of interaction of U.S. and ememy forces in Pacific during sustained phase of conflict, given "output" of initial phase

NOTE. — Output functions for European theater are comparable.

For convenience, the objectives of the tactical forces (the right-hand side of equations [17.2]–[17.5]) are expressed as the product of political objectives (R_{PI}, etc.) and the output of the relevant enemy forces ($O(Y_{PI})$, etc.). For example, if

$$O(X_P, Y_{PI}) \geq R_{PI}$$

and

$$O(X_P, Y_{PI}) = \alpha X_{PI}^{\beta} \ Y_{PI}^{\gamma} \quad (\beta > 0, \gamma < 0),$$

then

$$\alpha X_P^{\beta} \geq R_{PI} Y_{PI}^{-\gamma}.$$

The U.S. forces necessary to achieve a certain political objective, thus, will be a positive function of the effectiveness of the enemy forces. Equation (17.2) states that the output of the X_P forces in the initial phase of a Pacific conflict must be equal to or greater than the tactical objectives; the difference between the output and the objectives (which may be zero or positive) is the S_{PI} variable. Equation (17.3) states that the output of the X_P and X_C forces in the sustained phase of a Pacific conflict, given the output of the initial phase, must be equal to or greater than the tactical objectives in this phase. The inclusion of the S_{PI} variable in the production function for the sustained phase recognizes that the output of given forces in the sustained phase may be strongly dependent on the relative condition of U.S. and enemy forces at the end of the initial phase. The interpretation of equations (17.4) and (17.5) is similar. Equation (17.6) states that the sum of X_P, X_C, and X_E minus the newly procured forces (which may be zero or positive) must be less than or equal to the total tactical forces at the beginning of the planning period; this equation determines how much new procurement, if any, is necessary to meet objectives in this planning cycle. Equation (17.7) constrains all variables in the model to be either zero or positive.

This problem could be solved by the central manager (given the necessary second-order conditions) if all of the relevant information could be correctly and efficiently transmitted from the subordinate managers. At the present time, a planning format of this general nature is used to separately evaluate each of the functional components of the tactical forces — the ground forces, tactical air forces, navy forces, and logistic support forces. The choice of forces within each functional component is only moderately difficult, as the relative effectiveness of force elements within each functional type can often be satisfactorily estimated and the derived output relations can often be satisfactorily represented by linear functions. At the present time there is no formal planning procedure for selecting the efficient combination of the functional components on either an aggregate or a theater basis. The primary reasons for the failure of the Office of the Secretary of Defense to effectively plan the combination of functional forces, I believe, are the following: The output relations among the functional forces are more complex; less information is available on these relations at any level; and the information that is available at the theater commands is not effectively transmitted to the central manager.

Two characteristics of this tactical force planning problem also prevent the easy decentralization of planning to the theater commands:

1. Some part of the tactical forces in the continental United States may be employed in either the Pacific or the European theater during a sustained phase of conflict. The efficient level and composition of these reserve forces cannot be determined by any one theater commander, but they strongly influence the efficient level and combination of each of the theater forces. From the viewpoint of the theater commander, these reserve forces are a "public good." These forces provide an "external benefit" to both theater commanders. Acting independently, the two theater commanders would not choose as much reserve force as they would acting collectively.

2. The marginal cost of forces inherited at the beginning of a planning period is often substantially less than the cost of forces added during the planning period. In a general sense, this problem is not unique to the Department of Defense. As many defense assets are quite specific and the Department of Defense is a monopoly, however, the internal value of defense assets

(both equipment and training) is often much higher than the value of these assets in other uses. As a consequence, the total and marginal cost functions of individual force elements have the general characteristics shown in Figure 17.1. As no theater commander has a vested claim on the lower-cost inherited forces, the costs of forces to one theater command cannot be determined without information on the demand for these forces by another theater.

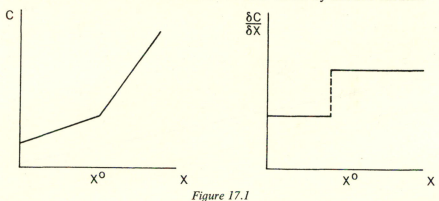

Figure 17.1

In the absence of the first problem (i.e., all forces are unconditionally committed to one or the other theater), this problem could be resolved by the standard decentralization procedures using shadow prices of the inherited forces. In the absence of both the first and second problems (i.e., such that the solution is in the region of either inherited forces or new forces for all elements), the decentralization problem is trivial, although the force planning problem of the theater commanders may still be difficult.

So, what might conceivably be done to decentralize tactical force planning, given both of these problems? One should begin by recognizing that there is a substantial cost of both information transfer and iteration in the defense planning system. Under most conditions, the following force planning process, I believe, would converge to the region of the correct solution.

1. A separate planning exercise would be conducted for each functional component (ground forces, air forces, etc.) of the tactical reserve forces X_c. A planning model similar to that described above would be used for each functional type. The objective for each force type in each theater and conflict phase would be based on the estimated present *capability* of the theater and reserve forces approved in the previous period. (As mentioned above, the functional force planning models are relatively straightforward to develop.) Although these separate functional force planning models would include the theater-committed forces, the primary purpose of these models would be to develop the level and composition of the tactical reserve forces (as well as, possibly, to evaluate research and development alternatives). No use would be made of the information specific to theater-committed forces from such models.

These planning exercises could be conducted by the tactical reserve commands responsible for each functional force, largely on the basis of previously developed information. No guidance from the central manager is necessary. Information from the theater commands may be helpful, however, in establishing the aggregate capability of previously approved forces.

2. Planning exercises would then be conducted for the combination of tactical forces committed to each theater, given the level and composition of the tactical reserve forces developed from the functional force planning exercises $\bar{X}_C$. *The cost of the theater forces would include the full investment cost attributable to the planning period.* Two types of planning models could be used by the theater commanders:

a) The theater command planning problem may be formulated to select the set of tactical forces committed to that theater which minimize

$$C(X_P) \tag{17.8}$$

subject to

$$O(X_P) + S_{PI} = R_{PI}O(Y_{PI}), \tag{17.9}$$

$$O(X_P, X_C, S_{PI}) \geq R_{PS}O(Y_{PS}), \tag{17.10}$$

$$X_C \leq \bar{X}_C, \tag{17.11}$$

$$X_P, X_C, S_{PI} \geq 0. \tag{17.12}$$

For this formulation, the theater commander would need the following types of information from outside this command: First, the central manager would provide the objective criteria *and level* for U.S. tactical forces in that theater (the R_P vector), the planning threats (the Y_P vector), and any relevant constraints on the use of specific weapons, tactics, and bases. Second, the reserve force planner would provide the level and composition of the tactical reserve forces (the $\bar{X}_C$ vector).

In this case the theater commander would inform the central manager of the theater force budget and theater forces necessary to achieve the specified objectives. It would also be valuable for the theater commander to give the central manager information on the dual values on the output constraints; these dual values are estimates of the marginal cost of achieving the specified tactical objectives. No information about the theater production functions need be transmitted.

b) Alternatively, the theater command planning problem may be formulated to select the set of tactical forces which maximize one specific theater objective — for example,

$$\text{Maximize } O_i(X_P, X_C{}^i S_{PI}) \tag{17.13}$$

subject to

$$O(X_P) + S_{PI} = R_{PI}O(Y_{PI}), \tag{17.14}$$

$$O_{\neq i}(X_P, X_C, S_{PI}) \geq R_{\neq i, PS}O(Y_{PS}),\qquad(17.15)$$

$$C(X_P) \leq C_P,\qquad(17.16)$$

$$X_C \leq \bar{X}_C,\qquad(17.17)$$

$$X_P, X_C, S_{PI} \geq 0.\qquad(17.18)$$

For this formulation, the theater commander would need the following types of information from outside his command: First, the central manager would provide the objective criterion to be maximized, the criteria and level for other theater objectives, the planning threats, any relevant constraints on the use of specific weapons, tactics, and bases; *and* the total budget for the theater command (C_P). Second, the reserve force planner would provide the level and composition of the tactical reserve forces $(\bar{X}_C)$.

In this case, the theater commander would inform the central manager of the capability that could be achieved against the primary planning objective and the set of theater forces which maximizes this capability within the constraints of the other objectives, the budget, and the reserve forces. Again, it would be valuable for the theater commander to inform the central manager of the dual values; the dual values on the output constraints are the marginal cost of the tactical objectives, and the dual value on the budget constraint is the marginal output per budget unit in terms of the primary objective.

Under most conditions this second formulation is preferred. One objective criterion is usually recognized as more important than the others. More important, the central manager usually has a better idea of the budget he is prepared to commit than of the level of the primary objective (this indicates that his elasticity of demand for the primary objective is closer to -1 than to 0). This formulation reduces the leverage of the theater commander to "game" the central manager for more resources and reduces the number of iterations necessary to achieve the output-budget combination acceptable to the central manager.

3. Since the budgets of the theater commands are expressed in terms of the costs of *new* forces, a third step may be necessary to ensure that enough of the inherited resources are maintained in the program. If the tactical reserve forces include either none or all of the inherited amount of a specific force element, no additional step is necessary; in either case, there will be no lower-cost inherited resources to allocate to the theater commands. If the tactical reserve forces include some, but not all, of the inherited amount of a specific force element, the remaining inherited amount of the specific element should be allocated to the theater commands, reducing by an equivalent-capability amount the new forces of the same functional force type.

4. A new planning cycle in the next period would start by repeating the first step. The tactical reserve commands for each functional force would conduct a new set of planning exercises based on the aggregate present capability in each theater of the reserve forces plus the respective theater

forces approved in the previous cycle. Changes in the amount of the functional forces planned by the theater commanders, thus, lead to changes in the objectives against which the reserve forces are planned in the next cycle without any direct intervention by the central manager.

Conclusion

The force planning process summarized above is only in a preliminary conceptual stage. At the present time I do not understand either its complete mathematical properties or some of the problems of implementation. An important problem not discussed in the above section—the necessary condition to induce subordinate managers in a bureaucracy to either minimize budget or maximize output—is discussed in several other papers I have written.[1] In the Department of Defense the most powerful means to improve the consistency of objectives is to encourage several services to compete in providing forces to the theater and reserve commands and to be prepared to relieve the theater and reserve commanders for poor cost-output performance. The Office of the Secretary of Defense would be well advised to focus on improving the force planning process, clarifying the guidance to subordinate managers, and monitoring aggregate cost-output performance, rather than try to reproduce the understanding and information of the subordinate managers. The prospects for improved efficiency in the Department of Defense, I believe, will be dependent on such a division of labor, and the potential for improved efficiency is enormous.

1. William Niskanen, "The Defense Resource Allocation Process," *Defense Management*, Stephen Enke (ed.) (Englewood Cliffs, N.J.: Prentice-Hall, Inc., 1967); "The Peculiar Economics of Bureaucracy," *American Economic Review*, LVIII (May 1968), 293.

VII

Postscript: Some Future Developments

Designing Organizational Structures for Interorganizational Decision Making

A number of federal agencies – HEW, HUD, OEO, and DOL – offer grant-in-aid programs to states, cities, and citizen organizations. The aid granted would be used to remedy shortcomings in health care, education, housing, and employment in inner-city urban and rural poverty areas. Responsibility for any given program is located within one of these agencies. A total program for a community must be put together from the offerings of the respective agencies.

A number of solutions have been proposed to the agencies for directing their delivery of a confusing array of potential services to where they are most urgently needed and in a combination which will do the most good in each instance. Among the proposals considered or tried by the agencies are a "supermarket" model, a project management model, a committee model, and a centralized authority model.

The supermarket model of interorganization decision making is just what its name implies. The programs of the agencies are advertised, and the coordination is carried out by the recipient community just as a housewife would coordinate a meal by her food selection in a store. The project management model assigns the lead decision role to one of the involved agencies, making it somewhat "more equal" than the others. The lead agency views the solution of a community's problems as a single project, coordinating but unable to command the delivery of services from the several agencies. This procedure corresponds to the Model Cities approach.

The committee model is exemplified by the regional council approach. The agencies, or at least the boundary personnel, must exchange information, reach a consensus, and then obtain action, in isolation from their own agency. The centralized authority version of this model is an attempt to interject a

287

Federal "presence" into the regional council. Thus, by having a man from Washington present, it is felt that the benefits of decentralized decisions may be preserved while the direction of a central authority is imposed to assure action. This model raises the expectation that the action will be facilitated through arbitration of disputes, attention to agenda items, and, if need be, threats of budgetary alterations for a recalcitrant agency.

Each of the proposed models has some merits and some drawbacks. None has been wholly and enthusiastically tried. Since behavioral and technological issues are involved in any attempt to design a new organizational structure, an approach to the problem with a coordinated interdisciplinary research team would seem to be indicated.

Interdisciplinary and Empirical Requirements

The above example of an interorganizational decision problem may illustrate the need for both interdisciplinary work and for empirical work in organization design.

Obviously, the continuation of the work reported here is essential for the further development of a complete theory of interorganizational decision making as we noted in the Preface. But the effort represented by this collection of papers was able to achieve only multidisciplinarity; for a fuller theoretical development truly interdisciplinary studies will have to be undertaken. Perhaps only by following such an interdisciplinary strategy can both physical and behavioral constraints on coordination be confronted in single models. This is not to say that the authors of the papers in this volume were unaware of the need for interdisciplinarity. However, one could not but feel a sense of frustration as their work probed but failed to break through the disciplinary boundaries.

This volume has used a theme in which the research efforts were directed at structure, behavior, and decision technology. It may be that interdisciplinary research efforts directed at these aspects of the joint decision problem would prove fruitful.

The editors are aware that interdisciplinary attacks on the problem area do exist. The above paragraphs are intended as encouragement for existing efforts and a plea for additional work. Some researchers have already advanced to the stage of formal organizations. For example, the Association for the Study of the Grants Economy and the Public Choice Society are organizations dominated by economists working at the discipline boundaries to study decisions by government units. A new discipline is emerging: Policy Sciences is the study of top level goal setting and decision issues in the public sector. The discipline arose because of the need to project the influence of behavioral scientists, especially political scientists, into political policy-making; the need to study large, complex, open systems with an eye to the intersectoral linkages and the second-order reactions which occur; the need for improvement of top level decision making technologies; and the frank desire of persons with a variety of skills to improve government decisions at top levels.

There is a need for experiments in organization design for joint decision making. Experimental and quasi-experimental work would refine and validate model construction. An empirical phase is particularly important in modeling which encompasses both physical and behavioral constraints.

The need for behavioral studies in otherwise structured situations was pointed out in Baron's paper in this volume. In his discussion of decision technology he raised a number of questions which were behavioral in nature. The usefulness of any decision technology may be circumscribed by lack of imputs of behavioral variables. Presumably a behavioral scientist could research some of these model shortcomings in isolation, but it would be much preferred if the work could be done in cooperation with a competent decision technologist.

Baron raised several questions of subunit motivation to fully participate in a decision technology designed elsewhere in this volume. For instance, he questions the extent to which persons in the large decision system would supply misinformation to the central coordinator. Similarly, the effectiveness of decision models could be subverted if any participants refused to play by the rules, but rather sought to maximize some more limited objective than that indicated by the model. Finally, there is a question of how willing people are to implement a decision made by someone else. The resolution of these questions lies in empirical behavioral research, but the results must be incorporated in future decision technologies if improved system decisions are to result.[1]

Some substantial work remains to be done on decision technologies. Some models are now well developed, but empirical testing remains to be done before they can be accepted with confidence. For example, Baron noted that without empirical tests he could not state anything about the complexity of the actual problems the models would be called upon to solve, the time required to carry out a number of iterations, or the cost of these iterations (in terms of information acquisition and processing and foregone opportunities).

Formally, there a number of extensions of the decision models which need to be worked out. Loehman and Whinston suggest several for the model they have developed. In their case, two firms are involved in the decision, but they indicate that it would be possible to extend the analysis to more than two firms. It is also possible to explore the decision under uncertainty by making

1. See, for example, the work on "Implementation" by Churchman, Radnor, and others: C. West Churchman and A. H. Schaiblatt, "The Research and the Manager: A Dialectic of Implementation," *Management Science,* II (February 1965), 369–78; and M. Radnor, A. H. Rubenstein, and D. A. Tansik, "Implementation in Operations Research and R and D, in Government and Business Organizations," *Operations Research,* XVIII (November–December 1970).

one or more variables stochastic. Finally, some of the variables might become control variables in the sense that these variables may be manipulated as a result of the decision process.

Dynamic Model Requirements

The discussion of extensions of existing models has up to this point been in terms of static models, though at times the dynamic nature of the decision problem has been recognized. An obvious need for further work is in the development of dynamic models.

There are at least two directions dynamic analysis may take. The first is in simply extending existing models to explicitly recognize the passage of time. Thus, questions of how often the model must be solved and the costs of resolving must be explored. Where the model is designed to generate a time path, as in Model II in the Loehman and Whinston paper, the use of numerical analysis to study the time path is needed. The relevant structural equations must be estimated, numerical analysis must be used to approximate the time path, and the stability of the system should be ascertained in order to complete this line of investigation.

Another approach suggested by Loehman and Whinston would be to convert the integrals to summations and the differential equations to difference equations. Then the dynamic of the models could be investigated by less demanding mathematical techniques. These include the use of nonlinear programming, gradient ascent methods, the generalized Newton-Raphson technique applied to the Euler-Lagrange equations, and dynamic programming.

There is another dynamic problem which needs to be examined. Not only do external conditions change over time, but internal conditions change as well. Thus, there is the need to examine the monitoring system of the decision model. There is a tendency for the goals of the subsystems to change, either simply due to the passage of time or as a direct result of the decisions emanating from the decision model. To be effective the model must compensate for these expected changes. Further work on how and why subsystem goal sets change within an operating decision system and the impact these changes have on the effectiveness of the decision model is necessary.

Evaluation Criteria Requirements

Hurwicz developed the criteria of desirability and feasibility for evaluating interorganizational decision systems. In addition, some formal evaluative measures, such as have been developed for single-system models, need to be developed and applied so that competing interorganizational decision models may be critically compared.

Actually the above paragraph suggests a more basic question which still requires some empirical examination. Certain advantages of decentralization have been discussed. Empirical examination of the relative merits of centralized and decentralized structures has produced mixed results.[2] Further research is clearly required into the conditions under which and by how much decentralization is superior to centralized decision making. Similarly, decentralization by guidelines was discussed, but again, the cost-benefit discussion proceeded in a priori terms. The questions of whether improved decision models are worth adopting by any criteria or measurement standards (and what these standards should be) must be investigated further.

Multi-Institutional Requirements

Finally, the need for and the application of interorganization decision models in other types of systems than those included here needs additional study. Two additional application areas were suggested previously in this volume. They were health-services delivery systems and educational systems. Other areas, no less critical, may be identified and studied.

A Final Note

The above discussion of open issues is far from exhaustive; rather, it was intended to be illustrative and inspirational. It is the hope of the editors of this volume that it will stimulate a considerable increase in interdisciplinary research in this area.

2. See H. Baker and R. R. France, *Centralization and Decentralization in Industrial Relations* (Princeton, N.J.: Princeton University Press, 1954); M. Radnor, "Control of R&D by Top Managers in 48 Very Large Companies," in *Operations Research and the Social Sciences,* J. R. Lawrence (ed.) (Tavistock 1966); A. H. Rubenstein, "Organizational Factors Affecting Research and Development in Large Decentralized Companies," *Management Science,* July 1964, 618–33; and H. A. Simon, H. Guetzkow, G. Kozmetsky, and G. Tyndall, *Centralization vs. Decentralization in Organizing the Controller's Department* (Controllership Foundation, 1954).

Name Index

Subject Index